MARVA COLLINS' WAY

MARVA COLLINS' WAY

Marva Collins and Civia Tamarkin

Foreword by Alex Haley

Jeremy P. Tarcher/Perigee Books

Jeremy P. Tarcher/Perigee Books
are published by
The Putnam Publishing Group
200 Madison Avenue
New York, NY 10016

Library of Congress Cataloging-in-Publication Data

Collins, Marva. 1936-
    Marva Collins' way
Marva Collins and Civia Tamarkin;
Foreword by Alex Haley. — 2nd ed.
    p. cm.
Includes bibliographical references and index.
ISBN 0-87477-572-8:
    1. Collins, Marva. 2. Teachers — Illinois — Chicago — Biography.
3. Educators — Illinois — Chicago — Biography. 4. Westside Preparatory
School (Chicago, Ill.) I. Tamarkin, Civia. II. Title.
LA2317.C62A3 1990
372-11'092 — dc20
[B]   90-43008
                                             CIP

Authors' Note: Some of the children's names have been changed to protect
their privacy.

Jeremy P. Tarcher, Inc.
5858 Wilshire Blvd., Suite 200
Los Angeles, CA 90036

Design by Mike Yazzolino
Publishing consultant: Victoria Pasternack

Manufactured in the United States of America

s 10 9 8 7 6 5

OCLC 5/3
1067093

To our children and all children,
may they find their own way.

CONTENTS

Foreword

To say *critical* is to understate how poorly most of our public education is serving our youth today. Indeed time and again in starkly clinical appraisal, our captains of industry have warned our sources of education that unless the U.S. produces higher-level graduates, American industry inevitably will be thrust into further jeopardy. They point out that today we confront a competition that is better motivated, better trained, and *smarter* than we have ever met before. Moreover, this new breed of competitor nation makes it their governmental policy to maintain their educational standards in a pursuit of greater excellence.

It is against this background that this book presents Marva Collins, whose opinions of what is and is not effective teaching afford us a palette of insights into why she must be regarded among America's foremost educators. Surely, no other secondary school principal ever has been offered the post of Secretary of Education by two consecutive U.S. Presidents. Marva Collins turned down both of these offers, preferring to remain her own woman, unencumbered by politics and bureaucracy, as the founder and the principal of the Westside Preparatory School.

The challenge that motivates Marva Collins is to prove that something positive and constructive *can* be done about the deplorable rate of dropouts, which is preceded by an attendant level of scholarship among most minority youth. But the inadequacy of U.S. public education of minorities is scarcely less than the inadequacy of public education in general. Even the most elite schools of higher-education perennially cry out against the poor quality of students of all ethnic descriptions who apply for entrance. A chilling statistic recently reported by American industries states that over 30 percent of their job applicants must be rejected because they are not able to fill out the application form properly.

Time and again, Marva Collins has issued this bold challenge: "Give me any class in any city. Give me the lowest-achieving students, those who have done poorly. Tell me nothing about those students, not even what they're studying, and I can go into that classroom and connect with those students."

The results achieved by Marva Collins' students are even more dramatic than her challenge. Since she began her school fifteen years ago, *every one* of that grammar school's graduates is today either attending some outstanding prep school on full academic scholarship, or has gone on to an outstanding college or university.

These are young Americans who without such schooling likely would have drifted into the surrounding world of drop-outs, public assistance, and addiction.

Little wonder that education administrators from around the world travel to Chicago to visit an inner-city school and expose themselves to the program developed by a dedicated and committed teacher and principal who is doing her utmost to offer something new to education.

What Marva Collins thrusts into the minds of her students is that whomever they are, and wherever they live, they can achieve quite literally whatever they can dream—no matter what anyone else may say to the contrary.

Why is this book by Marva Collins so important? It is because this book represents her life, her convictions, and her work. Indeed, America would be infinitely better served if Marva Collins' philosophy of education somehow could become franchised and implemented on a national scale.

Alex Haley
June 14, 1990

Preface to the
Second Edition

When I first wrote this book in 1982, I thought that education in America was about as bad as it could be. However, in the past eight years I have had many opportunities to observe schools throughout the country, and I have found that the situation is worse than I realized. What I once assumed to be inferior education for the poor and underprivileged has become a nationwide malady that afflicts the middle and upper classes as well. I have found bad education in the places I least expected to find it.

America faces an education crisis of frightening proportions. Only recently, in the spring of 1990, Education Secretary Lauro F. Cavazos deplored the nation's "indifference, complacency, and passivity." Responding to a survey of test scores and dropout rates, Secretary Cavazos called for radical reforms of the educational system.

One prestigious study after another has documented the sad facts with alarming statistics. One of every four American students drop out before entering the work force, as compared to Japan, where 96% graduate from high school. The Project on Adult Literacy estimates that twenty to thirty million Americans are unable to "read, write, calculate, solve problems or communicate well enough to function effectively on the job or in their everyday lives."

The Educational Testing Service concludes that about 1.25 million young adults between the ages of 21 and 25 cannot read at the fourth-grade level. Another six million (nearly one third of those measured) were unable to write a letter to a store about a billing error or to command enough simple arithmetic to balance a checkbook. Worse, 440,000 youngsters in that age bracket could not even read well enough to be tested. Most alarming, projections indicate that these problems will get worse as today's students enter the work force.

In addition to the lamentable decline in literacy and test scores, educators have also pointed out that the average student's grasp of simple geography (such as the location of familiar countries), history (such as when the Civil War occurred), and fundamental math and science is woefully inadequate. U.S. students consistently score near the bottom in mathematical achievement when compared to students in other developed countries. One study showed that *elite* twelfth graders in America understand math on the same level as their *average* Japanese counterparts.

When one considers that the future of our nation is being forged in today's classrooms, it is clear that our education crisis is the single greatest issue we face. America can no longer tolerate failure, rampant mediocrity and the tragic loss of potential brain power. Where will we be in twenty-five years when today's students are adult citizens who can barely read and compute? No wonder that responsible leaders from the President and Mrs. Bush to the Secretary of Education to corporate executives and local parent groups are all searching for solutions.

Although we hear a great deal about educational reform today, we are still not doing enough about it. It seems to me that we have been trying to improve our schools with the equivalent of using a toothbrush to clean up after an earthquake. It is as though we expect our schools to improve through some sort of magic. As Robert C. Winters, Chairman of Prudential Insurance, states, "The time has come for systematic . . . education reform. In fact, what we really need is not just reform, but a revolution."

Our children are not the culprits; they are the victims. My twenty years of experience in education have convinced me that children want to learn and can learn. Provide them with the right environment, the right motivation, and the right materiel, and children will demonstrate their natural ability to excel. Nor is this merely one woman's opinion. Dr. Jerome Bruner, the eminent educator and author of the influential book, *The Process of Education,* cites studies showing that the way a school is run makes a difference in the students' performance. "Where the school shows that *it* cares, the students care," says Dr. Bruner. "They respond with regular attendance, better behavior, and higher academic achievement."

No one, not professional educators, politicians, or parents, is to blame for the current predicament. No classroom teacher, principal, or school superintendent wants to be part of a bad school system; no politician wants inferior schools in his or her district; no parent wants to see his or her children grow up illiterate and undereducated. Unfortunately, we have all become quagmired in a system that fails more children than it helps.

Who is to blame then? Everyone. To solve our education crisis, we need to work on improving the entire system and every cog in the wheel. We need skilled, creative, persistent leadership at the top on both the local and national levels. We need a much higher degree of parental involvement, not just in the home but in volunteer capacities at every school in the country. We need strong principals who care more about children than about personality polls, politics, or job preservation. And, most important of all, we need dedicated, well-trained, highly respected, well-compensated teachers in front of our classrooms at every level and in every strata of society.

In the eight years since this book was written, I have found that the convictions expressed in it have been strengthened by experience. Students do not need to be labeled or measured any more than they are. They don't need more Federal funds, grants, and gimmicks. What they need from us is common sense, dedication, and bright, energetic teachers who believe that all children are achievers and who take personally the failure of any one child.

Such teachers are the key to the success of the Westside Preparatory School, whose founding and development is documented in this book. It has been most gratifying to see our approach validated by the hundreds of teachers from around the world who visit us each year or attend our teacher-training workshops.

Naturally, Westside Preparatory has no monopoly on quality teaching. There are thousands of excellent teachers in the country with valuable techniques of their own. What all good teachers have in common, however, is that they set high standards for their children and do not settle for anything less. The academic program at my school consists simply of the three Rs in the context of a total program that teaches each child that he or she is unique, special, and much too bright ever to be less than he or she can be. My teachers live by the credo, "I will never let you fail."

We must begin focusing on our children again. We must reevaluate our perceptions of them and learn to recognize that they can be motivated to achieve their potential, whatever it may be. It is too easy and too convenient to conclude that bad students are poorly motivated or stupid. This conclusion is a poor excuse, and it runs counter to the truth. A good teacher can always make a poor student good and a good student superior. The word *teacher* has its roots in the Latin word meaning *to lead* or *to draw out*. Good teachers draw out the best in every student; they are willing to polish and shine until the true luster of each student comes through.

Over the years, some of my ideas have become controversial, some have been hotly criticized, and some have been recognized for what they are: effective common sense. What is indisputable is the success of the program we have created at Westside Preparatory School. The school remains at full capacity—244 students—and we have to turn applicants away. Most gratifying, every one of our former students, most of whom were drawn from inner city Chicago, is now either employed or attending high school or college. Not one of our graduates has subsequently dropped out. And, since we taught them all that responsible citizens should give something back to their communities, most of them now spend time helping out at the school, tutoring the current students.

I wrote this book because I believed that others can benefit from my failures and successes. I stand behind everything in these pages. In fact, I believe the book is as relevant for the nineties as it was for the eighties. There is nothing we do at Westside Preparatory School that cannot be duplicated in any school in the country. This fact has been demonstrated by the hundreds of educators who have taken our workshops and returned to their schools with a fresh attitude and an arsenal of simple but effective techniques.

When my publisher and I discussed the preparation of this new edition, we tried to think of ways to update it. I was surprised (and relieved) when he suggested that we let most of it stand as is, since, to my gratification, it has come to be considered a *classic* in the education field. Therefore, apart from this new preface, the only updating is the material at the back of the book: two appendices—one addressed to parents, the other to teachers—with practical suggestions for how to foster quality education and create a brighter, more successful future for all children in America.

I sometimes wish that the whole world could see what I have seen in my classrooms: all children are born achievers. All they need is someone special to believe in them and draw out the best in them. Just today, when my class of three- and four-year-olds read the classic Greek myth of Daedelus and Icarus, one child said, "Mrs. Collins, if we do not learn and work hard, we will take an Icarian flight to nowhere."

In that child's observation is not only a lesson for each of us to live by, but a message to everyone concerned about the education of future generations.

Prologue

I first met Marva Collins in February 1980, when I was reporting a cover story on education for *Time* magazine. It was a period of upheaval in education. Everything that had been festering for years seemed to be coming to the surface. What was emerging was a major crisis, the result of a rash of school system bankruptcies, the politics of court-ordered busing, declining public school enrollments, low reading scores, and rampant teacher incompetence.

As a stringer in *Time*'s Midwest bureau, I had convinced the editors to take a hard look at what was going on in classrooms around the country. I was looking at the situation not only through the eyes of a journalist but also as a former teacher and as a parent who was dissatisfied with many of the teachers my daughter had had, first in the Chicago public schools and later in a private school. To find out what had gone wrong with American education and what could be done about it, I and other *Time* correspondents interviewed parents, teachers, students, school board members, and academics across the nation.

In my investigative odyssey, one of the teachers I talked to was Marva Collins, the brash, outspoken founder of Chicago's Westside Preparatory School. Marva had already been taken up by the media, hoisted onto an educational pedestal, and hailed as education's heroine. Scores of newspapers and magazine articles and several television features, including a segment of CBS's *60 Minutes,* had named her the miracle worker who had succeeded where other teachers had failed. Anxious to get her views on education and to find out if she was indeed different from other teachers, I accepted her invitation to come out to Garfield Park to see just what it was she was doing.

As I pulled off the expressway and entered the Garfield Park neighborhood, I could see it was a hazy vestige of its former self, a part of Chicago that stood forlornly like some dowdy spinster who had been jilted of her prime. The warren of streets and boulevards hugging the park's perimeter, four miles west of the city's downtown loop, was crowded with run-down greystones, six-flats, twelve-flats, and courtyard apartment buildings. Most of the stately old mansions along Hamlin Avenue had been abused, ignored, and haphazardly chopped up into apartments. Many of the front lawns were now dry dirt plots strewn with broken glass or covered with knee-high weed thickets. A Star of David carved over the doorway of the Morningstar Baptist Church, which used to be the Wilno Synagogue, was the only hint of the neighborhood's ethnic past.

On the corner of Springfield and Adams streets was Delano Grammar School. It had been one of the best schools in the Chicago system, and former graduates, now grandparents, still remembered teachers like Mrs. Wilson, who stayed an extra hour every day for a year, teaching her eighth-grade class to play Hohner harmonicas.

The school now loomed ingloriously, a clumsy, pathetic hodgepodge of mismatched building annexes sprouting from its side. Its playground—once the gathering place and training ground for such neighborhood celebrities as Tom Hayes, Sid Rosenthal, and Saul Farber, all-american basketball stars, and Saul's brother Eddie, who played professional baseball for the Cleveland Indians—was now buried beneath the annexes, so that all that remained were patches of gravel planted with rusted swings and slides.

If it hadn't been for Marva Collins, Garfield Park would have remained a forgotten neighborhood. But she had replaced all the old heroes. Marva Collins was a powerful force in that neighborhood. I found that out as soon as I pulled up in front of her house. Four young men in their middle to late teens were loitering across the street. One of them approached me as I got out of the car.

"You going to see Mrs. Collins' school?" he asked.

I nodded uncomfortably. After all, Garfield Park was the kind of place you drove through with your car doors locked and your windows rolled up.

"OK," he said. "You don't have to worry about anything. We'll watch your car for you."

I was struck by the respect they seemed to have for Marva. Later I related the incident to her and asked what her secret was.

"There's no secret," she answered. "I just deal honestly with children. They know I don't turn my nose down at them. They listen to me because I'm not some outsider who comes over here and talks down to them about what it is like to be poor. I'm right here working with them all the time. If everyone in the neighborhood treated these children with the same consistent interest, the children would do for them what they do for me."

What I eventually came to realize about Marva was that she was a teacher all the time, not just in the classroom. For her, being a teacher had turned into a fixed idea to which she obsessively referred all things and all experiences. If some found her single-mindedness overbearing, her students and the other children in the neighborhood saw it as a sign of her implacable devotion to them. And they, in turn, were fiercely loyal to her.

Meeting Marva, I was reminded of something Dr. Ralph Tyler, a former dean of social sciences at the University of Chicago, had once told me. "Teaching," he had said, "is not just a job. It is a human service, and it must be thought of as a mission." Marva seemed to see it that way. With an overwhelming dedication—which, I might add, could easily be mistaken for self-importance—she allowed teaching to consume her. As I got to know her, I saw that her life was so wrapped up in her teaching and in her students that she seldom needed anything else. She drew most of her pleasure and pain from her children. Oddly, people could accept that quality in a parent, but they had difficulty understanding it in a teacher. To many, Marva would often appear too good to be true.

When I first saw her in action in the classroom, she was every bit as impressive as the media had made her out to be. Actually, I had been wary of her miracle image, dismissing it as the stuff of media hype. But watching her perform, I suddenly understood how that image had come about. It was really a question of semantics. While Marva Collins didn't work "miracles," she was indeed a miraculous teacher. She had an exuberance, an energy about her that was both captivating and contagious.

The control and rapport she had with her students amazed me. From my own years as a high school English teacher, I knew that was no simple thing to achieve.

Marva's approach appeared so natural. There was a sense of maternalism about it. She was constantly in motion about the class, patting heads, touching shoulders, hugging and praising her students. There were more than thirty students in that room, yet no one seemed to be lost in the crowd. Somehow, during the course of the day, Marva managed to give each child personalized attention. She didn't just teach them, she nurtured them. And from the way the children responded, I could tell Marva wasn't merely putting on an act for a visitor. There was an incredible bond between her and her students.

Learning in Marva Collins' class was clearly an exciting, shared experience. The children were eager to learn. They waved their hands and jumped up and down in their seats, asking her to call on them. It had been a long time since I had seen a class work as well as this one. Many of the students were below average; some, in fact, had been tagged with learning disabilities. But their motivation was impressive.

Much of the media attention Marva Collins received focused on *what* she taught—on the fact that she had seven-, eight-, and nine-year-old ghetto children reading and reciting William Shakespeare and Geoffrey Chaucer. But I was more intrigued by *how* she taught and *why* her approach worked. There was a method there, but it was not readily definable. To understand it, I knew I would have to spend more than just one day in her classroom.

I wasn't naive enough to think Marva Collins had the

cure-all for the ailments of education. The problems were far too complex and chronic. Students' reading and other test scores had been declining since 1963. More than thirty million adult Americans were functional illiterates; some twenty million Americans over the age of eighteen could not read well enough to understand a want ad or a job application. The U.S. illiteracy rate was three times higher than that of the Soviet Union. American students were scoring lower on achievement tests than students from other industrially advanced nations, such as Germany, Japan, and Great Britain.

But after I watched Marva Collins and after I did all the interviews and research in connection with the *Time* story, one thing became clear: the teacher in the front of the classroom made the difference. For years educators had pointed an accusing finger at parents, at television, at the schools' lack of funds, at children's home lives and backgrounds, and at what the National Education Association described as "the distractions which characterized American life in the past decade or so." Now, suddenly and dramatically, the public was no longer willing to accept the blame. Instead, teachers themselves were coming under scrutiny.

The previous summer, headlines announced that half of the first-year teachers in the Dallas school system had failed to pass the Wesman Personnel Classification Test, an exam measuring verbal reasoning and mathematical abilities. The Houston Independent School District discovered that half its teacher applicants scored lower in math than the average high school senior, and about one-third scored just as poorly in language skills. And the situation wasn't limited to Texas. One-third of the teachers in Florida County flunked eighth-grade math tests and tenth-grade reading tests. And only half of the applicants for jobs in the Mobile, Alabama, schools passed the National Teacher Examination. A much-publicized study by W. Timothy Weaver of Boston University confirmed that college students majoring in education scored lower on the Scholastic Aptitude Test than majors in almost every other field.

The spotlight on school finances also underscored the deteriorating quality of American education. Faced with school closings, program cuts, teacher layoffs, and possible tax hikes, parents began to take a critical look at the kind of education their children were getting. In a number of instances across the country, parents sued school districts for malpractice. There was a renewed push for minimum competency testing of teachers as well as of students. State legislatures began passing bills requiring teachers be tested for their basic skills. Teacher colleges came under attack for seemingly handing out diplomas as though they were Green Stamps. Parents stormed school board meetings to demand teacher accountability. Others turned to private schools, and some even yanked their children out of the classroom altogether and taught them at home.

Marva Collins had come to the public's attention. From the ivy-covered walls of Princeton to the grade schools of Wyoming, educators clamored to attend her workshops, and they flocked to her classroom from as far away as Germany and Spain to observe her technique. Publishers were after her to endorse textbooks; manufacturers wanted her to advertise educational products. A Hollywood producer planned to make a movie about her, and a group of entrepreneurs tried to set up a franchise of Marva Collins schools. Distraught parents sought her advice, and politicians solicited her help. Weeks before I met her, she had been offered the post of Los Angeles County superintendent of schools as well as a seat on Chicago's Board of Education. Within the year, she would be invited by President Carter to a White House conference on education and be tapped for a cabinet spot in then President-elect Reagan's administration.

It was a celebrity status never before accorded a simple grade-school teacher. Everyone saw in Marva Collins what he or she wanted to see. Journalists viewed her as a maverick up against the system. Taxpayers, tired of subsidizing the growing cost of education, liked Marva's no-frills, no-gimmicks, basic approach to teaching, particularly when she was quoted as saying that more government spending was not the answer to the problems facing schools. Parents of low achievers looked to her as someone who offered hope to their children. Minority groups regarded her as a champion of equal opportunity. Conservatives seized upon her self-reliance, her traditionalism, and her insistence that old-fashioned values be taught in the classroom. And to liberals, she was a romantic idealist out to right the wrongs of society. Some teachers found her an inspirational model, while others saw her as a charlatan, a quitter who had gone outside the system, and even a threat to public education.

Perhaps no teacher deserved such attention. The headlines were calling her "super-teacher" and referring to what she did as "blackboard magic" and "miracle on Adams Street." Two years later she would make headlines of a different sort.

It took me more than a year of observing her teaching, of following her students' progress, and of talking to parents, psychologists, and other educators to separate the real Marva from her myth. She wasn't perfect, she wasn't a superwoman. For that matter, she was neither an academic, a scholar, nor the perfect grammarian. But what could not be disputed was that Marva Collins motivated children and made them want to achieve. That is what this book is about—a teacher teaching.

Civia Tamarkin

Marva Collins got Freddie Harris to take off his St. Louis Cardinals jacket and hang it on the back of his chair.

It was shortly after the bell rang on the first day of school, and teachers at Delano Elementary School on Chicago's Near West Side were being unusually tolerant of students because no one was up to a challenge so soon. In fact, short of a knock-down fight, teachers were overlooking just about everything as they shuffled class cards and gave out seat assignments. No one wanted to march a student into the principal's office and admit things had already gotten out of control just ten minutes into the new 1974–1975 school year.

It didn't seem particularly significant whether or not Freddie was wearing a jacket in class, until Marva noticed how defiantly his fists were shoved into the pockets. Actually her only concern was that it was too hot for him to sit in class all day wearing that jacket. The room was already choking in a late-summer heat that promised to get worse by midmorning. When she moved closer to him and saw how tightly his lips were pressed together and how his shoulders were hunched up around his neck, she realized that Freddie Harris was working hard at being tough.

Freddie expected his stay at Delano, and in particular this class, to be brief. At nine years old he was a repeater in second grade, a troublemaker whose file down in the office bulged with psychologists' reports and harsh evaluations from previous teachers. Last May he was suspended for the remainder of the school term for fighting. The time before, he was kicked out for throwing food in the lunchroom. Before that, he had cussed at a teacher. He was readmitted now for the new fall semester with the principal's warning that the next infraction would get him thrown out of Delano for good.

That suited Freddie just fine. He didn't like school, and he didn't like the other children any more than they liked him. The children his age thought he was a baby for being stuck in second grade, and the second-graders thought he was just big and dumb. Besides, he figured, once he was out of Delano, he would be finished with school. His old lady, he thought, wasn't going to pay for any private school, and she didn't like churches much so there was no chance of his being sent to a parochial school. All he had to do was get kicked out of this class and he could hang around all day and do what he wanted.

So when Marva asked him to take off his jacket, he just slumped further down in his seat, his fists stuffed into his pockets and his legs stretched out under the chair in front of him.

"Peach," Marva said softly, "you don't need to wear that jacket in class. Let's take it off and get out a pencil so we can do some work." She knew Freddie was trying to bait her, and her technique in this kind of situation was to be matter-of-fact. She was not sure yet how far Freddie would push it. Was he just introducing himself or trying for something more? She looked hard at him, wondering how many other teachers had fueled his fight.

Freddie turned his head away sharply, fixing his stare on the broken pane of glass in the third window.

"Sweetheart," said Marva, "it's so hot in here you're going to roast yourself."

He didn't move. She reached out and teasingly mussed his hair. "Besides," she said, "you're such a handsome, strong boy, I don't see why you want to cover up those big muscles of yours."

Marva thought she saw his mouth relax slightly, even hold back a smile, so she cupped his face in her hands and slowly drew him toward her. New children have such dull eyes, she thought, such sullen looks and empty expressions. At seven, eight, and nine years old they have already resigned themselves to failure.

Freddie refused to look up at her, though he allowed her to caress his face.

"Come on, peach, we have work to do," she said, standing straight and tall before him. Marva always stood tall, being easily six feet even without the high heels she liked to wear, never stooping under her height, not even when she was a long-armed and skinny-legged child with a size twelve shoe and the other children teased her that she could knock the roof off the church. "You can't just sit in a seat and grow smart," she said. Her eyes, which could turn dark and cold when she was angry, were soft on his face.

Then, because he hadn't jerked away from her touch, she let one hand fall to the collar of his jacket, and with the other she started to pull apart the front snap. His hand shot out of a pocket and locked tightly around her wrist.

"You are so very angry," she murmured gently, "but I know you're not angry with me, because I haven't done anything to you. We all have a good me and a bad me inside us, and I know that you have a good you. Will you help me find it? I'm your friend and I'm going to help you all the time and I'm going to love you all the time. I love you already, and I'm going to love you even when you don't love yourself."

She pulled him close to her, his head resting against her hip. Her long fingers kneaded the tension from his shoulders and stroked the back of his neck. Marva worked painstakingly to know each child, training herself to catch the gesture, look, or remark that would tell her what a child needed.

Freddie pushed back into his chair, sat up tall, and with quick, short pulls began popping apart the snaps on his jacket, slipping his arms out of the sleeves. Marva bent over him, balanced his chin on the crook of her finger, and tilted his head back so that he was looking straight at her. The subdued tone of her voice gave way suddenly to a new firmness. "I promise, you are going to *do,* you are going to *produce.* I am not going to let you fail."

Marva walked up to the front of the class. She had been teaching for fourteen and a half years—two at Monroe County

Training School in Beatrice, Alabama and twelve and a half in the Chicago public schools; and while she had grown to hate the teaching profession as a whole, she loved to teach. Septembers were always the same. She expected the anxiety would have worn off by now. It never did. She didn't sleep the night before school started, uneasy as a child going off for the first time.

With every new class there was so much to do. Somehow her room at Delano had become a way station for the castoffs the other teachers didn't want. There were always children like Freddie Harris, the discipline problems. Last year she had her hands full with James Thomas. James had acted up all through kindergarten and first grade, and most teachers couldn't stand him.

When James misbehaved in her class during the first week of school, Marva called him over to her.

"James, do you know how to spell your name?" she asked.

The child nodded that he did.

"Well, fine," Marva said, "you go over to the file cabinet, open the drawer, and see if you can find your cumulative record card and read it."

James took out the card, glanced at it, and brought it to Marva with a puzzled look on his face. School had just started and Marva had already given him a grade of "Good" in conduct.

"Do you think you deserve that grade?" asked Marva.

"No," he answered.

"Do you want that grade?"

"Uh huh," he whispered.

"Then you go back to your seat and earn it."

James Thomas was not a problem the rest of the year.

Besides the troublemakers, Marva had children like Bernette Miller, the heavy-set, slow-moving girl in the first row, whose drawn-out speech prompted a previous teacher to dismiss her as a child with a learning disability. And there were children like pigtailed Wanda Lewis, who had never learned how to spell her name or which side of the notebook paper to write on. She had been passed on to the next grade simply because she was so quiet.

Marva stopped beside Bernette Miller's desk. She said nothing, but the children instantly shuffled around in their seats and faced forward. She had a commanding authority, an almost hypnotic presence.

Marva was a striking woman with high cheekbones and strong angular features, which she inherited along with a love of jewelry from a great-grandmother who was a Choctaw Indian. Slender though not willowy, Marva was immediately discernible in a crowd—even without the visibility afforded by her height—for she had acquired a poise and sophistication that gave her appearance a deliberate style.

Marva would rarely wear slacks, and she never wore loose-fitting shifts or casually assembled blouses and skirts. Sloppy dressing showed disrespect for oneself, for the children, and for the profession. From the first day of class Marva was teaching that self-respect is the most important thing a person can have. For herself and for the children Marva dressed impeccably, favoring cashmere sweaters, suits, and herring-bone tweeds. Her clothing was tailored and stylishly simple, but she usually added an ornamental touch: a carved belt cinched over a sweater, a gold medallion on a chain, an organdy boutonniere, or perhaps a lace handkerchief fanned in pleats across a pocket and held in place by a beaded lion's-head brooch. In Marva's opinion, it was important to have a unique imprint. She felt she was different from most people and delighted in her difference. It was an attitude often mistaken for arrogance.

"I am a teacher," she said to the class on this first day. "A teacher is someone who leads. There is no magic here. Mrs. Collins is no miracle worker. I do not walk on water, I do not part the sea. I just love children and work harder than a lot of people, and so will you.

"I know most of you can't spell your name. You don't know the alphabet, you don't know how to read, you don't know homonyms or how to syllabicate. I promise you that you will. None of you has ever failed. School may have failed you. Well, goodbye to failure, children. Welcome to success. You will read hard books in here and understand what you read. You will write every day so that writing becomes second nature to you.

You will memorize a poem every week so that you can train your minds to remember things. It is useless for you to learn something in school if you are not going to remember it.

"But you must help me to help you. If you don't give anything, don't expect anything. Success is not coming to you, you must come to it."

The children looked puzzled. They were accustomed to warnings, threats, and rules of order on the first day of class. If nothing else, Marva vowed she would get through to these children because she was so determined. Or just plain stubborn. She was, in fact, more strong-willed than most, maybe even a bit too strong-willed for her own good. Over and over her mother used to warn her, "Marva, you'll never come to any good 'cause once your mind is set, there's no telling you what to do."

Marva Collins was not going to let any child make her a bad teacher.

"The first thing we are going to do in here, children," Marva told her class, "is an awful lot of believing in ourselves."

Freddie Harris decided to give this teacher a try 'cause she sure was different from all the other teachers he had messed with and 'cause it seemed like he was getting nowhere by acting up, at least, not for now. He finished helping Marva hand out excerpts from Emerson's "Self Reliance." Freddie and all the other children began riffling through the mimeographed pages, shaking their heads in disbelief at all the print, mumbling an occasional "Wow" or "No way, man."

"What are you all getting so worried about?" Marva said. "I don't expect you to know how to read this. I will read it to you, but you must listen to what it says."

She liked to begin the school year with "Self Reliance." Marva believed that it was one of the most important things a student, especially a black student, could ever learn.

"Now let's look at the title. The first thing you must always look at is the title. What is the first thing you must look at, children? The t——."

"Title," a sprinkling of voices offered shyly.

"Very good." Marva walked to the blackboard, picked up a piece of chalk, and printed "Self Reliance" across the newly washed surface. "The title is 'Self Reliance,' " she repeated, marking the vowel sounds with colored chalk. "These are called diacritical marks, and they show us how to pronounce vowel sounds. The *e* in *self* has the short sound *eh,* so we put a breve over it. The first *e* and the *i* in *reliance* have macrons, which tell us those vowel sounds are long; the vowels say their own names."

Marva moved down the aisle by the windows. "Now we are going to read an essay called 'Self Reliance.' What is the title?" Marva asked the boy in the fifth seat of the third row, who was rubbing his fingers along the edge of the desk. The boy lowered his head, chin resting against his chest, and moved his fingers up and down in a nervous rhythm, waiting for his turn to pass.

"What is the title, sweetheart? Don't just sit there with your mouth shut. If you don't know, then say, 'Mrs. Collins, I don't know.' Don't ever be afraid of making a mistake. If you can't make a mistake, you can't make anything."

She sidled around the desks until she was beside him, her hand resting on his shoulder. Then she asked the same question of the child behind him.

" 'Self Reliance,' " the girl answered.

"Very good," said Marva, unfastening the girl's barette and repositioning it to hold back a few stray strands of hair. "Let's keep the hair out of your eyes, pet, so you can see." Marva continued down the aisle, asking each child in that row to tell her the title, getting each child accustomed to speaking in class, and with each answer she said, "Very good," *"Très bien,"* *"Laudo,"* or *"Sehr gut,"* explaining that she was praising them in French, Latin, and German.

"Now," she said, "self-reliance means to believe in yourself. What does self-reliance mean? To be——."

"To believe in yourself," echoed a few faint voices.

"Everybody, in big outdoor voices, what does it mean?"

"To believe in yourself," the children said, more boldly.

"Very, very good, children," Marva told them in a steady businesslike voice, her eyes looking down on the paper as she calmed their rising enthusiasm and signaled them on to the next thought. Marva could lead with her eyes and her voice, winning control by a look or an inflection. Now her tone seemed to belie the praise she had just uttered, as if she were warning the children not to be too satisfied with one small success but to remember how much more there was to learn.

"The author of 'Self Reliance' was a man named Ralph Waldo Emerson," she continued. "You must always read the author's name. If you like what an author writes, but you don't know the author's name, then you won't be able to find any more of his stories to read." She paused, gauging the children's interest. A few were wriggling in their seats. Wanda Lewis, in the back of the class, seemed lost in herself, staring out the window, tapping a pencil against her pudgy cheek.

"Darling," Marva motioned to Wanda, "if you just sit and look, you are going nowhere. Come up here beside me so we can keep track of one another." Marva helped the girl push her desk up the narrow aisle, manuevering it to the front of the row as the other children shuffled their desks aside.

"All right, children," she quieted the class. "Mr. Emerson was a writer, a poet, and a lecturer who lived in the 1800s. A lecturer is someone who talks before an audience or a class." Marva wrote the word on the board, underlining *lecture*. "The base word is *lecture*, which is a talk or a speech. Someone who gives the talk or speech is a *lecturer*. Freddie, what is a lecturer?"

"Someone who gives a speech to a lot of people," Freddie murmured, smiling.

"That's very, very good, sweetheart," Marva told him. "See, you're so used to being wrong, you're afraid to be right. But speak more loudly next time. When you whisper, it means 'I don't like myself. I don't believe what I say.' What you say is important. Each of you is the most important child in the world.

"Now, children, Mr. Emerson was born in Boston in 1803. Where is Boston?" She waited for a response. "Come on, children, think, think, shake your brains! James, come up here to the map and show us where Boston is."

A stocky boy with short-cropped hair walked hesitantly to the wall map. Marva straightened his collar, telling him what a handsome shirt it was. She put her arm around him. With her free hand she guided his index finger to the correct spot on the map.

"That's wonderful, James. Boston is the capital of Massachusetts. Thank you, James, you are just so bright," she told him as he sat down grinning. "Ralph Waldo Emerson was born in Boston, Massachusetts, and his father was a minister. Where was Mr. Emerson born, children?"

"Boston," they answered.

"Very good. Boston. Now when Ralph was not quite eight years old, as old as some of you, his father died. The family was so poor that Ralph and his brother had to share the same winter coat. Yet Ralph and all of his three brothers studied hard and they all went to Harvard College when they grew up."

She moved around the room as she spoke, patting a head or caressing an arm. "When he graduated, Ralph Waldo Emerson became a teacher for a while to help pay for his brother William's college education, and then he became a minister. Mr. Emerson was always questioning life, and he didn't always agree with the church or the other ministers. How many of you question life? How many of you wonder why things happen the way they do?"

Two students immediately raised their hands. The rest watched curiously, surprised by their classmates' willingness to respond.

"Do you mean to tell me that only a few of you question the way things are?" Marva asked, exaggerating her amazement. "Well, I guess most of you think life is wonderful. Everyone always has enough to eat, a good place to live. There is no suffering, no poverty . . ."

Her words were muffled by the children's groans and giggles.

"Of course, you don't," she continued slowly. "Every time you say 'That's not fair' or you wonder why something is the way it is, you are questioning life, just as Mr. Emerson did. He believed that every person has a free will and can choose to make his life what he wants it to be. I believe that. I believe that you can make your life anything you want it to be."

Marva read aloud passages from the essay. She felt the children's restlessness as she read. Their eyes were roving around the room. A few had their arms slung over the backs of their chairs, their feet swinging sideways into the aisles. But

Marva continued. When she finished, she sat on the edge of a child's desk and looked at the class.

She said in a lower voice, "So you think this work is too difficult for you? Well, do not expect to do baby work in here. School can teach you how to lead a good life. We all come here to make life better. And the knowledge you put in your heads is going to save whom? You, not me. Mr. Emerson is telling us to trust our own thoughts, to think for ourselves and not worry about what other people tell us to think. Tanya, what does Emerson tell us to do?"

"Trust ourselves," replied Tanya.

"Very, very good, Tanya," Marva said. "James, what does Emerson tell us to do?"

"Trust ourselves."

"Very good, James. You're so clever, but I don't want to see you put your head on the desk. If you are sleepy, you should be home. This is a classroom, not a hospital or a hotel. I don't ever want to see any of you napping in your seats or just sitting with your hands folded, doing nothing. This is not a prayer meeting. If I see your hands folded, I'm going to put a Bible in them."

The children giggled and Marva smiled. A bond was beginning to grow between them. What she said and did this first day would determine the rest of their year together. She left nothing to chance.

It was Marva Collins' attitude that made children learn. What she did was brainwash them into succeeding. She was forever saying "You can do it," convincing her students there wasn't anything they could not do. There were no excuses for a child's not learning. There was no point in fixing the blame on television, or parents, or a child's environment. The decisive factor was the teacher up in front of the class. If a child sensed a teacher didn't care, then all the textbooks and prepackaged lesson plans and audio-visual equipment and fancy, new, carpeted, air-conditioned building facilities weren't going to get that child to learn.

"Children," she began, "today will decide whether you succeed or fail tomorrow. I promise you, I won't let you fail. I care about you. I love you. You can pay people to teach, but not to care.

"Some teachers sit behind a big desk, like a king in a castle, and the children are like the poor peasants. The desk isolates them from the children. But I don't sit behind a big desk in front of the class. I walk up and down the rows of desks every day and I hug each of you every day.

"Have you ever been afraid to go up to the teacher's desk? Did you think someone would laugh at you if you made a mistake?"

Marva didn't wait for an answer. She knew each child was following her closely. "Tell me when I'm wrong. You must never be afraid to tell a teacher if she is wrong. I'm not God. My mouth is no prayerbook. We shall work together. How many of you have been afraid to ask other teachers questions?"

Hands immediately went up.

"Why were you afraid to ask, Michele?"

"I was afraid the teacher would holler."

"Why were you afraid, Jerome?"

"I was afraid I would get hit with a ruler," he said flatly, expecting the snickers that came from his classmates.

"When you were afraid of a teacher, Bernette, what were you afraid of?"

"I was afraid she would make everyone laugh at me. My other teacher used to act like she was perfect or something. She used to make me feel dumb."

"Sometimes I don't like other grown-ups very much because they think they know everything. I don't know everything," Marva said. "I can learn all the time."

There was excitement building and Marva worked the momentum, like an entertainer who felt the pulse of an audience. "Oh, I love to see your eyes dance," she said. "New children have such dull eyes, but yours are already coming alive." She continued more seriously. "How many times did you feel old enough or smart enough to do something and then some grown-up told you 'You don't know how to do that'? I never like to hear grown-ups say that to a child. I don't know what you know. I can't wriggle down inside your skin or get into your brains. I am just another human being who has lived longer than you. I'm not smarter. I'm not greater. I bleed when I'm hurt, and I'm tired when I don't get enough sleep. But I am always here, to what? To help you. Freddie, tell me what you learned from Mr. Emerson's essay."

Freddie looked attentively at Marva but didn't answer.

"You have a right to your opinion. You say what you think," Marva told him. "Don't care what anyone else thinks. What's inside of you is important."

"I learned about self-reliance," Freddie whispered.

"Speak in a big voice, peach. What does self-reliance mean? Believing in ———."

"Believing in yourself?"

"Of course it does, but say it with confidence so we all know you believe in what you're saying. Let us all know how bright you are," Marva said, nodding. "Chris, what did you learn from Mr. Emerson?"

"To trust my own thoughts."

"Very good, Chris. See how much you already know? Marcus, what did you learn?"

"If you don't think for yourself, other people will tell you what to think."

Marva's eyes glistened. She laughed, sweeping her arm dramatically to her brow as she held herself up against the window sill, feigning a swoon. "Oh, I just can't stand it. You're all so bright. You're all so sagacious. *Sagacious* means smart and wise. What does *sagacious* mean, children?"

"Smart and wise," they chanted.

"And who is sagacious?"

"We are," they shouted.

"You certainly are." Marva put a throaty emphasis on *certainly* as she walked the rows of desks ruffling hair, pinching a cheek, squeezing a shoulder.

It was a beginning. The skills would come later with the daily drills of sounds and words over and over until Marva was tired of the litany. First she had to convince the children she cared about them, convince them to trust her, and make them believe they could do anything they wanted to do.

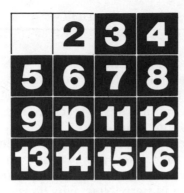

On the second day of school, Marva taught the English folk tale "The Little Red Hen and the Grain of Wheat." She had long believed that fairy tales and fables were effective in promoting emotional, intellectual, and social development. Most of the students were intrigued by the modulation of her voice and the changes in her face as she read aloud, shifting from one character to the next.

After the fourth round of quacking and squeaking and grunting "Not I," Marva noticed that Bernette Miller had taken off her locket and was looping the chain around her fingers, twisting it into a Cat's Cradle.

"You knew how to play with a chain when you came to school," Marva said. "Playing with a chain is a good way to get a job, isn't it? Put it away and listen to the story. I am not reading it just to entertain you. There is a lesson here. And we all better start paying attention to lessons like these, or this world we live in is surely headed for trouble."

Marva added, "I love you children all the time, even though I may correct you or disagree with you some of the time."

Marva finished the story. She closed the book, clasped it to her with one hand, and raised the other, index finger extended like a maestro's baton. Without losing the intensity delivered in the last line of the story, the discussion began.

"Do you think the little red hen was right in not sharing her bread with the duck, the mouse, and the pig?"

Heads nodded in agreement.

"Why was she right?" There were various demonstrations of squirming and fidgeting but no volunteers. After a while they would enjoy the heaping doses of teacher-student dialogue, but for now it was still a new and intimidating proposition. "Come on, come on," Marva said, "I am not going to leave you alone to become workbook idiots. You are not going to spend your time in here pasting and coloring and circling pictures. We're going to do some thinking in here. Now, why do you feel the hen was right?"

"She done it all. They was lazy," came a voice from the back.

"She *did* all what? She did all the work, didn't she? She had to sow and cut and thresh the wheat, and she had to carry it to the mill to be ground into flour, and she had to bake the loaf of bread. The other animals *were* lazy. They didn't want to help do any of the work. They only wanted to help eat the bread. What is the moral of this story? What lesson does it teach us? If we don't work, we don't eat. If we don't work, we don't ——?"

"Eat," came the unanimous reply. There was safety in numbers. Getting a child to take a chance and venture his or her own answer was another matter.

"Now, what would you say if I told you I think that hen was being selfish. She should have shared what she had with the other barnyard animals. What do you think about that?"

"No." They all shook their heads.

"Why not? Don't grown-ups always tell children that they should share their toys or their cookies or their candy? Freddie?"

"It ain't the same," he said.

"*Isn't*, sweetheart, it *isn't* the same. Children, listen to me for a moment. To succeed in this world, you must speak correctly. I don't want to hear any jive talk in here or any of this stuff about black English. You must not just think of yourselves as black children or ghetto children. You must become citizens of the world, like Socrates.

"Now, Freddie, why do you think there is a difference between the little red hen who did not share her bread and little children, who are always being told they should share their toys with others?"

"The hen had to work hard for the bread."

"That's wonderful, Freddie. You are absolutely right. The hen earned what she had. There is no comparison between the two situations. They are not analogous. You all know the word *same*. Let's try to learn some big words. *Analogous* means same or similar.

"Suppose I ask a child to help me do some chores, and when the chores are done I give the child some candy. Does that child have to share it with you because you say 'Give me some?' "

They shook their heads again.

"Of course not. You have a right to be rewarded for your work, for your efforts, and you also have a right to keep what you have earned. You don't have to give it away every time someone comes up to you with a hand out asking for something. A person who has his hand out today is going to have that hand out tomorrow. You are not going to solve his problem by giving him something free. He has to learn to solve his own problem. If you give another student in this class the answer to the homework, are you helping that student? No, you are cheating him out of learning how to find the answer himself.

"So the lesson of the story is one of the most important lessons you can learn. The person who does the work will be the one who has plenty of food, good clothes, and a fine house. The lazy person is always going to be standing there with his hand out. You have the choice, the right to choose which kind of person you want to be."

There it was. Marva had played her full hand. A teacher had to sell children on the idea of learning.

Oddly, Marva had not planned on becoming a teacher. She had not, in fact, given much thought to what she would do. As a child she had had the usual fleeting sort of girlish aspirations. One day she wanted to be a nurse, the next a secretary. With a child's fickleness she moved on to each new thing, her wishes shaped by a character in a book or a picture in a magazine. In that she was no different from other children. But what distinguished Marva's life from those around her—from the black children living in the wooden shanties with whom she went to school—was that she could entertain the vagaries of ambition beyond the age when others had to reconcile or surrender theirs. Necessity made no such demands on her. She grew up wealthy, pampered, and sheltered by small-town innocence and a doting protective father. She lived the freedom other people only dreamt.

★　★　★

I was born on August 31, 1936, in Monroeville, Alabama, about fifty miles north of Mobile. I grew up during the Depression, but while I can remember hearing the grown-ups talk about how times were hard and there was no money, none of that really affected my own life.

My father, Henry Knight, was one of the richest black men in Monroeville. We lived in a six-bedroom white clapboard house that had polished wood floors, store-bought furniture, and oriental rugs. Ours was one of the finest houses in the northern end of town, which was where all the blacks lived. People used to joke that our house was so fine you had to take your shoes off before going inside. My mother, Bessie, dressed me like a doll in ruffled, ribboned dresses and crisply pleated store-bought school dresses tied in back with an ironed sash. Because I looked so different from the other children, I had to put up with a lot of teasing. My schoolmates were mostly dressed in clothes their mothers made from the empty twenty-five-pound flour sacks they got from my father's grocery store.

There was determination in my family. We were always a family of doers and achievers. My mother's father, William Nettles, farmed all night and peddled meat door to door during the day, and he was the first black man in town to have a car, a crank-up Model T Ford. Everyone else rode around in mule-drawn wagons. My other grandfather, Henry Knight, Sr., owned a store and several houses and lived off his rental properties. He was a patient, thrifty man who always looked successful in a suit and tie, a gold watch chain, and well-shined shoes. I remember wondering why he always wore Sunday clothes.

I believed my father was the greatest man who ever lived. I would never meet anyone I admired more. He was the moving force in my life and we had a very special relationship. Of course, I loved my mother, but we weren't as close. My mother was very prim and proper, not as free with the hugs and kisses as my dad. She showed her love and concern for me by making sure I ate the right foods and wore the right clothes. I knew she loved me, but I missed hearing her tell me that she did. As an adult I have come to understand how important it is to be openly affectionate with a child, to be sensitive to a child's feelings. I couldn't talk things over with my mother, which was especially frustrating since I was the only child in the family until I was fourteen and always needed someone to talk to. My father was always there. I could say anything to him, even if it was silly, and he would patiently listen. I never felt I had to prove anything to him. I always knew where I stood. But I could never quite please my mother. I was not as ladylike or as well-behaved or as pretty as she wanted me to be. Parents don't realize how they can nag and pick away at a child until there is nothing left to pick. My dad was always supportive, constantly telling me how smart and pretty and special I was, even when I wasn't, so I felt good about myself. However, I did become an overachiever, and I attribute that to my mother saying I would never come to any good.

My father had only a fourth-grade education, but he was the smartest person I ever knew. He was a risk-taker with an instinct for business. Taking over his father's grocery store, he parlayed the assets into a thousand-acre cattle ranch and the town funeral parlor. He was a clever businessman, and even when he didn't have enough collateral, he somehow convinced people to go along with him on faith. When products were scarce on every grocery shelf during the Second World War, my father made a deal with an A & P down in Florida that could buy goods in larger quantities. He was the only merchant in Alabama—black or white—who had steaks, nylon stockings, chocolate, and chewing gum for his customers.

The black community in Monroeville existed apart from the white community. Blacks who were engaged in business were important and had a lot of influence. Since my father was the only black undertaker and the only black proprietor of a grocery store, he was a leader in the black community. The white businessmen respected him, and among blacks he was well respected though he was not particularly liked. Many people were envious of him. Sometimes people said they didn't want to shop in his store and make him any richer, yet those same people came to him when they didn't have money because they knew he would give them credit.

If someone got into trouble in town and was headed for jail, my father stood the bail bond. Not only blacks but many whites—some who owned the big stores downtown—would sneak into our house after dark to borrow money from my father. They didn't want anyone to know they were having anything to do with blacks, much less borrowing money. My father never chased me out of the room or said "This is none of your business," so I learned very early in life that white society was not the bright paradise other black children thought it was.

My father treated me the same as he would have treated a son, mainly, I guess, because I was always following him around. I didn't have a lot of playmates my own age because the other children had to work in the cotton fields after school and during vacations. I used to beg my parents to let me go to the cotton fields with the other children. Once my father let me go and I caught a bad cold. My father said he had to spend more money for the doctor than I earned in two days picking cotton, so he didn't let me go back. It was just as well because the foreman had told me not to come back to his field. He didn't like my bright ideas for making my cotton weigh more, such as putting stones in the bottom of the sack or pulling the whole cotton boll, branch and all. The other children took their job seriously because they had to.

Another reason I spent so much time with my father was that my mother constantly shooed me out of the house. She was a fastidious housekeeper, impatient with an awkward child who always seemed to spill and break things. "You can't keep a house in order," she would tell me. "I hope I live to see you grow up 'cause the buzzards are gonna fly over your house." My mother didn't try teaching me to cook and sew. She later said she realized it was a mistake because when I first married Clarence Collins, he had to take charge of the cooking and sewing. The funny thing is that I picked up my mother's housekeeping habits and I now find I have many of the same quirks.

From the time I was eight I woke at dawn and went with my father to open the grocery store. The people in town would buy bread before they set off to work in the fields. Late afternoons I helped him add the day's receipts. I counted the pennies and quarters and put them into rolls, and I helped haul out the empty cartons and sacks, which my father burned in a huge bonfire. Sometimes we'd roast potatoes or hotdogs over the flames. When my father slaughtered a cow in the large yard behind the house, I was out there with him, sprawled across the overhanging limb of the chinaberry tree.

Sometimes I sat there daydreaming about travel to exotic places. Or I imagined myself grown up and married with children of my own. For all my tomboyish ways—climbing the plum and chinaberry trees, throwing the hard green berries, playing in dark, cool caves—I was always sure I wanted to get married and have children with enchanting names like Chiquita Denise and Frenette René. Strangely, I ended up giving my children ordinary names—Eric, Patrick, and Cynthia.

At night when all the chores were finished, my father and I sat together and I would read aloud from *The Montgomery Advertiser* and *The Mobile Press* or *Aesop's Fables* or poetry books, until my mother waved me on to bed. And I would fall asleep thinking about the things I had read, pretending I was one of the characters in the stories.

On Saturdays I rode through town with my father, sitting next to him on the front seat of the new black Cadillac he bought each year for his funeral parlor. As we drove past the black men loitering in the town square, my father shook his head and said how undignified they looked. And when we saw black women carrying baskets of whitefolk's laundry on their heads, my father always said, "If I have to work all day and night, I'll never see my family doing other people's washing."

During the summer, from the time I was seven, I went on cattle-buying trips with my father. One day a week we would drive through the Alabama Black Belt, from county to county, through the rolling prairies filled with goldenrod and cane-brake. Sometimes we went to the livestock markets in Mont-gomery.

In the 1940s Alabama cattle auctions were segregated, like everything else. Although everyone bid on the same cattle, blacks and whites sat in separate buying sections. I grew up with that racism. You were always reminded you were black. You were always expected to know your place. Blacks had to use separate water fountains and rest rooms. We weren't served in restaurants. We had to go around to a back window if we wanted food. My father always said he would whip me within an inch of my life if he caught me getting food at a back counter. He also wouldn't let my mother or me go into a depart-ment store because white sales clerks gave black customers a hard time about trying on clothes. Black women had to put a piece of plastic on their heads before trying on hats. My father would not allow my mother or me to be humiliated. He did all the shopping and brought clothes home for us.

He was a proud man and a nonconformist. He did things that were unheard of in those days. He marched into the den-tist's office through the front door, though blacks were sup-posed to come in through the back. And he got away with it. No one said anything. I guess his money made the difference.

At an auction he outbid the buyers from Swift and Cud-ahy, the big meat packing houses. Afterwards, at the cashier's window, the buyers were waiting for my father. They shouted at him, backed him into a corner, and warned him not to come back to the cattle sales again.

I watched, frightened. Though I lived with the day-to-day realities of segregation and was used to hearing the word *nig-ger,* I had never directly experienced the violence and horrors of racism. I only heard about it. The grown-ups still talked about the Scottsboro boys. Occasionally I would hear about lynchings, or about people who were beaten up by the sheriff and dragged off to jail in the middle of the night. None of that had ever touched my own family. The first time I saw race hatred up close was when those buyers surrounded my father.

He did not apologize. He was silent, his eyes firmly set, not a muscle in him moving. He stood there tall and distinguished-looking in his starched shirt and creased trousers with the Stacy Adams shoes he always wore. He looked the men straight in their eyes and said he'd be coming back to the next auction. If they were going to kill him, he'd take one of them with him when he died.

I thought the men would hurt him then. They hesitated, asking each other what to do about "that nigger." Just then two other white men came by and broke things up. The buyers shrugged and walked away. On the way home my father told me, "I made an honest bid. If you believe in what you do, then you don't ever have to fear anyone."

Every sale after that, my mother pleaded with my father not to go, but he said, "I'm not going to stay away. I can't die but once." That was the kind of determination I learned from him. He was a man of strong values and uncompromising beliefs. I always believed strength was passed on from one generation to the next. I guess I felt secure and confident, maybe because I was Henry Knight's daughter, but also because growing up in a small town like Monroeville, Alabama, I was sheltered and protected from a lot of things. We didn't have the kind of crime they had in the big cities. We didn't worry about rapes or muggings or drugs. If those things were happening somewhere else, we only learned about it from the newspapers, and by the time we got the news from Mobile it was already history.

I lived in a town where everyone seemed to know and trust everyone else. Just about everybody was cousin this or cousin that. Like the other children in Monroeville I was free to roam from yard to yard collecting pecans and figs in the autumn, free to roam through the pine forests searching for cones, free to play in the low red-clay hills, sliding down mud banks, wading in creeks, building dams along the shore. It was a happy, carefree childhood.

When I was twelve, my parents separated. My father remained in Monroeville, while my mother and I moved forty miles south to Atmore. I don't really know what went wrong between my parents. Maybe I have just blocked the whole thing out of my mind. But somehow I was able to cope with their separation. My father had already taught me to be a survivor. He taught me that whatever happens in life, a person has to go forward. Perhaps I forced myself to adjust so I could show my father I was just like him.

I remained close with my father, and he continued to be the strongest force in my life. I visited him summers, weekends, and sometimes during the week. He was never farther than a phone call or a short drive away. In the meantime Atmore became home. I spent my adolescence there with my mother, her new husband, and a new baby sister, Cynthia.

But the years in Monroeville were the great, great years of my childhood. Those were the years that made me what I am.

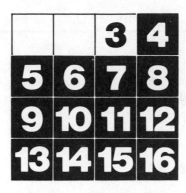

Marva moved up and down the rows of desks. "I could just cry that you have no sounds," she said, "for sounds make up words, and words are thoughts. Ideas. And the thoughts and ideas in your heads make you what you are.

"Well, you will have the sounds. You will never have to guess at them. Sounds are like keys, opening the door to words. If you don't have the right key, you can't open the door to your house, can you? If you don't have the right sounds, you can't pronounce a word."

Marva twirled around to the board and wrote *The catamaran sailed around the ait.* "What does that mean?" she asked. The class looked lost. "All right, let's see what we have. Let's syllabicate *catamaran.* The first vowel sound is a short *a,* as in cat. The next two vowel sounds are *uh,* which we mark with this sign, called a German schwa. It looks like an upside-down *e,* but I don't ever want to hear any of you calling it an upside-down *e* sound. It is called a German schwa. All right, the last *a* also has a short vowel sound, *ran.* Catamaran. A catamaran is a kind of sailboat.

"The catamaran sailed around the ait. The vowels *a* and *i* make one sound, the sound of a long *a.* The rule is: when two vowels go walking, the first one does the talking; it says its name. Ait. An ait is a small island in the middle of a river or lake.

"So now you know that the sailboat sailed around the small island. See how you were lost in words? That will never happen to you again. You will learn all the rules so that words will no longer be a mystery. You will be able to talk to anyone, no matter how smart, no matter how rich, no matter how pretty. You are all clever bright children, and there's nothing you can't do.''

★　★　★

I learned to read before I was old enough to go to school. My grandmother used to read aloud to me from her Bible, sounding out words by syllables. She had learned to read and spell by syllables when she was in school. By listening to her and imitating what she said, I learned the letter sounds and how to blend them together to read printed words. Once I discovered how to sound out words, I tried reading everything I could get my hands on: labels on cans and boxes, the farmer's almanac, newspapers, books of fairy tales and fables, and especially Grandma Annie Knight's huge black-leather Bible. My favorite was the story about Joseph and his brothers. I read it over and over until my grandmother—"Mama-Dear," as I called her—would shake her head and say, "Baby, you read so much I'm afraid you're gonna lose your mind." The old people in the South had a superstition that a child who was too studious— *prissy* was their word for it—was headed for trouble.

My introduction to literature began with the Bible stories I heard from my grandmother. Mama-Dear read her Bible every day. Down South everyone was religious. I grew up during the time of the big revival meetings when going to church was serious business. If you didn't go, you were an outcast. But Mama-Dear was the most pious, prayerful person I ever saw. Every morning and every night she got down on her knees beside her high, four-poster bed and said her prayers. When Mama-Dear wasn't praying or reading her Bible, she was walking around the house singing "Precious Lord Take My Hand" and "What A Friend We Have In Jesus." She was forever reciting proverbs. Time and tide wait for no man. Good that comes too late is good for nothing. "Baby," she would say to me, "a good name will go farther than you will." I got so tired of hearing those proverbs when I was a child. Now I use them all the time. Sometimes they are the best way of saying what needs to be said. I teach them to my students. I have a collection of proverbs for class discussions and writing assignments.

I spent a lot of time with Mama-Dear and Grandpa Daddy Henry. Some nights the three of us sat in front of the fireplace as the flames cast shadows that danced on the walls. The scent of burning pinecones floated lightly through the living room while Mama-Dear recited poems like "Hiawatha" or "Paul Revere's Ride." She had memorized them as a schoolgirl and was still proud of knowing them by heart.

I was smitten with poetry and literature. But there were no libraries for black children in Alabama. The only books I could get were the ones I bought, borrowed, or received as gifts. When my parents took me visiting to someone's house, I would disappear, rummaging through cabinets and shelves in search of books. A book was a treasure, and I lost myself in every one I found—a basic reader brought home from school, a *True Confessions* magazine, or even a dictionary. I read Nancy Drew mysteries, gothic romances, Richard Wright's *Black Boy* and *Native Son,* and Booker T. Washington, who I thought was the second greatest man next to my father. And I loved Erskine Caldwell's *God's Little Acre,* though my mother didn't approve of my reading such books. I bought half a dozen copies of *God's Little Acre* with the money I earned helping in the store. I hid them in different places as insurance. Every time my mother found the book and threw it away, I would take out another copy and continue reading.

It was Aunt Ruby Jones, my mother's sister, who introduced me to William Shakespeare. Aunt Ruby had gone back to high school after marrying and having two children. When I was at her house playing with my cousins, I would see her studying and reading from her schoolbooks. One night I overheard Aunt Ruby talking to Uncle Robert about someone named Lady Macbeth. Then she opened an old gray book and began reading:

She should have died hereafter;
There would have been a time for such a word.
Tomorrow, and tomorrow, and tomorrow,
Creeps in this petty pace from day to day. . . .

I was only nine at the time, but I was enthralled by the lines. For days after that I walked around with "Tomorrow, and tomorrow, and tomorrow" spinning in my head. The next visit to Aunt Ruby's, I asked if I could borrow that gray book. I read through *Macbeth,* and while I was not able to grasp its full meaning, I was fascinated by the action and the characters of the play. I thought it was such fun to say "Double, double, toil and trouble." My interest in Shakespeare wasn't encouraged until I reached high school. We never read Shakespeare in the lower grades. Most students still don't.

Along with the other black children in Monroeville I spent the primary grades at Bethlehem Academy, a clapboard building with unpainted walls and a woodburning stove in each room. There were two grades to a classroom. Books were in short supply, and most of our teachers had only a tenth grade education themselves.

Out of all the teachers at Bethlehem two left a strong impression. I got off to a bad start with my first teacher, a heavy-set woman who often wore a blue dress patterned with red, green, and yellow alphabet letters. In the first week of school when we were learning arabic numerals, I kept making the numeral 2 backwards. Each time I drew it wrong the teacher rapped my fingers with a ruler. I never understood why she kept hitting me. If I had known how to do it right, I would have. She acted as though I had made the mistake deliberately.

I never forgot that experience. It has influenced the teaching methods I use with my students. To me an error means a child needs help, not a reprimand or ridicule for doing it wrong. No child should ever be told "That's stupid" or "You can't do it" or "You don't know what you're doing." Adults should take a positive approach with children. The most important thing we can do as parents and teachers is build a child's self-confidence. Any child can learn if he or she has not already been taught too thoroughly that learning is impossible. Children need reassurance and encouragement. They have to be told that it is all right to make mistakes because mistakes are part of learning. I tell my students: "If you knew everything there is to know, then you wouldn't have to be in school."

Praise is essential in developing the right attitude toward learning and toward school. We all know this in theory. In practice we often forget the importance of praise in dealing with children. We forget how sensitive children can be and how fragile their egos are. It is painful for a child to be told "This is wrong." Rather than punishing, teachers and parents should encourage continued effort: "This is good. It's a wonderful try, but it is not quite right. Let's try correcting this together."

I praise every child's effort. I put every child's paper up on the wall or the bulletin board, not just the perfect ones. And I never put a failing grade or red marks all over a paper. That is a sure way to turn a child off of learning. Put yourself in the place of a child who is handed back a paper with a low grade while the other children have received high marks. Imagine how that child feels when everyone asks each other, as children always do, "What did you get on your paper?" That child wants to crumple the paper and throw it away. That child wants to get away from school. I write "very good" or "wonderful work" or make a smiling face on every paper. Then I handle errors by working individually with each child. We correct errors on a separate piece of paper, on an individual work sheet, or at the blackboard. I learned the value of blackboard practice from my fourth grade teacher, Mrs. McGants.

Mrs. McGants was a patient, good teacher. She had her students work at the blackboard so she could correct mistakes as quickly as they were made. Children need immediate feedback, especially in math and language where they need to master one skill before they can go on to the next. I do not wait days before returning papers. Errors will mean nothing to a child several days later when the class has moved on to something new. Delay in correcting errors only makes the child fall behind.

I find that children often understand a concept better when you take them to the blackboard rather than trying to show them at their seat. This practice helps the rest of the class at the same time, especially the shy child who will never come out and say that he or she does not understand. I draw a large part of my curriculum from these errors, not from the teaching guides. One child's errors become a lesson for the whole class. If one child is having trouble with something, it is likely that others are also, and all can benefit from a review.

My teaching methods evolved, in part, from my own experiences as a student. My first grade teacher was a model for what not to do. My fourth grade teacher showed me what to do. Miss Rolle, my tenth grade teacher at Escambia County Training School, was my favorite. She was probably not as beautiful as I then thought, but the way she walked and moved made her seem very sophisticated. I wanted to be just like her. Though Miss Rolle was from Alabama, she did not have a thick southern accent. I was so impressed by how articulate she was and how she enunciated her words that I practiced imitating her. I studied vocabulary from the dictionary all the time. Townsfolk used to tell my father, "The way that girl puts words together is like something out of the pages of a book." The white salesmen who came from Mobile to take purchasing orders for cans of beans and boxes of chickens would come into my dad's grocery store and ask, "Henry, where's your girl? I sure do like listening to the way she talks."

I suppose it is because of Miss Rolle that I stress proper speech and pronunciation with my own students. I try to get them in the habit of using correct grammar when they speak, and I have them read aloud every day so I can check pronunciation as well as comprehension. Having children read silently in class only allows their mistakes to go unnoticed. I have heard children read *capa-city* for *capacity, denny* instead of *deny,* or *doze* instead of *does,* treating the final *s* as though it pluralized the word *doe.* Children frequently reverse letters when they read. For example, they confuse *sacred* and *scared, diary* and *dairy, angel* and *angle.* If children read silently, they continue to make those mistakes.

Another reason for reading aloud is to build vocabulary. A child reading silently skips over big words he doesn't know. When I am there listening to a child read, I can interrupt to ask the meaning. The whole class benefits as we can look up the definition, the base word within the larger word, and the part of speech. I also have my students read aloud for tone, inflection, and punctuation. Reading aloud helps a child realize the difference between a comma, a period, a question mark, and an exclamation point. Children who are just learning to read tend to read individual words, not groups of words or phrases. That limits comprehension. I encourage my students to become idea readers, not word readers. By reading aloud children learn to understand words within the context of a sentence, and they see how words connect with each other to express an idea. This practice promotes not only good reading but good writing.

My students read everything orally—literature, science, social studies, and history. I even have them read their compositions aloud every day. It makes children more conscious of sentence structure, allows them to proofread for punctuation errors and word omissions, and helps them develop a certain presence and authority in front of an audience. Miss Rolle used to make us stand and read our papers to the class.

Except for Miss Rolle's and Mrs. McGants' classes, my schooling was typical of the separate and unequal education black children received in Alabama during the forties and fifties. Yet I found my own way around the inequities.

At Escambia County Training School—all high schools for black students were called training schools—girls did not graduate without taking home economics. I suppose it was the whitefolks way of saying all black women would never be anything more than homemakers or domestics. I refused to take it and signed up for a typing course instead. Shortly before graduation the principal called me into his office to say that unless I took the required course, I would not receive my diploma. I told him that I already knew enough about housekeeping. I didn't know what I was going to do when I went out into the world, but typing was going to be of more help than home economics. I never knew what made the principal change his mind. I was the only female student who ever graduated from Escambia County Training School without taking home economics.

From the day I became aware of what college was, I made up my mind I was going. My parents never stressed college degrees, not having had a high school education themselves, but they stressed learning.

I chose Clark College in Atlanta, an exclusive, all-black liberal arts school for girls. My father had no objection. He was proud of my being the first one in the family to go to college, and he believed it was his duty as a parent to make sure his child had the best. From the way the neighbors carried on, my father might have committed a cardinal sin. "What are you sending that girl to college for?" they asked him. "You'll never get your money back, 'cause that girl's never gonna do a thing for you."

Everything at Clark was very southern and very proper with a certain finishing-school mentality. How a student dressed was just as important as what she learned. My house-mother made certain I wore hats and white gloves, and she once sent me back to my room to change because I had made the "mistake" of wearing suede shoes with a leather jacket. To this day I am very conscious of clothes and appearance.

I don't believe I learned very much at college. It was my own fault. I went to college not really knowing what I wanted to do. At the last minute I decided to major in secretarial science. It seemed the practical thing to do. With a business sense picked up from my father and a knowledge of typing and book-keeping, I expected to get an office job upon graduating from Clark. I also took some education courses because they interested me, though I had no intention of becoming a teacher.

In June of 1957 I returned to Alabama with my degree and discovered that the only office positions available to blacks were civil service jobs. None of the private companies wanted to hire a black secretary. I filled out a civil service application. I turned down the one available job because it was in Montgomery and I wasn't ready to leave home again. Still, finding some kind of job was a matter of pride. After the way people had chided my father about paying my way to Clark, I was not about to let that degree collect dust.

I finally found a job teaching typing, shorthand, bookkeeping, and business law at Monroe County Training School, and considered myself fortunate. In those days teaching jobs were hard to come by in Alabama. Teachers seemed to live and die in their jobs. More than just a proper occupation for a woman, teaching was one of the only occupations at the time for an educated black woman. For all my attempts to be different, I finally had to settle for that. I had to accommodate myself to the realities of life in Alabama.

Some things are meant to be.

From the very first day, I felt comfortable teaching. With some experience conducting Sunday school classes at church, I was used to standing up and speaking before a group. I liked being around people, working with them and helping them understand things. I had always been fascinated with learning, with the *process* of discovering something new, and it was exciting to share in the discoveries made by my tenth, eleventh, and twelfth grade students at Monroe County Training School.

I didn't know anything about educational theory, and I have often thought that worked in my favor. Without preconceived ideas and not bound by rules, I was forced to deal with my students as individuals, to talk to them, listen to them, find out their needs. I wasn't trying to see how they fit into any learning patterns or educational models. I followed my instincts and taught according to what felt right. I brought my own experiences to the classroom, trying to figure out how I had learned as a student. I remembered what had bored me and what had interested me, which teachers I had liked and which ones I had disliked, and applied it all to my teaching.

Not having any formal theory or textbook methodology to follow made me receptive to new ideas. I was constantly learning along with my students, always looking for new ways to make a lesson more exciting. My colleagues were very helpful, offering suggestions and sharing their methods. They all seemed to care so much about their students. I may have been naive or too idealistic, but at the time the whole teaching profession seemed inspiring.

The principal at Monroe really taught me how to teach. He was especially hard on new teachers. He sat in my classroom every day for two months observing, shaking or nodding his head and taking notes. After class he would sit me down and lecture me as though I were one of the children. He told me to get to the point of a lesson more directly. He would say, "Well, you lost the boy in the third seat of the last row." He trained me to watch the students' faces, to see by their eyes if they understood. I learned that a good teacher knows the students, not just the subject.

After two years at Monroe I liked teaching but wasn't ready to commit myself. I was immature. Staying with my father on weekends and with my grandparents during the week, I was still too unsettled to dedicate myself fully to anything.

As a teacher I now try to teach children how to deal with life. More than reading, writing, and arithmetic, I want to give them a philosophy for living. But at twenty-one I was too sheltered and too protected to know how to deal with life myself. Though I earned a salary, my father continued to give me spending money—which I continued to accept—and he bought me expensive clothes, did everything for me. He even warmed up my car in the morning and filled the gas tank at the pump behind his store.

At some point my dependence on my father began to bother me. I felt constricted by small-town life. After four years in Atlanta I found Monroeville too confining. It was time to grow up and be on my own.

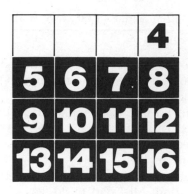

In June 1959, at the close of the school year, I left for Chicago to visit my grandmother's cousin, Annie Townsend, for a two month vacation. I did not plan on getting a job, finding a husband, starting a family, and settling down in Garfield Park.

After a few days in Chicago, I got tired of being a tourist. On an impulse I read through the want ads in the newspaper and applied for a job as a medical secretary at Mount Sinai Hospital. I was hired. I didn't know anything about medicine, but I began teaching myself Latin to understand the medical terms. The job was so exciting I decided to stay in Chicago. I took an apartment in a large, U-shaped courtyard building on Hamlin Avenue, overlooking Garfield Park. It was a small apartment with a Murphy bed and a sunny kitchen. It seemed elegant to me, but the best part was that this place was truly my own. My first apartment was close to the hospital, close to Cousin Annie, and close to Clarence Collins.

Clarence lived with his parents next door to Cousin Annie. I was first attracted to him by his devotion to his family. He was one of eleven children, eight boys and three girls, a close-knit family. When I met Clarence, he was working as a draftsman for the Sunbeam Appliance Company, a job he would keep for close to twenty years. While he did not have a college education and was not as well-read as I, he was just as determined. He was also more level-headed. And he was kind and gentle. All the neighborhood children gathered around him, and several went with us to Riverview Amusement Park on our first date. I knew that any man who could be so patient with someone else's children was bound to be a good father and a good husband. Within a year we were married.

I continued to work as a secretary, but soon I missed teaching. I missed the classroom. I missed the excitement of helping students discover the solution to a problem, of seeing the pieces fit together.

I went downtown to the Board of Education and filled out a teaching application. All I had to do was send for my college transcripts and my Alabama teaching credentials. Since I had not taken methodology courses, I was not eligible to take the certification exam. It didn't matter because teachers in the Chicago school system didn't have to be certified. There was a teacher shortage at that time, so as long as you had a college degree, you could teach. If you weren't certified, you worked as a full-time-basis substitute which meant you were assigned to a school but had no seniority and were not guaranteed permanent placement. Years later the Chicago Teachers' Union pressured the school board to grant automatic certification to those who had been in the school system for three years.

I received a letter telling me to report to Calhoun South Elementary School on Jackson Boulevard, where I was given a second grade class. I didn't have any experience teaching such young children, but I assumed the principles were the same as in teaching older students. I had to motivate the children, create a desire for learning. I had to make them understand why it was important to learn. And I had to make them feel worthwhile and confident.

I drew on my own childhood memories, recalling the things that had made me feel happy, sad, excited, hurt, or afraid, the things that made me want to laugh or cry. And I tried to be sensitive to those feelings in my students. I found that hugging and touching and saying "I love you" immediately made them feel secure and comfortable in the classroom, establishing a bond between us and also among the children.

Children are quick to mimic adults. If a teacher ridicules or picks on a child, chances are the children will pick on each other. And of course the reverse is true.

At first I followed the Board of Education curriculum.

Soon I thought the work was way below the children's ability. They could learn much more. So I expanded the curriculum. If a lesson called for the children to locate all the triangles on a page and color them in with crayons, I would tell the children to put a green capital *D* above the second triangle and to color the fourth triangle red and the seventh one blue. Then I would have them write the words *red* and *blue* above those triangles. The children were learning not only to recognize shapes but to follow directions, to think, to count, to distinguish colors, and to write. The group activity also kept them more attentive than they would have been if I had left them alone to work quietly by themselves.

After a few weeks my students were bored with the required second grade reader. I couldn't blame them. There were no real stories in those books, nothing to occupy a child's mind or stimulate thought. The pages were filled with pictures of boys and girls playing, and below the pictures were sentences like "Run, Pepper, run" and "See Pepper run." There was no reason for the children to bother reading the words. All they had to do was look at the pictures.

Never having taught second grade before, I didn't know very much about how to teach reading. I didn't know about the debate between advocates of the phonics method, in which children learn to decode vowel and consonant sounds in a word, and the look-say method, in which they identify words with pictures and build a "sight vocabulary" by reading sentences that use the same words over and over. It seemed to me that the natural thing to do was teach the children to sound out words. That was how I had learned to read, so that was what I taught my second graders. I disregarded the teaching guide, which followed the look-say method.

It seemed to me that the children would be more anxious to read if they were interested in what they were reading. I didn't have any expert studies to go by. It was just common sense. Why would a child want to put out the effort just to read "See Pepper run"? I stopped using the required reader and brought in books from the library and from bookstores. My children read from *Aesop's Fables, Grimm's Fairy Tales,* Hans Christian Andersen, La Fontaine's *Fables,* and Leo Tolstoy's

Fables and Fairytales. I chose those stories because they teach values and morals and lessons about life. Fairy tales and fables allow children to put things in perspective—greed, trouble, happiness, meanness, and joy. After reading those stories you have something to think over and discuss. More than anything, I wanted my students to be excited about reading. I wanted them to understand that reading is not an exercise in memorizing words but a way to bring ideas to light.

I had my students draw their own pictures to illustrate the stories. Sometimes we acted out the fables, or we made up our own ending. We even composed our own fables. I would start and then each child would add a sentence. I felt my way along, trying out new ideas and experimenting with different methods and lessons. And I loved it. I loved watching my students' faces when they discovered the solution to a math problem or recognized on their own the parallel between two stories. There was an effervescent quality to their excitement.

I taught at Calhoun for a year, leaving when I became pregnant with our first son, Eric. I knew I would go back to teaching.

While I was at Calhoun, Clarence and I bought a gray-stone two-flat at 3819 West Adams Street. It was down the street from Delano Elementary School and just around the corner from my apartment on Hamlin Avenue.

Garfield Park was a nice, respectable neighborhood of mostly Jewish, Italian, and Irish families. We were one of the first black families to move in. Looking back, I suppose I should have realized how fast the neighborhood was changing. The bank on Madison Street closed down. Steel grates appeared across some of the storefronts at night, and there were "For Rent" signs in many of the shop windows. At the time I didn't know anything about changing neighborhoods. I had grown up in a town where people mostly stayed in the same place all their lives.

In 1962, a year after we moved into the house, Eric was born. Three years later we had a second son, Patrick, and in 1968 our daughter Cynthia came along. By that time Garfield Park had turned into another Chicago ghetto. Prostitutes and street gangs staked out the area. There were razed lots, boarded-up windows, and vacant buildings. The worst destruction took place in April 1968 during the riots that followed Martin Luther King's death. People went crazy. They ran through the streets breaking windows, looting, and setting buildings on fire. It was terrifying. We locked ourselves in the house for days. When the rioting was over, there wasn't much of anything left in Garfield Park. All the stores were closed down. Clarence had to walk nearly a mile to get a gallon of milk.

With small children and a growing family Clarence and I simply could not afford to move away from Garfield Park. A lot of our friends began to move away. Maybe it was my rebel streak, but the more I saw people run off and forget about their old friends and neighbors, the more I resolved to stay, even later when we had enough money. I had put down roots in Garfield Park, and I wasn't going to give up that easily.

In the years since then I have been fighting an attitude, the apathy. No one seems to have any pride anymore. I don't understand what happens to people in urban areas like Garfield Park. In Alabama the poor blacks used to wash down every inch of their unpainted wooden shacks with Octagon Laundry Soap. They swept under their porches, even if they didn't have store-bought brooms. They cut down branches from trees and tied them together with rags or string to make brushbrooms. People in Alabama would shake their heads in disgust if they saw a dirty mop hanging out to dry on someone's porch railing, or greying sheets dangling from a clothesline. My mother used to say you can just look outside a person's house and tell what he is.

The one thing everyone in Alabama had was pride. That pride was a consistent part of a southern upbringing. The poor children came to school with neatly sewn patches on their clothes. Their clothes may have been old, but they were clean. If your children were dirty, you didn't belong anywhere in the social order of the town. If you had a dirty water bucket, you were a disgrace, and if you drank from the dipper instead of a glass, you were considered a heathen. If you didn't mow your lawn or clip your hedges, you were ostracized. When the neighbor next door saw you mowing your lawn, he would mow his. And on Sundays, after the church services, each family set out a picnic dinner and everyone saw who could have the best food. If your dinner didn't spread out well, you were disgraced.

Neighborhoods like Garfield Park are made up mostly of people from the South, like myself. I don't understand why my southern pride stuck while theirs didn't. Part of the problem is that people are looking for easy solutions. They have been led to believe that someone else is going to do things for them. Too many black people have fallen into the pattern of listening to the self-proclaimed leaders who find it in their own best interest to make people feel there are "free rides" in this world. If so many foreign immigrants could come to America and make it, so can people like those in Garfield Park. But unfortunately, so many blacks are waiting for white America to be their Messiah.

I don't think politicians are going to change things. And I don't think marching or violent protest accomplishes anything in the long run. I tell my students all the time: "If you raise your fist and yell at someone today, he may give you something because he feels sorry for you or is frightened of you, but what are you going to do tomorrow and the next day and ten years from now?"

I am convinced that the real solution is education. We have to teach children self-reliance and self-respect. We have to teach them the importance of learning, of developing skills, of doing for themselves. I am always reminding my students that if you give a man a fish, he will eat for only a day. If you teach him how to fish, he will feed himself for a lifetime. That's why I stay in Garfield Park. The legacy I want to leave behind is a generation of children who realize that you can't get something for nothing, who are proud and resourceful enough to take care of their own. In this messed up world, the only children who are going to make something of themselves are those who come from strong parents or those who have had a strong teacher. One or the other. Or both.

I went back to teaching in February 1963, when my son Eric was six months old. I didn't like leaving him with a baby-sitter all day. But I had to work. Without my salary, we had a hard time meeting the mortgage. Fortunately, I was assigned to Delano Elementary School, just down the street from my house. It enabled me to come home at lunchtime or in case of an emergency. I had a sixth grade class the first year, a second grade class the next, and later I settled in as a second grade teacher. Except for two brief maternity leaves when Patrick and Cindy were born, I stayed at Delano for several years. The job at Delano offered the best of all worlds. Eventually it turned into a nightmare, not because of the students but because of the other teachers.

When I started at Delano I was impressed by the principal, an older German man, a classical scholar who read the *Iliad* to students during lunchtime. He held faculty workshops where he recited Donne, Yeats, and Byron, stopping in the middle of a poem to ask his teachers to supply the next line. When they couldn't, he waved his hand with disgust and said, "Some of you aren't worth a Sam Hill." I learned a lot from him, and I began teaching poetry and classical literature to my students. Above all the principal taught me that a good teacher is one who continues to learn along with the students.

I got along well with most of the teachers at first, particularly the older ones whom I learned from. I used to sit at lunch with a woman from Arkansas and discuss ways to get children to like reading. Her advice to me was to involve the children in the story and never to let them stare passively at words on a page. She told me to have them take the place of one of the characters in a story and then ask them questions about what they thought and felt. She also suggested that I have the children write a letter to one of the characters. To this day I find these are excellent ways to get a child excited about a story.

Over the years the faculty at Delano changed. Some teachers retired, some transferred to other schools voluntarily, some were shifted around the city by the administrative bureaucracy. Their replacements were a different breed of teachers, people who really didn't care or know what they were doing. Several were young men who became teachers to avoid the draft and Vietnam. Many others were quick to admit they didn't really want to teach but couldn't think of anything else to do. All they wanted was to get by.

A new principal came to Delano. He didn't pay much attention to what went on in the classrooms, as long as things were quiet and orderly. Practically the only time he came into my room was to tell me the shades on the windows weren't even. He said it made a poor impression on people passing by the school. One time he interrupted a child reciting Robert Frost's "Fire and Ice" to tell me I had better get my class outside for the fire drill. It was the sixth fire drill in two days. On his way out the principal walked over to one of my girls and told her she could not sit in class with her shoes off. What do a child's shoes have to do with her brains? That child had created havoc in two other classrooms. Finally she had settled down to learn.

The longer I taught in the public school system, the more I came to think that schools were concerned with everything but teaching. Teaching was the last priority, something you were supposed to do after you collected the milk money, put up the bulletin boards—which must never display spring flowers in January or a leftover winter scene in March—straightened the shades and desks, filled out forms in triplicate, punched all the computer cards with pre-test and post-test scores, and charted all the reading levels so they could be shipped downtown to the Board of Education. Everybody was test crazy. It seemed as though the administrators only wanted to probe IQs and rank test scores. It didn't matter whether the children learned anything at all. Nothing was important except their performance on standardized tests. Teachers were supposed to teach skills specifically for those tests. The strange thing was that if a child didn't learn, no one held the teachers responsible. If an eighth-grader didn't know how to read, no one went back to that child's first, second, or third grade teacher to ask what went wrong. No, it was always the child's fault.

I couldn't stand all that. I couldn't stand the pretense that there was teaching going on, that children were getting an education. The children were merely being pushed ahead, unprepared, to make room for more failures. They couldn't read and they couldn't write, but they were passed along to the next grade anyway.

I became convinced that the many poor readers in the Chicago school system were casualties of the look-say method of teaching reading. The method was first used in the 1830s to teach deaf-mutes to read. Then some educators, including

Horace Mann, had the bright idea of introducing the look-say or whole-word or sight-reading method into the public schools, reasoning that if deaf children could learn to read by this, then surely it would make reading simpler for all children. By the 1920s sight-reading was adopted by many school systems and accepted nationwide. It has been popular ever since. Rudolf Flesch's 1955 classic *Why Johnny Can't Read* argued that the look-say method with its Dick-and-Jane books was producing generations of children who couldn't read, couldn't spell, and had no sense of grammar. His argument didn't dissuade many schools. Neither did the growing number of illiterate children.

I could never understand how anyone expected a child to learn to read by recognizing "sight" words. Take away the pictures that illustrate the words and the familiar word sequence, and reading turns into guesswork. With the look-say method a child is taught to memorize a controlled vocabulary. He or she isn't taught the rules for vowel and consonant sounds, so the child can't figure out new words independently. For example, learning the word *look* without learning the double *o* sound, the child is helpless when confronted with *took* or *book*. He or she has to wait to memorize those words later on.

Rather than have a child rely on a memorized vocabulary, I always thought it better to teach a child how to attack a word phonetically. Over the years I saw that children became better readers and spellers when they learned by phonics. But they had to learn intensive phonics—all the regular and irregular sound patterns in the English language—not some bootleg version for sounding out the first and last letters of a word. I saw that if a child knew the rules for vowel and consonant sounds and for syllabification, and the exceptions to the rules, then that child could pick up anything and read it.

So I didn't follow the look-say teaching guide. In fact I went beyond the required curriculum in many of my lessons. For example, I taught my students how to add and subtract, but I also taught them that *arithmetic* is a Greek word meaning to count and that numbers were called *digits* after the Latin word *digitus,* meaning finger, because people used to count on their fingers. I taught them about Pythagoras, who believed that mathematics made a pupil perfect and ready to meet the gods. I told them what Socrates said about straight thinking leading to straight living. I read aloud to them from *The Great Quotations* and *101 Famous Poems*. We talked about Emerson's "Self Reliance," Bacon's "On Education," and parts of Thoreau's *Walden:* "If a man does not keep pace with his companions, perhaps it is because he hears a different drummer."

But I did not teach my students these things to be pedantic. I hoped that what they read and learned would affect their whole lives, teaching them how to live. I tried to introduce my children to a world that extends beyond the ghetto of Garfield Park. Until you reveal a larger world to children, they don't realize there is anything to reach for.

My approach was to teach the total child. A teacher should help develop a child's character, help build a positive self-image. I was concerned about everything—attitudes, manners, grooming. I made sure my students' faces were clean, their hair combed, their shirts tucked in, and their socks pulled up. I told them to walk with their heads up and their shoulders back, to have dignity and confidence. And I cautioned them that what a person thinks of himself will determine his destiny. Those were the things my parents told me, and I still believe them.

I was brought up to follow my own convictions and not to change myself in order to please others. But because I did things my own way, the other teachers at Delano resented me. I faced that same kind of problem my whole life. My strong will always seemed to distance me from people, even when I was a child.

At Delano the hardest battle I ever fought was to be me. Somehow, everything I did annoyed my colleagues, from the way I dressed to the way I taught. As more criticism began to build up, they even questioned my intentions. I drew away from them, becoming completely absorbed in my teaching. However, my retreat only made things worse. When I kept to myself, the other teachers were offended by my standoffishness.

Each year, I became more discontented at Delano. Apart from the politics—the bickering and pettiness among teachers over who got which students, who got supplies, who was going to work recess or lunch duty—I was frustrated like so many teachers in so many schools by the bureaucracy, the record-keeping, the "Up the Down Staircase" syndrome. Where do they find all the minutia that keeps you from teaching?

The curriculum changed with the passing of each fad. And the textbooks changed. Somebody, somewhere decided to water them down. Textbooks were being written two years below the grade level they were intended for. Why? Because students couldn't read. Instead of challenging students with materials that might improve their skills, the new books made it easier, using more pictures and fewer words. And simpler words. One textbook that used *enormous* and *apprehension* in a story came out in a revised edition that replaced those words with *big* and *fear*. The standards fell lower and lower.

I never thought I'd look back to the 1860s with awe. I came across a *Rhetorical Reader* published in 1862 that included works by John Ruskin, Oliver Goldsmith, John Milton, and Leo Tolstoy. It was intended for children in elementary school. Today these classical works are considered too difficult. Even the vocabulary in first grade readers has been reduced. A first grade reader from 1920 introduced 345 new words. Today one of the most popular first grade readers introduces only fifty-three words for the entire year. Yet a child starting school at age five already has a vocabulary of about 4,000 words.

There is a lot of money to be made from miseducation, from the easy to read easy to learn textbooks, workbooks, teacher manuals, educational games and visual aids. The textbook business is more than a billion-dollar-a-year industry and some of its biggest profits come from "audio-visual aids"—flash cards, tape cassettes, and filmstrips. No wonder the education industry encourages schools to focus on surface education.

Quite a few of my Delano colleagues felt the same way I did about the school system, but most were apathetic and afraid to make waves. That included the principal. Principals by nature are forever looking for harmony. Often they only want to serve their stint in a school as peacefully and with as few complications as possible, aspiring to a job in the district office. They handle their faculty with kid gloves, afraid of giving unfavorable year-end evaluations and afraid of adding an extra student to a classroom. The last thing in the world any principal wants is trouble with the teachers' union.

All of this added to my frustrations. After a certain point I became more outspoken, which seemed to isolate me even further from the other teachers. If I complained about the textbooks and curriculum, they were annoyed. If I complained about the excessive number of fire drills or the dirty lunchroom conditions or the lack of toilet paper in the student washrooms, they chided me for wasting time at the faculty meetings. They told me to close the door to my classroom and forget about it. But I couldn't.

Eventually, the tension deepened. Whenever I walked into the teachers' lounge, there was an uncomfortable and mean silence. The other teachers, sitting on the sofas drinking coffee and swapping stories about their students, cut their conversations short the moment I entered. Though I have always felt pretty confident of myself, I wasn't immune to their coldness. I hated feeling like an outcast. It brought back the same pain I experienced as a child when my classmates poked fun at my fancy clothes or ridiculed me for being tall and awkward. I didn't know how to make peace with my colleagues. I just wasn't good at small talk. It bothered me to sit around talking about some boy who was repeating sixth grade for the third time or about a new transfer student who had been to seven other schools without learning how to write his name. Those things weren't funny to me. I used to hear some teachers say "I hate these damn kids." That comment would destroy me. As a mother I would hate to think I had gone through the trouble of getting my children dressed and fed and sent them off to a school where the teacher's attitude was "I hate these damn kids." No matter what it cost me personally, I couldn't be like that.

It was a depressing situation. Several times I thought about looking for a job in another school, but I didn't want to teach in another part of the city. I wanted to work with the children in my neighborhood. By September 1974 I had resolved to survive by concentrating on my students. The new semester got off to a great start, and by the sixth week of school my students were eager for learning. I felt it was going to be a terrific year.

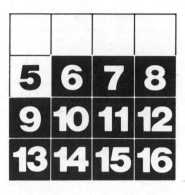

Marva stood in the doorway welcoming the children as they squeezed past her into the classroom. "I love your sweater," she told one of the boys. "Hello, sweetheart," she said, her large hand cupping a girl's chin, "who fixed your hair in such beautiful braids?" She told a boy who tried to push ahead of the others, "What good-looking shoes you have. Tie the laces, darling, so you don't fall and hurt yourself." Marva made sure she found something to praise in each of the children every day, even if it was nothing more than the color of their socks, a new pencil, a bright smile, or a good job of washing the back of their neck.

The children scrambled to their seats and began rummaging through their desks, putting lunches inside and taking out papers and pencils. Four boys huddled in the back of the room making plans for after school. A girl in the front row was combing her hair. Passing the child on her way to the blackboard, Marva took the comb from the girl's hand.

"Darling, put the comb away. Do you see me combing my hair in class? Do what you see me do. We don't comb our hair in public. How would it look if I came to class with a wet washrag and starting wiping my face? Washing our faces and combing our hair and brushing our teeth are all the things we do in private."

Marva looked around the room, saw that everyone was present, and began. "Who can tell me what homonyms are?"

"The second bell didn't ring yet," complained Jerome.

Jerome was like a nagging conscience, forever calling Marva's attention to points of order—pinpointing where they had left off in a story the previous day, reminding Marva to collect homework, notifying her that it was five minutes before lunchtime and the class should start putting away their books.

"Do you need a bell to tell your brain to start working?" Marva asked. "There was a Russian scientist named Ivan Pavlov, P-a-v-l-o-v." Marva wrote the name on the board, pointing out the short vowel sounds. "Pavlov tried the experiment of ringing a bell every time food was given to a dog. Pretty soon the dog learned that a ringing bell meant he would get some food. The dog associated the bell with food. What did the dog do? The dog *associated* the bell with food."

She printed the word *associated* on the board with its phonetic spelling. "The base word is *associate*. German schwa sound on the *a*, then macron *o*, macron *e*, macron *a*. *Associate*. And what does *associate* mean?"

Marva directed her question at Jerome. "Baby, what does *associate* mean? The dog associated the bell with the food. The bell made the dog do what? Think about the———."

"Think about the food," Jerome answered.

"Very good. *Associate* means that one thing makes you think about something else. *Associate* means to connect or join together. We associate Halloween with pumpkins. We associate Santa Claus with Christmas.

"Now Dr. Pavlov's dog associated the bell with the food. It became such a habit that his mouth watered when he heard a bell, even if he was not given any food. The bell rang and the dog acted hungry. Jerome, you don't need a bell to tell you that you are hungry, do you? Of course you don't. You're bright enough to know that by yourself. You don't need a bell to tell you when to start thinking either."

In the past six weeks, since the semester had begun, Marva's students had become used to these digressions. She never reprimanded a saucy remark like the one Jerome had made. She saw it as a test, a personal challenge. She liked to think she could transform anything into a learning experience.

A boy who kicked a classmate while going out to recess

had to look up the etymology of the word *kick* and report his findings to the class. When Wanda Lewis was chewing bubble gum and popped an enormous bubble all over her chin and nose, Marva had her look up the history of gum chewing and tell the class all about chicle and sapodilla trees.

The incident sparked a classroom discussion of botany, geography, and international trade. Marva told her students that sapodilla trees are evergreens, which differ from deciduous trees like the maples, oaks, and elms that grow in Garfield Park, because evergreens don't lose their leaves in the autumn. She pulled down the large world map and showed her class Mexico, Central America, and the tropical areas of South America where the sapodillas grow. She went on to explain how these countries sell the chicle from the trees to the United States in exchange for goods they don't have—"The word we use is *export.*"

It was typical of the spontaneous lessons Marva treated her class to daily. Nothing was irrelevant if it could be used to pique a child's intellectual curiosity.

Just as quickly as she had begun it, Marva dropped the discussion of Pavlovian psychology and brought the class back to the lesson on homonyms.

"Homonyms are like twins, but they are not identical twins," she said. "They are words that sound alike but have different middle vowels and different meanings. Anthony, use the homonyms *meet* and *meat* in sentences."

"Meet you next week?" answered Anthony, a small quiet boy, the kind of child who is easily overlooked in a classroom.

"Use a complete sentence, sweetheart. We must always speak in complete sentences. Can I meet you, when?"

"Can I meet you next week, Mrs. Collins?" Anthony replied.

"Very, very good."

"Mrs. Collins, Mrs. Collins," Freddie Harris shouted, stretching his arm as high as he could and bouncing in his seat. "I've got one, I've got one."

"All right, Freddie," Marva said, "why don't you give us a sentence using the word *meat,* the homonym with *ea?*"

"Dr. Pavlov's dog eats meat," Freddie said, sitting back in his seat very pleased with himself.

"Oh, you are so bright, so bright," Marva told him. "I can't believe no one ever told you what a brilliant child you are."

Marva had guessed the story of Pavlov's dog would find its way into the lesson. That was her method, to pool as much information as possible, to bombard the children with names and facts and anecdotes they could draw upon later. Of course the children wouldn't remember everything. Exposure to knowledge was what mattered. Some of it would sink in.

The children were learning their sounds. Each day in unison, like yogis chanting their mantras, the children followed Marva's lead, repeating the vowel sounds, the consonants, and the consonant blends—*br, bl, tw, spr.*

To a beat of one-two, one-two-three, they worked on the long vowel sounds: *"a, e—i, o, u.* I like reading, how about you?" Next they did the short vowel sounds, which Marva believed were especially troublesome for black children to pronounce: *"at, et, it, ot, ut.* Let's push the last door shut."

To link the sounds with spelling Marva printed several example words on the board.

"The vowel sound is *a* and the word is *ate.* The vowel sound is *a* and the word is *tail.* The vowel sound is *a* and the word is *may.* The vowel sound is *a* and the word is *straight.* The vowel sound is *a* and the word is *eight.*"

The class picked up the rhythm of motion and sound, and soon the excitement of a revival meeting spread through the room. The chorus of voices rose and fell accompanied by bobbing heads and clapping hands. The energy was contagious.

"Play and *stay. Play* and *stay,"* they sang. "I see two vowels, one, two. I see two vowels, one, two. I see two vowels and the sound is *a.* The word is *play.*"

So it went through the long and the short vowel sounds and then the consonants, each with an associative key. The letter *b* was the heart beat sound; *c* and *k* were copycats, both sounding like cracking nuts; *d* was a knock on the door; *f* a fighting cat; *g* a croaking frog; *h* a running boy panting. They chanted down the list to *z,* a buzzing bee.

Heart beat, heart beat, bh, bh, bh
Cracking nut, cracking nut, ck, ck, ck
Knock on the door, knock on the door, dh, dh, dh

Fighting cat, fighting cat, fff, fff, fff
Croaking frog, croaking frog, gh, gh, gh
Running boy, running boy, huh, huh, huh

Marva clapped her hands to keep up the pace, sustaining the children's energy and excitement. When they had finished, Marva praised her children, reminding them, "If you know the vowel and consonant rules, you will be able to spell and read every word."

★　★　★

By November, I saw the daily regimen of phonics drills beginning to work. It was a tedious, repetitive method of teaching reading, tedious for me as well as for the children. But there was no substitute for its effectiveness. The rhythmic tapping and hand clapping relieved some of the monotony. Before long, the children were almost as familiar with the chanting of vowel and consonant sounds as they were with the jingles on television commercials or the songs on the latest Stevie Wonder album. Once in a while, I would hear some of my students in the lunchroom or in the hallway singing their own jazzed up versions of "Cracking nut, cracking nut, ck, ck, ck. Buzzing bee, buzzing bee, zzz, zzz, zzz."

In class the children were now blending vowels and consonants and sounding out words. They were beginning to read, using the text *Reading Is Fun,* the first book in the phonics-first series published by Open Court Publishing Company. The former principal at Delano had ordered the books years before and had encouraged his teachers to experiment with them. Most of the teachers declined, feeling that the Open Court books were too hard for their children. When the new principal took over, the phonics-first readers were packed away in the storeroom.

I liked the Open Court series because the poetry and story selections aimed to teach values as well as vocabulary.

Say well and do well

End with the same letter.

To say well is fine,

To do well is better.

Like the old *McGuffey Reader,* the Open Court series taught a lot more than "Look, look. See me." So my students worked through poems, fables, and stories like "Dick Whitington and His Cat," in addition to the selections that I read aloud to them daily right after lunch. The children sponged up information as though they were on their way to a children's version of College Bowl. They knew that trolls and elves came from Scandinavia, pixies lived in England, leprechauns came from Ireland, goblins were found in France, and poltergeists were noisy little German spirits. They learned that there are 343 different versions of the Cinderella story and that the first was printed in China in the year 340.

The book you give to a child who is learning to read determines what he or she will read later on. If we give children the boring Dick-and-Jane type of stories, how can we spark their curiosity in further reading? Fairy tales and fables whet a child's appetite for more reading, and they are an excellent means for teaching the rudiments of literary analysis. In fairy tales there is always a conflict or problem, the forces of good poised against the forces of evil. I teach my students to identify the protagonist and the antagonist. I also point out that in fairy tales there are often elements of three—three bears, three pigs, three wishes, Cinderella's three nights at the ball. I explain that the number three is widely symbolic, representing many things. One example I usually give is the three parts to our personality—the id, the ego, and the super-ego. I tell the children that the id is the person we are when we are first born, before we learn anything. The ego is our present self, the person we think we are. And the super-ego is our conscience, the person we feel we should be.

Even young children love to analyze a story this way, working out a puzzle and seeing how all the pieces fit together. The children suggest other associations for the number three, such as three strikes to an out in baseball or three meals a day. The search for connections between what they read and what they see around them gets the children's minds clicking for classroom discussion, which is the heart of the lesson. I remind my students that they each have an opinion and that their opinions are important. I don't tell them what to think. I try to teach them how to think. It is useful in these discussions to introduce a question without a clear-cut answer, a question to stimulate critical thinking. Did Goldilocks have the right to go into someone's house without permission? Was she right to destroy the bears' beds and eat their food?

To limber up their minds, I put my students through warm-up exercises. During an arithmetic lesson, for example, I might ask, "If it takes me three minutes to boil one egg in a pot of water, how long will it take me to boil two eggs?" Someone usually pops up, "We don't know times yet." Another student might venture, "It'll take two times as long."

I say, "You're going to have overcooked eggs if you do that. Stop and think. If I'm putting an egg in some water and bringing that water to a boil, what difference will it make if I put in two eggs instead of one? It will take the same amount of time for the eggs to cook, won't it?" The object is to get children to think, use not only book knowledge but common sense. Sometimes, I give my students incomplete questions with facts deliberately omitted. I do this to teach them how to evaluate information and to get them to realize that not every question can be answered. They eventually learn to tell me there isn't enough information.

★　　★　　★

The progress being made by Marva's students became obvious, one day, during a discussion of "Jack and the Beanstalk."

"Well, what about Jack?" Marva asked. "What kind of character do you think Jack is?"

"That Jack, he was sure dumb," said Chris.

"Yeah," laughed Freddie, "messing with that old giant. He could of been dead for sure."

"So you don't think he should have taken the chance and gone to the giant's castle?" Marva asked.

"I think he shoulda gone 'cause he got his daddy back and his daddy's things," Bernette replied.

"Aw, all he was thinking about was swiping those things," Freddie argued. "How'd he know for sure the money and the hen with the eggs was his dad's?"

"*Were* his dad's, darling," Marva corrected.

"Yeah, they were his dad's."

"He was no good," agreed Jerome, sitting back in his chair with his arms crossed on his chest. "He was just lazy. He didn't want to do no work, see, so he's looking to get by. Like you always telling us, Mrs. Collins, he's the one with his hand out looking for something he don't earn."

"He went begging the lady giant for food," whispered Anthony. A second later he seemed startled to realize that he had answered in class.

"Anthony, aren't we getting so brilliant!" exclaimed Marva.

"Shoot, I still think Jack was dumb," burst out Chris, who had been shaking his head during the other comments. "You don't give away no cow for some beans some dude says is magic till you make him show you how they work. Man, that Jack was getting set up!"

Chris was raising a whole new issue from the story. There was no holding them back now.

The dedicated teacher knows that feeling of epiphany, when all the pulling and pushing and coaxing and laboring over lessons finally take effect and the children go on their own. Marva watched the children's eagerness, thinking what a long road it had been to bring them to this point of openness. That first day of school they were shells of children with toughened faces and glassed-over eyes, devoid of hope and joy. Now they had enthusiasm.

"I don't know what St. Peter has planned for me," she said, "but you children are giving me my heaven on earth."

★　　★　　★

Naturally my optimum goal was to get the children in this class to see the intrinsic value of an education, so that they would want to learn for the sake of learning. That would come eventually. They were still seven, eight, and nine years old. While I had no use for bribes, I strongly believed in rewards. Praise—every day for every task—was the main incentive. But every so often, when it was earned and unsolicited, a little something more didn't hurt.

My students had been working hard, so I arranged for them to visit a local fast-food restaurant. We had been studying a science unit on how man gets his food, and the field trip seemed to fit right in. The owner agreed to take the children on a behind-the-scenes tour of the restaurant, showing them how food was prepared and how the business was run, treating each of them afterward to lunch. I had already cleared everything with the principal, who said it was a fine idea. "Those kids are always eating that junk food," he laughed. "Maybe they'll get a chance to see what goes into it."

This franchise restaurant was using a clown in its advertising campaign, and at 11 A.M. the clown came to class to lead the children to the restaurant. They were all squeals and giggles as they left Delano, though they were trying awfully hard to act like mature ladies and gentlemen. Tripping and shoving were kept to a minimum as the children attempted to heed my reminder that they were all ambassadors of the school and must be on their best behavior.

Just as our procession was turning the corner, the principal came rushing down the sidewalk, calling to me to stop. He was clutching his suit jacket together to keep it from flapping. He looked more out of sorts than usual.

"Marva, you can't go," he said, panting. "You have to bring your class back to the building. I've got a lot of trouble with the other teachers. They're giving me a hard time about letting you go."

"But you already gave permission," I said.

"I know, I know, but I didn't expect it to cause such a fuss."

"Look at these children, look how excited they are. I am not going to disappoint them. When you make a promise to children, you keep it, or you don't promise in the first place."

So I continued on to the restaurant with my children. I had to pay dearly for that decision. The principal apparently went back and said he had not given me permission to take my class on the outing. From then on it was open warfare with the faculty.

Someone started the rumor that I beat my students into behaving. When my second-graders were studying a science unit about dinosaurs, I posted their papers on the bulletin board outside the class, and some teachers spread the word that I had made up those papers myself. They said it was impossible for my students to write about the brontosaurus and the pterodactyl and the tyrannosaurus when their own classes were still struggling with the first thirteen words in the basal reader.

The harrassment kept up. Twice I found hate notes in my school mailbox: "You think you're so great. We think you're nothing." They were signed "A Colleague."

Some days, standing at the blackboard, I felt dizzy. I began to have trouble sleeping at night. There was a pulsating pressure against the sides of my head. I would sit up suddenly unable to breathe, gasping and then exhaling in quick spurts. I felt like I was dying.

I spent most of my time wondering what it would be like if I quit teaching altogether. I knew I would have to find another job. Even with my teaching salary we had barely enough money. A lot of it went to pay for summer camps and private schools for Eric, Patrick, and Cindy. As it was, Clarence had to work two jobs, getting up at 2 A.M. to mix cement at a construction site before going to his regular job at Sunbeam. I often typed medical reports on Saturdays to bring in extra cash. It would have been much easier if I had enrolled my children at Delano, but by the time Eric was old enough for school I had already been teaching at Delano for more than four years, and I realized that that school would never provide the kind of education I wanted for my children.

I was sure there were other things besides teaching. I considered finding a job in an office, working for a textbook publisher, or writing for one of the newspapers. I wrote some letters of inquiry, but it was no use. Every time I had an idea, it was driven from my head by one prevailing thought—there was no way I could leave the children in my class. Not in the middle of the year. Not when they had just come alive. Continuity was so important for these children.

I didn't think I could endure the tension much longer. I was tired of no one talking to me. Tired of the whole world hating me. I was glad when Christmas vacation finally came.

Over the holidays, Clarence and the children did everything they could to cheer me up and get my mind off my problems at Delano. Without their support, I probably would have fallen apart completely. I've always had a quick temper and I often panicked about things. But Clarence, in his calm, comforting, common sense way, never failed to remain steady in a crisis. That was what I needed. Even my son Eric reassured me. "Now look, Mom," he said, "you're the one who's always telling us to be strong. Well, you've got to be strong yourself." He was only twelve at the time, but he already had a certain take-charge manner.

I wandered through the house trying to understand what was happening to me. For a few days I nursed self-pity. Then came the doubt, even guilt. Was I self-righteous? Too rigid? All my life I had been serious, too serious. I wished I could be more like everyone else. I even practiced being more casual about things, leaving the dinner dishes overnight in the sink. I ended up washing them before I went to sleep.

When I was sure I was right about something, I just couldn't back down or even compromise. As a teacher my sympathies were only with my students. Could I have done more to understand my colleagues? I was confused. The simplest values, things I had always understood, were now complicated.

After a while I began to see that it wasn't only the conflict with the faculty that had unleashed these emotions. It was everything about today's education. The indifference and the bureaucracy had made the daily struggle to educate children that much harder. I was also frustrated as a parent. I was having trouble finding a good school for my own children, getting them a decent education.

At the time I was sending my children to a Lutheran school miles away from Garfield Park, paying taxicabs and neighbors to drive the children there and pick them up again. Yet I wasn't pleased with the school. It was the fourth I had tried in less than seven years.

First I had sent Eric and Patrick to a Catholic school at the other end of the city. It cost $60 a month in tuition and more than $100 for a private cab to take them there. I thought it was worth it. They were getting a good basic education—Latin, grammar, and plenty of old-fashioned discipline instead of gimmicks and games.

From pre-school through first grade they had good teachers. By the time Eric was seven the school began opening up its curriculum to more "progressive" teaching methods and hiring lay teachers chiefly to attract more students. When I saw my sons doing word-picture games and coloring in workbooks rather than building their reading skills and vocabulary, I enrolled them in another school.

For all its prestige the private all-boys prep school quickly proved disappointing. Eric and Patrick were not learning phonics but were being drilled to memorize words on flash cards. They were reading from a basal text without classroom discussions, exercises, or questions to stimulate critical thinking. Worse, they were using look-say readers. Patrick, who was an eager reader when he transferred to the prep school in first grade, began to act as though a light bulb had clicked off inside. He stopped learning, he lost interest in reading, and the school tried to convince me that he needed a remedial class.

I met with the headmaster. I wanted to offer some assistance, not as an expert but as a concerned parent. I felt that if parents were willing to get involved—to help with more than fund-raising and chaperoning field trips—then maybe the children would start getting a better education. The headmaster appeared to be interested. In fact he asked me to draw up sample lesson plans and reading guides for teaching phonics. I did, though I had the feeling he was humoring me.

Nothing changed. At the end of fourth grade Eric was stumbling over words that he would have been able to sound out if he knew phonics. And Patrick was having problems reading. I worked with them in the evening, mostly trying to undo what they had done all day at school. So I told Clarence I didn't want the boys returning to the prep school the following semester. He found it difficult to comprehend my relentless pursuit of a good school. I think he believed that somewhere along the line a normal parental concern had become a cause célèbre. He assumed that as long as his sons were attending an expensive private school, they must be getting a solid education.

I understood how easily someone who was not in education, not in the classroom working with children, might think I was overreacting. Everyone thinks a school is a place where children learn. What else is a school for? People still believe in the tradition of dedicated, self-sacrificing school teachers. They don't know how the profession has changed.

The search for a school for my own three children opened my eyes: the public schools had no monopoly on poor education. Miseducation was a problem everywhere, a galloping epidemic that was infecting every school from the city to the suburbs whether public, parochial, or private. What was once the poor man's burden had become everyone's.

With this came another realization, that I couldn't escape the problem, as a teacher or as a mother. These parts of my life were inextricably interwoven; at Delano I was fighting for the kind of education I wanted for my own children. As a parent I tended to be protective, and I always felt that same driving concern as a teacher. I could never walk out of Delano at 3:15 and leave the school and the students entirely behind me. Were my students going home or would they wander the streets? Were their clothes warm enough? Would their stomachs be full tonight and would they have sheets on their beds?

During recess I watched from the doorway to make sure no child was being picked on by classmates or excluded from games. And when I saw anyone standing off alone, I took the child's hand, called the other children over, and began a new play circle. It was important to me that the children feel accepted in their group. I knew all too well what it felt like to be ostracized.

When I returned to Delano in January, I was more determined than ever to teach. Two weeks after school was back in session, everything came crashing down.

On a Friday afternoon the principal sent up a message saying he wanted to see me immediately in his office. I couldn't imagine what was so urgent that it couldn't wait until the end of the day. Did I forget to fill out some form? Was one of my students in trouble?

The principal was sitting behind his desk, looking very formal and very official. He was a short man; behind the desk he looked even smaller, swallowed up by filing cabinets and stacks of papers. He told me to sit down. I knew I wasn't going to like what he had to tell me.

He was taking my class away from me. Because of funding cuts, the school had lost some supervisory positions, so he had to put one of the master teachers back into the classroom. And he was giving her my class and switching me to another. She was retiring in June, he explained, after thirty years of teaching, and he wanted to make her last few months as easy as possible. I half-heard some backhanded compliments on how well my children were doing and how well behaved they were. She would have no problems.

What about the children? I flew upstairs to my class. My heart was pounding. I closed the door behind me, leaned against the wall, staring around the room cluttered with books, papers, posters, and plants. Some visitors might not have found it esthetically pleasing, but everything in it was for the children. My eyes went to the posters on the wall: *A Winner Never Quits and a Quitter Never Wins! Winners in Life Respond Positively to Pressure. If Life Gives You Lemons, Make Lemonade.* Each day the children repeated those sayings. Each day I proclaimed the message, driving home the importance of a positive attitude. I expected it of my students. Suddenly I no longer had it myself.

★   ★   ★

The children could see that Marva was upset.

"What's happening, Mrs. Collins?" Freddie asked.

"You okay, Mrs. Collins?" Anthony whispered, his brow furrowed. She rested her hands on his shoulders.

"Children, I have always been honest with you, so I'm not going to fool you now. The office is making some changes." Her grip tightened on Anthony's shoulders. "You are going to get another teacher, and I guess I am going to get another class."

She expected the moans, the chorus of noes, and the head shaking. Tears ran down Anthony's cheeks. Freddie slammed his hand against the side of his desk, shoving it against the wall.

"I'm never coming back here!" he shouted, his lips pursed tightly together, his arms and shoulders moving in quick angry jerks. "I'm gonna break every window in this place."

"Is that what my teaching has come to? Is that what I have been doing here all these months, teaching you how to break windows and slam desks? When you go looking for a job, some employer is sure to say, 'My, my, look at this young man. He certainly is qualified for the job because he went to school and learned how to break windows and slam desks.' "

A few giggles broke the tension. Marva walked over to Freddie, pushed his desk into the row, and put her arm around him.

"I love you," she told him. "I love you all, and I am going to continue to love you and care about you and worry about you. Sometimes things happen in life that we can't do anything about. We don't let them get us down, do we? We go on doing the best we can, making something of our lives. If you stop learning, if you stop building your minds, then everything I have been teaching you is wasted. Then you will make me a failure as a teacher."

★　★　★

When the children had gone home, I rolled up some of my posters and packed up a few of my books and plants. I decided I'd come back for the rest or send Clarence to pick them up. Relief was beginning to wash over me.

I had seen it all. Children coming to school so dirty I had to take them into the bathroom and scrub their arms and elbows with alcohol. A parent barging into the school with an extension cord to beat a child. I had worked hard, worked until I was exhausted, trying to change it, trying to give the children something more to look forward to in life than they could see in Garfield Park. If I was as strong as I thought, then I was strong enough to admit defeat.

A student's mother walked into the room. She told me that parents had already heard about the principal switching the children around. One of the teacher's aides had gotten the word and started making phone calls. There was a group of angry parents downstairs in the office. They were angry at the idea of disrupting two classes and sixty children just to find a place for one teacher.

While she talked, she kept her eye on the box of plants on my desk. She said, "Mrs. Collins, when you start packing up your plants, I know you're ready to go. But we want you to stay." The other parents were downstairs with the principal insisting on it.

I didn't answer. I tried to imagine the shouting and fussing in the office. The thought of the principal being swarmed over by those parents made me smile. Poor man, he never expected it. He probably figured the parents would ignore things as they usually did—not so much because they didn't care but because so many of them were easily intimidated by teachers and school administrators. They were afraid of not knowing what to say, afraid of looking dumb, embarrassed by their own lack of education. Too often they were self-conscious about the way they talked, about the way they looked or dressed, expecting the teacher to laugh at them. I was glad the parents were taking a stand. However, I was no longer going to be involved. I had settled the matter for myself and had started to feel comfortable with my decision.

I put on my coat, turned off the lights, and closed the door of the classroom. Downstairs I heard the commotion. Hoping no one would see me, I turned and ran out of the building. I needed serenity so badly. The last thing I could have endured at that moment was fighting and arguing. What I had to do at that point was hold on to my reason, my dignity. My sense of personal identity depended on it.

That night Clarence and I talked it over, and I told him I had made up my mind to resign from Delano. He said I had to do what I thought was best, but I suspect he was more relieved than he let on. I went to bed thinking everything was finally resolved, and for the first time in weeks I slept soundly.

The next morning several parents telephoned to ask about the rumor that I was leaving. They told me if I didn't come back to school, they weren't going to send their children back either. They would boycott the school and keep their children home.

Whether or not they meant it, I was alarmed. Things could get out of hand in a place like Garfield Park, and I was afraid a boycott would prove dangerous. Not that I doubted the parents' intentions, but I was worried that some of the older boys in the neighborhood might use it as an excuse to start trouble. I did not wish to be the cause of anything.

On Monday I returned to Delano. The principal gave me back my class and I resumed teaching. Neither the children nor I mentioned what had happened.

For me that was the end. All I wanted to do was make it through to June. I couldn't fight any longer. As the weeks and months passed, I became steadily more depressed. It got to the point that I dreaded walking into the school building. On Friday evening I was already worrying about Monday. By Sunday I was tearing through my house like a whirlwind, cleaning and scrubbing and polishing. Or I fell silent. My family had to put up with a lot of moodiness from me. I alternated between shouting, complaining, and crying. I was holding on for June.

Those last few months of the school year were the most difficult. Relief was so close, I could see it ahead. But each day was so long and painful. I gave all my remaining energy to my students. There was nothing left for me. I didn't fix my hair and often went without washing it. I stopped caring what I wore and forgot about makeup. Mornings, I would grab anything, even a pair of blue jeans. And there were times I wore the same clothes two days in a row, something I had never done before.

Naturally my students saw the change. I didn't hide my feelings from them. I told them that sometimes I hurt inside and felt like crying but it wasn't because of anything they had done. It was important that they understood because children, especially young ones, are quick to assume they are responsible for whatever might be troubling the adults around them. Sometimes the class was a kind of group therapy session. They shared their experiences, and I was open in talking about mine. I never believed a teacher should pretend to be perfect. A teacher who never displays any human weaknesses makes children self-conscious about admitting their own. A perfect teacher, like a perfect parent, is an impossible model for a child to live up to.

Yet my students were learning, learning to read, to do math, and to exercise their minds. In September my second-graders had started out with the first book in the Open Court series; in June they finished up in the middle of the fifth grade reader. They knew of Aristotle, Aesop, Tolstoy, Shakespeare, Poe, Frost, and Dickinson. If I had changed, my teaching methods had not.

On the last day of school I hugged and kissed each of the children goodbye. I gave them a list of books to read over the summer. "You are the brightest children in the whole world," I reminded them one last time, "and you must never forget that. Remember, no one can take your knowledge from you. You are the only ones who will determine whether you succeed or fail in life. You must never give up. Always try to fly."

It was past noon when I gathered my things together and walked out of Delano. The children milling around in the front of the building ran up to me, tugging at me. "I love you," I called to them, crossing the street. That was the truth; they were the only reason I had held on for those last months. But I promised myself I was never going back. As long as I lived, I would never set foot in that building again.

My departure from Delano was no great gesture of protest. I was almost thirty-nine years old. I wasn't some young upstart out to prove something to myself and to the world. I still liked teaching, but it had to be in a place where I could be comfortable. I was willing to stay in the public schools and try to make the system work, as a lot of teachers do. But I no longer had the energy to do that and take on my colleagues too.

After spending the past fourteen years learning how, I wasn't about to give up on teaching. I figured I would take the summer to unwind, and then I'd consider the other possibilities. I had a feeling things would work out.

In July a group of neighborhood women organizing a community school came to see me. Dissatisfied with the public schools, they wanted to start a private elementary school for children in the Garfield Park area. They asked me to be director. It sounded wonderful. I had some strong opinions about what a school should be, and here was the chance to apply those ideas. I accepted their offer immediately, without even considering what it took to get a school started. It seemed to me that all I needed were students, some books, and a blackboard.

None of the women knew much more about setting up a school than I did, but the president of a community college on the West Side, Daniel Hale Williams University, offered some assistance. He agreed to provide our new school with a basement classroom rent-free, and he let us use some typewriters and mimeograph machines.

Next we met with the director of the Alternative Schools Network, an organization of community-participation schools in and around Chicago. Unlike the free schools that grew out of the antiestablishment mood of the late sixties, the ASN schools evolved in the early seventies as part of the back-to-basics movement. The government-funded Alternative Schools Network paid my salary as director and curriculum developer, and their staff showed us how to open a private school.

During the last weeks of August I raced around trying to collect books. I bought some in secondhand bookstores and borrowed others. One day when I was passing the Delano schoolyard, I noticed the trash bins were filled with books, the very books I had used with my students, the Open Court readers. None of the other teachers had any use for them. I rescued the phonics-first series from the garbage, confident that I could use them to save children from a similar fate.

On September 8, 1975 Daniel Hale Williams Westside Preparatory School opened its doors. Though we had spread the word around the neighborhood, enrollment was not overwhelming. Parents were leery of chancing a new school. Many were put off by the $60 a month tuition. I wasn't discouraged. Aristotle said, "The heights of great men were not attained by sudden flight." I would work with what I had. I had only four students, ranging from second grade to fourth grade. One of them was my daughter Cindy. If the school was going to be good enough for other children, it had to be good enough for my own.

I had thought about the effects of teaching my own children, and I decided that whatever difficulty there might be in having your mother for a teacher, it was certainly no greater than the problems Cindy would face trying to learn in some other school. As for my sons, Eric would stay where he was because he was in eighth grade and due to graduate at the end of the year. Patrick was enrolled in a private school near Lincoln Park. I felt he would benefit by being on his own, out of the shadow of his older brother and his younger sister.

I didn't know very much about my other three students and didn't really want to know their backgrounds. Knowing a child's previous record can sway a teacher's expectations. Each child came to me with a clean slate. Still, from the initial interviews I had with the children and their parents, I could tell that each had had a problem of one kind or another.

Gary Love was angry and defensive at nine years old. He talked back to his mother and to me during the interview and made it very clear he hated school.

Eight-year-old Allen Pratt was being raised by a father who was a member of a motorcycle gang. I didn't know why Mr. Pratt enrolled his son in the school. He never told me. I suspected it may have been because he didn't have a permanent address, which might have posed a problem in registering Allen in a public school. When I asked Allen to read a sentence in the reader, he didn't even know the words *and* or *the*. On top of everything else, Allen was the dirtiest child I had ever seen. His hair was matted down; he had dried food on his mouth and chin and streaks of grease on his arms. The boy looked as though no one had washed his clothes in months.

My third student, Tracy Shanklin, was seven years old and had been passed into second grade at Delano. She couldn't read a sentence like "Sam sat at a mat," and she didn't know how to do simple addition. She was a quiet girl, very submissive and downcast. Everything about her seemed to say "I'm a nobody." Mrs. Shanklin was impatient with her daughter's progress at Delano. She enrolled Tracy in Daniel Hale Williams Westside Preparatory after hearing about it from a woman who lived in her apartment building.

From one point of view, having so few students was an ideal teaching situation. Any teacher who had to keep track of thirty or forty children would have gladly traded places with me. But the size also presented a problem. How would I turn four students and one classroom into a real school? I decided to use the same style of teaching I had developed at Delano. To me the four students sitting in the classroom that first morning might just as well have been forty. I was ready to teach.

★ ★ ★

Cindy was already sitting in the front row opposite Marva when the other children started to arrive. Tracy Shanklin, holding her mother's hand, was the first. Her mother stood in the doorway and gave Tracy a gentle nudge to go inside. The girl looked up hesitatingly, then dropped her eyes to the floor and walked into the room, heading slowly for the last seat in the last row. Mrs. Shanklin whispered to Marva that at Delano her daughter had been seated in the back of every classroom she was in, overlooked by teachers because she was such a quiet child. It was a pattern Marva recognized repeatedly in slow learners. She hurried over to Tracy, catching her before she settled into the chair. Hugging the child close to her, Marva led her to a desk beside Cindy.

"I love you too much to have you so far away from me," Marva said. "I will be lonesome if you sit in the back of the room."

Marva was introducing Tracy to Cindy when Gary Love, big for his age, bounded into the room, swaggering and snapping his fingers behind his back, jiving to some imagined music.

"Sweetheart, is your hip broken? If it isn't, there's no reason to come in here walking that way, slopping and popping your fingers. Why don't you come sit over here?" Marva patted the back of one of the front seats.

Gary plopped into a desk in the middle of the room. "You make me."

Marva shrugged. "I don't make children do anything. You make yourself what you are. You must decide for yourself what you want to do in here, peach. You have the right to learn. You also have the right to fail, if you choose."

Marva stopped, letting him think the matter over, and went to usher Allen Pratt to a desk. She was about to put her arm around Allen when a wave of sweat hit her nose.

Turning to the others, she said, "Children, look through the books on your desk. I will be right back." She took Allen's hand, whispering, "Come with me, darling," and she led him down the hall to the women's washroom. Embarrassed, Allen refused to go inside. Marva shoved open the door, shouted hello, and waited for a response. When no one answered, she said, "It's all right, sweetheart. No one is there. You're such a handsome young man, but we can't see just how good looking you are beneath all that dirt. Let's scrub you down and find the real you."

Coaxing him over to the basin, Marva wet some paper towels, rubbing the grease and sweat off the child's neck and arms. He pulled away. She kept talking to him, asking him about his summer, about his former school, about his father's motorcycle, anything and everything she could think of to make him relax.

When she had finished, Marva handed the boy a dry towel. "All right, tomorrow I'm going to bring you some clean clothes. Starting today and for the rest of your life, you're going to have to wash your own face."

She hugged him as they walked back to the classroom. Allen scooted into a chair. Cindy and Tracy were talking quietly and seemed to be getting along well. Gary had shunted himself off to the far left corner. From the look of the zig-zagged rows of desks, it seemed he had tried out every chair in the room before settling there. Gary's eyes were closed as his head swayed and his fingers snapped, keeping beat to a tune playing silently inside him.

"Darling, no one is going to be handing out the good jobs to someone who sits there popping his fingers," Marva said, ruffling Gary's hair. He recoiled, turning his body to the wall. "You have a right to sit there all day staring at the wall if you want. You'll never become a millionaire that way, but you can stare away if it pleases you. However, you cannot sit here snapping and tapping because you are interfering with everyone else's right to learn."

She walked up to the front of the room to commence her customary first-day-of-school pep talk. In her tailored suit, hoop earrings, and high-heeled shoes, she was as imposing a figure as she had been at Delano. Daniel Hale Williams Westside Preparatory may have been a makeshift school, but there was nothing informal about the teacher or her classroom. Perhaps as a consequence of her southern background, Marva subscribed to the idea that formality established a tone and decorum that encouraged her students to see a school, regardless of its setting, as hallowed ground, a place of learning.

"You are the best and brightest children in the world and there is nothing you can't do," she began. She rated their former schools for failing them, promised that she would not let any of them fail, sympathized with their fears and frustrations in school, told them she loved them, and then "tossed the ball into their court"—they had the choice of learning or sitting on the sidelines. Her speech was peppered with such similes as "Life is like a football game: you have to hit the line hard." She piled up aphorisms, partly out of habit but mostly because they helped children remember ideas.

"No one is going to hand you anything on a platter, not in this classroom. Not in this life," she said, revving up her students. "You determine what you will be, what you will make of yourselves. I am here to help you, but you must help me to do that. You can all win if you do not spend too much time trying to fail.

"In your other schools you probably started out each day saying the Pledge of Allegiance. Here we are going to start each day making a pledge to ourselves."

It was something Marva had composed herself. She asked the children to listen closely and repeat each line after her. "This day has been given to me fresh and clear ..." Marva waited. Cindy belted out the words. Tracy followed, mumbling softly. Allen's voice picked up the word *clear*, but Gary was close-mouthed, sitting in a defiant posture with his back against the wall.

"I can either use it or throw it away," Marva continued. "I promise I shall use this day to its fullest, realizing it can never come back again." Except for Gary, the class repeated in voices that were getting stronger. "I realize this is my life to use or to throw away."

When the children finished their refrain, Marva took a sweeping step over to Allen's desk, positioned her hands solidly on each side of it, and hunched over to look the child squarely in the eye.

"Are you going to throw away your life?" she asked.

Allen crouched in his seat and giggled.

"This is not funny. What you do with your life is not a joke. Are you going to throw your life away?"

Allen sat upright with a frightened look. He rapidly shook his head no. Sometimes Marva came on too forcefully. Sometimes, she knew, there was too much anger in her teaching—

anger not at the children but at the desolation in their lives. She smiled, flicked her finger ticklishly under his chin, and slid over to Tracy, making the same inquiry. Sheepishly Tracy whispered no. Then Marva asked Cindy, who responded dutifully. Weaving among the desks, she approached Gary.

"Sweetheart, what are you going to do? Use your life or throw it away?"

Gary sat stonefaced, his arms across his chest.

"Of course it's your life to do with as you please," Marva reminded, "but there is a whole world out there calling you. If you throw away your life, you're just letting society have its way." She spun around to face the other children. "You know, boys and girls, there are some people who look at places like this, neighborhoods like Garfield Park, and they say 'Oh, children from there are not very smart. They aren't going to grow up to be anyone or do anything special.' If you decide to waste your lives, you are letting all those people be right. No one can tell you what you will be. Only you have the power to decide that for yourselves."

From that point Marva pushed on to Emerson and "Self Reliance." As before, she spent most of the first morning trying to convince her students that they wanted to learn. Her approach was to make the children see the link between an education and a job, a way out of the ghetto. She seldom missed a chance to draw the connection, because it was a reason they already understood.

When Tracy rummaged through her lunch sack a half hour before noon, Marva reminded, "Don't worry so much about feeding your stomach. Feed your brain first and you'll always find a way to get food for your stomach.

"Children, you are not in school for your parents, for your teachers, or for anyone else. You are here for yourselves. Your education is going to help you, not me." She swung over to the bookshelf and reached for a Bible that was nestled among *Plato's Republic, The Odyssey of Homer, Little Women, Candide, Charlotte's Web, The Brothers Karamazov,* and *Charlie and the Chocolate Factory.* Opening the text to the underlined passages, Marva quoted: "Proverbs, Chapter 3, verse 35 says 'Honor is the portion of wise men, but fools inherit shame.'

Chapter 6, verse 6: 'Go to the ant, O sluggard, study her ways and learn wisdom.' Chapter 10, verse 4: 'The slack hand impoverishes, but the hand of the diligent enriches.' "

Marva paused and looked out at the children. "What do you think those proverbs mean?" She knew there would be no flurry of hands waving. Not yet. These children had never had a dialogue with a teacher before. They were not accustomed to anyone asking them what their thoughts were. "All right, Cindy, would you please tell us what they mean?"

"A lazy person will be poor and won't have anything," Cindy blurted out quickly, repeating one of her mother's pet phrases.

"Very good." Marva sat on the edge of Tracy's desk. It was an intimate pose, suggesting that she might be about to share a secret. "The proverbs tell us that the wise man will advance in learning and will be able to take care of himself. But the fool destroys himself. A people without vision—without knowledge, without education—will perish.

"Children, that is why you are here. You must have an education to live a good life. To survive. You may not believe what I am telling you. And you may not believe what your parents and other adults tell you. But surely you believe what the Bible tells you."

For a few moments the children sat in awed silence. Even Gary was having some difficulty trying to look cool and aloof. Marva said it was time for lunch. The pensive mood lost out to the rustling of brown paper lunch bags and voices bartering Twinkies for potato chips.

Except for Cindy, the children were not reading at the level appropriate for their age. Marva started them with the most basic lesson, going over the alphabet, pronouncing the vowel and consonant sounds. Next Marva selected two consonants and one vowel, writing them on the board and saying their sounds.

"Consonant *m*," she said. "Mmm is the sound you make when something tastes delicious. Vowel sound *e*. In this case we have two *e*'s, so we put a macron over the first *e* to show that it says its name, and we put a slash through the second *e* to show it is silent. Next we have consonant *t,* which makes the sound of a clock ticking.''

The children repeated each sound as Marva watched their pronunciation, showing them that with the sound of *m* their lips had to be pressed together, with *e* their mouths had to be open, and with *t* their tongues had to hit the roofs of their mouths.

She wrote *Meet me.* Allen, Tracy, and Cindy each took a turn reading the words aloud. Gary refused. He was busy twisting a pencil between his fingers, as though he were winding the propeller of a model airplane. Marva didn't force him. She said, ''If you pay attention and learn, you will have choices in life.''

Turning her attention to the other children, she asked them all to go up to the blackboard to take dictation. Her technique was to teach reading, writing, and spelling concurrently.

Still reveling in the novelty of having her mommy for a teacher, still not certain whether she was playing school or going to school for real, Cindy raced up to the blackboard. Allen gave a shrug, as if to say ''Oh, why not,'' and found a spot for himself. Tracy squeezed in next to Cindy. With a piece of chalk in her hand, Tracy began to whimper. She couldn't do it, she said.

''I love you,'' Marva told her. ''You have no reason for crying in here. We don't shed tears, we just go ahead and try to do it. No one is going to shout at you or laugh at you for making a mistake.''

Tracy said she would try. Marva decided it was time to invite Gary into the lesson. She walked over to him, placed a hand on each shoulder, and whispered, ''I'm not going to leave you alone. I care about you. Let's try to do some work.''

''I'm not gonna do any damn work!'' he shot back.

''You are too important to be left all alone. You are the most important child in this world, and people have left you alone for too long already. The Lord gave you a head to use, and if you care about yourself at all, and I know you do, then you will use it. I am not going to give up on you. I am not going to let you give up on yourself. If you sit there leaning against this wall

all day, you are going to end up leaning on something or someone all your life. And all that brilliance bottled up inside you will go to waste."

Marva took his arm and led him to the blackboard. He stood there, still determined to do nothing. She considered it a victory. He had not run back to his seat or, worse, out the door.

"All right, children," she began, "let's first make a capital letter *M*, mmm. Why a capital? Because we are beginning a sentence. Vowel sound *e,* then vowel *e* again, then consonant *t.*" As she spoke, Marva moved from child to child, guiding their hands with her own, helping them to form the letters. "Now you have written the word *Meet.* Put your finger down on the board so you can leave a space for the next word. All right, finger space, then consonant *m, mmm, vowel sound e,* and period because it is the end of a sentence."

When she finished, Marva glanced back at Gary, who was still standing in place with his hands in his pockets. Though she preferred to win her students with affection, she was no pushover. She felt that children needed and wanted discipline. Towering beside Gary, she spoke matter-of-factly, carefully measuring her voice so he would not mistake her firmness for hostility.

"There is no one on this earth who is going to make me a poor teacher," she said. "If you do not want to participate, go to the telephone and tell your mother, 'Mother, in this school we have to learn, and Mrs. Collins says I cannot fool around, so will you please pick me up.' "

Gary considered her statement for a moment, broke off some chalk, and scribbled *Meet me.* He returned to his seat, deliberately bumping into other desks along the way. Marva squelched the desire to reprimand him, asking him instead if he hurt himself. Her question was the last thing Gary expected to hear from his teacher. There was even some disappointment in his voice as he muttered, "I'm okay." He sat down.

On that first afternoon the quartet of students got their first taste of literature, *Aesop's Fables.* Before Marva began reading aloud, she prepared her students for the story. She explained the Latin origin of the word *fable* and defined the term, pointing out the difference from a fairy tale.

"Aesop," she continued, "was a Greek slave who lived on Samos, which is an island that belongs to the country of Greece. Some people think Aesop was black, or at least dark-skinned. He had a heavy nose and thick lips, and he was rather homely looking. When we describe a person's facial features and the way a person looks, we are describing physiognomy." Marva printed the word *physiognomy* on the board and placed the diacritical marks over the vowels.

"Now, Aesop is said to have lived about 600 years before Christ, which means he lived more than 2,500 years ago." She paused. Allen was staring at the clock, his head propped up against his hand.

"We don't sit in here daydreaming our lives away." She took his hand from the side of his face and held it in her own as she continued. "Even though Aesop was a slave, he was a very wise man. The story goes that Aesop was standing with two other slaves while a master was choosing which one of them to buy. The master asked the slaves what they could do. One slave said, 'I can do anything.' The next said, 'I can do everything.' When it was Aesop's turn, he said, 'I can do nothing.' The master asked why not. Aesop replied, 'If this one can do anything, and that one can do everything, then that leaves nothing for me.' "

The children giggled. Gary grinned also, but when he caught Marva watching him, he immediately assumed a deadpan look.

"The master thought Aesop was the most clever man he had met, so he bought Aesop. After a while the master set Aesop free because he was so impressed by Aesop's wit and wisdom."

Marva let the last line sink in for a moment. It was a good example of making the most of your abilities. "At the time Aesop lived, people were very *disgruntled*—they were very upset—with the government and the politicians. Let's try to use as many new words as we can, children. Let's expand our vocabularies. What does *disgruntled* mean? It means upset. Even though the people were disgruntled with the government, they were afraid to complain. Instead of complaining, Aesop poked fun at the government through his stories, using the animals in his fables to describe the behavior of people. Now, a story that pokes fun at something is called a *satire*. What is it called?''

"Satire," answered Cindy.

"Very good. There is another word to describe how we make fun of something, either by our language or by the tone of our voice, and that word is *sarcasm*. When we see a fat man stuffing a piece of cake in his mouth, we might say, 'He really *needs* that piece of cake, doesn't he?' That is using sarcasm. We are making a sarcastic remark."

By the time Marva's students were ready to hear the fable of "The Frogs Asking for a King" they had already been exposed to a smattering of etymology, vocabulary, literary terminology, and Greek history. The fable itself was not much longer than half the printed page, but Marva's telling of it took almost twenty minutes. She stopped at words to explain their meaning, dissecting prefixes, asking for synonyms. She broke off after certain phrases to check for comprehension or add more background, roving into the knowledge of related studies.

"Who did the frogs ask to find them a king?" she asked.

"Zeus," Allen answered, looking at the floor as he spoke.

"That's right, but don't talk to the floor, talk to me. No one trusts a person who can't look you in the eye. They asked Zeus because he was the most important Greek god. The ancient Greeks believed in many gods. They had a god of the sun and a different god for the moon. A god of love and a god of war. We are going to learn all about these gods when we study Greek mythology. Zeus was the king of all the other gods. He ruled over them and he ruled over humankind. The Greeks built beautiful temples and shrines to honor Zeus. The most famous statue of Zeus was considered one of the Seven Wonders of the World."

Marva continued with the fable, interrupting and starting again, asking questions and prying up responses: "Do you think it was a good idea to give the frogs a log for a king? What could that log do for them? Could it hear their complaints? Give them advice or tell them what to do? No, it could only sit there, couldn't it? Sometimes the people running our government act like logs, don't they? They don't always seem to hear what we are saying. Did you ever hear the expression *like a bump on a log?* What does that mean? It means a person is lazy, or *indolent,* doesn't it? And what does that new word *indolent* mean? It means lazy, doesn't it?"

Marva followed the Socratic method, in which a teacher asks a series of easily answered questions that lead the student to a logical conclusion. To the philosopher's method she added her own brand of energy, pacing up and down the aisles, patting a head, touching an arm, rattling off questions, complimenting answers, and employing grand histrionics. The lesson did not end with the last line of the fable. It was time to strike the moral.

"What do we learn from this fable, children? What is Aesop trying to tell us?" There was silence. "Well, what about the two kinds of kings in this story? First we had a log that did what, Tracy?"

"Nothing," the girl whispered.

"Darling, you have to speak much louder than that. If you don't, I'm going to have to climb on top of a desk and stretch all the way to the ceiling so you can practice shouting up that high."

The children laughed and Marva laughed with them. "All right, all right, let's finish up this story. So we had a log that did nothing, and then we had a stork who came to be king but ended up doing what?"

"Eating the frogs," said Allen.

"One ruler was too lazy and the other was———."

"Evil," shouted Cindy.

"It didn't do the frogs any good to wish for a king, did it?" All but Gary shook their heads no.

"Wouldn't the frogs have been better off learning how to take care of themselves? The fable shows us we have to lead ourselves instead of looking for others to lead us. If we don't think for ourselves, others will do what? They will do our thinking for us. We must each be the captain of our fate and the master of our soul."

From that day forward everything the students read or wrote would bear upon that theme, the keystone of Marva's teaching. Whether it was vocabulary, reading, mathematics, or literature, from Aeschylus to Zola, Marva's highest aim as a teacher was to endow her students with the will to learn for themselves.

By the end of the first day she knew exactly where each child was. Before she dismissed them that afternoon, she passed out sheets of math homework and phonics exercises, tailored to each child's needs. Allen was the first to catch the discrepancy.

Leaning over to look at Tracy's papers, he said, "I don't have those things. How come I don't have the same papers she does?"

Marva narrowed her eyes, furrowing her brow. "You don't look like her, do you? What makes you think you should do the same work she does?"

Making her way over to Gary, she placed three sheets of homework on his desk. He examined one of them curiously. "You got to be kidding," he said, throwing all of his wallop into the word *got*. "You want both sides of the paper for homework?" His voice cracked in disbelief midway through the question.

"Both sides?" Marva said, affecting a throaty drawl. "When your mother gives you dinner, do you want only half a chop? When someone hires you for a job, are you going to get only half the work done?"

Gary didn't answer. After the children had filed out the door, Marva found his homework papers on the floor under his desk. This boy had to change his priorities, but she wasn't going to force him. Eventually, with lots of praise and lots of hugging, his defensiveness would melt. The one thing all children finally wanted was the chance to be accepted for themselves, to feel some self-worth. Once they felt it, children became addicted to learning, and they had the desire to learn forever.

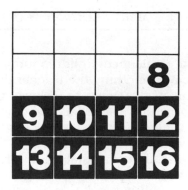

In my view the main thing is to get children reading. A child who doesn't know how to read can't do anything. But children do not learn to read by osmosis. It requires work—hard boring work without any shortcuts. It is drill and more drill. Repetition and memorization. Children must learn how to use key sounds to unlock words and they must recite long lists of words that have the same *a* sound as in *apple,* the same short *i* sound as *Indian* and *it,* the short sound of *u* as in *umbrella,* the short sound of *o* as in *ostrich,* or the sound of short *e* as in *eskimo.*

On the first day of school the children learned to read, write, and spell *Meet me.* On the second day I used the same method to introduce a new initial consonant, the letter *s.* The children pronounced the consonant and vowel sounds in *See me,* and then they went to the board and wrote the words as I dictated. Having learned the *ee* spelling for the vowel sound *e,* the class went on to learn that *ea* also says *e.* I wrote *e* on the board, putting a macron over the *e* and a slash through the silent letter. And the children read and wrote *See me eat.*

Day three, the children progressed to reading and writing *See me eat meat.* Day four, I taught them the consonant *h* and the children read and wrote *See me heat meat.* On the fifth day I reviewed everything, pretending I didn't know the sounds myself. By pretending that it was just as difficult for me to learn I was able to bait the children into reciting the sounds on their own. It was a way of informally testing them and at the same time building their confidence. Children jump at the chance to show that they know something the teacher doesn't.

"Children, as many times as I have gone over these sounds, I keep forgetting them. My old brain isn't working right. I think the sentence says *see-ee me ee-ate me-ate*. Is that right?"

Of course the children all started laughing. "You mean that's not right? Well, what did I do wrong?"

"You said the silent letters," they shouted.

"I did?" I said surprised. "You mean I forgot the rule that when two vowels go walking, the first one does the ———."

"Talking and says its name," they bellowed.

By the beginning of the second week of school the children advanced from pronouncing initial consonants to consonant blends. I explained what a blend was with an easily visualized image: "When Mommy bakes a cake, she doesn't just plop the eggs and the sugar and the flour into the bowl, does she? She stirs everything together, she blends the ingredients to make a cake. We are blending two letters, putting two letters together to make one sound."

I started them off with *th*, showing them how to put their tongues between their teeth to say the sound. We practiced putting our tongues between our teeth: thirty, thirteen, three, that, they, the. I wrote the word *the* on the board, underlining the blend *th*. The next step was to have the children incorporate this lesson into one they had already learned. At the board they wrote *See me heat the meat*.

From there we went on to the *igh* spelling of the vowel sound *i*. Following the same method I had used with *ee* and *ea*, I put a macron over the *i* and a slash through the silent letters *g* and *h*. So that the children could identify the sound with something concrete, I had them all take a deep sigh. I put an *s* in front of *igh* and had the children say the word *sigh*. Next I added the final consonant *t* so that the word was *sight*.

The children learned the family of words in which *igh* says *i*: night, right, might, tight, light, fight. Building on the previous sounds, they were able to write *See the night light*.

I told the children that now they were on their way to reading. They would want to learn another consonant blend, *fl*.

To show how the blend *fl* changes a word, I had the children say *fat* and *flat, fight* and *flight*. I reviewed *th* once again and then had the children combine everything they had learned thus far by saying and writing *See the night flight.*

The third blend was *br,* and the children read and wrote *See the bright light.* After that it was back to the vowel sounds to learn the long *i,* as in mine and kite, and the long *a,* as in gale. I explained that these vowels become long when they are followed by a consonant and an *e,* formulating this as the *i blank e* rule and the *a blank e* rule. Putting it all together, the children read and wrote *I might take a night flight.*

These lessons were the kernels of reading. The children progressed through the entire alphabet in the same way. They learned all the long vowel sounds and the short vowel sounds through compounding and repetition. They learned all the beginning consonant blends and then word endings like *ble, gle, tch, nk, ng, dge,* and *tion.*

They studied all the vowel and consonant rules and the exceptions to the rules. They knew, for example, that the letter *c* says *s* when it comes before *e, i,* or *y* and that in all other instances it says *k.* They knew that at the beginning of a word the letter *x* says *z,* at the end of a word *x* says *ks,* and after the letter *e* it says *gz* or *ks,* as in textile and exist.

The children had the sounds and the rules coming out of their ears. They were starting to wriggle in their seats at the routine, but I kept coaxing them on. "This is not baby work. These are the tools of language. How are you going to build anything without the right tools? Every word you will read in Shakespeare or Cicero or Dante is made up of sounds like these. You have a choice. You can learn these sounds and become literate lifters of mankind, or you can be lazy leaners all your life, turning to the next person to help you get by."

The expressions "literate lifter" and "lazy leaner" usually brought out a chuckle. Children like alliteration. I often have my students practice their initial consonant sounds by reciting tongue twisters like "Peter Piper picked a peck of pickled peppers" and "Betty Botter bought butter." I used the phrases "literate lifter" and "lazy leaner" so many times that the children began saying them on their own. More than once I heard Cindy and Allen teasing back and forth, asking one another, "Are you gonna be a literate lifter or a lazy leaner?"

After a month I started all four children on the second grade reader in the Open Court series, *A Trip Through Wonderland*. They read aloud every day as I checked their pronunciation and comprehension. Cindy, as I expected, breezed through the reader. I had worked with her from the time she was three years old, reading aloud to her, playing word games, and going over the sounds of the alphabet. She had started to read at age five, but her teacher at the Lutheran school discouraged her, making her self-conscious because none of the other kindergarteners knew how to read. Reading wasn't part of the kindergarten curriculum. When she passed into first grade, Cindy was still so far ahead of her classmates who were learning to read with the look-say books that she just lost interest. My big job with her was to awaken her enthusiasm.

Allen also caught on quickly. He was a very bright child, but he had been ignored and allowed to daydream. The sad truth is that children who are dirty or physically unattractive are often passed over in a classroom. I had to keep after Allen about his grooming, sending him to the bathroom to wash his face and scrub under his fingernails. I brought him some clean clothes—pants and shirts my son Patrick had outgrown—and I took his own soiled things home to wash. Little by little he seemed to take more care to keep himself clean. One morning I saw him in front of the drinking fountain trying to wash the stains off his pants.

Tracy and Gary, however, were both a problem. Tracy didn't want to read. She cried and complained of headaches. I saw that the reader was too difficult for her, but when I tried to give her the easier first grade book, she wouldn't take it. She and Cindy had taken to one another immediately and become fast friends; Tracy wanted to do the same work Cindy was doing. I reasoned it might be better for her to start at the higher level and build up her self-esteem than to feel she was behind her newfound friend.

Still it was a struggle to get her to read. She kept saying, "I can't do it, I can't do it." And I kept telling her how pretty and bright she was and reminded her of the story "The Little Engine that Could." When it was her turn to read, I put my arms around her and praised her for each word she read. As soon as Tracy finished three or four words in a row correctly, I had her stop, lest the fifth word prove too difficult. I did not want Tracy discouraged. Until she had a better opinion of herself, Tracy had to be insulated from failure.

Where Tracy became weepy, Gary would get angry. He'd take one look at the exercises or homework papers, shake his head, and shove them under his desk. I didn't make a big deal about it. I handed him the same paper along with the new one on the next day. It took about five days for Gary to see he was getting nowhere. He wasn't getting rid of the papers and he wasn't getting me upset. I wanted Gary and the other children to know I was always in control of the classroom. When Gary threw a batch of papers on the floor, I saw an opportunity to set things straight.

"I know children are always testing their limits," I said, "because when I was a child, I was always testing mine, always trying to see what I could get away with. There isn't a trick you can pull on me that I don't know. I probably did it myself when I was your age because I was full of mischief and always getting ideas in my head. My mind was always clicking, but it wasn't always to my advantage."

Stretching the facts a bit, I told them how I dumped a bushel of plums down a neighbor's well. Hiding behind a berry hedge giggling, I watched as an old woman pulled up a bucket of purple water and ran screaming into the house crying Jesus had given her a sign. The children laughed uproariously, including Gary. I described how I would occasionally turn back my parents' living room clock so I could have an hour longer to play outdoors. And I told them how I hated to go to Sunday chapel when I was in college. To avoid going I would put my coat on over my nightclothes, march out the front door of the dormitory, and sneak back inside when the housemother wasn't looking.

"But one morning the housemother caught me and I had to sit through the entire chapel service on a hot Sunday morning with my overcoat buttoned up to my neck, hiding my nightclothes. You see, I wasn't so smart after all, was I? I was the same as all children, always testing adults, always testing my teachers. The teachers who didn't know what they were doing had a hard time with me. And when a teacher would let me get by, I did just that. I remember handing in the same paper ten times to the same teacher, who never knew the difference.

"In elementary school I used to keep steel marbles in the pocket of my dress, and when the teacher's back was turned, I would rattle them making all sorts of noise. I also kept half a dozen Mr. Goodbar candybars in my desk. I would take all the wrappers off the candy beforehand so they wouldn't make any noise, and when the teacher wasn't looking, I would pass out pieces of melted chocolate to the other children.

"Now, I am not going to let you be so bored that you have time for that kind of foolishness. You will never turn in a paper that I do not read. You will never be asked to read something that I have not also read. So don't try to fake the characters or the story. No one will try to put anything over on anyone in here. That is not what we are here for. You are here only to learn, so you can make something of your lives."

I didn't expect my speech to have an instantaneous effect on Gary. I knew that for him to keep his pride intact, any initiative would have to appear to be strictly his own doing. To save face, he couldn't allow me to think that anything I said or did had changed his mind about school. The rest of that afternoon went much as usual. I handed him papers and he tossed them on the floor. I called on him to read and he sat there silently. I said, "That's your right, Gary."

It was the same the next day. But the day after, when I called on him to read, Gary decided to give it a try. He made it through the first few words. As soon as he had trouble, he flung the book across the room.

"You have to take stumbles before you can learn to walk," I told him. "It's all right to make mistakes. I make mistakes. I'm only a poor mortal and I don't have all the answers. I don't always understand things. I'm counting on you to help me with my mistakes and I'll help you with yours. However, I do not have all the money in the world to spend on books, and you have no right to destroy the ones we have. If you do not wish to use them, then someone else will, but you have no right to ruin them for others."

He picked up the book. When he settled down, I leaned over him, rubbed his arm, and pronounced the words aloud with him as he read.

As the weeks passed, Gary found it difficult to remain hostile. No matter how many times he shouted to me, "I hate you and I'm not going to do the damn work," I always answered, "I love you all the time, even when you behave like this." I guess it took the fun out of fighting. A fair fight was one thing; taking swipes at someone who wasn't fighting back was quite another. Gradually Gary began to do the work. He still had an attitude. And he didn't get along with the other children.

★ ★ ★

On October 16, 1975 Daniel Hale Williams Westside Preparatory School accepted its fifth student, Erika McCoy. In a way it was Erika who brought Gary into line—not because of anything she did but because of what she was. She was in awful shape. A chubby girl of not quite six years, Erika seemed intent on destroying herself, and everything else in sight.

The moment the other children saw her in the doorway, licking the mucus that was running from her nose, they broke into laughter. For Gary it was a moment of reckoning. A look at Erika gave him a quick shot of confidence. Until then he hadn't known how well off he was. If he wasn't a wiz like Cindy or even as good as Allen, he sure was ahead of this new girl. He got up from his desk at the back of the room, climbed into a seat next to Allen, and joined in the giggling and shaking of heads.

"You may know where you're going now, but that doesn't mean you forget where you came from." Marva gave the four students a hard look. Of course she understood their laughter—she was aghast herself—but she couldn't allow it. "Are some of you forgetting the problems you had?" She directed her look at Allen. "Did you like it when people in other schools laughed at you? We don't laugh at each other in here. We support each other and help each other. We are all part of the same family in this school. And people in a family help each other all the time."

As she walked into the room, Erika deliberately bumped

right into a wall. She had been dressed up prettily in a velveteen jumper, white knee socks, and patent leather Mary Jane shoes. Her mother had braided her hair with ribbons, but Erika looked completely disheveled. Her socks were hanging down around her ankles, and her feet were half out of her shoes as she broke their backs with her heels. One hair ribbon had been loosened. She was chewing on the other.

She staggered into the classroom, knocking desks and turning over chairs. She was behaving like a severely disturbed or retarded child. Clinically she was neither. Somehow she had been made to feel that she was supposed to act like that.

Erika McCoy had spent most of her nearly six years living with her grandmother in Mississippi. She had moved to Chicago over the summer to live with her mother. Ella McCoy did not know her daughter very well. As a public school teacher she thought she knew children, but she didn't have the slightest inkling of a problem when she enrolled Erika in the first grade at a nearby Lutheran school. She had chosen a parochial school because she had no faith in the Chicago school system.

Each afternoon when Mrs. McCoy picked up her daughter at the parochial school, she would faithfully ask the teacher how Erika was doing and whether there was anything she needed to help her daughter with at home. Each day, just as faithfully, the teacher told Mrs. McCoy, "No, everything is fine." Then came the phone call. The teacher was requesting a conference to discuss "Erika's problem."

Mrs. McCoy was beside herself. It was only three weeks into the semester. What could be wrong? She drove to the school that evening. The teacher said, "Erika cannot read and she will probably never learn to read. We are taking her out of first grade and putting her into a special class."

Mrs. McCoy didn't hear another word. Her daughter was only five and a half years old and already these people were writing her off. Dazed, Mrs. McCoy went home to work with Erika. Erika shook her head, "No, I can't do that. My teacher said I can't learn how to do that." No matter how much Mrs. McCoy tried to coax her daughter, bribing her with ice cream, candy, and a new toy, Erika would only repeat, "Oh no, Mommy, my teacher said I can't do that. I can't learn that."

Mrs. McCoy spent three sleepless nights worrying about her daughter. On Sunday evening she happened to watch a local television program on alternative schools. Part of the show dealt with the school Marva was running in a basement classroom at Daniel Hale Williams University. Mrs. McCoy looked up Marva's phone number and called. Marva told her to bring Erika to the school.

The following morning Marva settled Erika at a desk and told her, "Don't you worry about a thing. You are a very smart girl. You will soon be doing what everyone else in here does. Right now they have a little head start because they have been here longer. I will work with you and teach you. Soon you will be reading and adding and subtracting numbers, too."

The class began with arithmetic.

"What is arithmetic? It is a Greek word meaning what?" Marva asked.

"Skilled in numbers," came a chorus of four voices. Gary was joining in for the first time, and his participation certainly did not go unnoticed.

"My goodness, Gary, we've come a long way. You see how well you can do when you try?" Marva smiled and Gary too looked pleased with himself.

Marva wrote 2+3=5 on the board.

"Which number is the sum, children?"

"Five," they answered.

"And two and three are called what, Allen?"

"Addends," he said.

"Très bien." Marva printed *addends* on the board and placed the diacritical marks over the vowels. Phonics was incorporated into everything from math to science.

"An addend is a number that is added to another number. You must remember the words *sum* and *addend* because they are used on all the standardized tests. Those words trip up many students. If the question was 'Find the sum of the addends two and three,' what would your answer be?"

"Five," they responded.

"Very good." Marva handed out math worksheets.

The children were working at different levels in math.

Cindy was doing two-digit addition, learning to carry tens. Tracy was still having a difficult time with simple addition. Gary and Allen were both on multiplication. Marva moved from child to child, teaching each one individually.

Tracy was drawing sticks beside each problem, counting up the sticks to find the answer.

"You are not going to count sticks or blocks or circles or rabbits in here," Marva said, bending over Tracy's desk. "Look, sweetheart, six and seven cannot possibly make eight. Eight is only one more than seven. You want to add six to seven. Count out loud with me: eight, nine, ten, eleven, twelve, thirteen. Six and seven make thirteen."

Tracy began erasing her wrong answer.

"No, darling. Remember, we draw a circle around the error and put the correct answer above it. We proofread mistakes, we don't erase them. When you erase a mistake from the paper, you erase it from your mind, too, and you will make the same mistake over again."

Marva looked up and saw Erika had taken off her socks and was chewing on them instead of the hair ribbon.

"That's not how the brightest child in the world behaves," Marva said, taking the socks out of Erika's mouth. Handing her a pencil, Marva asked Erika if she could print her name at the top of the math paper. Erika shook her head and said she couldn't. "Don't say 'I can't,' " Marva told her. "Say, 'I'll try.' If you say, 'I'll try,' then we'll get it done together." Erika grabbed the paper, crumpled it into a ball, and threw it on the floor.

"I love you and I know you can do it," Marva said, taking out a fresh sheet.

"No!" Erika shouted, punching holes through the paper with her pencil.

At lunch Erika took the cap off her thermos and let the juice dribble all over her dress. She took apart her sandwich, licking the mayonnaise from the bread and getting it all over her face. The other children giggled and whispered among themselves.

"She's crazy," Gary said.

"I don't want to hear any name-calling," Marva told him. "God made us all special. If you don't like someone, then you write a letter to the Lord and say, 'Lord, you goofed on so-and-so.' "

Suddenly Erika looked straight at the group, a dab of mayonnaise smeared on the tip of her nose. "My teacher said I can't read."

"If you don't forget what that teacher told you, I'm going to get terribly angry," Marva shot back. Before her lay weeks of deprogramming, telling Erika over and over, "You are not a bad girl, you are not a stupid child." It wasn't going to be easy for either of them.

★   ★   ★

I estimated it would take Erika a month, about the same time it took most children to get started reading. Usually it took a month for the lessons on sounds to jell and for students to become comfortable expressing their thoughts in class. Erika was the most difficult child I had ever encountered. I couldn't seem to reach her. I had always been sure of my ability to move children, but my approach wasn't working with Erika. All the affection, the praise, and the encouragement seemed to hit deaf ears. By Christmas vacation, nearly two months after she had come to the school, Erika was no different than on the first day she arrived.

In the middle of a lesson she would get out of her seat, sit down on the floor, and scoot around the room on her behind. Often I had to hold her on my lap to keep her still while the other children read aloud. Erika rubbed against the board, covering her backside with chalk dust. If she wasn't stuffing socks into her mouth, then she was biting a pencil. She wrote all over her reader with crayola, and when I gave the children their first novel, *Little Women,* Erika chewed the edges of the pages. I told her to stop. She snapped, "I can if I want!" She tossed her head defiantly.

Mrs. McCoy told me her daughter was just as diabolical out of school. While riding in the car Erika would grab the steering wheel or throw a sweater over her mother's head. She would tear up people's houses wherever she went visiting. One time she replaced the assorted chocolates in a box of candy with rocks, to the dismay of an elderly neighbor woman. Mrs. McCoy had no control over her daughter and absolutely no idea how to handle her. Neither did I.

I wasn't upset with Erika but with myself for not being able to get through to her. Several evenings I burst into tears just thinking about that child. Clarence tried to console me, telling me to forget about it, but I couldn't forget. I was not going to let any child fall victim to a label of failure.

A few days after we returned from the Christmas holidays, Erika ran out of the classroom, up the stairs, and out of the building. I chased after her, grabbing her arms tightly. Holding her close, I said that was not the way to behave; children couldn't run out of school any time they wanted to. She pushed away from me and shouted, "I can do what I want! My mommy lets me. I say, 'Please, please,' and she lets me do what I want."

I realized then how blind I had been. I should have recognized the problem before. All the signs had been there, laid out before me in a pattern like the numbered drawings in a coloring book. I recalled that Mrs. McCoy had brought a pot of spaghetti for the whole class on Erika's second day in school. I recalled hearing that she took Erika to the movies or to an amusement park on weekday afternoons. No wonder endearments and praise hadn't worked. The child was used to hearing them all the time, indiscriminately, indulgently. In that moment I saw that Erika had been begging not only for attention but for discipline.

I took her by the hand, led her back inside the classroom, and sat her down at her desk. I distributed reading comprehension worksheets mimeographed from old editions of the California Achievement Tests. I frequently gave my students the old tests for practice, even at Delano. I didn't put much stock in standardized tests myself, but as long as so many other educators did, my students would probably have to take these tests at one time or another, when they transferred out of my school or went on to high school. Thus it was important for them to know how to take tests.

"I don't need any tests to show me how much you know. I see it every day by what you do in here. But we learn how to take tests because we live in a world that often judges us by how we perform on tests."

I was guiding the children through the first few examples when I heard paper tearing. Erika was ripping her sheet into long shreds.

"I saw a man yesterday giving a million dollars to anyone who could tear up paper. Employers pay a lot of money for someone to do that, don't they? You'll get the best job in the world knowing how to tear paper, won't you?" The other children shook their heads no. I took away the paper and gave Erika a new one. "I want you to circle the synonyms on this paper, right now."

"I won't!" she screamed.

I saw a lot of myself in Erika, the same strong will and determination. I had to show her that I was more determined than she. The four other children had forgotten about their own work and were watching. If I didn't do something fast, I was going to lose all of them. I whirled around, grabbing the first object that came to hand, an extension pipe from a vacuum cleaner left by the maintenance crew. Clutching the pipe in my hand, I stood over Erika and stared her dead in the eye.

"I'm going to kill you today if you don't finish your paper," I shouted. No sooner were the words out of my mouth than I was stunned at having spoken them. Still dazed by my rage, I heard one of the children gasp. They were all listening with large-eyed disbelief. There was a loud throbbing deep in my own throat and my whole body was quivering.

I didn't know what had come over me. I could never hit a child. Never. I had never in my life threatened a child. I wondered whether this desperation was for Erika or for myself. I wished I could drop the pipe to the floor and go on with the lesson as if nothing had happened. But once I had begun this thing, I had to see it through. The big question was whether the child would call my bluff.

Holding back the quaver in my voice, I told her, "Everyone says you are crazy. I don't believe that. But if you don't finish that paper, then I'll know you're crazy. You might as well be dead if you are going to go through life the way you are."

Erika's eyes were riveted on the paper. Her hands were planted firmly on it, palms flat and fingers pressed together. Her right hand jerked slightly, tipping the pencil off the desk. She leaned over, picked it up, and held it pinched between her thumb and forefinger. She hastily circled the word *throw* as a synonym for *pitch*. Moving on to the second question, she matched *silly* with *foolish*.

I wanted to laugh. Erika had been listening all along! All the time she had been acting up, all the time she had been tearing her papers and chewing her books, seeming not to pay attention, she had been listening and learning. I stood there until she finished the page. After the last question, Erika tilted her round face upward. "Am I in first grade or was I put back?"

I gaped at her. She understood perfectly about the label that had been put on her. I said that of course she was in first grade. "We don't ever go backwards in here. What is past is past. We only move forward."

Reassured, she handed me her paper, then pulled the ribbon from her pigtail and chewed on it. I decided to take care of one problem at a time.

Erika joined the other children in the reading group. Over the next few days she seemed to become a different child. Of course her change had really not come about suddenly. All those weeks Erika had probably been working things out in her own head, taking note of herself and the other students. And she had been sizing me up, testing my attitude, my trustworthiness, and my acceptance of her. It wasn't my threat that made her alter her behavior for the long run. What sustained the change in Erika was her own decision to settle down, a decision contingent on whether I came through for her. I did my best.

After a while Erika's seeming lack of interest was replaced by active curiosity, her lethargy turned into ambition, and her obstreperousness gave way to a measure of self-control. The potential had always been there. It exists in all children. The challenge for a teacher is to bring the potential out. There is no such thing as *the* way to reach a student. Any way is *the* way as long as it works for the individual child.

Some children, like Allen and Tracy, respond easily to affection and warmth. Others, like Gary, hide their fears and frustrations behind a wall of defensiveness; they have something to prove to themselves and everyone else. Erika seemed convinced that there was something wrong with her, that no one would accept her. Through her actions she issued a challenge: "Are you going to believe in me and accept me no matter what I do?"

I discovered that Erika was a pleaser. She did what people expected her to do; she became what they expected her to become. According to her mother, a previous teacher had told Erika that she was dumb, and that was exactly what Erika tried to be. She didn't try to prove her teacher wrong. I laid before her a different set of expectations. And Erika responded. Children rise to the level their teachers set, as numerous studies have shown.

Erika still had a thirst for attention, but she sought it now through precocity. Erika became a zealous student, sometimes overly zealous. Every time I asked a question, her hand would shoot up, waving frantically. "Me, Mrs. Collins, call on me, please!" When I had my students memorize a poem a week, Erika memorized three or four. She would turn in a paper and then ask to do it over again because it wasn't neat enough.

Once she began reading and saw what fun it was, there was no stopping her. She became addicted to books. If she wasn't reading one of the Judy Blume books or one from the Laura Ingalls Wilder series, then she was trying out *The Fables of La Fontaine* or *The Song of Roland*. One day, as I went around the class asking each child what new bit of knowledge he or she had learned that day, Erika said, "I'm like Socrates. The only thing I know is how much I don't know. I'm learning something new every day." As much as I praised her, though, I still had to keep after her.

Erika pulled up academically first. Socially she dragged behind. She didn't know how to talk to the other children, how to mingle, and her frantic enthusiasm put them off almost as much as her previous antics had done. It didn't matter to Erika. She knew I was determined to teach her and prove she wasn't stupid. For the time being, that was enough.

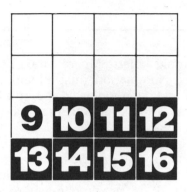

By January 1976, a little more than four months after the school started, the size of my class had almost tripled as a result of word of mouth and publicity from the television news feature and from an article in *The Chicago Defender,* a black-owned newspaper. Teaching became more complicated. I was running a one-room schoolhouse. In contrast to my teaching at Delano, where all the students had been in the same grade and around the same age, I now had boys and girls of all ages and abilities with an odd assortment of problems.

The new children were crammed together in the front half of the room. Theodore was the oldest, a beefy twelve year old who looked like the tackle on a football team. I had one year to build up his third grade reading level and get him ready to pass the high school entry exams. Next to him George Beecher slumped nonchalantly in his seat most of the time. A round-faced eleven year old, he walked with a waddle and could barely write his name. He could not add four plus one or read "bat" or "cat," even though his previous teachers at a Catholic school had promoted him to sixth grade with a report of "making fair progress." His five years in parochial school had been a waste. He gave the teachers no trouble and they left him alone. For five years he sat in the back of the room and listened to other students perform. I had seen that pattern before. Fat children, quiet children, dirty children, and children with unappealing or perhaps scarred features were hidden away in the back of a classroom and forgotten.

Frail six-year-old Janette Moore wouldn't talk. She sat and stared. No feeling. No emotion. Just a blank look. Her mother told me the child had been molested. I didn't talk about the incident with Janette. It took me four months to get her to smile when she was tickled.

Theodore, George, and Janette were representative of the thirteen new students. Not one was reading at the level appropriate for his or her age. Some had been labeled "unteachable" or "learning disabled" by previous teachers and psychologists and had been placed in or recommended for special learning programs. These children arrived at the school with satchels full of official memoranda documenting their behavior disorders and their emotional, psychological, or psychosocial problems. They were a band of misfits and discards, and nobody else seemed to want them. I needed students. I felt I could help them.

Most of their parents knew very little about me or the school. I don't think they were coming to me because of the curriculum or educational philosophy of the school. They came because we had an open door and empty desks. I was just one more alternative to be tried, probably not much different from the ones they had tried before or the ones they would have to try later, when I too gave up on their children.

Some of the parents came to me in a more desperate mood. For them our school was a last resort. Their children had been turned out of school, in some cases illegally, and they had nowhere else to go. I had the feeling that some of these parents were less concerned with what I could do for their children than with finding a place to dump their problems.

The first thing I did was toss aside all the reports and cumulative records. My experience had shown me that those reports were wrong more often than they were right. I had seen too many children with their personalities ink-blotted, their IQs probed, and their every move analyzed—children written off as losers.

One of the things I hated most about the public schools was how quickly teachers "blue-slipped" children for psychological referral. Every time they came across a child who was too hard to deal with, out came the blue slip, a convenient excuse. The private and parochial schools were just as quick to label a child. Erika McCoy was one example, one of many who came to our school. One mother told me her son's Catholic school principal recommended that the boy transfer to the Beacon School for emotionally disturbed and learning-disabled children. A teacher at Beacon told her, "Your son doesn't belong here. He is not emotionally disturbed. When a child misbehaves in the Catholic schools, they are quick to ascribe it to mental problems."

Too often teachers, school psychologists, and social workers have preconceived notions about children and pigeonhole them accordingly. Children with divorced parents run a high risk of being stereotyped, as do children from wealthy families, or those with working mothers, and black children living in neighborhoods like Garfield Park. Tell some people where these children live, and right away they assume that the children are abused or neglected, that they come to school hungry, have no clothes, and have never lived with a father. Some teachers assume that these children can never learn anything.

Over the years I've heard all the arguments from people in and out of education. What good is it to teach a ghetto child Shakespeare? Why bother teaching literature and philosophy? Just give them some vocational training, if they can handle that much.

We live in a label-conscious society where people are forever trying to categorize and classify each other. We tend to overuse terms like "learning disability," "developmental disabilities," "behavior disorder," and "hyperactive," bandying them about until they are stretched beyond validity. A child who fidgets in his seat isn't necessarily hyperactive. Maybe that child is bored. Maybe that child doesn't know how to do the work and is afraid to ask for help. Or maybe that child is just active. One boy's kindergarten teacher claimed he was hyperactive because he wouldn't put his head down during morning rest period. The child's mother, a pediatric nurse, argued that her son had twelve hours of sleep every night and simply wasn't tired during the day. Another teacher advised a mother not to feed her seven-year-old son sugar-coated breakfast cereal because the boy showed signs of hyperactivity. When the mother asked what the symptoms were—did her son have any trouble learning or was he a behavior problem?—the teacher replied no, the child was very bright but he had too much energy and she couldn't keep up with him.

Often a problem in the classroom lies not with the child but in the relationship between the child and the teacher. A teacher's assessment of a child is necessarily based on that teacher's life experience. That means certain children trigger a positive or negative reaction because of the teacher's past, a reaction having little to do with the children's abilities or personalities. For example, a child might remind a teacher of someone, perhaps a sibling or a classmate he or she didn't get along with.

Teachers are, after all, people, and there are times when they respond to situations not as teachers but as unhappy people. Occasionally a child gets stuck with a label because the teacher overreacts in frustration over behavior that might be nothing more than normal childish antics. Sometimes a teacher is just angry with a child and wants to retaliate. And all too frequently a teacher's personality, attitudes, and preferences color his or her response to a child.

A teacher can make or break a child, favor or stigmatize him. Just as there are teachers who are inspiring, who can spark interest and turn students on to learning, there are teachers who can turn a student off, not only to school but to himself. Not that it is done consciously. But a teacher has to be sensitive to all things at all times. Even such offhand remarks as "Your older brother was a brilliant student" or "You're the biggest one in class so you stand in the back row for the assembly program" can alienate a child.

I was aware of these issues as an educator and as a parent. Around the time my thirteen new students enrolled in the school, my son Patrick, who was ten, was having difficulty with one of the teachers at his new private school. For some reason Patrick's teacher didn't like him. She would display every child's paper but his. She kept him inside during recess taking tests, and she criticized him in front of the others, turning him into the class dummy. Eventually the other children supported the teacher's characterization, poking fun at Patty in the gym or in the lunchroom.

I knew Patrick could do the work. I sat with him at night as he read Chaucer's "Knight's Tale" aloud without any trouble. I couldn't understand why that teacher was riding the boy so hard. Clarence and I both wanted to pull Patty out of the school, but Patty kept insisting he didn't want to be a quitter and he didn't want to be pampered like a sissy. So I mistakenly gave in and let him stay, hoping the situation would ease itself and the teacher would have a change of heart. Meanwhile Patty began stuttering, and I'd have to say, "Take your time, baby, Mommy's here."

Several nights I got out of bed and found Patty sleeping fitfully, gnashing his teeth and mumbling, "Oh no, I can do it." I felt angry and guilty and desperate—the same feelings many of my students' parents had experienced. And like those other parents, I didn't know what to do. Since Patty was so determined to stick it out at that school, at least until the end of the year, how could I undercut his resolve? And if I did take him out, I didn't know where I would put him. Over the years I had pretty well exhausted the list of private schools in the city, and I thought the worst thing I could do would be to put him in school with me. He would surely feel like a defeated baby running back to his mother.

All I could do was comfort him and reassure him, trying to rebuild his shattered confidence each day. The whole family gave him all their love and encouragement and support. I hated Patty's teacher, more than I had ever hated anyone before. I wondered, if they are doing that to my child, how many others are suffering the same or worse?

For students the vast pool of teachers is like an educational lottery. A child is lucky to draw a good teacher and get off to a winning start, but there is no guarantee that another teacher the next year will keep the child on track.

My attitude toward teachers' evaluations—of my own children and those in my class—kept me from taking anybody else's word for what a child was or was not. I didn't have faith in aptitude tests either. Some children become confused and disoriented and can't perform when taking those tests. Patrick was one of them. Sometimes a child, worried about doing well and living up to a parent's expectations (set perhaps by an older brother or sister), freezes during a test.

And I didn't believe psychological tests were any more conclusive, especially since the results often depended on interpretation. For example, one of my students, a seven-year-old girl, had undergone a "mental status examination." Asked to draw a picture of her own choice, she drew a park scene—a yellow sun, two blue clouds, a green lawn, a big brown and green tree, and three flowers surrounding a figure of a child throwing something in a garbage can. According to the psychiatrist's evaluation, the "theme of the garbage can indicated perhaps preoccupation with being abandoned, thrown away." Yet another psychologist said the drawing could indicate a preoccupation with neatness and cleanliness. Who was the parent to believe?

Because of all the problems my son Patrick was having with his teacher, the school psychologist put him through a battery of tests, which included a human figure drawing. Because he had drawn the feet first, the psychologist concluded Patrick had a problem. However, I thought that was perfectly natural since Patty has big feet, his brother Eric has big feet, and I have big feet.

Knowing all the things that can contaminate an expert's judgment of a child, I refused to view any child as unteachable. I didn't know whether my new students had clinical dysfunctions. Maybe some did. But I was never going to teach them as though they did. I was not going to narrow my expectations. I was convinced that somehow, and in some way, I would be able to reach each child.

Like so many other children I had taught over the years, my thirteen new students all seemed to have the same feelings of worthlessness and insecurity. Whatever their individual problems, the one thing they all had in common was too much failure. I knew I would have to implant new success messages. I had to condition them to think positively, as I had done with all of my previous students.

There was one big difference with the entry of these new

children. Mine was not the only voice of encouragement; it was now backed by a chorus of support from my five original students. By now they were old hands at Emerson. They knew all the proverbs and quotations about believing in oneself. And they were rooting for the newcomers.

Before, I had been the only one saying "I won't let you fail." Now it was "We are not going to let you fail. We are going to be right there to help you along."

Turning to Cindy and Tracy and Erika and Gary and Allen, I asked, "There was a time in here when all of you did not what?"

"Did not know," they answered.

"And now you must do what? You must help whom?"

"Another child," they shouted.

Learning was to be a group effort. Everyone in the school was part of the team, and like any team, the school would only work if everyone pulled together. This was the first time I was dealing with so many different age groups and achievement levels. Without the all-for-one-and-one-for-all spirit, there was no way to get a twelve year old to feel good about sitting in the same room with children five, six, and seven years old.

More important, each child needed to feel loved and wanted. Each child needed the sense of belonging. Most were still suffering the stigma of being the outcasts and oddballs in their previous school. Our class had to be a support group, urging one another along and delighting in each other's small accomplishments, much the way a group of Weight Watchers rallies around a new dieter or an Alcoholics Anonymous meeting takes a new member under wing. I didn't want any of the children to feel that they were on their own. Therefore, I tried to turn the age discrepancies into an advantage, creating a climate where students would tutor and help one another.

By the end of February 1976, one month after they had entered the school, all thirteen of the new students were reading. Some were reading better than others of course, but all of them had a hold on the roots of phonics. I thought I would die when I had to go back to the very beginning all over again and teach the new children that sounds make up words and words stand for thoughts. But I did it, as I would continue to do with each new child, starting right in with the drills, the chanting, and the sing-song recitation of the vowel and consonant sounds. I was tired of the routine, but I never let it show. A good teacher has to be a ham. I always tried to appear as fresh and energetic as if I were teaching the exercises for the first time.

"What I do here is no miracle," I would tell my students. "It's simply hard work. My feet are killing me. My throat hurts from talking, and when you are asleep at night, I am up preparing your lessons."

Each child at the school got the work he or she needed. That was the only way I could effectively teach such an assortment of students. I would say, "We don't all wear the same size shoe, do we? When we go to the doctor, we don't all get the same kind of medicine, do we?" If a child was having difficulty with homonyms such as *to* and *too,* the appropriate worksheet would be on the desk the next morning. If a child was having difficulty adding dollars and cents or working out story problems, there were other worksheets. None of the individualized lessons could be prepared in advance because I never knew what specific need or weakness would surface each day.

The children's reading ability evolved from the embryo of phonics. Once children master the sounds and learn how to syllabicate, they progress rapidly. A first grade child who is taught intensive phonics can read four-syllable words within four to five months. Studies show that with phonics a first-grader can have a reading vocabulary of 24,000 words by the end of the year. A child learning the look-say method has a reading vocabulary of 1,500 words at the end of the fourth grade. The look-say vocabularly does not include such common words as *boil, brain, copy, pain, pity, pray, pride, puff, root, spare, stir, sum, tax, thirty, twelve, vote.* With phonics a first-grader can read those words after a few weeks.

Phonics enables a child to decipher words and so allows better reading comprehension. When a child understands the relationship between a series of spoken sounds and the printed word, the child will read for meaning. Comprehension is hampered with the look-say method because a child has to guess at words. Busy trying to identify each word from memory, the child can't concentrate on what a sentence means. With look-say there is a tendency to displace words and meanings. A child who has to rely on memory and context clues to recognize whole words is prone to misread words and make word substitutions. A study of misreading errors made by high school students—including students who had passed college entrance aptitude tests—showed that instead of reading *Solomon,* the students read *salami.* They misread *delicacy* as *delinquency, hurricane* as *hammer, groceryman* as *clergyman, inert* as *inherent,* and *imbecility* as *implicitly.* In total the study recorded approximately 100,000 similar misreading errors made by students ranging from first grade to college.

As soon as my students learned the sounds of words, they also learned homonyms, synonyms, antonyms, and spelling. The moment they were introduced to a vowel sound, the children put it to work, using the spellings for that vowel to form words. For example, using the spellings for the *a* and *e* sounds, they completed such words as ....t (a number),

_ _ t (we do this with food), h _ _ (we feed this to horses), f _ _ t (we walk on these), th _ _ (a plural pronoun), pl _ _ n (not fancy), and str _ _ _ _ t (a line that is not crooked).

Later the children progressed to transcribing words from the phonetic spelling. What might have looked like a foreign language to some students was perfectly clear to my brood. They knew that ə-noi is annoy, ə-myōōz is amuse, kāk is cake, frīt is fright, frē-kwant is frequent, i-rā-sər is eraser, myōō-zik is music, and ik-splō-zhən is explosion. I kept their reading and writing skills working in tandem. My students were never going to think by the mile and write by the inch.

Critics of the phonics method claim it can't teach children to read well because there are too many irregular sounds and spellings in the English language. The German schwa sound, for instance, has some thirty different spellings, including: *a* in *tidal, e* in *sicken, i* in *charity, o* in *come, u* in *typhus, ion* in *vacation, le* in *sickle, m* in *prism.*

I dealt with the irregularities by spotlighting representative words. When I taught a sound, I brought in all the spelling patterns for that sound. To teach the sound of *z,* I used words like *music, zebra, has,* and *treasure.* The three *f* spellings, as in *fight, phone,* and *cough,* were taught together. *Ck* and *ch* words were taught together when they both made the hard *k* sound as in *tack* and *ache.* Words like *sugar, tuition, permission, special,* and *ocean* were taught along with *sh* words like *ship, shall,* and *shelf* and words having the French *ch* sound, as in *challis* and *charlatan.* The soft *ch* sound, as in chime or cheese was taught separately.

In order for the children to practice distinguishing the sounds, I composed chanteys that they recited aloud in cadence, clapping twice at the end of each refrain:

Change and chord, change and chord
Change says *chuh* and chord says *ck.*

Chin and chagrin, chin and chagrin.
Chin says *chuh* and chagrin says *sh.*

Go and edge, go and edge
The vowel signal *e* changes *g* to *j*.
Beg and beige, gap and revenge.

Cap and rice, or can and nice
The vowel signal *e* changes *c* to *s*.

Sweater and pleasure, sweater and pleasure
The vowel *ea* now says *eh*.

Sit and site, sit and site
The vowel signal *e* hits the vowel before it
and makes it say its name, and makes it say its name.

Bread and knead, bread and knead
Bread says *eh* and knead says *e*.

Accumulate and quotient, accumulate and quotient
Accumulate says *q* and quotient says *kw*.

There are 180 rules for consonant and vowel sounds. We were constantly repeating drills and reviewing phonics. And we continued over the years, even when the children had progressed to reading things like *The Brothers Karamazov*. The phonics review allowed their spelling to keep pace with their reading.

I started off Theodore and George, my oldest students, in the sixth grade reader. The only way to motivate children is to make them stretch. Both these boys belonged in the third or fourth grade books, but there would have been no incentive for them to learn if they felt they were doing the same work as the younger children.

Cindy, Erika, Allen, and Gary pushed on to the third grade book by the middle of the year. So did Tracy. I had worked with her alone, tutoring her before and after school until I brought her up to where Cindy was. In class I continued to guard her reading, stopping her after a few sentences so she wouldn't make a mistake. Months went by with Tracy experiencing these small, controlled spurts of success. One day when I cut short her turn, she looked up at me doe-eyed and asked, "Please, Mrs. Collins, can I try more? Can I read one more sentence?" I was thrilled. She wasn't merely trying to please me. She had finally reached the point where she felt competent. Of course I let her go on reading aloud. When she came to the end of the para-graph, the rest of the class, led by Cindy and Allen, burst into applause. The support of her classmates sealed Tracy's confidence. From that day on she was out of her shell.

Meanwhile Janette and some of the other newcomers were working with the second grade book. As soon as they were able to read the material, I skipped them on to the more advanced reader. As a motivating technique I always told the children the grade level of the book they were reading. If they were reading well, I'd say they were not going to finish the book they were on, they were going to move ahead to the third, fourth, or fifth grade book. Little children always want to be like the big children. The incentive for the older children was to read at or above their grade level so they could be role models for their younger classmates to look up to. Somehow there was no competitive atmosphere.

By loving and touching and talking to each child, I tried to create an atmosphere of mutual caring. The children cheered one another when they recited or read aloud, and occasionally they even applauded me. And when a younger child moved up to a higher level, the older students offered congratulations. They were proud of their classmate's accomplishment. Allen, for example, proved to be such an excellent reader that by May I felt he could handle the sixth grade reader. Theodore and George took him under wing like big brothers.

We all shared in each other's success. No one laughed at or called attention to another child's shortcomings. And anyone who dared to try was immediately reminded of Coleridge's line from *The Ancient Mariner:* "All things both great and small . . . He made and loveth all." If a student tried to score points by tattling on a classmate, I immediately said, "If God had meant for you to see for me, he would have stuck our heads together."

★   ★   ★

Every two weeks the children had to report on a book they read outside class. Marva was accumulating a stockpile of books, some donated and some purchased at charity book fairs or used bookstores. The inventory was a literary mulligan stew, classical authors mixed in with writers of popular children's fiction. E. M. Forster, Somerset Maugham, and William Faulkner shared the shelves with Judy Blume, Roald Dahl, and Shel Silverstein.

On the second and fourth Fridays of the month Marva chose a book for each child, handing out copies of *The Jungle, Pride and Prejudice, O'Henry's Tales, Mysterious Island, Spring Is Here, Tales of a Fourth Grade Nothing, Lord of the Flies, 1984, The Fall of the House of Usher,* and *Great Expectations,* among others. Marva seemed to dispense the books arbitrarily. However, her policy was the older a child, the more difficult the book, even if the child's reading level was not quite high enough. Children used to failure needed goals if they were going to succeed. That was her rationale for giving Theodore, her twelve year old with the third grade reading ability, one of the thickest books on the shelf, *Moby Dick.*

"Hey, Mrs. Collins, I got the wrong book."

"No, sweetheart, I gave you the right book, *Moby Dick.*"

"But it's got so many pages and so many words on a page. It's got no pictures. This is a book for big kids."

"I think you're big enough."

"Naw, in the old school I always got easy books."

"Well, in this school we don't give young men like you easy books. We don't expect you to do the same work the little children do. Give this book a try. You don't have to understand everything in it, but see what you can do. It's made up of words and words are made up of what?"

"Sounds," Theodore grinned.

"That's right. And as long as you remember your sounds and know how to use a dictionary, you'll do fine."

At the end of the day Theodore left the school clasping the copy of *Moby Dick* so that everyone could see the title and the thickness. Marva wanted him to show it off. As far as she was concerned, all he had to do at the end of the two weeks was tell her the book was about a big fish. As it turned out, he told her Moby Dick was a big, white, man-eating whale.

It was through Operation Read, the forty-five minutes of free reading right after lunch, that Marva stimulated her students' interest in books, exposing them to a vast range of stories, topics, and authors. Each child read a chapter or two from a book or a short story or some poetry or a masterplot summary from *Digests of World Literature*. It was the only silent reading the children did in class. After the reading there was a period in which the children told about their individual reading.

They read and Marva read along, encouraging them to try new authors. She stocked her shelves with the very best stories possible, such as Ovid's *Metamorphoses* ("Don't get hung up on the long word; the book is nothing but the Greek myths all over again," she reassured the children), the *Satyricon*, Guy de Maupassant's stories, Greek drama, *Candide,* and *Crime and Punishment.* Marva knew the children would return to these books years later like lifelong friends.

After the quiet reading time, Marva would take the first turn at telling what she read. She would dramatize the stories, sometimes putting in things that weren't there to make the telling more vivid. Pacing across the front of the room, she explained how Raskolnikov carefully counted the number of steps from his house to the pawnbroker's apartment as he prepared for his crime.

"*Crime and Punishment* is a psychological novel," she said. "*Psychology,* which is the study of why people think and behave the way they do, comes from the Greek word *psyche,* meaning the human soul or mind. Now this is a story of guilt. No one knows for sure that Raskolnikov murdered the old woman and her sister, but he thinks they know, so he gives himself away. If you do something wrong, your guilty conscience makes you think everybody knows about it. Raskolnikov is poor and unhappy, and he doesn't have many friends. Children, is that a good excuse for getting bad thoughts in his head and committing murder?"

Another time she dramatized the sufferings of Candide, telling how he was expelled from the Baron's castle, captured and tortured by the Bulgarians, shipwrecked, caught in an earthquake, and flogged—all within the first few chapters. She told her students about *The Happy Prince* by Oscar Wilde, pointing up the lesson that a generous heart is rewarded. By way of contrast, she outlined the gloomier view taken in *Lord of the Flies.*

"You see what happens when you don't care about your

fellow man. All children like to be free of restrictions. You all think it would be ideal not to have adults around to tell you what to do. But we need restrictions; we all need order and discipline. Without them we would all be destroyed. Society would be chaos."

When Marva finished summarizing what she had read, some child would invariably say, "Oh, can I read that next?" And then a classmate would ask, "Can I have it after you?"

Her synopses were not confined to literature. Sometimes she told the children the stories behind operas such as *La Bohème* or *The Marriage of Figaro* or narrated ballets such as *Giselle, The Nutcracker,* and *Petrouchka.* The making of educated young men and women, she believed, required exposure to the full breadth of culture. How else would children from an inner-city ghetto learn about opera or ballet?

Then Marva went from child to child, asking what he or she had read that day. It was during one of these oral periods after Operation Read that George Beecher, the overweight and sullen eleven year old, finally opened up. George had been ignored for so long in his previous school that he found it hard to break the habit of not participating in discussions. Marva encouraged him but didn't push. When children were ready to come around, they would. She asked him what he had read, and suddenly he rose to the occasion.

"I read part of *The Pearl* by John Steinbeck," he mumbled. The children had to state the title and the author before they began explaining anything else.

"Speak up, darling," Marva told him. "Don't let someone else steal your thunder or you'll always be just a little raincloud."

"This guy Kino," he continued, "found the biggest and greatest pearl in the world. He was poor, and then he found the pearl and everyone wanted to be his friend. The doctor wouldn't take care of his sick baby before, but now he came to take care of it and be Kino's friend."

"Why wouldn't the doctor take care of the baby?" The question came from a classmate.

"'Cause the doctor only wanted to take care of rich people," George said, pleased by the other student's interest and confident of his answer. "Rich people had money and the poor people only had fish to give him."

"Yeah, I know a lady who got sick and the doctor didn't want to take care of her 'cause she was on public aid," chimed in Theodore.

"Everyone's always pushing poor people around," said Allen.

"When you're poor, the landlord turns off the heat and he don't care if you freeze," added Gary.

"Let's not cry about what's wrong with this world," Marva told them. "Complaining isn't going to change things. Learn all you can so you will become the doctors, the lawyers, the politicians, and the thinkers. Then you can change things yourself."

"Aw, politicians don't change things," said Cindy. "They have those picnics every year in the park and pass out free hotdogs, but they don't do a thing."

"Then you will have to be the ones to come back to neighborhoods like Garfield Park and rebuild them," answered Marva. "Now, George, go on with your story."

"Well, first everyone acted like they was Kino's friends, but it was fake 'cause they really wanted to get that pearl. And then someone went sneaking around Kino's house at night looking for the pearl and Kino had to fight him off and Kino's wife started to think the pearl was bad."

"Sweetheart, what do you think Steinbeck is telling us in this book?" Marva asked him.

"That people always want money and want to get the rich things someone else got."

"Very, very good. And what else is Steinbeck saying? He's showing us that having valuable things doesn't necessarily make us happy."

"Nope. When you got something good, it can turn out bad. It's like you always tell us, Mrs. Collins, life's not perfect."

George's philosophizing won him an ovation from his classmates. After that he became even more talkative in class, continually waving his hand to be called upon. He followed Marva around like a puppy, telling her about his latest book. One day he was shadowing her so closely that she jumped when he burst into a description of King Arthur and the Knights of the Round Table. Marva laughed and hugged him. Only months before, if that child had been sneaking up behind someone, it surely would not have been to discuss a book.

Some days there was no question that the children were learning. Other times I felt as though I wasn't really getting through to them. I invested all my energy and effort in trying to make my students special, trying to separate them from the others out on the street. Yet they seemed to backslide so easily.

Gary Love pouted and lapsed back into a defeatist attitude the minute something looked difficult. And Tracy Shanklin seemed to forget more than she remembered. She was trying to do the work, but it took me nearly four months to teach her how to subtract twenty-seven from thirty. Once in a while Allen came to class smelling so bad that no one wanted to sit next to him. Erika had come far with her academic skills, but she still lacked social presence. She still walked on the backs of her shoes, let her nose run, barked at the other children, and fought for the limelight in every discussion.

I had to keep reminding myself where these children had been; they had all taken giant steps forward. I could measure their progress in the small daily victories, as when Gary took homework papers home and returned them the next day or Tracy read aloud excitedly and enthusiastically. However, I needed more. Since I was running a one-room school without official accreditation (Illinois law did not require private schools to be registered or recognized by the state), I needed some traditional proof that my students were learning—in the form of test scores. If my experience at Delano had done anything, it had made me cynical enough to know that their achievement had to be documented in some way. Of course, what test could measure a change in their attitudes, their priorities, their philosophy about life?

Toward the end of May I led my students through practice runs of the Stanford-Binet and the Iowa Achievement Tests, just as older students study for college boards or the bar exam. I made sure my children knew how to follow directions. I reviewed the language used in test questions, words like *integer, inversion, transformation, obtuse angle,* and *acute angle.* And I went over the symbols for *greater than, less than, congruent, parallel, perpendicular, equal to, not equal to, equilateral,* and so on. I knew my children had the knowledge, and I wanted to make sure they would not be stumped by the phrasing of a test question.

When the day came for official testing, I administered the Stanford-Binet series. First I reassured the children that the tests were not going to show who was smarter than someone else. They were only a tool for me to use in determining which subjects needed more of our attention in class. When the results were tabulated, I was delighted.

I had not expected miracles, only solid improvement, and there was plenty of that. Even the children who had entered the school in January had increased their reading and math comprehension substantially in a matter of months. George Beecher, for example, who was at a third grade, fifth month (3.5) level when he arrived, jumped up to 4.2. Tracy and Erika showed even more dramatic gains. Neither had been able to read a word back in September. By the end of our first school year Tracy, at age seven, scored 3.7 and first-grader Erika tested at 4.2. The biggest surprise, however, was eight-year-old Allen, who tested at a seventh grade level.

It had been a wonderful year for the children. They had achieved in our one-room school as they could not have in schools with large budgets, resource centers, and all sorts of teaching aids and audio-visual equipment. The most important reason was that their attitude about school had changed.

On the last day of the school year I couldn't get the children out the door.

"What is this?" I laughed. "Don't you know that children are supposed to be excited about vacation? You're supposed to be happy about being out of school. Don't you know that?"

"No!" they sang out.

"What have I done to you? Lord, what have I created?" I teased, throwing my hands up in mock despair. "I love you all, but I need to get off my feet. And I've worked you so hard all year long, you deserve a rest, too. But remember, a rest from school is not a rest from what?"

"From learning," they chorused.

"And what are you going to do over the summer?"

"Read ten books."

"And I am going to read all twenty books on the list, because I won't know which ten you choose. At this school you can never what?"

"You can never fool Mrs. Collins," they roared.

At the end of that year I decided to take the school out of Daniel Hale Williams University. I appreciated the free space they had given us to get the school going, but I wanted to be independent. The university was involved too much in politics, and I thought it best to separate the school from that environment. The group of women who had helped organize the school said that since I had been running the school, I had their permission to take it over as my own. They told me I could take the students with me, some books and supplies, and even the name of the school.

When I first told Clarence what I wanted to do, he didn't say that I was crazy or even that having my own school was a crazy idea. I spent nights talking to him, discussing the finances of operating a school, the physical space requirements, and above all my purpose. After a few weeks of considering the project, I launched into the paper shuffling. First off, I shortened the name to Westside Preparatory School. I had to incorporate as a not-for-profit organization to get tax-exempt status. Then Clarence and I began hunting for a location. We drove around Garfield Park checking for space in day-care centers and churches, but we found the same dead end wherever we looked. Either the rent was too high or people didn't want the kind of children my school would have. They had visions of rowdy disruptive children stealing and vandalizing.

By the middle of July I had exhausted all the possibilities. I decided to use what I had—the vacant upstairs apartment in my two-flat house. Clarence did all the work. He pulled out kitchen cabinets and plumbing, removed the sink, stove, and refrigerator, knocked down walls and rebuilt new ones, and installed new lighting fixtures. He hammered and sawed long into each night and all through the weekends. By the end of summer I had my school—a classroom fashioned out of a kitchen and the adjacent family room.

For seed money to get the school started, I had planned on using the $5,000 I had withdrawn from my pension upon leaving Delano. However, the construction materials and the attorney's fees for incorporating the school had eaten up most of the money. There wasn't enough left for desks and blackboards and teaching materials.

Still, if the odds were against me in starting a school, luck was in my favor. In late August I received a call from a friend telling me about a suburban school district that was getting rid of desks and blackboards. This friend, who owned a chain of hardware stores and served on his local school board, bought up some of the desks and blackboards as well as a duplicating machine, a record player, and a set of children's encyclopedias. He sent them to me in the store delivery trucks. With this windfall and the books I had accumulated the previous year, Westside Preparatory School was nearly ready.

Taking my household money, I bought fifteen more desks. Then I began a letter-writing campaign to neighborhood banks and businesses, telling them about the school and its objective: to help the children in Garfield Park make something of themselves. I asked for whatever support they could give—not money but office supplies, an old typewriter, or perhaps a water cooler. The response was poor. All I received were reams of scrap paper, much of it from the probate court of Cook County. I used all that paper and more in mimeographing math problems, reading lists, word definitions, phonics exercises, and short stories (in lieu of textbooks). Still, the absence of any substantial public backing was a disappointment. From then on, whatever I had to do I would do myself. The school was going to make it. I would see to that.

In September I had an enrollment of eighteen children. Tracy, Erika, George, and Theodore returned, as did most of my previous students. Naturally my daughter Cindy was also there. I had lost Allen. His father refused to send him to a school in someone's house. Janette had moved to another part of the city, and so had another of my girls, nine-year-old Patricia Washington. Her new house was beautiful, her school was big and sprawling, but, as she told me in a phone call, "They don't hug and touch in the school out here."

There were three new children to take their places. One was an eleven year old named Laura Brown who spelled every word with jumbled letters. Then I had a pre-schooler, four-year-old Calvin Graham. And the third new student was my son Patrick.

I had begun to feel that Patty needed someone to challenge him more, to light a fire under him. Recently he had been doing well enough in a "progressive" private school, but I was convinced he could realize more of his potential in an environment where the educational aims were more clearly defined. Not every child benefits from a "progressive" education; some children need more direction and prodding than others. A child who is a self-starter, already ambitious and motivated, may do well in a situation where students have the freedom to set their own goals. For the child who isn't as well motivated, that freedom may result in goals that are set too low.

Over the years, I have come to believe that some of the problems plaguing modern education are the result of the emphasis placed on "progressive" teaching methods. In an effort to follow John Dewey's notion of a student-centered rather than subject-centered approach to learning, schools have too often sacrificed subject matter, being more concerned with how they taught rather than what they taught. During the late 1960s and the 1970s, when our society was becoming fascinated with pop psychology, many young men and women entered the teaching profession thinking "As long as I can relate to a child, what difference does it make if he or she can't spell *cat?*"

Dewey's philosophy has been misconstrued, misapplied, and frequently seized upon as a convenient rationale for not teaching fundamental material. When parents and school boards have challenged the subject competency of teachers and accused schools of not teaching basic skills, administrators and teaching theorists have rushed to the defense, claiming that "humanistic" education is more important than knowledge.

The problem is that some schools cannot strike a balance between "progressive" and "traditional" teaching methods. People wrongly assume that it has to be one or the other. If you teach the basics in a classical curriculum, you can still pay attention to a child's feelings and attitudes. Moreover, it is a mistake to assume that in order to stimulate creativity and critical thinking you must rule out any learning by rote. Memorization is the only way to teach such things as phonics, grammar, spelling, and multiplication tables.

There is a tendency in education to reject arbitrarily a method of teaching simply because it's old-fashioned. The fact is a teacher can combine both progressive and traditional approaches to learning, each enhancing the other. There is no reason why a teacher can't be sensitive to a child's needs and at the same time teach the child subject matter and skills. That blend has always been the basis of Westside Preparatory School.

School was scheduled to begin at nine o'clock. That held true only on the first day. By the second day, and always after that, school started as soon as the first child arrived, as early as 7:30. The first child would come into the kitchen with my family, and I would begin a review of whatever subject he or she was weak in. While I cleared off the table, combed my hair, and put on lipstick, the child would linger for a few minutes, sipping a glass of juice or eating leftover bacon or flapjacks. As I was finishing my morning household routine, we would begin the drills on math, questions about the readings, or working out the sounds of letters. Which *a* in cake? Which *o* in boat? Which *i* in light? I fired off the questions as I darted from the kitchen to the bathroom to the bedroom. And between bites of breakfast the child responded. Then we would move upstairs and write words on the board, putting in the diacritical markings, of course. I would look over the homework papers so that I could see whether the child was ready to move ahead to something new.

I gave homework every day, though never in massive doses. A child should not have to do thirty math problems overnight. Five or ten problems are enough to see if a child knows what he is doing. I didn't give homework as busy work, but to reinforce a lesson. And I never gave homework until I was certain that the child could do it successfully. I didn't want parents to have to help. Homework was for the benefit of the child, not the parents.

When I saw a child ready to leave at the end of the day without his or her papers, my standard comment was: "Unless you are a genius or your daddy is a millionaire, you cannot afford to leave your books here and not do your homework."

I never punished or reprimanded a child for not turning in homework. I simply reminded all my students that they would not receive their report cards (written evaluations instead of grades) if they did not turn in their daily homework. It was one more way of teaching them about what would be expected of them in the adult world, where rewards are based on performance.

"If you don't do your job, your employer will not give you a paycheck," I reminded them. "No one is going to pay you for something you don't do. Remember what Kahlil Gibran said: 'If this is your day of harvest, in which fields have you sown your seeds?' For now, going to school is your job, and doing homework is one of the responsibilities of that job. I don't want to hear 'The dog ate my paper' or 'My baby brother tore up my report.' We can't go through life giving excuses for what we don't do."

★ ★ ★

At Westside Preparatory School there was nowhere to escape learning. Even the bathrooms had phonics charts tacked on the walls. Marva's classroom was organized and efficient, yet it had the friendly comfortable clutter of a house. Thirty desks were squeezed into the cramped space. Paperbacks and worn hardcover classics were piled in teetering stacks on the floor and on the shelves of an old bookcase.

As in any one-room schoolhouse, different activities were going on all at once. During mathematics some children might be doing addition and subtraction, others multiplication, others long division, while still others might be learning to reduce fractions. Marva walked the aisles, reading over the children's shoulders as they worked. She didn't wait for them to ask for help. She made herself always accessible, for she knew that children are usually hesitant to walk the long mile to the front of the classroom and announce that they do not understand. Often the confused child stayed in his seat and forgot about solving problems until he fell so far behind that he gave up completely.

"Six times five can't be eleven," Marva said, spotting an error on one of the girls' papers. "Sweetheart, remember you are adding six *five* times. We're going to cheat you out of all your money if you can't multiply."

She glanced up and saw another girl chewing gum.

"Get the gum out of your mouth, sweetheart," she said firmly. Then lovingly, "Put it in the garbage and not in your pretty hands."

On her way to Laura Brown's desk she stooped to pick up some papers scattered on the floor beside George. She handed them to him. "I think we're just going to have to get you a secretary," she teased, "because you can't seem to keep your things in order." Mussing his hair, she moved to Laura, the girl who scrambled her letters like alphabet soup and made backward twos, fours, and nines.

"Peach, didn't anyone ever tell you not to go over the margin of the paper? You begin to the right of the red line, like this." She picked up the girl's pencil and printed Laura's name on the page. "See, we print our letters and numbers neatly on the paper. We don't make scratch marks all over it going every which way."

Looking up, she saw Calvin sitting with his index finger in his mouth. "Sweetheart, take your finger out of your mouth. You're a big boy now."

As she turned back to Laura, there was a loud scraping noise. Gary had scooted forward in his desk. "You did a good job of pushing that desk," she told him. "Mommy told you to get up this morning and go to school so you could push a desk, didn't she? You get good jobs pushing desks, don't you?"

Nothing escaped her. She was aware of all things at all times, and without losing her focus, she could address every one of them. She could tell a girl to stop combing her hair, tell a boy to tuck in his shirt, or another to blow his nose, without once losing the attention or concentration of the particular child she was working with. Marva just squeezed Laura's shoulder to remind her that the teacher was still there for her.

Reading lessons were in groups. While Marva worked with one group, pointing out words to watch and giving background on a story, the other students busied themselves with comprehension exercises, theme writing, researching an author or topic in the encyclopedia, composing sentences, and doing analogies ("Photograph is to caricature as fact is to exaggeration").

One morning during reading Gary announced, "I'm finished." He slammed his book shut on his paper, a letter to Robinson Crusoe offering encouragement and survival tips. He stood beside his desk with his hands in his pockets, looking as though he was about to take off for a leisurely stroll around the classroom.

Marva had been working with Theodore, tutoring him from a high school literature book so that he would be ready for the high school placement exam. She shot Gary a disapproving glare.

"Don't give me that 'I'm finished' business," she said. "We are never finished in life. We don't ever stand around idly or sit with our hands folded, acquiescing. God isn't finished with you and I'm not either."

"Okay, okay, don't have a coronary," Gary said, sitting down and holding up his palms in surrender.

Marva laughed. "I love your spunk. Don't ever let anyone break your will. Since you are finished, why don't you read us your theme?"

Gary withdrew the paper from his book and began to read aloud: "Dear Mr. Crusoe, You will feel better if you have courage, strength, and patience. You need tenacity."

"Tenacity!" Marva exclaimed. "Gary, that is terrific. Since you have done such a wonderful job of helping Mr. Crusoe, why don't you take one of the younger children out on the stairs and help him with his sounds. You help him the way I helped you."

The buddy system was an integral part of life at Westside Prep. It helped the new children feel more comfortable and adjust faster, and it offered the seasoned students a review of the material and developed their sense of responsibility. The buddy system was invaluable for Gary, who tended to become wrapped up in himself, and especially beneficial for Erika, who still didn't get along well with the other children.

The first time Marva solicited her help, Erika was leaning against the wall, rubbing her head up and down against it, and chewing on a pencil.

"We eat our food, not our pencils," Marva told her. Erika removed the pencil from her mouth but continued to rub her head against the wall. Marva handed her a copy of *Professor Phonics Gives Sound Advice* and asked her to go over the word lists with Calvin.

"Huh?" Erika wiped her nose on her sleeve.

"If you have a question, say 'What, Mrs. Collins?' And don't wipe your nose on your dress. Take a tissue. Do you see me wiping my nose on my dress? Do what you see me do. Now, I want you to help Calvin the same way I helped you. We have to pass on what we learn in here. We are all responsible for one another."

Erika shook her head. "I can't."

"By now you know we don't ever say 'I can't' in here. A year ago you said you couldn't read and now look at you. You are so bright and you learn so fast. I need you to help me with a new student."

Thinking it over for a moment, Erika led the boy to the stairs and did a perfect imitation of Marva as she coached Calvin through the long and short vowel sounds. Her voice was too loud but there was a reassuring, patient quality to it. Marva overheard her telling Calvin, "You can do it."

Ultimately, tutoring the other students drew Erika out. When Marva added more pre-schoolers to the class roster, Erika teamed up with Cindy and taught them beginning sounds, read them fairy tales, and pointed out the moral in such verses as:

> There once was a boy named Pierre
> Who would only say "I don't care."
> His mother said, "Stop pouring syrup on your hair."
> Pierre said, "I don't care."

In her desire to emulate Marva, Erika proved to be a natural teacher herself. And being responsible for other students seemed to make her more responsible for herself. She slowly became more fastidious about her appearance. Perhaps she reasoned that as a teacher she had to set an example, as Mrs. Collins did.

Four years after she arrived at Westside Preparatory School as a defeated, backward, asocial child, Erika McCoy wrote:

> If Fredrick Douglass can, so can I. If Fredrick Douglass could learn when learning seemed almost impossible for a black man, so can I. If Fredrick Douglass could free our people from the bondage of slavery, surely I can free my people from the bondage of ignorance. If Fredrick Douglass could conquer the impossible, surely I can conquer ignorance. If Fredrick Douglass could deliver speeches to thousands of people, surely I can deliver a speech to the few. If Fredrick Douglass could scale the high walk of success, surely I can too.

Throughout the year, as in every year of my teaching, my main goal was to motivate the students to make something worthwhile of their lives. Everything we said or did in class was directed toward that aim. More than anything I wanted to supplant apathy and defeatism with positive expectations. I didn't want my children to feel stigmatized by where they lived. I didn't want them to succumb to a ghetto mentality. If I had my way, they would dream and hope and strive and *obtain* success.

I was forever compiling lists of positive, motivating slogans:

You are unique—there is no one else like you
The world moves aside to let you pass only if you
know where you are going
Character is what you know you are and not what
others think you are
You know you better than anyone else in this world
People's ideas actually tell you how they feel about
themselves

And I was constantly reminding the children that some of the greatest people in history—Socrates, Milton, Galileo, Einstein, Edison, and Columbus—were ridiculed and told they would never amount to anything.

Every day I put a different quotation on the board:

What I do concerns me, not what others think of me
Hitch your wagon to a star (Emerson)

Vivere est cogitare (Cicero)
Speak the speech trippingly on the tongue (*Hamlet*)
Cowards die many times before their deaths; The valiant never taste of death but once (*Julius Caesar*)
The mass of men lead lives of quiet desperation (Thoreau)
He who eats my bread does my will

I felt it was as important to deal with attitudes as with any of the academic subjects. In fact it is probably more important. Without the right attitude, everything else is wasted.

I told the girls not to walk around with their socks falling down like a scrubwoman's or with their nail polish chipped. My eleven- and twelve-year-old girls were instructed not to wear plunging necklines or walk around looking like dimestore floozies. Everyone knew there would be no gum chewing, nail biting, unbuttoned shirts, loose shirt tails, jazzy walks, jive talk, or finger snapping.

I'd ask the children, "How are you going to run a corporation if you can't run yourself? Are you going to sit behind a conference table in an executive suite popping gum or sticking your fingers in your mouth? How are you going to keep your life in order if you can't keep your appearance or your desk or your notebook in order?"

My approach is to address a fault without ever attacking a child's character. Who they were was always separate and distinct from what they did. The gum chewing was displeasing, not the child. I might tell a child, "You are acting like a fool. Why? You are not a fool." With that difference clearly established, the children could open themselves to my comments and criticisms. A child could give up the behavior without giving up any dignity or self-worth. I tried to show the children that I wasn't sticking them with an arbitrary list of do's and don'ts. These were the rules of etiquette observed in the adult world.

"Do not ever mouth off to an adult," I warned. "I don't care how wrong the adult is, just say 'yes' or 'no.' I don't care what the rest of society is doing, I don't care how many people tell you not to take anything from anyone, I want you to know when to do and say the right thing.

"There is a time to talk and a time to shut up. A time to be proud and a time to be humble. When a policeman says stop, he means stop and not go. Black children get in more trouble because they mouth off. Why get beaten up or even killed because you didn't know when to keep your mouth shut? If I teach you Shakespeare and Cicero and Dostoevsky, what good is it going to do you if you don't live to tell it?"

I prepared my children for life. And I didn't mince any words in doing it. I didn't hesitate to discuss crime in the ghetto, drugs, prison, or teenage pregnancy. I told them welfare is just another form of slavery. I warned them not to hang out on street corners or places they didn't belong, because they could easily be picked up and arrested for something they didn't do. And I bluntly told them to face the fact that no one was going to hire them for a job if they walked into an office wearing picks in their hair, if they slinked into a room as though their hips were broken, or if the boys wore earrings or high-heeled shoes or wide-brimmed hats.

I think it's foolish and hypocritical that many people allow black youths to take on extreme styles and mannerisms under the guise of finding their black identity—without pointing out the social and economic consequences. I reminded my students that blacks don't go to work only for blacks. I encouraged them to become universal people, citizens of the world.

I did not teach black history as a subject apart from American history, emphasize black heroes over white, or preach black consciousness rather than a sense of the larger society. My refusal to do so was a sore spot between me and some members of the black community. As far as I was concerned, it was a waste of precious class time to teach a child that he or she was black.

I'd say to my students, "Is there anyone in here who doesn't know he's black?" And the children would shake their heads and laugh. Then I'd ask, "Is there any black child in here who plans on turning white?" Again there would be laughter. "In that case let's get on with the business of learning."

I'm opposed to teaching black English because it separates black children from the rest of society; it also implies they are too inferior to learn standard language usage. How many black youths are cut off from the job market because they do not have a command of the English language? I was convinced black English was another barrier confining my students to the ghetto, and I had no intention of letting them be confined. I cautioned my children, "When you don't know the language, people are always going to take advantage of you. It's like being a visitor in a foreign country."

Instead of teaching black pride I taught my children self-pride. All I wanted was for them to accept themselves. I pointed out that in many ways the ghetto is a state of mind. If you have a positive attitude about yourself, then no one can put you down for who you are or where you live.

The concept of self-determination goes hand in hand with self-discipline. The general rule in my class was that behavior contributing to the learning process or benefiting another child was acceptable. Anything that took away another child's right to learn was not. Talking in the classroom, for example, was not prohibited per se; my response depended on the nature of the conversation and when it was taking place. Certainly no one was free to interrupt me or anyone else who was speaking or reciting. If a child was talking about lunch or any other personal business, then the next child did not need to hear it. If the talk was about how to put together a car engine or about a character in a story, then it was helping me teach.

Fighting upset me more than anything else, and my students knew it. I told them that when they fought they didn't hurt each other, they hurt me. It meant I failed to teach them what values were important in life. I never took sides in a student scuffle, and I refused to hear who threw the first punch. Instead of listening to any feeble excuse about who did what to whom, I had the two culprits embrace and say "I love you" to one another. It was a fairly good peace-keeping technique—most of the time.

One morning in the beginning of November eleven-year-old Sonya walked into the classroom with fresh scratches across her face. She looked like a cat had attacked her.

"What happened?" I asked, putting cocoa butter on the wounds.

"Lynette did it," Sonya mumbled. "She did it on the bus."

"On the bus? You mean the two of you were fighting on the city bus?"

Sonya nodded.

"Didn't the passengers stop you? What did the bus driver do?"

"Nothing."

I was furious. The moment Lynette sauntered into the room, I called both girls over to me. "Wherever you girls go, you represent me," I told them. "Imagine, someone on the bus could have said, 'Those girls go to Westside Preparatory School.' I bet no one on that bus knew you girls read Shakespeare or Socrates or Emerson. All they saw were two wild cats clawing at each other in public. So all I have done, all that I have taught you has been for nothing."

"I didn't start it. She did," Lynette insisted.

"I don't want to hear that," I said. "I don't care who started it or who finished it. How much are you worth to yourself? Are you willing to destroy yourself to get back at someone? Do you have to prove to the crowd that you take nothing from no one? Do you have to prove you're tough? Don't throw away your life."

I was angry and the girls knew it. I made them apologize. They did it begrudgingly and quickly went to their seats. The scratching incident disturbed me because it was different from the usual sort of classroom skirmishes, where one child mischievously shoves another or sticks a foot in the aisle to trip a classmate. Theirs was a real fight, presenting something more hateful, more violent. I couldn't let the matter drop.

"Children," I said to the entire class, "when you're willing to destroy one another, how can you complain about society being racist? Until you learn to help and love each other, don't talk about what other people are doing to you.

"I don't believe in saying 'Oh, he's just a child' or 'She's just a child.' The way you act as children will determine what kind of adults you become. School is a miniature society where we learn and practice to become useful adults. You must use your time wisely. We can't begin to make something of our lives when we are filled with hate. It's not an easy thing, but you've got to learn to walk away from your enemies. If you don't, they will drag you down."

The children were all listening silently. I didn't think I was getting through to them. Suddenly I felt ineffectual.

I was shaken once again by the fear that I had made no real change in the lives of my students. Of course they were memorizing poetry and quoting the classics. Was it all mimicry? What I so desperately wanted to give them was the substance, not the trappings, of an education. The fighting episode was a painful indication that I might not have succeeded. It nagged at me all day. By evening it provoked me to compose a "school creed":

Society will draw a circle that shuts me out, but my superior thoughts will draw me in. I was born to win if I do not spend too much time trying to fail. I will ignore the tags and names given me by society since only I know what I have the ability to become.

Failure is just as easy to combat as success is to obtain. Education is painful and not gained by playing games. Yet it is my privilege to destroy myself if that is what I choose to do. I have the right to fail, but I do not have the right to take other people with me. God made me the captain of only one life—my own.

It is my right to care nothing about myself, but I must be willing to accept the consequences for that failure, and I must never think that those who have chosen to work, while I played, rested, and slept, will share their bounties with me.

My success and my education can be companions that no misfortune can depress, no crime can destroy, and no enemy can alienate. Without education, man is a slave, a savage wandering from here to there believing whatever he is told.

Time and chance come to us all. I can be either hesitant or courageous. I can swiftly stand up and shout:

"This is my time and my place. I will accept the challenge."

I had said all this before in many different ways. These maxims were the cornerstone of my teaching. Now they were solidified into something whole. The next morning I told the children they would recite the creed every day until they knew it by heart.

"My hope," I explained, "is not that you will *look* literate but that you will *be* literate. Remember the story of the emperor's new clothes? I don't want to turn you into a bunch of emperors running around without any clothes. I don't want you to pretend you are educated. I want you to act and *think* like educated people all the time."

Then I reminded the children of the lessons in Tolstoy's tale "The Three Questions."

"Who is the most important person?" I asked.

"I am," the children shouted.

"What is the most important thing?"

"To do good."

"And what is the most important time?"

"Now!"

A few months were sufficient to dispel all my romantic visions about starting up a school of my own. It was one thing to teach, another to be also principal, secretary, janitor, and pencil sharpener. The roughest part was keeping the school afloat financially. Though the school was in my house, the income from tuition was barely enough to cover the operating expenses. Only half my students were paying the full $70 per month tuition. Some paid what they could afford; others didn't pay anything at all. When the money came in, it was in dribs and drabs. Meanwhile there were monthly bills for utilities, insurance, and supplies.

Clarence gave me his full support. He never spoke a word of resentment about the eighteen hours a day I frequently put into my teaching. Only when he judged my enthusiasm had gone too far afield would he ask, "Whose children are you talking about? The ones in the school or our own?" It was his way of reminding me there was more to life than school.

Without him there would have been no Westside Preparatory School. He was the strong silent partner. I had one kind of strength, Clarence had another. When the bills added up and our money ran out, he rolled up his sleeves and took on part-time carpentry and construction jobs.

I found weekend work typing medical reports, as I had done before, but the financial pressures didn't ease. Besides the school costs, Clarence and I were having a difficult time managing our household budget. For the past year I had been receiving a small salary as a curriculum developer for the Alternative Schools Network, but it was $10,000 less than what I had earned at Delano.

On top of the monetary problems, I had to contend with a relentless parade of city inspectors knocking at the door with their building and fire codes. Despite the fact that Clarence had complied with the city's specifications when building the one-room school, the inspectors continued to badger me. I couldn't understand why they seemed so intent on making Westside Prep into the model for building standards when there were schools in the Chicago system that were downright hazardous. Several public schools long slated for demolition or structural renovation were still making do with falling ceiling plaster and rickety fourth-floor staircases. In some schools students were meeting in makeshift basement classrooms with exposed steam pipes sweating overhead.

I telephoned City Hall and complained. I said I wanted to be allowed to teach. I preferred to do it peacefully in my own school, but if I had to I'd teach on the steps of City Hall. I explained that my students were not costing the taxpayers any money; by educating these children I was in fact keeping them off welfare rolls in the future.

For months the inspections continued and so did my complaints. Eventually the inspectors stopped hounding the school. Maybe they had just tired of *my* persistence.

Between the bills and the city bureaucracy, each day was a contest for survival. I had to do whatever I could to keep the school going. I knew the school would work only if I made it work. And the children worked because I did.

My goal is to have my students know a little about everything. "The knowledge you put in your heads is like money in the bank," I told them. "You may not need it today, but it is there to use when you need it. You may not always remember everything you are reading and learning, but you are storing it in your minds for the future. Someday when someone mentions Dostoyevsky, you won't have to stand there looking surprised and thinking it's the name of a Russian dance."

Once children learn how to learn, nothing is going to narrow their minds. The essence of teaching is to make learning contagious, to have one idea spark another. A discussion of *Little Women* included everything from a lesson on the Civil War to an explanation of the allegory in *The Pilgrim's Progress,* which the little women in Alcott's novel loved to act out. When the children studied Aristotle, they learned the principles of logical thinking. Plato's *Republic* led to de Tocqueville's *Democracy in America,* which led to a discussion of different political systems, which brought in Orwell's *Animal Farm,* which touched off a discussion of Machiavelli, which led to a look at Chicago's city council.

Through the riddle of the Sphinx, which appeared in the second grade reader, the children were also introduced to Sophocles' *Oedipus Rex,* the Greek theater, and other heroes and legends of ancient Greece. Mention of the Roman deity Jupiter, lord of heaven and prince of light, triggered a science lesson on the solar system, which brought in the ancient geographer and astronomer Ptolemy, then Copernicus, then Isaac Asimov, Carl Sagan, and the U.S. space program. Archimedes' discovery of water displacement and specific gravity tied in to Sir Isaac Newton's work with gravity and light, which in turn spurred an introduction to Einstein's theory of relativity. When I taught Voltaire's *Candide,* I pulled in Pope's "Essay on Man" and Leibnitz and the "optimistic" school of philosophy. If I was teaching Chaucer, I introduced Boccaccio, telling the children how Chaucer drew his "Clerk's Tale" from Boccaccio's "Patient Grisel."

In one of the most unlikely progressions of learning I began talking once about triangles and ended up with Hinduism. The children learned that Pythagoras figured out how to measure the side of a right triangle, that Pythagoras was a philosopher who believed the human soul was immortal, and that his idea of the transmigration of souls was part of the Hindu religion.

For every story the children read in their basal readers, I brought supplementary material. I also pointed out every allusion in a story, not ignoring a single footnote at the bottom of a page. I blitzed the children with facts, but I did not go into all subjects in detail. Mostly, I hit upon them in a generalized way. I wanted to get my students to see the flow of knowledge.

★　★　★

Each day there were frenzied classroom exchanges between Marva and the children as she tested their memories and pushed them to draw analogies.

"What drug takes its name from Morpheus, the god of dreams?"

"Morphine," the children called out in unison.

"From where do we get the words *geography* and *geology*?"

"The goddess Ge," they answered.

"Who was Ge?"

"Greek goddess of the earth."

"The word *choreography* comes from which of the nine muses?"

"Terpsichore."

"Sacred hymns are inspired by which muse?"

"Polyhymnia."

"Which breakfast food do we get from the grain goddess Ceres?"

"Cereal."

"What does *museum* mean?"

"Temple of the muses."

"And what is a muse?"

"A Greek goddess."

"How many muses were there?"

"Nine."

"What else does the word *muse* mean, Laura?"

"To think about something," she answered.

"Let's give her a hand," Marva said. And the class applauded. Then Marva went on. "Which of King Priam's sons has a name that means to bully?"

"Hector," the class responded.

"And who killed Hector?"

"Achilles."

"How did Achilles die?"

"Paris shot him with an arrow in the heel," Gary shouted, before anyone else could put together a complete sentence.

"And when we use the phrase 'Achilles' heel,' what do we mean, Tracy?"

"A weak spot," Tracy said.

"When we have a weak spot, we are what?"

"Vulnerable," replied Erika.

"Which one of Ovid's stories is similar to Shakespeare's *Romeo and Juliet?*"

"Pyramus and Thisbe," the children chorused.

"George, which Bible story is like the story of Orpheus and Eurydice?"

"The story of Lot and his wife," he answered.

Theodore shouted, "Hey, Mrs. Collins, that's cool. Everything links into something else, doesn't it?"

Marva beamed. "Now you've got it. Every scholar, every writer, every thinker learned from those who came before. You are all becoming so erudite, we are going to have to dub you MGM—"Mentally Gifted Minors."

★   ★   ★

I read constantly in order to tie together fragments of information and interweave subjects. As a business major in college I had not taken many courses in the arts and sciences. My education was about the same as that of the average grammar school teacher, merely a sampling of some basic courses. I had to teach myself more. I read with an urgency so I could teach my students what they needed to know. I believe a teacher has to keep polishing his or her skills. You can't take the attitude "I know how to teach," and resist learning anything new.

I was always on the lookout for a new book to spark my children's interest. Teaching children to read was one thing; keeping them interested in reading was something else. I was forever reading up on new children's books in *The New York Times Book Review,* the local Sunday newspapers, and *The Library Journal.* I searched through *Masterplots* and *Children's Treasury for the Taking.* And I stalked bookstores and libraries on a regular basis.

I feel that to be a good elementary school teacher one needs to have a general knowledge about all fields of study. The best training a teacher can have is a solid liberal arts education. Instead of emphasizing methods courses, training institutions should require education majors to have a broad background in literature, science, art, music, and philosophy. The object of teaching is to impart as much knowledge as possible. Students can only give back what a teacher gives out.

Eventually my children began to recognize parallels and relationships on their own. Sometimes when they recited their compositions, they would summon forth a plethora of citations. Laura Brown, the girl who had written word salads when she first arrived at Westside Prep, wrote the following theme a year later:

> Pascal said, "A man without a thought is a stone or a brute. A man is a reed, but a thinking reed." Cicero was right—"Vivere est cogitare." To think is to live. Let us stand up and shout this is my time. We are fools to depend upon society to make us into what we refuse to mold ourselves into. Confused aliens are Hecate's delight.

A few days after we had read about Patrick Henry and our nation's founding fathers, one of my eight-year-old boys turned in the following book report on Maya Angelou's *I Know Why the Caged Bird Sings:*

> The caged bird sings because it wants to be free. It wants to sing like the other birds. It wants to swing on the limbs like the other birds. Give the caged bird freedom or give it death.

Drawing analogies and tossing off literary allusions became second nature to the children, appearing even in their jokes. Four-year-old Calvin accidentally wet his pants one day, and as I took him to the bathroom to clean him off, six-year-old Lewis shouted, "Out, out, damned spot!" Then there was the time George and Theodore were arguing. Reaching her arms beseechingly to the ceiling, Tracy called out, "Wherefore art thou, Themis, goddess of justice. We need your help, quick." One day the group was discussing how Medea tore her sons to pieces and got revenge after Jason left her and took a new bride. "Well, you know what they say," Erika wisecracked, "Hell hath no fury like a woman scorned."

Such learned extracts were applied as readily outside class. While Cindy and I were shopping in a department store, we saw a boy of about five crying and clinging to his mother's skirt as she tried to purchase some cosmetics. Cindy turned to me, shook her head, and coolly remarked, "Mommy, I think that boy has an Oedipus complex."

The children were showing off their newfound knowledge like a new toy. In the middle of the semester I took them to see the movie *The Man Who Would Be King,* based on the short story by Rudyard Kipling. Schools had been invited to attend a special screening of the film and hear a lecture on Kipling. My children were already well acquainted with the author. They knew his *Just So Stories* and *The Jungle Book,* and some had memorized "If" for their weekly poetry recitation.

As the children filed into the theater, the guest lecturer came running up to me. "Oh, there must be some mistake," he said. "Your children won't understand or appreciate this."

Looking around the auditorium, I saw that most of the audience was of high school age. "You just lecture the way you normally would to the older students. Don't worry about my children."

When the movie was over, the speaker began talking about Kipling's life, his schooling in Britain and his return to India at the age of eighteen. George began shaking his head vehemently. Suddenly his hand shot up. Squinting out into the audience, the man motioned for George to stand up. "Yes, young man, do you have a question?" he asked.

George shook his head no.

"Then what can I do for you?"

"I read in the encyclopedia that Kipling was seventeen

when he went back to India," George stated, taking his seat.

Applause mixed with laughter rang out from the audience. A few of the high school boys sitting with their feet propped up flashed a victory salute and shouted, "That's the way, kid, right on!"

In any other circumstances I would not have encouraged such pedantry. With the lecturer assuming that my children wouldn't understand, I made an exception and allowed them the spotlight. Cindy asked why Kipling was so British-oriented. And George, bolstered by the earlier success, took the floor a second time. "In whose memory was the Taj Mahal built?" he asked the speaker.

"It was built by the Shah Jahan in memory of his favorite wife, Mumtaz Mahal."

"That's right." George nodded, satisfied with the man's answer.

In late January there were a few changes. Two new students arrived and three others left. Theodore, who had come to the school the year before reading at a third grade level, passed the high school entrance exam and was admitted to a parochial high school. One father took his seven-year-old daughter out of Westside Prep because he could not afford the tuition. I offered to have the girl stay on a scholarship, but the father refused, saying, "I'm as proud as you are, Mrs. Collins. I don't believe in handouts any more than you do."

Another parent withdrew her five-year-old son because she was displeased that her child wasn't doing enough "creative things"—cutting out valentines and snowflakes and making paper bag puppets. She seemed to think that white children were doing that sort of thing in their progressive schools. I had no intention of having my students cut and paste and finger paint or march around with rhythm bands. Black children from inner-city neighborhoods cannot afford to spend time finger painting in school. When these children enter kindergarten, they are in most cases already behind socially and academically. Statistics show that they fall even further behind while in elementary school, so that by the sixth grade they are reading at a 2.2 level. The only way to combat that trend is to give the four and five year olds a strong start reading and writing.

That's not to say I stifle creative expression. My students were exposed to art, drama, and music but within the context of the basic curriculum, not as separate subjects. The children acted out fables and stories, wrote their own poetry and plays, and drew illustrations for the stories they read. Their reading selections included biographies of Mozart, Beethoven, Leonardo da Vinci, and Michelangelo. Our class discussions ranged from symphonies and sonatas to frescos and miniatures.

When I lost a student to coloring and cut-outs, I didn't try to dissuade his mother. Parents set their own expectations for their children, and they have to decide whether a particular school or teaching method suits their needs. Not all parents like the Montessori approach. Not all parents favor the Suzuki method of teaching children a musical instrument. So I didn't expect every parent to be satisfied with Westside Prep. I couldn't be all things to all people, and I didn't try to be.

Since my first year of teaching, my students have always learned to love Shakespeare. Even the boys who picked their teeth with switchblades and dared other teachers to make it safely to their cars in the afternoon always begged for more. At Delano I had to sneak in the lessons on Shakespeare, because they were never included in the curriculum prescribed by the Board of Education.

Many educators and textbook publishers seemed to think that children should not be reading Shakespeare or, for that matter, any other great works of literature. The prevailing thought among the curriculum experts was that the best way to teach inner-city children to read was through "realistic" story content: the recommended material for teaching reading skills included stories about stealing, sex, drugs, running away from home, alcoholic fathers, know-nothing mothers, children who lied and conned adults, and children who committed crimes.

For years, the textbook companies had published readers that were totally unrealistic. Parents never argued, Father always looked neat and tidy, Mother never worked and was always baking cookies, the house was always spick-and-span, and brothers and sisters never disagreed. Little Jane's hair was always perfect, and her shoes were never scuffed.

Then the publishers and experts tried to make readers more lifelike. But in the process they have gone to the opposite extreme. A selection from one popular textbook reads:

I found a piece of rope, made a noose, slipped it about the kitten's neck, pulled it over a nail, then jerked the animal clear of the ground. It gasped, sloppered, spun, doubled, clawed the air frantically; finally its mouth gaped and its pink-white tongue shot out stiffly. I tied the rope to a nail and went to find my brother.

I don't believe in sheltering children or limiting their reading to stories with a Pollyanna vision of the world. Life is chaotic and imperfect, and children should be taught to understand that. Topics like death, greed, and violence are not taboo. They are often themes of great literature. However, some of today's textbooks smack of educational hucksterism: offer children anything; just get them to read!

According to the curriculum experts, everything has to be "relevant." One mathematics textbook has a chapter on probability that asks students to determine: What are the odds that a cabdriver will get a counterfeit $10 bill? What is the probability that a girl will become pregnant if she is taking birth control pills that are 97 percent effective? What is the probability that a person living in a certain community has either syphilis or gonorrhea?

All that "relevance" undermines the very purpose of an education. It doesn't expand the children's horizons or encourage inventiveness and curiosity. Instead it limits perspective to the grim scenes they see every day of their lives. Children do not need to read stories that teach "street smarts." They learn enough on their own. What they need are character-building stories. They need to read for values, morality, and universal truths. That was my reason for teaching classical literature.

It is senseless to hand children prepackaged, specially designed reading material when there are so many relevant lessons to be plucked from the writings of great authors. But it takes a creative, hard-working teacher to ferret out those things, to focus on the content, not the mechanics of reading.

★　★　★

William Shakespeare's plays were a gold mine of meaningful themes, and the students at Westside Preparatory School loved reading them. *Macbeth* was a special treat. The children were intrigued by the action of the play, the witches, the ghosts, and the idea of a cold, calculated murder. They came away from the play fully aware that crime exacts a price.

Students of every age level were treated to *Macbeth*. For the younger children, ages four and five, Marva gave a digest of the story: "Now the witches can only hurt people if those people are already evil, and since Macbeth was already inclined to do evil, the three witches persuaded him to murder King Duncan while he was a guest at Macbeth's home . . ." Sitting cross-legged on the floor, their eyes glued to the storyteller, the children heard how the ghost of King Duncan haunted Macbeth and how Lady Macbeth tried to rub the imaginary bloodstains from her hands, crying, "Out, damned spot, out I say."

The students reading at a first, second, or third grade level received a narrative adaptation of *Macbeth* from *Favorite Tales from Shakespeare* by Bernard Miles. As always, the children read aloud, and periodically Marva asked each student to define a word, supply a synonym or antonym, or discuss the meaning of a paragraph.

"Did the witches make Macbeth do evil?"

"No," replied the children.

"The witches only predicted that he would do evil. Macbeth himself made the evil happen. Others can predict, but the individual determines his own life. Society predicts that you will fail. But you what?"

"Determine our own life," said Laura.

"Very, very good. Why do you think Macbeth is so depressed, so troubled?" Marva asked.

" 'Cause he thinks people are going to find out how he murdered King Duncan," answered Maria, who had joined the school in January.

"He has a guilty conscience," added one of the boys.

"That's right," Marva said. "The murder ends up destroying him. That's what happens in life. People may offer us glorious things, but they don't tell us the price we have to pay for them. After the deed is done, the weird sisters say, 'Macbeth shall sleep no more.' There is always a penalty to pay. If someone doesn't catch you, then your own conscience will. We don't like ourselves very much when we do something bad, do we?"

In Marva's hands Shakespeare became a vehicle for positive attitudes. The children reading the adaptation learned the themes by following the action of the play. The students reading at or above the fourth grade level pulled out meaning line by line from the original text.

"What does Duncan mean when he says, 'The love that follows us is sometimes our trouble?' "

"Sometimes we trust people and think they love us, but they turn against us," said Gary.

"Very good. And when Macbeth has second thoughts about killing Duncan, what does Lady Macbeth do?"

"She calls him a coward," said Cindy.

"She makes fun of him for not being man enough to do it," added Patrick.

"How many of you have had that happen to you?" asked Marva. "Did you ever have your friends call you a coward or a baby or a chicken because you didn't want to go along with something?"

A few of the boys looked around the room before they reluctantly nodded.

"So what does Macbeth do? What does he tell Lady Macbeth?"

"He gets her off his back by saying he's going to be a bigger man than anyone else," George said.

"So you see what happens, children? Macbeth ends up committing murder to prove he is tough. His wife ridicules him, she makes fun of his manhood, so he feels he has to go out and murder Duncan to prove he is a man. If he liked himself, if he had self-respect, he would not have had to prove anything, would he? It's the people who don't like themselves very much who make trouble for the others.

"The mess society is in today starts with people who don't like themselves. And when that's the case, nothing is going to help you, is it? Not drugs, not alcohol. Those things don't make life any better. You have to get your head on straight. Could the doctor give Lady Macbeth anything to cure her mind? Could he 'minister to a mind diseased?' ''

The children shook their heads.

"What did the doctor tell Macbeth?" Marva asked.

The children ran their fingers up and down the page looking for the line. Erika blurted out, "I've got it, Mrs. Collins. He says, 'the patient must minister to himself.' ''

"It's sort of like what Socrates says, isn't it, Mrs. Collins?" Gary said. "Macbeth should have known that 'Straight thinking leads to straight living.' '' Gary sat back, evidently pleased with himself.

All the children were proud of themselves. Reading Shakespeare gave them an enormous sense of self-worth. Some days Marva wished the whole world could hear them, especially the experts with theories about what inner-city children should not and could not read.

The children's acquaintance with Shakespeare didn't end with *Macbeth*. Eventually they went on to read *Twelfth Night, A Midsummer Night's Dream, Hamlet, Romeo and Juliet, Merchant of Venice, Julius Caesar,* and *King Lear.* In the meantime Marva made sure Shakespeare remained in the children's minds. Sentences such as "Shakespeare lived in England" and "The three witches in *Macbeth* were evil" were given as dictation exercises, and Marc Anthony's funeral oration became part of a lesson on rhetoric and propaganda. Several of the children memorized the funeral oration or Hamlet's soliloquy for their weekly poetry recitation. Lines from the plays and sonnets became topics for daily writing assignments.

William Shakespeare had already become an old friend to the students at Westside Prep when, one morning in the spring of 1977, Marva read a story in the *Chicago Sun-Times* about high school students in the suburbs who did not know who Shakespeare was, when and where he lived, or what he wrote. For example, one student wrote that "the global theater was a three-sided octagon." She clipped the article and brought it to class for her students to see. It was a great ego booster. The children shouted exultant cheers, drummed victory rolls on their desks, and clasped their hands overhead, hailing themselves champions. None of their day to day small triumphs in the classroom could match their first thrill of seeing how they compared to the outside world.

"Shoot, you mean those rich high school kids in the suburbs don't know Shakespeare was born in 1564 and died in 1616?" Gary's hubris might have been the fatal flaw in many of Shakespeare's heroes, but in Marva's students it was a hard-earned and welcome virtue.

"You see," Marva said, breaking through the noise. "You make your own success. Children can go to expensive schools, but it doesn't mean they learn any more or any better. Buildings don't teach, people teach. Everything works in here because we make it work. All the money in the world isn't going to make a difference."

That afternoon Marva gave in to some pride of her own. She wrote a letter to *Sun-Times* columnist Zay Smith, telling him that she had read his story and that she had students from "the allegedly fetid ghetto" who had a reading acquaintance with Shakespeare. She explained a little about her school. Marva followed up the letter with a telephone call several days later, inviting Smith to visit the school any time. "I'd match these students now with students anywhere in the suburbs," she added.

Unannounced, Smith dropped in on Westside Prep at nine o'clock the next morning. As he later wrote in his *Sun-Times* column, "I wasn't expecting any miracles. So I wasn't prepared for what I saw." Sitting quietly in the back of the classroom, Smith observed a typical day at Marva's school. He watched "four year olds writing sentences like 'See the physician' and 'Aesop wrote fables,' and discussing diphthongs and diacritical marks—calling them correctly by name." He heard "second-graders reciting passages from Shakespeare, Longfellow and Kipling," and "third-graders learning about Tolstoi, Sophocles and Chaucer."

Amazed at a teacher working such wonders, Smith interviewed some of the children. One girl said, "When I went to my old school I didn't learn anything. My teacher used to go around pinching our ears. Here somebody believed in me." And another girl told him, "We do hard things here. They fill your brain."

Smith's story on Westside Prep, along with a sampling of student writing (compositions on Michelangelo, Leonardo da Vinci, Aesop, and Hinduism), appeared on the third page of the Sunday edition of the *Sun-Times* on May 8, 1977. It went out on the *Sun-Times* wire service and was picked up by other newspapers around the country. Readers were touched by the story of children who had been discarded as "unteachable" climbing to superior achievement in a school that was always short of books, paper, pencils, and even chalk. And Marva was catapulted into an unexpected, though not entirely unsought, spotlight.

★   ★   ★

What pleased me the most about the publicity was having people see the kinds of knowledge my students were attaining, because it had become a common assumption that the liberal arts curriculum was beyond the capacity of black children. The public response to the newspaper article was overwhelming. People started sending me ten, twenty, and thirty dollar donations. One man sent me a check with a note saying that he had read the story aboard a plane on his way to Nevada. He was so moved by the work I was doing that he mailed the check the minute he landed at the Las Vegas airport.

The story struck different chords in different people. For some the contributions represented an endorsement of alternative education. I suspect other people responded to the portrayal of an underdog, a risk-taker, and educational maverick. Whatever the reasons, I was glad to get the contributions. I put every dollar into the school, buying such things as a set of *The Great Books* and dictionaries for every child in the class.

I had always had very strong opinions about education, and suddenly I had a public forum to air my views. Shortly after the story appeared in the newspaper, I received an invitation to speak before a gathering of educators in the Dade County, Florida public schools. They were even paying a $500 honorarium. A bit uncertain about the kind of response I would receive from my audience of teachers, I talked about phonics, recommended reading lists, and explained the methods I used to teach literature and writing skills. I discussed the importance of a positive attitude and stressed that any child could learn if a teacher cared enough to teach.

The audience reaction was mixed. Some of the teachers came up to me afterwards eager to share ideas. Others were antagonistic or just plain rude. They probably resented an ordinary classroom teacher standing up there telling them about *her* methods. It wasn't as though I were an expert from the Department of Education or a university professor who had researched countless learning theories. Sometimes teachers depend too much on the experts—some of whom have never taught in a classroom—instead of looking toward their colleagues for techniques and advice. Perhaps that's one of the problems with education today. There is often a reluctance among teachers to pool information and learn from one another.

The Monday morning after my first public speaking engagement, I walked into the class with my $500 check in hand and passed it up and down the rows of desks for the children to see.

"You see," I told them, waving the check, "people will pay you for the ideas you have in your head."

"You mean you got all that money just for talking?" Gary asked.

"That's right. I talked all about phonics and the dictation I give you and the quotations I put on the board and the poetry you recite . . ."

"Heck, *I* could've told them all that," he said.

"You mean those people *paid* you just to tell them what we do in here every day?" Tracy sounded incredulous. Listening to me preach about the value of an education was one thing; seeing the proof was quite another.

"Yes, they did," I said, recognizing a chance to expand on my major theme. "If you have the knowledge, if you have the skills, people will come to you. You will find work. You don't need to steal or wait for someone to give you something for nothing. A free ride is never worth very much anyway. If I give you some of my clothes, I don't give you my favorite dress, do I?

I'll give you something that's old and worn out, won't I? Just how much is that going to be worth to you?"

"But how come those people want to know what we do?" George asked. He and the others were still in awe of the $500.

"Because a lot of people are surprised at the kinds of things you children are learning," I told him. "Black America has been led to believe that we are supposed to fail. When we do fail, people look down on us, and that leads to a lot of hate. Things do not have to be that way. We can make them better. You were not born to fail. You were born to succeed. You were born to be millionaires! But you are going to have to learn. No one owes you a thing in this life. I don't want anyone to give you children anything—except your dignity."

By then the school year was nearly over, so the children were used to my sermonizing. Most of them had sat through two years of it, and it was taking hold. Children who had come to me lacking all confidence, convinced they couldn't do anything, were now talking about becoming doctors, judges, scientists, and teachers. Sonya, one of the girls who had been fighting on the bus six months before, insisted she was going to be the first black woman president of the United States. She and the other children walked around quoting from what they had read and boasting about what they knew. They'd come to me and say, "I know this big kid in high school, and he never even heard of Dante Alighieri." To some outsiders my children may have appeared to be little know-it-alls. I loved their spirit.

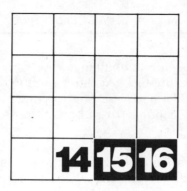

Despite the financial strain, the new Westside Prep had survived its first year, and every one of my children had made progress. Now nine, Tracy was long rid of her headaches and crying and was comfortable reading more than a year above her grade level. She was even writing themes on such subjects as "The Four Major Religions of the World," with lines like: "It is not possible, the Hindus believe, to achieve perfection in one lifetime. Therefore a man is born on earth again and again."

Laura Brown, the sixth-grader who had once written every word with jumbled letters, was reading from an eighth grade book at the end of the year. George was in a twelfth grade literature book, and four-year-old Calvin was reading at a second grade level. Erika McCoy was still having trouble keeping the shoes on her feet, and the other children seemed to tolerate her more than they liked her, but at seven and a half years old she was an insatiable reader, headed into a summer vacation with Dickens, Melville, and the Bronte sisters. And Gary Love, who once resisted learning anything, had become an ambitious writer:

> Somnus, god of sleep, please awaken us. While we sleep, ignorance takes over the world. . . . Take your spell off us. We don't have long before ignorance makes a coup d'état of the world.

That kind of success with my students made me push ahead with an almost maniacal fervor. Now, I had come to recognize, I *was* trying to challenge the system. And it was an inexorably demanding task. At times I felt exhausted and frustrated, I was afraid I had taken on too much. I worried about losing the school, about letting the children down, and about failing myself.

The summer offered little rest. After the Zay Smith article and my few speaking engagements, there was a steady stream of mail from people seeking my advice on educational matters. There were more offers to speak, reporters requesting interviews, and inquiries from parents who wanted to enroll their children in my school. By September 1977 Westside Prep had an enrollment of thirty students and a waiting list of almost the same number.

All the parents had stories to tell. Some of them came to me because they refused to accept the judgment of school officials who had said their children were mentally retarded, emotionally disturbed, or learning-disabled. Others came because their children had been expelled from school as behavior problems. One mother cried as she told me that her son had been suspended from school so often that he spent more time on the streets than in a classroom. She was sure Westside Prep was the only chance standing between him and reform school.

All the parents were frustrated and worried; some were desperate. One of the most distraught was Cathy Mullins' mother, who had heard about Westside Prep from a woman who happened to sit next to her on a city bus. She told me her eleven-year-old daughter, after falling far behind in school, had given up on herself. The child walked around crying all the time and had worked herself into such a nervous condition that her hair was falling out.

I took in Cathy Mullins. Ironically, I had an easier time with Cathy than with her father. He had disagreed with his wife over enrolling their daughter in the school and he objected to my methods.

"What are you doing to our girl?" he said one afternoon during the second month of school, bursting into the room just as the children were leaving. "She's messed up enough without you giving her all these big words to learn and the Latin and the poetry. She's a slow child. Don't you know she can't do that kind of work?"

"Any child can learn if she is not taught too thoroughly that she can't," I answered curtly. I believed in every one of my students. Why didn't their parents? Criticism from parents— even when it is unintentional—tends to lodge in a child's mind, particularly if that child already has self-doubts.

"The kind of work you want Cathy to do puts too much pressure on her," Mr. Mullins said.

"Did Cathy tell you that?" I asked him. Cathy was doing well. In two months' time her reading ability had gone from a second grade level to the fourth grade.

"Well, no. But going by what those other teachers used to say, I just figured . . ."

"Life is pressure, Mr. Mullins. There's no sense isolating these children or keeping them so sheltered that they won't ever be able to cope with anything. Other schools don't teach a child to push, to achieve. I do."

Some parents had the opposite complaint. They felt that I wasn't pushing their children hard enough and that the children weren't progressing fast enough. It amazed me that these parents could allow their children to get behind in school and then assume I could bring the children's skills up to the right grade level in only a few months. With some children it was possible, but others learned more slowly and needed more time to adjust and become motivated. A few times parents demanded to know why I had their child reading from an easier book or doing simpler math than the other children.

Others seemed to want to turn over all responsibility for their children to me. I believe it is the parents who must be strong and set the tone. Yet some parents don't spend time reading, don't read to their children, and don't have books around the house. Somehow they expect teachers to make their children into competent and eager readers. There are parents who don't set rules and limitations for their children, yet they expect the teacher to maintain discipline and order in the classroom. And some parents wonder why their children don't do homework, yet at home these same children are never given responsibilities or chores.

If I wasn't battling the parents' criticisms, then I was fighting their apathy. Some of the very same parents who had pleaded with me to rescue their children washed their hands of any further involvement once the children were in my school. Some even avoided paying the tuition. When there was real hardship, when a parent was out of work or ill, I accepted a child on scholarship. A few parents paid whatever they could afford each month. In lieu of tuition a few mothers helped out answering the telephone, opening mail, and copying selections from textbooks. The increased enrollment meant more work of all kinds, not just more teaching.

What infuriated me though, was that parents who seemed to have money to spend on other things, didn't seem to feel that paying for their children's education was a priority; they wanted an education for their children for nothing, without lifting a finger to help themselves. To a great degree, they too had to be educated.

In the meantime, I still had the burden of supporting my cash-starved school. I continually had to remind parents of their overdue payments. They responded by saying they had no money to give. I told them, if you are not willing to work for your child, please do not lean on the rest of us. Not all of my students had "caring parents." Some of them didn't give a damn about what happened to their children, though I struggled every step of the way to teach them. Yet, finally, when many of my students were reading and learning material well beyond their age level, there were parents who declared there had never been a learning problem in the first place.

However, I was determined not to let my students grow up having such short memories. What upset me was the idea of people forgetting where they had come from. So I repeatedly warned my students, "Don't you ever forget what you started from when you first came to this school. Don't forget how envious and ashamed you were because you couldn't read as well as some of your classmates. Don't forget, because when you grow up and finish college, you are the ones who are going to have to come back here to neighborhoods like Garfield Park and turn them into places people want to live in and not run away from."

The number of students really didn't make a difference.

Even with thirty children I ran the classroom the same way I had done the previous year. I struggled to parcel out individualized attention, while keeping up the momentum of the class as a whole. I moved from child to child, correcting mistakes on the spot and giving instant feedback on every paper as soon as it was completed. And still I tried to catch sight of everything: a child talking or throwing a paper clip, resting his head on his desk or even copying—"Your understanding must be your understanding and not your neighbor's, unless you plan on taking him with you every place you go."

As always, the emphasis for the new students was on phonics. Returning students worked in various reading groups. One group read legends, fables, Greek myths, and American tall tales; another studied selections from classics by Voltaire, Nietzsche, Goethe, Emerson, Thackeray, Dickens, Chaucer, Tolstoy, Flaubert, Swift, Dostoyevsky, Colette, Boccaccio, and Petrarch; a third group delved into biographies of Helen Keller, Harriet Tubman, Abraham Lincoln, and Frederick Douglass.

Math lessons ranged from algebra and geometry for the eleven and twelve year olds to numeration and telling time for the kindergarteners. In science some children were studying the planets and the galaxy; others learned about the earth and its history; still others worked on plant and animal life, biological adaptations, and classification. And social studies lessons were just as diverse, with kindergarteners learning about building strong communities, first-graders studying citizenship and national heroes, second-graders exploring the seven continents, third-graders looking at Chicago history and politics, fourth-graders learning about state and federal government, and fifth-through eighth-graders studying various periods of American and European history.

Running a multi-level one-room school was a constant juggling act. Yet it wasn't as complicated as it might seem. Whenever possible I tried to teach subjects not in isolation but as part of a central curriculum. Language arts (reading, writing, grammar, and vocabulary) were correlated with social studies and science. For example, when the children learned about the seven continents, they read a story from one of the countries under discussion. When they studied the solar system, they read about the lives of Galileo and Copernicus, compared Aristotle's theories to Galileo's, wrote reports about them, and analyzed the parts of speech in such sentences as *Copernicus showed that the planets revolve around the sun.*

I had always stressed vocabulary, encouraging the children to look for synonyms in the dictionary and thesaurus, teaching Latin and Greek derivations, and explaining the meaning of prefixes such as *ab* (away), *ad* (to), *com* (with), *dis* (opposite), *re* (again), and so on. That fall I discovered a secret weapon for building vocabulary, a book called *Vocabulary for the College-Bound Student.* As it happened, my son Eric, who was then a sophomore in high school, was using the book in his English class. I frequently perused my children's textbooks—it's important for parents to know what their children are learning—and this one turned out to be a gem. I ordered copies for all the students in Westside Prep.

"Words are ideas. They make up thoughts. If our words are limited, our thoughts are limited," I said, holding up the book and pointing to its title. "You see what this says? It says for the college-bound student, not the failure-bound student. To succeed in life, you must be a thinker, and to be a thinker, you must have vocabulary."

For their first homework assignment from this book the children studied and memorized five words and definitions. I said I wanted them to learn the words, but I didn't want them to write the words ten times and then say "Hallelujah, I'm finished!"

The next day the children were all flagging their hands, eager to shout out the definitions.

"What does *blithe* mean?" I asked.

"Happy and cheerful," blurted out Erika, jumping the gun on everyone else.

"Laura, what's *buoyant?*" I asked.

"Cheerful," she answered.

"Very good. Look how far you've come. Now who can tell me another word that means cheerful?"

Calvin, who had come to the school the previous January at the age of four, was waving and shouting, "Call on me, call on me."

"All right, Calvin, what's a synonym for cheerful?"

"Jocund," he said proudly. Everyone clapped. I couldn't help beaming. I told him he was probably the only four and a half year old in the world who knew that word.

I have always believed young children can grasp complicated words, as long as they know how to syllabicate and decode sounds. No word is too difficult if a child has the right phonics tools. The only thing standing between a young child and a difficult word is the child's fear of it. By exposing them to the complexities of language, I made sure my children were not intimidated by words.

I reinforced phonics by having my students repeat the pronunciation of words like *charlatan, bronchitis, Andromache, Petrarch,* and even *adiadochokinesis*—a medical term (describing a muscular disorder) some of my boys discovered on their own while playing a dictionary game which involved trying to stump one another over pronunciations. Every day I gave the children dictation, using such sentences as "The politician was accused of malfeasance" or "The president was lionized by the people." Whenever I spoke, I tried to supplement their vocabulary by serving up new words. And I urged them to incorporate the new words into class discussion and into their compositions.

Very often the children strung together the new words the same way they did quotations. When a few of the children were reading *Uncle Tom's Cabin,* the assignment I gave was to compose the kind of letter Eliza might have written to her son Harry when she overheard he was going to be sold. One paper read:

> My frolicsome, jocund son,
> This is a time of tribulation, not jubilation. I am disconsolate over your plight, but I do not want you to be glum, doleful, and dejected because you have nostalgia. You must be brave. I love you.

In November, spurred by a suggestion from its Chicago bureau, *Time* magazine ran a story about the school in its education section. The response was unbelievable. A television producer from Los Angeles donated a check for $5,000. Another $2,000 came in from a movie star who wrote that he was sending the money on the advice of his psychiatrist. There was a gust of $10 to $100 checks stapled to letters. In all, the windfall came to nearly $10,000. To me it was like the Irish Sweepstakes. The expansion of the school from eighteen to thirty students had sunk us into a financial hole. Clarence was working more part-time jobs than I could keep track of. We poured all of our savings into the school, ignored the upkeep of our house, and let our life insurance policies lapse. But these contributions enabled me to pay off some bills.

The aftermath of the *Time* article set the pattern for what would happen every time Westside Prep was featured in the mass media. Teachers wrote me asking my advice on how to teach a child to read or how to get a child to love learning. Some told me of their own frustrations with the educational system and with apathetic colleagues who criticized them for being "too optimistic" or ridiculed them for "wasting time caring about students." I also heard from corporate executives who complained about the illiteracy of employees and from college administrators appalled at the poor reading skills of incoming freshmen.

More than 2,000 letters came from parents—frightened, worried parents all calling for help. They told the same kinds of stories I had heard so many times before—only now I was hearing them from people all across the country, not just from black parents living in the inner-city. A mother from California wanted to know what to do for her son, who had been diagnosed in the usual way by his teachers: "hyperactive, brain damaged, bright but a poor achiever, immature, and not properly motivated." There was a letter from a woman in a small Michigan town, saying her teenaged daughter was "a casualty of our failing public school system—an A and B student who can't read and comprehend, think independently and has no clear understanding of our world and how it works."

There were pleas from parents who believed their children were wrongly categorized as retarded or learning disabled. Others wanted to know how they could pull their sons and daughters out of public schools and teach them at home. A St. Louis mother complained that her two boys "entered school

open and receptive" but "the school discouraged these quali-
ties." Another woman, from Maryland, said her teenage son
was being wasted in a learning disabilities class where all he did
was play and paint, doing nothing that could be described as academic all year.

I knew the poor shape education was in, but I had never
realized the extent of the public's desperation. One letter, written by a woman from upstate New York, seemed to sum it up:

> My son is in first grade. Already he dislikes school,
> which is causing him to be a discipline problem to his
> teacher. I know he does not receive her love and en-
> couragement. His teacher informed me she did not
> have the time with 28 other active youngsters in her
> room and besides he is 'too old' for this kind of treat-
> ment. It scares me and is tearing me apart. The sys-
> tem is losing him and as a result I am afraid I may
> also.

People were crying out for help, yet there was so little I
could do. What kind of remedy could I offer parents in a letter
or a long-distance phone call? Everyone was looking for a cure-
all, hoping for some quick-fix for a chronic problem. Parents
were so desperate that I sometimes got the feeling they'd buy
a snake-oil potion if it promised to turn their children into
readers.

Meanwhile, with thirty students my enrollment was nearly
up to the limit imposed by the city's building code. I could only
accept a handful of new students, squeezing in a few more
seats and having some of the four year olds sit on the floor. I
wanted to move the school into larger quarters, but I didn't
have enough money or a steady enough income from the school
to guarantee rent, and many landlords wanted the rent paid
months in advance.

Following the *Time* article, other publications did stories
on our school, including educational journals, the *Chicago Tri-
bune Magazine, People* magazine, and *Good Housekeeping.* The
publicity brought still more parents, teachers, school administrators, and more press filing into my classroom. The director of

the Free Schools in Europe read about Westside Prep in the European edition of *Time* and came all the way from Germany to observe my children.

Over the next two years the children and I were the subjects of articles in newspapers and magazines all over the country. We were also featured on local and national television. I appeared on ABC's *Good Morning America,* and in November 1979 CBS's *60 Minutes* aired a segment on Westside Prep. As a result of the *60 Minutes* broadcast I received more than 6,000 letters from desperate parents.

★　　★　　★

Marva's students reveled in the excitement of being neighborhood celebrities and seeing their pictures in newspapers and magazines. A few of the children had been interviewed by reporters. One boy gleefully told the class that his relatives in the South had read about the school. And two of the girls told how they had been walking to the playground one day when a woman stopped them on the street to ask: "Aren't you some of those Marva Collins children?"

Marva decided she had better set her students' priorities straight about all the attention they were receiving.

"People are always reading about the bad things that go on in Garfield Park, and it is our obligation to show a different side of our community. Everyone is coming to see you because you're so bright, but we can't afford to go sticking out our chests. We can't get too carried away with this publicity. We can't run around bragging and forget what we are here for, or we'll all end up like a bunch of Petunias. Who remembers the story of Petunia?"

"Petunia was the hen who went around telling all the other barnyard animals she knew how to read when she didn't," Cathy Mullins said. After seven months in the school Cathy had pulled up to reading at her age level. Her nervousness had disappeared, her hair stopped falling out, and she no longer shuddered and whimpered when someone looked at her. She had developed such confidence that months later, when the school year was over, she would take charge of organizing the year-end class party.

"And what happened to Petunia and the rest of the animals?" Marva asked.

"They all got blown up and ended up in the hospital or walking around on crutches," George answered. " 'Cause when the mailman brought a package to the barnyard, the other animals asked Petunia to read what was in it. And since she really didn't know how to read, she pretended it said candy."

"What did the package really have in it?"

"Explosives," the children chortled.

"Now we're not going to be Petunias sticking out our chests and bragging about how much we know, not without putting in the effort to learn it," said Marva. "Your picture appearing in the paper today is not going to make you happy for the rest of your life. Getting your picture in the paper or in every magazine in this country is not going to pay your bills. It's not going to put food on your table or keep you warm in the winter. People are impressed by what you have learned so far, but that doesn't mean you can sit back and congratulate yourselves and do nothing. The more successful a person becomes, the harder he or she has to work to stay there. Let's not worry about what people *write* about us. Let's just worry about getting things *right* ourselves."

Things settled back to a kind of normalcy, and in the weeks that followed, the children attended to their work, Marva raced and bounced around the classroom, and everyone tried their best to ignore the visitors who filed into the room and sat on the folding chairs in the back corner. When the children gave in to their curiosity and turned their heads to stare at a stranger or look over a reporter's shoulder as he was jotting notes, Marva quickly reminded them what they were in school for.

"You won't know that man ten years from now," she'd say. "His name isn't going to be on your paycheck." Her caveat was enough to spring all eyes face front. Never mind that their ministers were forever telling them "God will provide." Marva had taught them her own corollary: God will provide if you first have the brain to provide for yourself.

★   ★   ★

My children were drawing on everything they learned. One Monday morning twelve-year-old Renee Williams came to class with an observation inspired the previous day at church.

"Mrs. Collins," she said. "You know how Jesus in his Sermon on the Mount said, 'I come to fulfill you, not harm you'? Well, I bet that's where Shakespeare got the idea for the line 'I come to bury Caesar, not to praise him.' "

During a discussion of Euripides' tragedy *Andromache* I asked them how they thought the heroine felt when she went from being a queen to being a slave.

"She probably wanted to kill herself like Cleopatra did," Cindy said.

"And when a person kills himself, what is that called?" I asked.

"Suicide," the class answered.

"When Orestes killed his mother Clytemnestra, that was matricide," Gary added.

"And when you kill your father, that's patricide," Patrick said taking his cue from Gary.

"So killing infants is infanticide," Erika chimed in.

"Yeah, and killing pests is pesticide," said another voice, followed by a guffaw.

Aside from the children's academic progress there were changes far more subtle. They had a discernible pride not only in their work but in their school as well. The school, they felt, belonged to them and they displayed a proprietary sense about its upkeep. I was determined to instill a *we* mentality in my students and make them realize the school would only work if all of us stuck together to make it work.

I had told them that everything they tore up or lost would have to be replaced, then tuition would have to go up, and soon only the rich would be able to go to school at Westside Prep. To illustrate my point I brought the utility bills and invoices for school supplies to class. It was a simple but compelling economics lesson. Everything has a cost. As long as they were learning, the investment was well worth it. "See the bill from People's Gas Company? I want that much learning out of you today."

Despite all the attention I was getting from the media, my priority was still my students. Once I entered the classroom the rest of the world didn't exist. My students knew and understood me better than anyone else. They certainly knew me better than the media that was calling me "super teacher" and "miracle worker." I hated those epithets. I resented the way they made it all sound so easy.

There was no miracle or magic in what went on in our school. If it were that simple, then teaching would not have been such hard work for me, and learning would not have been so demanding for the children. It was because of all the effort and difficulty that the children savored every accomplishment. And once they started to succeed they wanted to succeed even more. They didn't ever want to turn around again.

Before the 1977–1978 school year was over George and Laura were both accepted by high schools, and Cindy and Erika won commendations in a statewide student writing contest. Both had written essays on the subject of violence, drawing upon the *Iliad* to make the point that violence has always been around. They were invited by the Illinois State Superintendent of Schools to read their papers at the Illinois Young Authors Conference.

Sitting in the auditorium as the girls presented their papers, I kept picturing Erika as she had been nearly three years before. The same child who had been called retarded was now expressing her thoughts before an audience.

Like every teacher I had days when I was impatient with my students' progress. There were times when I could not seem to break through to a child. And there were some lessons that fell on deaf ears no matter how much I banged on desks or waved my arms to get the point across. Yet I made certain that I never underestimated by children's intelligence or their ability to learn. I kept in mind the countless schools across the country that mislabeled children, simplified textbooks, diluted curricula, and created special curricula for "underprivileged" children. How many are victimized by an educational philosophy which presupposes that background and environment limit a child's capacity to learn? How many children are discouraged from pursuing an education because teachers have taken it upon themselves to judge who can achieve and who cannot? I wasn't there to judge my students. My job as a teacher was to get their talents working. And that's what I tried to do.

The following year the school had a waiting list of several hundred students. Otherwise life at Westside Prep continued much the same. New students replaced those who left, and like their predecessors these children had to be brought up to level. Some of them were real hellions. One boy, Derrin, couldn't sit next to someone without kicking him. After a while, as their brains began to click, the children's hands and feet became still. Order seems to evolve naturally once children realize why they are in school. Six months after Derrin came to the school, a reporter who was talking to him a bit too long heard the boy say, "I don't mean to be rude, but you are taking away my skills."

The children who had been with me for several years were like sponges soaking up everything I could give them. Just as I used to drill them, they now began to push me, constantly asking what does this mean and what does that mean. They were fascinated with words, and they hunted through the dictionary for the sheer joy of finding polysyllabic words to try out on one another.

The great books were their greatest teacher. While there are critics who claim the classics are too difficult for younger students to read—that an eleven year old, for example, can't understand something as complicated as *The Brothers Karamazov*—I have found that great literature not only teaches students to read but makes them thirsty for more and more knowledge. These books *are* over the head of the student reader; that is the purpose of reading them. We read to stretch the mind, to seek, to strive, to wonder, and then reread. We discuss the ideas contained in those books with others, and we temper our own thoughts. The great books are great teachers because they demand the attention of the reader. The mundane content of second-rate literature turns students off from reading forever.

However, I did not leave the children to read these books by themselves. They read a chapter aloud each day in class and a chapter each night at home. We went over these books paragraph by paragraph, often line by line, discussing the ideas and following the characters, action, and movement of the story. The literature they read became part of them. The more I worked with them and the older they got, they began to communicate with each other through the things they learned. Their street lingo began to disappear sometimes to be replaced with lines they had read.

To me they were beginning to sound like Rhodes Scholars—even when they were insulting one another. Once when a student told a lie in class, someone said, "Speak the speech trippingly on thy tongue," and another chimed in, "The false face does hide what the false heart does know." If a girl was acting too flirty, the other girls would accuse her of acting like the Wife of Bath. One day my son Patrick had a pimple on his face and his sister Cindy told him he looked like the Summoner in *Canterbury Tales.* Another time when a rubberband shot across the room, I asked Michael whether he had done it. He said no and blamed it on Phillip, who said, "Et tu, Michael? This was the most unkindest cut of all."

When the 1978–1979 school year ended, several students, including Cathy Mullins, passed into high school, skipping from seventh to ninth grade. Upon finishing fifth grade, Tracy Shanklin was reading two years above her grade level. Erika and Cindy, in fourth grade, were reading high school books.

That year I had sent all my students aged eight and above to be tested independently at a nearby Catholic school. They took the California Achievement Test, Form 18-C, which was valid for students between seventh and ninth grades. Ordinarily only my older students took that test, but I felt it was also a good experience for the children below seventh grade, whose scores were adjusted upward in accordance with their age.

The results of those tests showed that most of the children had made extraordinary improvement in vocabulary, spelling, reading comprehension, and math. In a few instances a student's test score jumped four years after one year at Westside Prep. Not all my students were reading above grade level. Some were still quite far behind. However, all showed significant improvement from where they had been. There were sixth-graders reading at a fourth or fifth grade level, but those students had started the year struggling with second and third grade material. They had made wonderful progress. I was pleased.

★   ★   ★

The Catholic school admissions director, Harvey Gross, who administered the California Achievement Test to students from more than seventy Chicago area schools, noted that Marva's Westside Prep students scored higher and showed greater progress than any other group he tested. Yet he was quick to say that test scores alone didn't tell the whole story. One had to watch Marva's students in the classroom to see the full effect of her energy and her conviction that children can learn.

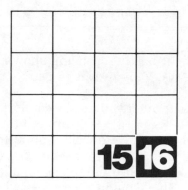

The one question that ought to be asked on a teaching application is: do you love children? To me that's the most important criterion for a teacher, more important than credentials or college degrees. A devotion to children was the quality I looked for in all the people who applied for teaching jobs at Westside Prep. Often I didn't sense it in the most seasoned teachers, long-time veterans of public, private, or parochial schools. Others without any formal training or teaching experience sometimes struck me as having the personality and enthusiasm that made an effective teacher: one of those was Lillian Vaughn, a CETA (Comprehensive Employment Training Act) worker placed with me for training by the Alternative Schools Network.

At the time I was anxious to have an assistant to help me with the four and five year olds, who naturally worked at a slower pace than the older students. The job was made to order for Mrs. Vaughn. A short, quiet, rather shy woman of thirty-eight, she was eager to work with the children, which was reason enough for me to try her out. It didn't matter that Mrs. Vaughn had only had a year of college or that her only previous experience was as a teacher's aide, going from school to school to assist in the administering of standardized tests. It was all the better. There would be no bad habits to contend with, no professional ego to bruise.

Lillian Vaughn seemed to love children; she was gentle and patient with them. Further she was receptive to learning my methods without balking at being shown what to do. The first thing I told Mrs. Vaughn was to get a pair of comfortable shoes.

"To be a good teacher you need a comfortable pair of shoes and a strong pair of legs to get you through the day. No teacher sits in this school. You have to walk around to each and every child, not just the ones in the front seats. You have to check for errors in the back as well. Remember, children only want to finish their work. They couldn't care less whether they get it right. They don't want to be bothered. They will tell you they understand when they really don't."

I gave Mrs. Vaughn explicit directions that every child had to be praised and patted, hugged and touched each day. Slower children needed to be praised for something daily just as much as the brighter child. I told her to think of something positive to say before going over a child's errors. Then I started Mrs. Vaughn the same way I started with any new student, teaching her the phonics drills. I gave her guidelines on how to draw morals and analogies from fables, fairy tales, and poetry. I wrote out elaborate lesson plans and then led her through each step from beginning to end.

The first few months Mrs. Vaughn stayed in the classroom with me, following my moves and tutoring the children. I watched her like a hawk, the same way I watched my students. Once when she was reading a fairy tale to the little children, I heard four-year-old Andy cry and say he was afraid of the witch in the story. Mrs. Vaughn told him not to act like a silly baby.

I left the reading group I was working with and called her aside. "Never make children feel that their fears or questions are silly," I told her. "The fears are real to them. And try not to embarrass a child in front of the other children. They don't like to be ridiculed in front of others any more than we do."

"But I never meant to embarrass him," she apologized.

"I'm sure you didn't, but we have to be conscious of everything we say to children. You have to make yourself aware of how they might interpret something that we say very innocently."

Another time Jimmy Tucker and Donald Ellis were fighting over a pencil and I overheard Mrs. Vaughn tell them she was going to send notes home to their mothers. I interceded. First I scolded the boys, "Don't go on about 'This is mine and This is yours.' If you spend your time learning instead of fighting over a pencil, then someday you'll each be able to own your own pencil factories."

Later I explained to Mrs. Vaughn that as a teacher she had to take care of problems herself. "Remember, if you take the problems to the parent, you and the child will not learn to trust each other and work together. Children respect teachers who do not always send notes home to parents."

I went on for weeks overseeing everything Mrs. Vaughn said and did. I stressed that phonics had to be taught daily; no religious fervor for just one day. When I felt she wasn't putting enough expression into the reading of a story, I urged her not to be afraid to become a good actress. A teacher must excite the students about learning.

After a while I felt that Mrs. Vaughn was ready to take charge of the youngest group, the pre-schoolers and kindergarteners. I set up space for her class in what had been the living room of the second-floor apartment, down the hall from my classroom. There were no desks and chairs. The youngsters sat on the carpet, surrounded by piles of books and papers, and Mrs. Vaughn kneeled beside them, inching from child to child, helping each to print the upper and lower case letters and to sound out words.

"You have to get down to a child's eye level and talk directly to that child," I insisted. As tall as I was, I was forever stooping and bending down when I talked to a student. "Children, especially the little ones, are easily intimidated by someone towering above them and speaking from on high."

Teacher training was a new area for me. The simplest part was explaining my curriculum. It was far more difficult to show someone how to understand children, how to be sensitive to their needs. Just as a teacher knows his or her own family members, he or she must know the students, their needs and their interests. Each child is unique.

My methods were a far cry from those endorsed in most teacher training institutions, where the emphasis is mostly on abstract theory and professional jargon. To this day I don't understand how hearing about "learning interference due to ret-roactive and proactive inhibition" will ever help a teacher get through to the freckle-nosed boy with the crooked teeth and make him feel confident and motivated. Many teachers who are honestly looking for ways to improve their techniques walk away from the in-service training sessions overwhelmed with information but without any answers. It's like asking directions to the bus stop and getting a lecture on mass transit sys-tems.

The fancy dressing of "education-speak" has even spread to job titles. Every profession has its lexicon of fancy job de-scriptions, and education is no exception. There are curriculum facilitators, master teachers, test administrators, LMC (Learn-ing Materials Center) supervisors, TESL (Teaching English as a Second Language) instructors, LD (learning disability) spe-cialists, and EMH (Educable Mentally Handicapped) coordina-tors. The serious side of it is that while everyone is closely guarding his or her own title, the children are left to fend for themselves.

When teachers turn to the education experts for help, they rarely seem to offer any practical advice. The experts are busy trying to build professional reputations based on some new gimmick. Each has had its fling: new math, teaching machines, continuous progress and non-graded classrooms, open class-rooms, team teaching, core curriculum, back-to-basics, black English, and bilingual instruction. One school superintendent had his local community declare an annual "Teachers Day" to improve teacher morale and enthusiasm. What about student morale and enthusiasm? Another superintendent's favorite gimmick was getting businesses to sponsor schools.

That is typical of the American approach to problem-solv-ing. People seem to think that if they throw a few more dollars at a problem it will go away. It is like putting a band-aid on a hemorrhage. When the Chicago public schools were in the throes of a financial crisis, the Chicago School Finance Au-thority, charged with overseeing school funds and expendi-tures, hired a consulting firm to make a $33,000 study on cost-saving recommendations. Then, the next year, after the school board failed to do anything about the recommendations, the city allocated another $200,000 for a second study on how to cut school costs.

I remember a time, years back, when schools and teachers tried to deal with their own problems. Then federal dollars became available and suddenly everyone had a problem he couldn't solve and was writing grant proposals. People got billions of dollars to study problems, and when those studies didn't work out, people got more government money to do a new study to find out what went wrong with the first one.

Countless studies have been done on how to teach inner-city students. To me it seems perfectly plain that inner-city children should be taught the same way other children are taught, because all children want the same things out of life. A ghetto child learns in the same way as any other child and is equally capable of reading Dante, Homer, Pascal, or Chaucer. A child—any child—may not go on to college or become a great scholar, but there is no reason he or she can't gain some appreciation for literature or get something worthwhile out of discussing the great books.

I don't hold with a "ghetto approach" to teaching. The experts claim that correcting an inner-city child's grammar will damage his or her identity. I believe that not correcting grammar will damage that child's whole life. While others lowered their standards for inner-city students, I made mine higher.

Busing is another example of a self-defeating approach to black education. It only makes minority children ashamed of themselves and their neighborhoods, as though only schools in white neighborhoods can teach. My goal is to make my students proud and to involve them in improving their community.

Busing doesn't accomplish anything useful. It is merely another way of side-stepping the real problem—ineffective teachers are everywhere. Statistics clearly show that many white, middle-class children are graduating as functional illiterates. In 1976 a Hudson Institute study reported that the most precipitous decline in student achievement was among the brightest and most advantaged children—those from middle-class families. Miseducation is not a function of a child's race or neighborhood but of the teaching methods he or she is exposed to from kindergarten on.

New methods and theories are not the solution. In fact they have been the primary cause of miseducation. In the mid-1960s many educators supported a trend away from the use of books towards "experiential learning activities." They said students needed to experience concepts and ideas instead of just reading about them. One educational psychology textbook used in teacher training courses stated: "Today's schools probably depend far too much upon reading as a data gathering technique." Why then were educators surprised when students went all the way through school without being able to read? And why was everyone surprised when those same non-readers became teachers themselves and spawned a whole new crop of miseducated students?

No amount of money or theory or gimmickry will cure what is wrong with education. Teachers need to stop looking for excuses and teach. They have to read and prepare and learn what they do not know, and then they have to bring that knowledge to their students, taking as much time as necessary to make sure every child learns. Any teacher who leaves a child as she found him negates her duty as a teacher.

I trained Mrs. Vaughn and eventually other teachers by giving them the same advice I gave my students. "You can't weep or talk your way through a mess," I said. "When you come up against a problem, you have to work your way through it."

★   ★   ★

Ella McCoy came to the school for a few days as a parent volunteer, helping to answer the phone and sort the mail. She ended up staying on as a teacher, becoming Marva's protégée. She quit her job after six years of teaching in the public schools. The last straw was overhearing the principal call to a student, "Hey, you fool, come here!"

Having witnessed the transformation of her daughter Erika from a six year old who had been considered retarded to a ten year old who read twenty-three books over the summer, including *Tale of Two Cities* and *Jane Eyre,* Ella resolved to stick with Marva to repay that debt. She wanted to give other children the same hope that had been given to her child.

Ella did not know where to begin. Although she had graduated from a midwestern teachers' college, she did not know how to syllabicate words. She knew nothing about literature or poetry. Like any one of Marva's students and like Lillian Vaughn, Ella needed to start out with the basics—the phonics, the drills and memorization, the vocabulary, the spelling and grammar rules. She studied the fables, mythology, and classics as though she were cramming for an introductory course in English Lit.

Ella trained in the classroom with Marva, trying to help with the children. "I couldn't really help them," she confessed later, "because I didn't know the material myself." When the school day was over, Ella became Marva's pupil. Marva taught her when a vowel sound was long and when it was short, when to double a consonant and when not to. Before, it had all been a matter of guesswork for Ella: she had never had a method for determining whether the word was *hoping* or *hopping*.

More than the fundamentals of language, Ella felt she was learning how to teach for the first time—how to motivate children and get them going. "Everything works when the teacher works," Marva told her. "It's as easy as that, and as hard. It's your duty to find a way to reach each child. If the child doesn't move, it's the teacher's fault."

Ella watched Marva and did what she did. Ella praised the children, patted them, scolded them, hugged them, prodded them, joked with them, was firm with them, held their hands, and pumped them full of confidence and love. Her rapport with the children came naturally. All she could think about was reading and studying and finding ways to move each child. She had never realized teaching was so demanding.

"Each teacher must prepare, prepare, prepare, and prepare some more," Marva had told her. "We never assign to children what we do not understand ourselves. Never assign children books that you haven't read. Remember, written book reports are often copied. The child copies the front of the book, the middle, and the end. Have the child describe the book orally, and be ready for the child to test you to see if you have read the book."

Because she had not read many of the classics herself, Ella became a steady customer at the library. Marva encouraged her to "look through old anthologies, the kind that kept children interested in school before the publishers watered them down and choked so many children on boredom."

After the first day she taught on her own, taking over half of Lillian Vaughn's class, Ella was exhausted. Her legs weren't used to walking up and down all day. However, she knew she couldn't be a teacher at Westside Prep and sit behind a desk, wondering what the child in the back was doing. She had to get up and see for herself. In Marva's school errors had to be checked immediately or a child would fall behind. Ella found energy she never thought she had and she trusted her legs would get stronger and the ache in her lower back would eventually go away. The children needed her full attention now.

A new student, Arnold Rogers, reminded Ella of Erika as she had been before. The child's previous teachers had disposed of him as a lost cause at eight years old. If ever there was a child who had been trampled by armies of specialists clashing over diagnoses, it was Arnold. He had gone through the educational system like a lab rat in a maze, scrutinized by psychologists, audiologists, ophthalmologists, speech pathologists, and social workers. Arnold did have a physiological problem: surgical correction of a cleft palate had left him with speech and hearing difficulties. No one was certain whether these difficulties prevented Arnold from learning.

His principal and teachers saw Arnold merely as a child with "severe behavior disorders," and they wanted him placed in a special school for emotionally disturbed and retarded youngsters. When a psychologist from the Chicago Board of Education examined Arnold, he kept asking her, "Why are you so *obese?*" The psychologist later said to his mother, "So many of our black boys end up in jail . . ."

To his public school teachers Arnold was a clear-cut case, which they had chronicled for months:

11/10/78 Playing with cough drops. Passing them all around to classmates instead of doing seatwork.

When told his work was not finished he scribbled everything black.

Grabbed Michael Lane in lunch line and tried to lift him up.

Put his lunch tray in Michael Lane's face.

Playing with spider ring of Derrick's.

During math, Arnold was imitating everything I said. He was playing with his pencil and flipped it onto the floor.

Pushing Beverly's desk back.

11/14/78 Arnold began his A.M. work with little difficulty. He did come up to ask me words 3 times, however.

11/15/78 While walking to lunch, Arnold stopped at water fountain and turned on faucet.

2:30 P.M.—Pushed down all the boys in line while standing at the door, for no apparent reason.

2/16/79 During Black History assembly, Arnold seemed confused as to where he was to stand and what he was supposed to say. While on stage, he was looking around— somewhat detached and disinterested in the program.

Note that Arnold needs constant reminding to complete one entire task. During a regular class day he must be spoken to often.

2/21/79 During assembly program, Arnold was holding his hands over his ears. When asked whether the music was too loud— said yes. Several times got out of seat to walk away. Had to be reminded to sit quietly.

3/26/79 Arnold had 2 hours to do three papers. He played with his ink pen and ball for those 2 hrs. instead of working.

Miriam Rogers didn't care what kind of "evidence" the teachers had against her son. She was determined to prove he did not have a behavior disorder. She couldn't understand how a teacher could allow a child to dawdle at his desk for two hours playing with a ball. Why didn't the teacher simply take the ball away and tell Arnold to get busy? As Arnold's father told the principal: "My son understands what you are trying to do to him. He is not crazy, but you are trying to make him crazy."

Arnold's parents got a lawyer from the Legal Assistance Foundation to fight having their son placed in a special school for emotionally disturbed children. They argued their case before representatives from the Board of Education at a special due-process hearing. They won. The hearings officer ruled that there was insufficient proof of a behavior disorder, although there was ample evidence that Arnold had "serious learning disabilities in the areas of visual-motor perception, visual processing and eye-hand coordination."

Arnold remained in school with the same teacher and received speech and visual therapy from the school clinician. Two months after the hearing there were problems once again. Arnold was suspended for throwing food and fighting in the lunchroom. Having had her fill of the public schools, Miriam Rogers tried to enroll Arnold in Westside Prep.

Marva was out of town. Ella, who had been working at the school for seven months, met privately with Mrs. Rogers and surprised her by showing little interest in Arnold's history of misbehavior: "As far as I'm concerned, your son is an eight-year-old child who *will* learn." When Marva telephoned, Ella said, "Please, Mrs. Collins, let's squeeze Arnold in. We'll find the space somehow." With only three weeks left before the school closed for the summer, Marva agreed to take Arnold until the end of the term without any fee.

Marva met Arnold and his mother at the door. "Why were you suspended from your other school?"

"For fighting and throwing food." His mother spoke for him. Arnold was too ashamed of his speech impediment to attempt more than a one-word answer to any question.

Marva nodded. "Arnold, sweetheart, you already know

how to fight. If you want to spend your time throwing around food and garbage, if you want to be a garbageman all your life, then you don't need an education."

"Huh?" Arnold looked up at Marva, confused.

"I beg your pardon. We don't say 'huh' in here. We speak in sentences." Marva kneeled next to him, her eyes level with his, her hands on his shoulders. "Your mother can't be with you your whole life and neither can I. You must make it on your own. Love, you are going to learn in here every day starting today."

Arnold stared in amazement.

"Now, sweetheart, can you spell *cat* for me?" Marva asked.

"C-a-t," he answered hesitantly.

"Very, very good. You're so bright," Marva said. Then she turned to Mrs. Rogers. "There is nothing wrong with your son that time and patience can't take care of."

Arnold became one of Ella's students. She sat him down and said, "Arnold, sweetheart, from now on you're going to learn. Children don't fail in here because I don't let them fail. You will learn to read so you can have choices in life."

The other children were reading *Aesop's Fables.* Arnold refused to open the book. He bolted out of his seat and into the bathroom where Cindy and Tracy were sitting on the edge of the bathtub reading. Cindy looked up from her book. "Do you want to use the bathroom?" she asked.

He shook his head. He spied a hammer that Clarence had left on the floor beside the toilet. He grabbed it and took a swing at Cindy, hitting her on her arm. She screamed and ran out of the room with Arnold chasing after her.

"I'll take that hammer, Arnold," Marva said. What surprised Arnold even more than the suddenness of her appearance was her tone. She spoke calmly and softly, yet something told him she meant business. He shoved the hammer at her and started to turn away. Marva held him by his arm while she consoled Cindy and checked for injuries. Satisfied that Cindy wasn't hurt, Marva turned back to Arnold. "In this school we put our energy in our brains, not our fists and certainly not in hitting others with hammers or sticks or anything else."

Arnold raised his head to look at her, wondering if she was crazy.

"This is your last school, darling," she continued. "You are here to stay. No one is putting you out. But you are going to produce, you are going to read, because if you can't read, then you can't do anything in life." She tucked in his shirt and started to walk him back to Ella's classroom. "I know there's a good you locked up inside that angry you. It's just waiting to come out if you will only let it.

"There once was a famous sculptor named Michelangelo. Do you know what a sculptor is?" Arnold shook his head without lifting his eyes. "Well, a sculptor is someone who carves and chisels statues out of blocks of wood or stone. Michelangelo liked to make things out of marble. And he would walk around the streets of Florence, Italy, where he lived, and every time he saw a piece of marble he would think of the beautiful angels he could carve from it. Just as Michelangelo thought there was an angel locked inside every piece of marble, I think there is a brilliant child locked inside every student in this school."

Marva sat Arnold down at his spot in the second classroom. Ella was giving dictation. Ella paused and held his shoulder: "You can do it. You can do it." She printed his name at the top of a paper and wrote out the last sentence of dictation: *Aesop wrote fables.* Taking Arnold's chin in her hand, she said, "Now let's say the first word together. The *a* is silent so we begin with the *e* sound. Say *ee.* You have to open your mouth in a smile."

Arnold repeated the vowel.

"Oh, that's good. Now *sss,* make the sound come through your teeth. Then *ah,* open your mouth wide. And *puh,* make a popping sound with your lips. Now put all the sounds together and say *Aesop.*"

"Aesop," Arnold said.

"Very good. Aesop, Aesop," Ella repeated.

"I know it's Aesop. How many times ya gonna tell me? Wads duh nex' word?"

Ella laughed and mussed his hair. "You're going to do just fine."

Marva was watching this scene from a distance, looking on with pride in both the child and the teacher.

At the end of the first day Ella sent Arnold home with a sheet of math problems for homework. She didn't expect him to do them all. If he did one, it would have been something. But he finished the page. By the end of the week Arnold was starting to read. He was taking dictation and writing on the lines of the paper, which he had never done before. He came in scrubbed and with his shirt tucked in. Once he discovered that no one made fun of the way he talked, he began to answer questions and read aloud—drawing cheers and applause from his classmates.

His mother didn't know what to make of it. Arnold had always been such a frustrated and angry child. He used to say he couldn't wait until he got to be sixteen years old so he could drop out of school. Now he woke up in the morning excited about going to class, telling his father to drive faster. He didn't mind staying late in the afternoon to finish work. Sometimes Ella would drive him home and stop for a hotdog or milkshake. He looked forward to Ella's tutoring him over the summer; as he told his mother, "I got to learn 'cause I'm going to go to college and do a lot of things when I grow up."

One morning the bubble burst. Arnold came to school upset. The sparkle was gone, replaced by his old belligerence.

"What happened, baby?" Marva asked.

Arnold told her he forgot his homework and his father had yelled at him in the car for it.

"Who runs this school, your dad or Mrs. Collins?" Arnold had never seen her so angry—not even the time he hit Cindy with the hammer.

"Mrs. Collins," he answered.

"That's right. And you know what we say in here: if you can't make a mistake, you can't what?"

"Make anything."

"Good. Now get a smile on that face. I can't stand to be around sad children."

That afternoon, Marva telephoned Arnold's father. "Mrs. McCoy and I are trying so hard to build confidence in Arnold," she told him, "but by shouting at the boy you are going to undo everything we have done so far. Arnold has been called every name in the book and now he needs praise and plenty of it—from everyone."

A few days later came the end of another school year. It had been five years since Marva left Delano to begin an alternative school. The students who had first come to her as ornery, scared, bored, underachieving children were now stepping into adolescence as confident and determined young men and women. Erika left for the summer handing Marva a copy of a newly published biography of Sacajawea. "Mrs. Collins, you've got to read this book. It's terrific."

Gary Love said his last goodbyes to Marva and Westside Prep. Gary, who used to insist he couldn't do anything, had won a scholarship to a private academy in the northern suburbs. Marva's son Patrick was also going to high school in the fall.

There were other changes afoot for September. Clarence was leaving his job at Sunbeam to help Marva manage the school's business affairs. Westside Prep had grown into a full-fledged educational institution, and Marva was finally moving it out of her house. The *60 Minutes* feature had opened a financial spigot that allowed her to make plans for accommodating some of the children on the waiting list, which had swelled to about 700 students. Almost $50,000 in contributions had rolled into Westside Prep, including a $10,000 check from an anonymous donor whom Marva jokingly called J. Beausfoot Tipton from the TV series *The Millionaire*. Another $75,000 came from a film production company that bought the rights to make a movie about Marva and the school. The contributions, the movie money, plus the income from her workshops and speeches enabled Marva to rent space on the second floor of the old, and practically vacant, National Bank of Commerce Building, a few blocks away on Madison Street.

In September 1980 Westside Prep would have an enrollment of 200 students. Marva had said all along that Westside Prep was not the "one-room fairy tale" some of the press had labeled it. She was going to prove that good education could happen on any scale.

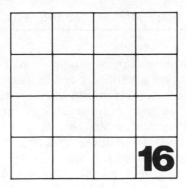

16

I had dreamed of expanding the school for nearly three years, ever since I had to draw up that first waiting list with thirty names. Yet when it finally came about, the expansion happened so fast I felt as though I were whirling on a merry-go-round and couldn't catch my breath. The school didn't just grow. It seemed to explode. We jumped from 34 students in June to an estimated fall enrollment of 200, with a waiting list of over 500 more.

The summer was chaos. Everyone was swept up in moving the school. Clarence, Eric, and Patrick worked frantically, painting, building bookshelves, hanging blackboards, and carrying all the desks, books, and filing cabinets from the upstairs of our house to the second floor of the bank building. Cindy, Tracy, and Erika unpacked cartons of new textbooks and supplies. Ella, Mrs. Vaughn, and I made class lists, wrote up lessons, mimeographed worksheets, arranged desks, and put up posters and phonics charts. Some of the parents pitched in too, helping out with registration, phone calls, and office work.

Expansion on this scale made it necessary that I do something about the other sort of parents, those who remained uninvolved in the education of their children, to the point of never paying tuition. One father seemed to typify their attitude when he said, "I know you won't put my child out if I don't pay tuition. You like children too much." I flatly informed the parents we would have to change that policy in the fall. Tuition was the only reliable source of income for the school. I couldn't count on contributions and lecture fees to pay the monthly rent or salaries for my staff. The parents agreed to form an association to deal with delinquent tuition and to do some fund raising.

My chief concern that summer was hiring and training new teachers. Ella and Mrs. Vaughn were working out beautifully, though both needed to develop more initiative in handling student problems. They tended to run to me with everything, from a child who needed a band-aid for a scratch to a student who was disrupting the class, but they were hard-working, dedicated teachers. Most important, they believed in the children. I wanted to find two other teachers just like them.

I had a stack of resumés from people all over the country, even a few inquiries from Europe. Resumés and letters couldn't tell me what I wanted to know. I was interested in attitudes, not credentials. I didn't want people who pitied poor little black children. Nor did I want teachers who had limited expectations of what children could achieve.

Since August had to be set aside for training new teachers, I didn't have time to go through a long interviewing process. Fortunately I didn't have to. I hired one teacher, Patricia Jurgens, on a referral and recommendation from a friend of mine. The other teacher I decided on was Marcella Winters, the mother of one of my students. She had gone back to school and had just completed her degree in education. I knew and liked her as a person before I ever knew her as a teacher. She was outgoing and high spirited, a bundle of energy. The main reason I hired her was that she had an interest in the school and believed in what we were doing. Her daughter had been enrolled in Westside Prep for two years.

I drilled the new teachers in my methodology. "The teacher who can only work with the well-motivated child and the well-behaved child has no place at Westside Preparatory School," I told them. "I want teachers who will make the slow student become good and the good student become superior."

★　★　★

A wig emporium and a Frederick's of Hollywood-style lingerie shop flanked the entrance to Marva's new school in the National Bank of Commerce Building. In the lobby an elderly security guard sat at his post by the iron-gated doorway to the empty bank. The bank had closed nearly twenty years ago, when everything else in Garfield Park shut down.

The building's only tenant was Westside Prep, installed in the mezzanine overlooking the unused teller cages. Marva paid $2,400 a month to rent the windowless, musty space that was too hot in the fall and spring and too cold in the winter. It was a stiff price, but that was a fact of life in that neighborhood.

By 2:30 in the afternoon, when the children filed out of school, hawkers had set up their wares on card tables in the outer vestibule, hustling parents to buy rhinestone rings and gold-plated chains. Outside, car exhaust mixed with the smells from the fried chicken franchise across the street, and customers were already seeking out the taverns around the corner.

It was an improbable setting for a school, perhaps even more improbable than the apartment above Marva's house. Yet Westside Prep was drawing students from all parts of the city and even from Chicago's western and far-southern suburbs. Many parents now felt that the only place their children could get a high-quality education was in the heart of a ghetto.

One student commuted by train from Elgin, Illinois, thirty-five miles away. Eighth-grader Sandra Parsons—a former junior high school student who performed at a fourth grade level in both reading and math—made the daily sixty-mile round trip from East Chicago, Indiana. And nine-year-old Brian Shoemaker came from the Lincoln Park area, a neighborhood of lakefront condominiums and $250,000 Victorian rowhouses, whose residents included the likes of Governor James Thompson. Brian had attended the Lincoln School, one of the highest rated of the city's public schools, where he had been a fourth-grader reading at a first grade level.

Westside Prep's 200 students were divided among five classes. Some classes had more than forty pupils—ten to fifteen more than the Chicago Teachers' Union allowed in the public schools. Lillian Vaughn, Patricia Jurgens, and Marcella Winters took charge of the pre-schoolers, kindergarteners, and first-graders—about half of the school's enrollment. Most of these younger children did not have any difficulty learning; their parents were sending them to Westside Prep in the hope that they never would. The few who had problems had drastic ones. Mrs.

Vaughn had a six-year-old student who showed signs of being autistic. According to his grandfather, who raised him, Charles had never talked. All he did was grunt.

Marva and Ella taught the older students, the hard-core problem children. Besides not having academic skills, some of these youngsters had enough emotional disorders to fill the glossary of a psychology textbook. One boy had been in and out of thirteen schools in four years. Another youngster, who had a penchant for stabbing other children with pencils, had been thrown out of the Drusso Mental Health Center. Then there was "The Slasher," an eight year old who would remove the blade from pencil sharpeners and run around cutting up his classmates' coats, hats, gloves, and scarves.

Tommy, at twelve, was in a constant depression, hating himself, hating his brother, hating everyone for not liking him; he even hated his last name, which he refused to use. The word *kill* nearly always came up when he spoke. If Marva said, "How do you feel today?" Tommy would say, "I feel like killing myself." When Marva said, "Have a nice weekend," he'd answer, "If I don't kill myself falling off my bike" or "If I don't kill myself getting hit in the head with a soccer ball."

Marva kept a straight face and praised him, saying he was handsome or she liked something he was wearing. She believed that he was not really self-destructive; he wanted attention. Marva resolved to show him there were more positive ways of getting it. Their exchanges began to sound like a cross between a Burns and Allen sketch and *Waiting for Godot*.

"I *don't* like myself. I want to kill myself."

"My, what a beautiful shirt you have."

Tommy would shrug and try again. "My brother hates me. I'd like to kill myself."

"Oh, what lovely eyes you have." Marva replied.

It went on for months. Then one afternoon Marva wished him a good evening.

"I . . ." Tommy paused.

What was it going to be this time? Marva wondered.

"I . . . I love you, Mrs. Collins," Tommy shouted, throwing his arms around her in a bearhug.

★   ★   ★

That first breakthrough was a joy to me, but it was only a beginning. Tommy inched into learning, still elusive, still testing and feeling his way. He spent part of the day in Ella's class, working on phonics and math and then came to mine for social studies and science. During one of the social studies lessons, while the students were taking turns reading aloud, I called on Tommy to read a short passage that I had selected especially for him. It contained eleven words that I was sure he could sound out. As he read, I stood beside him squeezing his shoulder. And when he finished, the whole class applauded.

"I gotta see Mrs. McCoy. Can I go see Mrs. McCoy?" he said excitedly, already half-standing. When I gave the okay, he bounded out the door and rushed into Ella's room. "I knocked 'em dead in Mrs. Collins' class. I sure knocked 'em dead!"

Seeing Westside Prep's *wunderkinden* splashed across the TV screen and featured in newspapers and magazines led some skeptics to accuse me of hand-picking only the brightest students. They saw only how far the children had come, not where they had been.

In a way I did hand-pick the students. Often the severity of a child's problem speeded up admission to Westside Prep. An older student took precedence over a pre-schooler or kindergartener for two reasons. First, the older child needed more immediate attention, sometimes having only four or five months to develop his or her skills to qualify for high school. Second, the pre-school and kindergarten enrollment had ballooned, and I didn't want my teachers to have more students than they felt they could handle.

Sometimes I gave priority to a child who wasn't even on the waiting list, and that selection policy brought on a barrage of complaints from parents who had long-standing applications on file. I also drew fire from some parents and members of the black community when I accepted some white students to Westside Prep. I tried to be fair, but I couldn't please everyone. It was up to me to make the decision on each new enrollment.

It was my school and I felt the public had no right to tell me how to run it. That especially meant government bureaucrats and special interest groups pushing minority rights. I live in the middle of Garfield Park, they do not. They do not know what works here, I do. People who have never set foot in this neighborhood always seem to think they know exactly what is good for it. All the do-gooders come in and criticize what is wrong. But do they ever come up with better alternatives?

Some people criticized my kind of "tough love," but I did not need any outsiders telling me I was too firm with my students. I felt just as sorry as they did for those children. No one knew better than I what kinds of homes some of them came from. But I was doing something constructive about it. I wasn't just passing out candy, rubbing the children's heads, and telling them how cute they were. I was trying to give them the skills to survive, forever telling them that each person must decide what he or she is going to leave to society for the privilege of living here. It was through the children in my school that I hoped to change the attitude of future generations.

The school itself represented the kind of determination, perseverance, stick-to-it-iveness, and pride I wanted the children to have. Sometimes, as I walked through the classrooms or when I overheard four and five year olds running around saying, "I'm a universal citizen," I was amazed at what we had accomplished in five years.

Westside Preparatory School had come full circle. With an enrollment of 200, operating a school that size became complex and demanding. I suddenly had an enormous overhead, a payroll, and all kinds of administrative duties. I had to deal with the newly formed Parents Association, occasionally being the referee at their meetings. One father simply could not get along with the other parents, and finally I had to ask him to withdraw his two children from the school. Once or twice I even had to put an end to bickering and resentment among my staff—the same kind of dissension as at Delano. I had to remind my teachers that they were not the important ones, that only the children mattered.

The 1980–1981 school year was a period of transition. I found myself pulled in a dozen directions. I had to oversee what my staff was doing, but I couldn't be in every classroom every minute of the day. I had to run the school as a whole, in addition to teaching my classes. I kept reminding myself that people were sending their children to this school because they wanted the kind of education demonstrated in the one-room school on Adams Street.

Of course the school lost some of the intimacy of a one-room setting, but I made sure I knew every one of the 200 children. I was determined not to lose sight of the philosophy on which the school was founded—we were there to serve the individual needs of each child. I kept telling my teachers that they should be the ones sharpening pencils and washing the blackboards. The children were there to learn, and learning was a full-time job.

I also had to remind my staff that whatever a child should have learned in a previous school didn't matter. Their duty was to start that child up from where he or she was. There were times when I had to caution my teachers not to write a child's name on the board for talking. Most of all I stressed the importance of praise and positive reinforcement.

I didn't want to be a principal. I fought the remoteness of being an administrator. The hours I spent in the classroom teaching were all the more precious because they kept me from losing touch with the children. Yet I had to be a principal. One of the newer teachers proved to be reluctant to follow my methodology, though I hoped she would eventually come around. I was especially anxious not to dismiss her in the middle of the year because children need continuity in their education. Schools have always moved black children around like pawns on a playing board, and I was not going to do that. If the other aspects of their lives were in chaos, then it was up to me to give my children the stability they needed. Unfortunately the teacher did not work out and she left the following year.

By January the school was operating with a certain momentum of its own. For the most part the teachers were carrying on my methods—especially Ella, who had a strong enough personality to take charge when I had to be away. The children themselves were the best indication that the school was working. At eight years old Calvin Graham, who had started at Westside Prep four years before, was reading at a ninth grade level. The older children had adopted him as a sort of class mascot, and I could barely keep a straight face at some of the things that came out of his mouth. One afternoon I was going around the class asking the children to give me a thought for the day. In turn they recited quotations from Emerson, Shakespeare, and Socrates. When I came to Calvin, he said, "To associate with fools is like going to bed with a razor." Surprised, I told him I wasn't familiar with that line. He said he made it up himself.

Arnold Rogers, the child Ella had worked so closely with, blossomed during that year. His mother said he hated to miss school, even when he was sick. Once he had the stomach flu but refused to stay home. In class he had an unfortunate accident, and when I took him to the washroom, he said to me, "Oh, Mrs. Collins, I'm so chagrined. I'm so humiliated." I told him that any eight-year-old boy who had the word *chagrin* in his vocabulary had no reason to be humiliated about anything. Several months later that same child, who had struggled to overcome a severe learning disability associated with a speech impediment, stood before an auditorium filled with people and recited the poem "Invictus."

I was proud of all the children. Their accomplishments spoke for themselves. Sandra Parsons, for example, the thirteen year old who had arrived in September doing fourth grade work, tested a few months later at a tenth grade level and was admitted to the freshman class at a private high school in Indiana. Another girl, who came to me in the fall from one of the city's most acclaimed public schools, where she was scheduled to repeat seventh grade, scored at a tenth grade level in vocabulary and at an eleventh grade level in reading comprehension when she took the California Achievement Test in January. And in June 1981 Tracy Shanklin, who had started with me six years before, was accepted into a parochial high school—a year above her age level—and was slated for advanced algebra and sophomore biology classes.

Former students of mine were now attending a variety of private, parochial, and public high schools, where most of them were holding their own. Some did only average work. A few had a difficult time adjusting and had to work hard to pull up their grades. Still, considering all these students had been so far below average when they first came to Westside Prep, the progress they had made was remarkable.

Somehow people have a hard time accepting the fact that inner-city children can achieve on a higher plane than most schools require. It was precisely that myth that I wanted to shatter. With that in mind, I took on children from the Cabrini-Green housing projects in the summer of 1981.

★   ★   ★

Cabrini-Green is the essence of Chicago's mean streets, a graffiti-scrawled stretch of high-rise public housing where murder, rape, and gang terror are daily events. In March 1981 Cabrini-Green caught nationwide media attention when Mayor Jane Byrne moved into one of the apartments in an effort to curtail the violence and pacify frightened residents.

Trying to keep things cool over the summer, city officials stepped up the police patrols, built a new baseball field to get the children off the streets, and also sponsored a tuition-free Summertime Institute for 140 Cabrini-Green area youngsters, kindergarten through sixth grade.

Mayor Byrne asked Marva to organize the eight-week summer school program. She accepted without hesitation, asking specifically for students who had behavior problems or were reading at least two grades below their age level. This time critics would hardly be able to accuse her of selecting the brightest students.

Marva used the same textbooks and teaching materials she used at her school, not the ones the city school system wanted to provide. She set up the curriculum, prepared the lesson plans, and hired the teachers. There was one catch: her staff had to include five teachers from the public schools, a concession to the Chicago Teachers' Union.

More than two dozen applied. Some of the interviews were brief. One applicant demanded a classroom with windows. Another was dismayed that the Byrd Elementary School, where the program was being held, was not air-conditioned. A third wanted to know how many aides she would have. Others balked when Marva told them they would not be able to sit behind a desk. Needless to say, those teachers weren't hired.

Organizational details were taken care of the day before

the program started, much to the irritation of some teachers who didn't want to show up before the children. Marva refused to waste any class time passing out books and papers. By 8:30 on the first morning Marva and her staff were ready to begin teaching.

Marva was to supervise the seven classrooms. During the first week she spent most of the three-hour daily session with the sixth-graders, the oldest students and the by now chronic non-learners. To see her then was to see the quintessential Marva at work—preacher, flatterer, aphorist, quipster, booster, parent, and teacher.

"Good morning, I love you," Marva greeted the students. "You are all very special students and you are going to learn here . . ." Beginning with an introduction to phonics, she raced excitedly around the room, urging the children to an enthusiasm that matched her own. "Show me a teacher who is dragging," she reminded her staff, "and I'll show you a listless class."

Though it was summer, no one in class was ever allowed to sleep or daydream. "Wait a minute," Marva said, stopping in the middle of an explanation of the vowel reversals in *diary* and *dairy*. "Sit up everybody. Sit up and look alive."

One boy was leaning over his desk, his head resting on his arm. Marva went over to him and gently lifted his head. Nudged out of his nap, he angrily pushed Marva away.

"If you touch me again, I'm gonna kill you!"

"Good, I've lived too long anyway." Marva remained calm.

"Why don't you beat him? His teacher last year always hit him with a stick," a child called from across the room.

"Because that is not the way human beings should treat each other. I am a teacher. I wasn't trained to be a jailer or a disciplinarian. School is not a place where we beat people. It's where we go to learn to have a better life. Beating someone doesn't do any good. When you are finished beating someone, how much better off are you? How much richer are you?"

Marva turned back to the boy. "What's your name, darling?"

He didn't answer.

"Sam, he's Sam," a classmate said.

"Now look, Sam," Marva continued, "you are going to sit up if I have to spray you with cold water. I will not have you drooping and wilting on me. I do not droop and wilt on you. You will learn here. You have no choice."

Standing beside Sam, her hand on his shoulder, she turned to address the whole class. "Some of you are in sixth grade and you can't even read at a first grade level. I'm not saying that to put you down. I'm telling you the facts as they are. When you go back to your regular schools in September, you will be the brightest children in your class."

Marva walked to the front of the room, handing one boy a tissue as she passed him and reminding another to take the pick out of his hair. Pointing to the words she had printed in long lists on the board, Marva explained that the letter *e* at the end of a word makes a middle vowel long. She recited the words and the children echoed: "Rod and rode, pin and pine, cut and cute, sit and site, dim and dime, cub and cube, man and mane, kit and kite, mad and made, pal and pale, fin and fine."

A boy wearing a gold Superman tee-shirt started making faces and laughing and whispering to the child next to him. Both of them giggled. Marva stopped.

"Is it funny when we fail?" she asked. "Is it funny when we have no food? Is it funny when we have no money to go to the doctor?"

Marva glowered at the student who created the distraction. "Is it funny when we haven't got a dollar?" she repeated. The boy shook his head. "Well, then, stop clowning because this is money up here," Marva said, pointing to the vowel sounds on the board.

Moving to the second boy, she asked, "Why are you paying attention to him? Don't grin at him. He's sad. Get on your knees and pray for him. Children who keep clowning do it because they can't do anything else.

"Children, you are foolish to spend school time clowning and grinning. Teachers come in here wearing nice clothes, and they drive away from here in nice cars. They get all that from you, from the public paying their salaries. You pay them to teach. If you just sit there grinning and not learning, you are paying them for nothing."

Taking the arm of the boy in the gold tee-shirt, Marva eased him out of his seat. "Now, let's go to the board, and we'll do these vowel sounds together."

Slowly the boy followed, and with Marva helping him he sounded out the list of words. He strutted back to his desk with an air of success.

Marva told the class to open their readers to the story of *Peter Rabbit* by Beatrix Potter.

"Do we copy the whole story?" asked a girl.

"Copy the story?" Marva was puzzled.

"Sure, we always copy the story and do the questions in the back."

"You don't copy anything from a book. You learn what the book has to teach you. If you are used to copying, you are not used to thinking. You are going to think in here. You are not going to be looking at a picture and filling in a word. You are going to do things that require brains."

Marva gave the children background on the author, telling them that Beatrix Potter grew up in England. "England is in the British Isles. 'England, Ireland, Scotland, and Wales, four little dogs without any tails.' That's how you remember the British Isles." Continuing, Marva told about the author's lonely childhood, reflected in the point of view of her stories. "And what is point of view? It's the attitude an author shows in a story."

Marva highlighted words to watch, giving the pronunciation and the definition. "*Implored* means begged. What did I do if I implored you?"

"You begged," the class said in unison.

"Exert. The *ex* has the sound of *eg*. The *ert* sounds like *zurt*. *Exert* means to try very hard. What does it mean?"

"To try very hard."

"Oh, you are so smart. Now we are going to read a story about a rabbit who was naughty. What happens to people who do bad things?"

"They come to no good," answered a thin girl wearing a long-sleeved blouse.

"So it is better to stop a bad thing before it gets started, isn't it?" As she spoke, Marva walked over to the girl and began rolling up the sleeves of the child's blouse. Leaning down to her ear, Marva whispered that it was too hot to have on long sleeves.

"I want all eyes on the books. Don't lose your place reading. You will get lost in the world that way."

She called on a child to begin the reading of *Peter Rabbit*: "Once upon a time. . . ." When he finished the first few sentences, Marva stopped him to check for comprehension. "Who is this story about?" she asked.

"Rabbits," a chubby boy in the front seat answered.

"There are lots of rabbits. What are these rabbits' names?"

"Aw, this story is taking too long," complained a boy as he banged his book shut.

"All year you have been copying a story out. That is why you have problems with reading. I have read this story at least sixty times. I have been using this book for fourteen years. It's easy for me as a teacher to sit behind a desk and ask you to answer the questions at the end. It is much easier than standing here and asking what everything means. If the story is too long, life is too long. How many of you want to die this minute? You need to take time to learn. How many of you would tell me to stop if I were putting $20 bills on your desk? Well, don't tell me to stop teaching you either. Everything I teach you is like money in the bank."

The children read half the story. Sensing their interest flagging, Marva told them to close their readers and take out Bernard Miles' *Favorite Tales From Shakespeare*. She launched into an introduction to *Macbeth*.

"The witches predict but people determine," Marva said. "Everyone said, 'Oh, Cabrini-Green,' when I told them I was coming here to teach. They tried to predict something. They tried to predict that I would find trouble here. But you determine. You determine what you are going to be and what you are going to make of Cabrini-Green. You can be as great as you want to be. And this neighborhood can be as good or as bad as you want it to be."

A child in the back let out a groan. "If you have a headache or a stomachache, go home. No one pays you for aches and pains. People will only pay you to do work."

"Is it almost lunchtime?" blurted another child.

"Are you children worried about getting one free carton of milk and one free sandwich from the city, when I am teaching you so that you can get your own milk and food your whole life?"

Marva stood beside the child who had asked about lunch. "I love you," she told him, "and I am not going to go home and talk about you behind your back. I am going to tell you the way it is right to your face. See the torn shirt you are wearing? Without an education you will always have a torn shirt. I am going to bring you a shirt tomorrow, and I expect you to act like someone who wears good clothes, starting now. Right now."

The class read part of *Macbeth,* saving the rest for the next day. They went on to work on synonyms. At a quarter of twelve Marva began passing out homework sheets.

"I already got one," said the boy with the Superman shirt, clowning again.

"Do not say 'I already got one.' Say 'I have one.' But don't tell me to stop giving you homework. I asked you before would you tell me to stop giving you money? You know, you are a handsome boy. You don't have to stretch your mouth back like that in a grin. You were born to win, so don't make yourself a loser."

Hearing papers rustling, Marva looked up and saw some of the boys folding their homework and shoving it into their back pockets.

"Don't crumple your papers into little pieces," Marva said. "Big people take their papers home flat. How would it look if some lawyer or executive brought important papers home looking like that? All of you sit down and straighten those papers. You all have such a poor image of yourselves. Be proud of your work. Be proud of what you do."

As the children were leaving the room, Marva intercepted the boy in the Superman shirt. Putting her arms on his shoulders, she said, "You are in sixth grade and your reading score is 1.1. I don't hide your scores in a folder. I tell them to you so you know what you have to do. Now your clowning days are over. You haven't done a thing to me. You've done it to you. If I have to love you more than you love yourself, I'll do that."

Marva's biggest problem at Cabrini-Green was not the children but some of the teachers. Some had no enthusiasm. They watched the clock, let children fall asleep, and acted as though it was killing them to move. One woman quit after four days, telling Marva it was just too difficult: she was too tired and uncomfortable standing all morning. Marva had to replace a second teacher, a woman who claimed to be a reading specialist. As it turned out, she didn't know a thing about phonics. Marva discovered she was giving her students busy-work instead. On one occasion Marva walked into this woman's classroom and found her assigning a composition on "My Trip To A Foreign Country." She expected the students to write about traveling to a foreign country when some of them had never traveled more than a few miles beyond Cabrini-Green. Worse than inappropriate, the topic was boring. It was standard who-cares fare, like the traditional "How I Spent My Summer Vacation."

Marva wasn't about to let the project fail because of poor teachers, so she brought in reinforcements. Ella McCoy came in to help supervise. Even Erika did some tutoring. She walked up and down the aisles supplying a synonym or an antonym, assisting a younger child to read aloud and offering encouragement. One of the eight-year-old boys said the work was too hard and he couldn't do it; Erika looked at him sternly and said, "Yes, you can. There isn't anything you can't do if you try. You're the brightest child in the world."

Over the course of the summer a lot of children dropped out of the Summertime Institute. But by the end of eight weeks the children who had remained in the program improved their skills. They had been given a test of vocabulary, spelling, and reading comprehension at the beginning of the session, and their post-program scores all showed increases. In a matter of weeks some of the students had jumped to readers a grade level higher.

On the last day of the program the assembly hall at Byrd School was crowded with media and city officials as Mayor Byrne presided over the awards ceremony, passing out certificates of achievement to eighty-seven students. Later the press surrounded several children.

"What did you learn?" a TV correspondent asked.

"Norse gods and Greek gods," answered one boy.

"I learned Shakespeare, *Macbeth,* reading comprehension, and dictation," said another. "Learning was fun."

"I'm going to keep on studying and learning words," eight-year-old Dorian Hudson told a newspaper reporter. And an eleven-year-old girl said, "I want to take some of what I learned back to my own school and teach it to others."

When the reporter asked the girl what her name was, the child answered, "Chatapne Calvin. There is a long mark over the vowel *e.*"

Epilogue

In September 1981, Westside Preparatory School moved into its own permanent facilities—two adjoining one-story brick office buildings that blended in with the factories, warehouses, and storefront churches along Chicago Avenue on the outskirts of Garfield Park. From its facade, no one could tell it was a school. But everyone knew it was there just the same.

It was Marva's school, but it seemed to belong to the whole neighborhood. People saw it as a beacon of hope on the West Side, a stand against the transience and waste that had plagued the area for nearly two decades. And they were proud of it. How many schools in the middle of a ghetto had ever been a model for achievement? In Marva, the children of the neighborhood had someone to look up to who was not a hustler, entertainer, or sports figure. She and Westside Prep were abiding proof that a person didn't have to be a Dr. J or a Lena Horne to make it.

Not everyone saw her that way. Marva had her share of scoffers and detractors. Most of her critics were within the teaching profession. Her visibility and her incriminations against the educational system understandably made her a prime target. From Albert Shanker, President of the United Federation of Teachers, to her former colleagues at Delano, critics took issue with Marva and with the "success claims" of her students. They accused Marva of exaggerating her students' accomplishments, of fixing her pupils' test scores, and of raising her school's average test scores by getting rid of poor achievers. There were also charges that she was running an educational sweatshop, and that her students were not learning to read, think, and discuss the great works of literature, but that they were merely memorizing passages by rote.

The more the press and the public extolled Marva, the more vocal her critics became. Both the praise and the criticism built to a crescendo following the airing of a television docudrama about Marva in December 1981. *The Marva Collins Story* touched off a backlash from some Chicago public school teachers who felt the movie was an affront to them and to public education in general. In defense, they set out to discredit her.

Two months later, a newspaper published by an organization of substitute teachers printed an exposé charging that all the publicity surrounding Marva and Westside Prep was the result of a "carefully constructed" five-year "media hoax" that was "aimed at further crippling public education here and around the country." The article alleged that press coverage of Marva had been inflated and misleading. It claimed that Marva's school was not taking the rejects of the public school system but that Westside Prep's student body was made up of middle-class children handpicked for high ability. At the same time, it questioned Marva's acceptance of CETA money when all along she had been an outspoken critic of federal aid.

A few of the local media jumped on the story, attacking Marva with the same hyperbole they had used in praising her. They went after her personality—depicting her as egotistical vindictive, and quick-tempered—and they began looking for the proverbial skeletons in her closet, treating her as if she were a high-profile politician. In an interview, one newscaster went so far as to ask whether Marva was "a sinister woman." Another columnist, angered by Marva's statements that "money isn't the answer to educational problems" and by her endorsement of publicly funded tuition vouchers, accused Marva of "playing into the hands of the right wing" and allowing herself to be used by politicians to support school funding cuts.

Two radio and television reporters hit the hardest with a litany of allegations. Quoting a handful of disgruntled parents and a former Westside Prep teacher, they contended that Marva had misrepresented her credentials; that she had plagiarized another educator's ideas for an opinion column she wrote for the *Sun-Times;* that Westside Prep teachers mistreated students; that Marva refused to release her students' test scores for verification; and that she pressured parents for tuition and barred from the school pupils whose parents had not paid the monthly fees.

Because of Marva's enormous reputation, the controversy became a national story covered by *The New York Times, The Washington Post, The Wall Street Journal,* and *Newsweek.* But all of the news reports were not negative. In fact some journalists defended Marva. Chicago *Sun-Times* columnist Mike Royko called the complaints against Marva "nitpicking—the kinds of gripes that might be kicked around during a teachers' coffee break. But nothing worth screaming headlines." He added that the "complaints didn't alter the basic fact that Collins was and is getting the kinds of results in her school that would delight most public school principals."

Correspondent Morley Safer, who did the *60 Minutes* report on Marva in 1979, stood by his original reporting. He told *Newsweek* the critical stories aired on the Chicago outlet of his own network were "outrageous" and "loaded with inaccuracies" and he said, "I'm convinced that Marva Collins is one hell of a teacher."

The Wall Street Journal saw the controversy as "a story about the politics of education in this country, especially education in the inner city, where the public schools have failed miserably. Mrs. Collins's private success invited reaction because it became a reproach to that failure." The article concluded that "it's clear her critics have more on their minds than her personal foibles. They know that her success showed that poor black children can learn outside the public schools—with little money and without the bureaucracy."

Newsweek summed it up by stating that perhaps Marva had taught the nation at least two lessons. "The trivial one is that not even the heroes of television docu-dramas are guaranteed to be free of human flaws. The important one is how much trust, faith, and hope the nation will invest in a teacher who holds out the simple promise, once taken for granted, of teaching kids to read."

Initially, Marva refused to respond to the charges. She told reporters, "My best defense is what I do. These children can read." But friends and supporters urged her to answer her critics and eventually she did so on a special two-part *Phil Donahue Show*. Meanwhile, Westside Prep parents and community supporters held rallies for Marva, and newspapers received letters to the editor calling the criticism "a witchhunt."

The controversy only lasted a few weeks. When it was over, Marva was battle-fatigued, yet she and Westside Prep were unscathed. The school still had a full enrollment and a long, growing waiting list. She still had enormous public support and legions of admirers. As far as most people were concerned, the only thing the uproar had proven was that Marva was human and not a superwoman—which was what she had maintained all along. In an interview with *The New York Times* she said: "I've never said I'm a superteacher, a miracle worker, all those names they gave me. It's unfair to expect me to live up to it. I'm just a teacher."

For all their attempts to tear down Marva's image, her critics had never once questioned her commitment to teaching. And it was only through that commitment that she cared to be judged. The sneers and insinuations would never diminish her real achievement: Children who were educated, motivated, confident, and determined to make their own way in the world. They were her legacy.

Questions From Parents

Parents, you are the first teachers your children experience. You are also the most influential teachers they will ever have; everything you say and do is a model for what they will ultimately become. Therefore, the way you interact with your children has a tremendous impact on what they learn, both in and out of the classroom.

Over the years I have consistently been asked certain questions by parents who take their children's education seriously. What follows are the most frequently asked questions from parents and my answers.

QUESTION: How can I best prepare my children for the day they enter their first classroom?

ANSWER: The child that gets a head start at home is a step ahead when he or she begins school. Create a climate where curiosity is encouraged and learning is fun. If your children are naturally inquisitive, don't discourage them. Never shut them up or say, "Stop asking so many questions." Curiosity is essential for learning, and questions are a sign of an active, inquiring mind. Rather than squelch their inquisitiveness, compliment them for asking intelligent questions. Remember, if they can't talk to you, who can they talk to?

Even when your child is very young you can transform ordinary activities into learning experiences. For example:

- Teach your child shapes such as circles and squares. You can purchase inexpensive books in the supermarket to help you with this activity.
- Have your children accompany you when shopping, and introduce them to numbers and units of measurement.
- When going up or down stairs, have your children count the steps.
- Play games of rhyming words with your children.
- Turn car trips into learning experiences: categorize objects you pass and count them, e.g. how many red cars, how many churches, etc.
- Always speak in correct English and complete sentences, and insist that your child do so as well.
- When reading stories and nursery rhymes, ask your child questions to cultivate the habit of *active* listening. For example, when reading "Jack and Jill," ask questions such as, "What were the names of the children who went up the hill?" "Who went up the hill first?" "Who fell down?" You can also use stories to stimulate their imaginations by asking provocative questions such as, "What do you think they saw on the way up the hill?" or "Where do you think their parents were?"

QUESTION: How can I be sure my children learn to read?

ANSWER: Perhaps the most important thing you can do is to set a good example by making sure your children see you read often. In addition, read something to your children every day, no matter how old they are. Even adolescents need and often want you to read with them, or to have them read to you. Reading to, or with, them is a good way to discover their strengths and weaknesses. Follow the reading sessions with questions, such as, "What happened in that story?" and "What do you think will happen next?"

With very young children, put pictures on cards with the words that describe the picture. Show the child the picture of a duck, for example, and say the word and spell it. Do this every day until the child masters the process, then begin to encourage the child to say and spell the word without the pictorial clue.

Play vowel games with your child. Say words such as cat, fig, pot, pet, rid, red, rut, etc. and have the child name the vowel in each word. This activity not only improves reading skills, but speaking skills as well.

When your children are old enough to read on their own, insist that they set aside at least thirty minutes a day to read in a quiet place and take the time to discuss with them what they have read.

Use a dictionary to teach your child three new words a day. A rich and varied vocabulary is essential for good readers and speakers. Make sure your children are familiar with, and use, more than one word to describe the same idea. For example, instead of letting them say *big* all the time, supply synonyms such as *huge, enormous,* and *gargantuan.*

When engaged in everyday activities, teach your children words and how to spell them. For example, when cooking, ask them to name the first letter in the word *pot, corn,* and *steak.*

Read challenging, positive stories that instill values and morals, not banal books with no instructive value beyond "See Dick run." For example, *Petunia* teaches the importance of learning to read and think for yourself. *The Pied Piper of Hamelin* teaches the importance of keeping your word. The story of *Pierre* teaches children to care about life.

QUESTION: What can I do to help my child develop positive self-esteem?

ANSWER: Building self-esteem and confidence in your children is one of the most important things a parent can do. You can build self-esteem by continuously reminding your children that they are special, intelligent, worthwhile individuals. Never be afraid to hug them or tell them that you love them. Don't take it for granted that they know how you feel; tell them consistently and often.

Frequently, parents single out only the things their children do wrong. We should also praise them for the things they do *right*. For example, "I like the way you cooperated when getting dressed this morning," or "You did such a good job helping out with the dishes tonight."

Every day, tell your children what you like about them, and ask them what they like about themselves. Having done that, you can then go into the behavior you would like them to change or improve—and ask them what they would like to change about themselves.

When you send your children off to school in the morning, boost their self-images with encouraging words like, "Be all that you can be today" and "Remember, whatever happens, you are a winner and I love you very much."

When your children are faced with a difficult task, never say things like, "You can't do that," or "You're too small to do that." Let them try what they want to do. If they don't succeed, praise them for their efforts and say, "You did a wonderful job, but let me give you some help."

When your children make mistakes with their homework, or misuse a word, or add two figures incorrectly, don't just say, "That's wrong." Instead, say "That was a good try, but it wasn't quite right."

QUESTION: How can I discipline my children without damaging their self-esteem?

ANSWER: Every parent has to correct their children or reprimand them, but the way you do it is crucial. Discipline them in a loving manner; never demean, degrade, or humiliate. If your patience has been tried to the limit, say "I love you very much, but right now I do not care to talk to you" or "I love you all the time, but right now I am disappointed with your behavior."

Instead of reprimanding them in a purely negative way, try "You are much too bright to do that. I must punish you, but I want you to remember that I love you all the time, even though I disagree with this behavior."

If your child has a temper tantrum, try saying, "I don't know that person who is acting out right now, but I am sure that my bright, well-behaved child will return very soon, so I'll just leave the room until he comes back."

Even discipline can be used as a learning experience. Rather than spewing forth negatives you might later regret, if your children are old enough to write and spell, have them take a sheet of paper and write down ten reasons why they are too special to have exhibited such behavior. Then hang the paper in a prominent place as a reminder to the children.

QUESTION: What can I do if my child is having a problem at school?

ANSWER: Remember, there is safety and strength in numbers. If your child's school has a parents organization, become an active member. If it does not, consider organizing one yourself. At the very least, stay in touch with the parents of your child's classmates. Discuss with them what goes on in the school and do some research to determine exactly what kind of education you want for your children. Parental pressure does make a difference.

If a problem arises with a particular teacher, bear in mind that confronting the teacher directly can cause problems for your child, who has to be in that classroom every day. Instead, see the principal. Also, check to see if other parents are having similar problems and, if they are, go to the principal together. Whether in a group or alone, have the principal agree not to divulge the identities of the parents who issued the complaint.

However, you should not wait until a problem arises to pay close attention to your child's schooling. Parental involvement should be routine from the first day in school. One good way to keep well-informed is to have your children tell you every day three things they learned at school.

And don't just look for the negatives. If your child's teacher is particularly dedicated, let her know you appreciate her efforts. You might even organize other parents to reward excellent teachers with prizes or awards. Use them as examples to give other teachers the incentive to excel.

QUESTION: What should I do if I'm told my child is hyperactive or has a learning disability?

ANSWER: Get a second opinion, and if necessary a third and a fourth. Those conditions are often misdiagnosed. Many children are told they have learning disorders when the only thing wrong is how they are being taught. With proper teaching of the basics, a large number of children who are thought to have learning disorders develop quite normal skills.

With respect to hyperactivity, too many children are incorrectly labeled. In many cases, the children are very bright and energetic, but poorly motivated. Some are simply smart enough to finish an assignment before their classmates. Bored and restless, they are called *disruptive,* or are mistaken for hyperactive, when they are just being kids. Sadly, many of these children are then sedated with drugs, often turning into little zombies as a result. In an age where we are urging kids to "just say no" it is astonishing that we should so freely dispense drugs to control their behavior.

Questions From Teachers

Teachers, you are the infantry in the battle to improve education. Yours is a difficult job, but it can also be the most rewarding of all. You have the ability to be Pygmalions in your classrooms; you can mold those young, impressionable minds into the best possible adults they can be.

Sometimes, we worry too much about the system and what others are doing instead of pursuing excellence in our own corner. Despite all the systemic problems—the bad homes, the low budgets, the poor pay, and lack of respect for the jobs you do—every teacher can strive for excellence in his or her classroom and make a real difference in their students' lives. And each little point of light becomes a greater ray through example.

QUESTION: What would you say is the key to your success with children?

ANSWER: I believe in my children. If a teacher believes her students cannot learn, then her students will not learn. If a teacher believes that children from underprivileged homes cannot achieve very much, then those children will not achieve very much. On the other hand, if you create a positive environment for your students, you will see miraculous things take place. If you tell your students that they are bright, intelligent winners, they will act like bright, intelligent winners.

At Westside Preparatory School, we rinse out the negative brainwashing and replace it with positive reinforcement, consistently telling our pupils that they are unique and special, that they were born to win, that they come from *royal blood,* and that there is nothing they can't do. We mean it, and because we believe in them, the students come to believe in themselves.

The importance of the teachers' attitudes and expectations has been demonstrated in laboratory studies. Harvard psychologist Robert Rosenthal randomly divided grade-school students into two equal groups, carefully matched by age, sex, ethnic background and IQ scores. Rosenthal then told the teachers that one group of students consisted of fast learners, while the second group was merely average although both groups were the same. A year later, when he compared the achievements of the two groups, Rosenthal found that the supposed *fast learners* far surpassed the *average* students. The difference in their academic success was attributed to the expectations of the teachers; they treated one group as if it were actually outstanding and the students performed accordingly. Here are some ways to reinforce your students' belief in themselves.

When a child gets something wrong, don't simply redmark the paper; take the student aside and help him get it right. Remember, if he knew how to do it correctly, he would have done so in the first place.

Make sure students know that if they can't make mistakes, they can't make anything. Create a positive classroom ambience so that your students know it is more courageous to make a mistake than to play it safe by not responding.

Use the word *proofread* when going over their writing, rather than merely correcting errors.

Don't be afraid to admit when you are wrong. Students should know that even teachers make mistakes and that no one can have all the answers all the time. Encourage them to proofread what you write on the blackboard.

Protect yourself from any surrounding contaminating negativity. If your fellow teachers have a dim view of their students, stay away from the faculty lounge, where your expectations might be lowered by jaded naysayers.

QUESTION: How can I be a better teacher?

ANSWER: These are ten basic principles of good teaching:

Faith. Just as faith moves mountains, faith in your students can move them to heights never imagined.

Harvesting. Make each and every day a great student harvest. Refuse to let your pupils fail.

Faithfulness. Insist that your students faithfully perform every little act. The way they enter the room, the way they keep their desks, the way they head their papers, the way they dress—all such things should be done with élan. Getting the little things right makes the bigger things easier as well.

Don't be a Judas. Never betray the confidence of your students. You are their teacher some of the time, but you should be their friend *all* of the time. So, for example, never write negative comments on their records that could damage them in the future; instead, take the time to polish every mind until the luster shines through. Today's problem student might become tomorrow's leader.

Teach even the least of them. Teach as if every child, regardless of his or her background and family conditions, is the son or daughter of a Harvard or Yale graduate.

Teach because you can't help it, not for what you are paid. Teach with passion. Teach with devotion, dedication, and a steel-trap determination that will not allow your students to plunge into mediocrity or failure.

Go into the schools and spread your gospel. Teach so well and so diligently that even the most recalcitrant student drops his or her indifference and becomes motivated.

Teach as if your life depended on it. Positive attitudes are catching. When you make a lesson come alive with what I call *hot teaching,* every child becomes a winner.

Come as a teacher who is there to save students, not fail them. Any ordinary teacher can fail a student. Superior teachers make the poor students good and the good students superior. If others have declared a child a failure, dare to say, "I will be the one to save you, child."

Never give up. If at first you don't succeed with a child, keep trying, knowing that one more effort can make all the difference.

QUESTION: What is your view of current reading materials?

ANSWER: At Westside Preparatory School, we have always used a distinctive reading list. We believe in challenging the students and in having them read meaningful works that are rich in life lessons. We can't expect children to read, write, and think critically if we expose them to such banalities as: "See the ball. See the big ball." Of course they see the ball; a huge picture of it is there on the page. We have our students read stories that have instructed people of various cultures for centuries. If you use them properly, classics such as *Macbeth* enable you to teach not only reading, but morality and values as well. You will find our reading list in this book.

QUESTION: How do you discipline your students?

ANSWER: I believe in discipline. However, I believe that discipline should be instilled with a loving touch, or else it leads to bitterness and resentment, not maturity. Here are some guideposts to developing a disciplined classroom.

Try to prevent discipline problems by making friends with all students and winning their trust. Find something positive to say to every student every day, such as "What nice gym shoes" or "I missed you yesterday." Rather than eat with fellow teachers or staff, sit with your students— either the entire class or with a different child each day.

Offer to help the slower students with their work. It is usually the slow students who create havoc in the classroom and make it difficult for teachers to give the most to other children. Give those slower students extra teaching time after school or before school.

When a pupil misbehaves, instead of having her write punitive lines such as "I will not chew gum in class," have her write a composition or deliver a three-minute speech on the etymology of gum. Additionally, ask the entire class the question "Why aren't you going to misbehave in class?" Then have them respond in unison, "Because I am too bright to waste my time." After you teach them this routine, they will respond properly without being reminded.

When you have to enforce discipline, try to do it in a way that does not just punish, but instructs. For example, if the class ridicules a fellow student who makes a mistake, tell the one who is being derided that he or she is very courageous. Explain that it takes much more courage to speak out and risk being wrong than it does to laugh at other people. If a student does not pay attention, say "I am not here to entertain you. There is a lesson here, and anyone who does not pay attention to these lessons is surely headed for trouble. I love you all the time, even though I may correct you sometimes."

QUESTION: How can we teach well with so many students in the classroom?

ANSWER: A high student-teacher ratio can certainly make things difficult, but it can also be used as an excuse. A good teacher can teach fifty students effectively; a poor teacher can do a bad job with ten.

QUESTION: Can you tell us about your teacher-training workshops?

ANSWER: The Westside Preparatory School National Training Institute has been very successful. Teachers, principals, and superintendents from all over the country have attended, many of whom work in well-funded school systems. The workshops, which we hold once a month, last three days. On the first day, participants sit in on our classes and observe our teachers in action. The next two days involve intensive workshops in teaching methods, curriculum design, and related subjects. Anyone interested can write the school for an application. We accept sixty to eighty participants per month.

QUESTION: What can we do to improve the quality of education in our country?

ANSWER: We have been labeled *a nation at risk* because of the magnitude of our educational problems. The crisis is so big and the causes so complex that it would be ludicrous to propose an easy formula. However, in my experience, I have come to believe that certain steps must be taken. These steps are some of the most important ones.

Inspire more of our brightest college undergraduates to pursue careers in teaching. This action would require not only better pay for teachers, but a strong message from citizens and government that we respect and value the role that teachers play in our society. Our schools should be hiring the best of the crop, not the dullest graduates who cannot find employment in other fields.

Rethink and restructure the way teachers are trained. Pedagogy today does not relate to the reality of the classroom. Teachers should spend more time with real students in real classrooms during their training, so they get a taste of what day-to-day teaching is all about.

Make greater use of the educational potential of television, particularly for students with special needs. But, at the same time, we must stop looking for new gimmicks and high-tech devices and start making the most of the innate tools we already have: the natural curiosity of our students, our own brains, and a determination to give our children the best possible experience in the classroom.

Extend the school day so it runs from 8:00 to 4:00, and hold Saturday sessions for poor achievers.

Pay teachers according to performance. Students drop out because elementary teachers did not give them the motivation or the fundamental tools they need to do well in later grades. Teachers should be held responsible for children who read below grade level at the end of the third grade.

Increase the amount of reading and writing in classrooms. Children should write a composition every day beginning in kindergarten, and they should make regular oral presentations, speaking standard English in grammatically correct sentences. In addition, make greater use of oral examinations, giving attention to pronunciation, inflection, emphasis, and pause.

Develop uniform curriculum and achievement standards for the country as a whole, prepared by excellent teachers, not by theoreticians who have never taught a day in their lives. Also, legislate a national compulsory education act that requires all students to remain in school until they master the ninth grade curriculum—not according to age, but according to ability.

Retrain or retest all teachers every two years. This step would keep teachers learning and prevent them from settling into complacency. Also, create more opportunities for new teachers to learn from experienced, successful colleagues.

Require students to tutor others who are younger or less advanced. This requirement would benefit both groups and drive home an important lesson: we all must give something back.

Create schools that are truly supportive of children. We must teach the total child, do justice to his or her full potential, and make the school day something to look forward to. As long as the average student hates school, we have failed our children.

Recommended Phonics Books

Foltzer, Monica *Professor Phonics Gives Sound Advice.*
Cincinnati: St. Ursula Academy, 1965, 6th ed., 1976.
_____ . *A Sound Track to Reading.* Cincinnati: St. Ursula
Academy, 1976.

For information on phonics programs and materials,
contact:

The Reading Reform Foundation
949 Market Street, Suite 436
Tacoma, WA 98402

Reading List
for Children Ages Four, Five, and Six

Title	Author
Pierre	Maurice Sendak
Chicken Soup and Rice	Maurice Sendak
Tales from Shakespeare	Charles Lamb and Mary Lamb
You Will Go to the Moon	Ira Freeman
Twenty-Three Tales by Leo Tolstoy	Leo Tolstoy
Fairy Tales and Fables by Leo Tolstoy	Leo Tolstoy
Grimm's Fairy Tales	Wilhelm and Jacob Grimm
Russian Fairy Tales	Pantheon Books (publisher)
The Wonderful Story of Henry Sugar and Six More	Roald Dahl
The Silver Pony	Lynd Ward
Cricket Magazine	Open Court Pub. (publisher)
The Marvelous Misadventures of Sabastian	Lloyd Alexander
The Prince and the Pauper	Mark Twain
Hitty: Her First One Hundred Years	Rachel Field
The Royal Book of Ballet	Shirley Goulden
Stories of India	Dolch Series (publisher)
Stories of England	Dolch Series (publisher)
The Secret Garden	Frances H. Burnett
Famous Poems of Henry Wadsworth Longfellow	Doubleday (publisher)
Charlotte's Web	E. B. White

Title	Author
The Arbuthnot Anthology Children's Literature	Zena Sutherland
The Firebird	Viking Press (publisher)
Castles and Dragons	Crowell (publisher)
Pilgrim's Progress Retold for Children	Laurence Morris
The Water Buffalo	Pearl S. Buck
Mike's House	Julia Sauer
Rain Drop Splash	Alvin R. Tresselt
Hi, Mr. Robin	Alvin R. Tresselt
Spring is Here	Lois Lenski
Summer Day	Lois Lenski
I Like Winter	Lois Lenski
The Wonderful Egg	Dahlov Ipcar
Against Time	Roderic Jefferies
The Animal	Abingdon Books (publisher)
Among the Dolls	William Sleator
Animals You Will Never Forget	Readers Digest Press (publisher)
The Bad Times of Irma Baumlien	Carol Ryrie Brink
Baker's Hawk	Jack Bickham
Benjamin the True	Claudia Paley
The Best Christmas Present	Barbara Robinson
The Cay	Theodore Taylor
The Crack in the Wall	Karl H. Meyer
The Fiddler on High Lonesome	Brinton Turkle

Reading List
for Westside
Preparatory School

Books without publishers are available in many editions. Books marked with an asterisk are no longer in print but may be available at your library.

Adams, Russell L., *Great Negroes, Past & Present,* 3d revised edition, Afro-American.

Adler, Irving, *Mathematics,* Golden Press.*

Aesop, *Fables.*

Aldington, Richard, *Oscar Wilde Selected Works,* Arden Library.

Alexander, Lloyd, *The Marvelous Misadventures of Sebastian,* Dutton.

Alighieri, Dante, *Divine Comedy.*

Aristophanes, *The Plays of Aristophanes.*

Armstrong, Sperry, *Call of Courage.**

Asimov, Isaac, *Inside the Atom,* Harper & Row.

Aurelius, Marcus, *Meditations.*

Austen, Jane, *Pride and Prejudice.*

Bach, Richard, *Jonathan Livingston Seagull.*

Bamberger, Richard, *Physics Through Experiment,* Sterling.

Barr, George, *Research Ideas for Young Scientists,* McGraw-Hill.

Bendick, Jeanne, *The First Book of Time*, Franklin Watts.*

Blackwood, Paul, *Push and Pull: The Story of Energy*, McGraw-Hill.*

Bleeker, Sonia, *The Masai: Herders of East Africa*, William Morrow.*

Bond, Michael, *A Bear Called Paddington*, Houghton Mifflin.

Bontemps, Arna, *Frederick Douglass: Slave-Fighter-Freeman*, Alfred A. Knopf.*

Bowie, Walter, *Bible Stories for Boys & Girls*.*

Brent, Robert, *The Golden Book of Chemistry Experiments*, Western Publishers.

Braidwood, Robert J., *Archeologists and What They Do*, Franklin Watts.*

Bronowski, Jacob & Selsam, *Biography of an Atom*, Harper & Row.

Bronte, Emily, *Wuthering Heights*.

Buehr, Walter, *The First Book of Machines*, Franklin Watts.

Bulfinch, Thomas, *Book of Myths*, Macmillan.

Bunyon, John, *Pilgrim's Progress*.

Carson, Rachel, *The Sea Around Us*, New American Library.

Cervantes, *Don Quixote*.

Chaucer, Geoffrey, *The Canterbury Tales*.

Chekhov, Anton. *Complete Plays*.

Clarke, Arthur, *The Challenge of the Sea*, Holt, Rinehart & Winston.

Cleary, Beverly, *The Mouse & The Motorcycle*, William Morrow.

Cleator, P. E., *Exploring the World of Archeology*, Children's Press.

Clymer, Eleanor, *The Second Greatest Invention; The Search for the First Farmers*, Holt, Rinehart & Winston.

Colum, Padraic, *The Children of Odin*, Macmillan.

Cottrell, Leonard, *Land of the Pharaohs*, World Publishers.

Cousteau, Jacques & Frederic Dumas, *The Silent World*, Nick Lyons Books.

De LaFontaine, Jean, *Fables of LaFontaine.*

Dickens, Charles, *Great Expectations; The Old Curiosity Shop; David Copperfield; Bleak House.*

Dickinson, Alice, *The First Book of Plants,* Franklin Watts.*

Dostoyevsky, Fyodor, *The Brothers Karamasov; Crime and Punishment.*

Drisko, Clark, *Unfinished March.**

Dunbar, Paul L., *The Complete Poems of Paul Laurence Dunbar,* Dodd.

Eaton, Jeanette, *Marcus and Narcissa Whitman,* Harcourt Brace Jovanovich.*

Edel, Abraham, *Aristotle,* University of North Carolina Press.

Emerson, Ralph Waldo, *The Portable Emerson.*

Epstein, Sam & Beryl, *Harriet Tubman, Guide to Freedom,* Garrard.

Faulkner, William, *Light in August.*

Felton, Harold W., *Nat Love, Negro Cowboy,* Dodd, Mead.*

Field, Rachel, *Hitty, Her First Hundred Years,* Macmillan.

Flauber, *Life of Thoreau.*

Fleming, Ian, *Chitty, Chitty, Bang, Bang;* Amerion Ltd.

Foster, Genevieve, *Augustus Caesar's World 44 B.C. to A.D. 14,* Charles Scribner's Sons.*

Franklin, Benjamin, *The Autobiography of Benjamin Franklin.*

Freeman, Ira & Mae, *The Story of Chemistry,* Random House.

Golding, William, *Lord of the Flies.*

Gallant, Roy A., *Exploring the Universe,* Doubleday.

Goldsmith, Ilse, *Anatomy for Children,* Dover.

Goldston, Robert C., *Legend of the Cid.**

Gregor, Arthur S., *The Adventures of Man: His Evolution from Prehistory to Civilization,* Macmillan.*

Gunther, John, *Death Be Not Proud,* Harper & Row.

Harte, Bret, *The Luck of the Roaring Camp,* Jamestown.

Harrison, George Russell, *The First Book of Light,* Franklin Watts.

Haviland, Virginia, *Favorite Fairy Tales Told Around the World,* Little, Brown.

Henry, O., *The Gift of the Magi.*

Hardy, Thomas, *The Return of the Native.*

Hogben, Lancelot, *The Wonderful Book of Energy,* Doubleday.

Homer, *The Odyssey* (do background on Homer first; explain the term *odyssey,* which now means long voyage)

Hugo, Victor, *Les Miserables.*

Huxley, Aldous, *Brave New World.*

Heyerdahl, Thor, *Kon-Tiki,* Books, Inc.

Irving, Washington, *Rip Van Winkle; The Legend of Sleepy Hollow.*

Judson, Clara Ingram, *Andrew Carnegie.**

Juster, Norton, *The Phantom Tollbooth,* Random House.

Knight, David C., *The First Book of Air,* Franklin Watts.*

Knight, Eric, *Lassie, Come Home,* Dell.

Kohn, Bernice, *The Peaceful Atom,* Prentice-Hall.*

Kosinski, Jerzy, *The Painted Bird,* Bantam.

Krylov, Ivan, *Krylov's Fables,* Hyperion.

Lamb, Charles, *Tales from Shakespeare,* New American Library.

Lee, Harper, *To Kill a Mockingbird,* Warner Books.

Leonard, William E., *Aesop & Hyssop* (Fables in verse), Open Court.*

Lindgren, Astrid, *Pippi Longstocking; Pippi Goes on Board.*

London, Jack, *White Fang.*

Lowie, Robert H., *Indians of the Plains,* University of Nebraska Press.

Mandell, Muriel, *Physics Experiments for Children,* Dover.

Marlowe, Christopher, *Dr. Faustus.*

Morgan, Alfred, *First Chemistry Book for Boys & Girls*, Charles Scribner's Sons.

Mead, Margaret, *Anthropologists and What They Do*, Franklin Watts.*

McCloskey, Robert, *The Canterberg Tales*, Penguin.

Mullin, Virginia L., *Chemistry Experiments for Children*, Dover.

Murasaki, Lady, *The Tale of Genji*, Random House.

North, Sterling, *The Wolfing*, Scholastic.

Orwell, George, *Animal Farm; 1984*, New American Library.

Olbracht, Ivan, *Indian Fables*, Paul Hamlyn.*

Peare, Catherine Owens, *Helen Keller Story*, Harper J.

Plato, *Five Dialogues*, Hackett.

Plutarch, *Plutarch's Lives*.

Poe, Edgar Allan, *Ligeia*.

Potok, Chaim, *My Name Is Asher Lev*, Fawcett.

Rabelais, Francois, *Gargantua & Pantagruel*, Penguin.

Rawlings, Marjorie, *The Yearling*, Macmillan.

Reeves, James, *Fables from Aesop*, Bedrick Books.

Rogers, J. A., *World's Great Men of Color*, volumes I, II, Macmillan.

Rollins, Charlemae H., *They Showed the Way: Forty Negro Leaders*, Crowell Junior Books, Harper J.

Scott, Walter, *Quentin Durward; Ivanhoe*, Airmont.

Seldes, George, *The Great Quotations*, Lyle Stuart.

Serwer, Blauche, *Let's Steal the Moon; Ancient Folktales from Around the World*, Shapolsky.

Sophocles, *Oedipus the King*.

Spenser, Edmund, *Saint George & the Dragon*.

Stevenson, Robert Louis, *Treasure Island*.

Scherman, Katherine, *The Slave Who Freed Haiti: The Story of Tousaint Louverture*, Random House.*

Tennyson, Alfred, *Poems of Tennyson,* Houghton Mifflin.

Thoreau, Henry David, *The Portable Thoreau* (Essays); *Walden.*

Tolstoy, Leo, *Fables & Fairy Tales* (Ann Dunnigan, translator), New American Library.

Tolstoy, Leo, *War and Peace.*

Twain, Mark, *Puddin' Head Wilson; The Prince & the Pauper; A Connecticut Yankee in King Arthur's Court* (explain the word *pseudonym* and that Mark Twain, George Eliot, and others wrote under a pseudonym).

Vivian, Charles, *Science Experiments & Amusements for Children,* Dover.

Voltaire, Francois, *Candide* and *Memnon.*

Von Loon, Hendrich Willem, *The Story of Mankind,* Liveright.*

Williams, Jay, *Song of Roland.**

Wilson, Mitchell, *The Human Body,* Golden Press.*

Wise, William, *The Two Reigns of Tutankhamen,* G. P. Putnam's Sons.*

Wohlrabe, Raymond, *Crystals,* J. B. Lippincott.*

Wyler, Rose, *First Book of Weather.*

Poetry

Children should be encouraged to memorize famous poems of their choice, for example: "Abou Ben Adhem" by James Henry Leigh Hunt, "House by the Side of the Road" by Sam W. Foss, "If" by Rudyard Kipling, "Invictus" by William Ernest Henley, "Keep a-Going" by Frank Slanton. These poems can be found in *101 Famous Poems.*

Title	Author
101 Famous Poems, Contemporary Books. (These should be used as daily readings just as basic readers. Far too many schools deprive children of the opportunity for reading good poetry.)	Roy J. Cook (editor)

Library of Poetry and Song, Ayer.	William Cullen Bryant (editor)
A Galaxy of Verse, M. Evans.	Louis Untermeyer (editor)
Edgar Allan Poe's Selected Stories & Poems	Edgar Allan Poe
Poems of William Shakespeare	William Shakespeare
Selected Poems	Langston Hughes
Poems of Emily Dickinson	Emily Dickinson
Poems for Young People	Paul L. Dunbar

Epics
Introduce epics and that all epics begin in medias res (Latin for "in the middle of things"). That is, when all epics begin, much of the action has already taken place. This is a good time to introduce a little of Milton's *Paradise Lost.*

The Epic of Gilgamesh
Medieval Epics
The Story of Roland

Biography
Several biographies are usually available for these people.

Jane Addams
George Washington Carver
Frederick Douglass
Sir Francis Drake
Amelia Earhart
Gandhi, Fighter Without a Sword
Chief Geronimo
Helen Keller
Martin Luther King, Jr.
Nat Love
Thurgood Marshall
Mary, Queen of Scots
Peter the Great
Pocahontas
Marco Polo

Acknowledgments

I would like to thank my husband Clarence, my children Eric, Patrick, and Cynthia for being so patient with me during the months while I worked with Civia on this book. I am grateful to the students and parents of Westside Preparatory School, who enabled me to realize my dream, and to my own personal class who gave me much of the background for this book. Particular thanks to Lorraine Shanklin, Eileen Wells, and Patricia DeBonnett. I am grateful to the numerous visitors who came to the school, liked what they saw, and spread the word about what I was trying to do. To my mother, Bessie Maye Johnson, who always insisted I do everything the right way. To Robert and Nancy Soukup, who have followed my teaching career from the time of Delano until now. To Louise Godbold, who saved me thousands of dollars in psychiatric care. To Lillian Vaughn, who saw the school from its humble beginnings to the present and never missed a day of work. To Ella McCoy, who has taken on half the burden of running the school. And to my entire staff, who are patient and energetic enough to do without a desk and chair all day. Finally, I would like to thank all the wonderful people throughout the nation who have sent me letters of support.

Marva N. Collins

This book could not have been written without the help and cooperation of Marva Collins, her family, and the students, parents, and teachers of Westside Preparatory School. Evaluating the work of one teacher also required an understanding of the overall educational climate of this country, and I am grateful to the numerous teachers and former teachers, psychologists, parents, and students who contributed to that understanding.

I would like to express my deepest gratitude to my editor, Victoria Pasternack, for her faith, understanding, guidance, and above all, friendship. Grateful thanks are also extended to Janice Gallagher for her editorial advice and assistance, and to my publisher, Jeremy Tarcher, for being sensitive to the needs of a writer. My sincere appreciation to Benjamin Cate, my former bureau chief at *Time Magazine,* who encouraged my pursuit of a story on education that eventually led to this book, and to Lyn DelliQuadri and Larry Green, who first suggested I write it.

For their generous support, counsel, and encouragement, I offer many thanks to Edwin Black, Elizabeth Black, Renee Dolezal, Hubert Dolezal, Mort Edelstein, Marcia Fensin, Beverly Frankel, Ronald Futterman, Pamela Futterman, Esther Levin, Ira Levin, Iris Moscowitz, Judith Shapiro, and Eugene Wildman. Most of all, I wish to thank my husband, Bob Tamarkin—my best teacher, editor, critic, and friend—for taking time away from his own book to look over my shoulder, and my daughter, Elisa, not only for her patience and enthusiasm, but for her shared insights into schools and teachers.

Civia Tamarkin

DATE DUE #2

A
Promise
of Hope

Amy Clipston

Book Two

ZONDERVAN®

ZONDERVAN.com/
AUTHORTRACKER
follow your favorite authors

We want to hear from you. Please send your comments about this book to us in care of zreview@zondervan.com. Thank you.

ZONDERVAN

A Promise of Hope
Copyright © 2010 by Amy Clipston

This title is also available as a Zondervan ebook.
Visit www.zondervan.com/ebooks.

This title is also available in a Zondervan audio edition.
Visit www.zondervan.fm.

Requests for information should be addressed to:
Zondervan, *Grand Rapids, Michigan* 49530

Library of Congress Cataloging-in-Publication Data

Clipston, Amy.
　　A promise of hope / Amy Clipston.
　　　　p. cm. – (Kauffman Amish bakery series ; bk. 2)
　　　　Summary: An Amish widow with newborn twins discovers her deceased husband
　　had disturbing secrets. As she tries to come to grips with the past, she considers
　　a loveless marriage to ensure stability for her young family ... with her faith in God
　　hanging in the balance.
　　　　ISBN 978-0-310-28984-5 (softcover)
　　　　1. Amish – Fiction. I. Title.
　　PS3603.L58P76 2010
　　813'.6 – dc22　　　　　　　　　　　　　　　　　　　　　　　　　2009051036

Cover design: Thinkpen Design, Inc
Cover photography: iStock / Shutterstock
Interior design: Christine Orejuela-Winkelman

Printed in the United States of America

12　13　14　15　16　17　18　/DCI/　22　21　20　19　18　17　16　15　14　13　12　11　10　9　8　7　6　5　4　3　2

In loving memory of my father-in-law,
Joseph Martin Clipston Jr., who left us too soon.
You're forever in our hearts.

Note to the Reader

While this novel is set against the real backdrop of Lancaster County, Pennsylvania, the characters are fictional. There is no intended resemblance between the characters in this book and any real members of the Amish and Mennonite communities. As with any work of fiction, I've taken license in some areas of research as a means of creating the necessary circumstances for my characters. My research was thorough; however, it would be impossible to be completely accurate in details and description, since each and every community differs. Therefore, any inaccuracies in the Amish and Mennonite lifestyles portrayed in this book are completely due to fictional license.

Glossary

ack: Oh
aenti: aunt
appeditlich: delicious
boppli: baby
bopplin: babies
danki: Thank you
dat: dad
Dietsch: Pennsylvania Dutch, the Amish language
    (a German dialect)
dochder: daughter
Englisher: a non-Amish person
fraa: wife
freind: friend
freindschaft: relative
gegisch: silly
gern gschehne: You're welcome
grossdaddi: grandfather
gut: good
Gut nacht: Good night
Ich liebe dich: I love you
kapp: prayer covering or cap
kind: child
kinner: children
kumm: come
liewe: love, a term of endearment
maedel: young woman
mamm: mom
mei: my
mutter: mother

onkel: uncle
Wie geht's: How do you do? or Good day!
wunderbaar: wonderful
ya: yes
zwillingbopplin: twins

Prologue

Luke Troyer blew out a sigh and wiped his brow. The swelter-ing heat of the carpentry shop choked the air. The heaviness of sawdust, the pungent odor of stain, and the sweet smell of wood filled his nostrils. Tools and loud voices blared while a dozen other men created custom cabinets in the large work area surrounding him.

He placed his hammer next to the cabinets he'd been sand-ing and headed toward the small break room in the back of the shop. It held a long table with chairs, a refrigerator, and a counter with a sink. He fetched his lunch pail from the large refrigerator and pulled out a can of Coke.

"How are those cabinets coming along?" Mel Stoltzfus asked, leaning in the doorway.

Luke shrugged and gulped his cool, carbonated beverage. "All right, I guess. I'm about halfway through." Lowering him-self into the chair at the small table, he glanced across at a folded copy of *The Budget*, the Amish newspaper, and sudden memories of his father gripped him. Pop had read *The Budget* cover to cover every Wednesday.

"You have plans tonight?" Moving into the room, Mel sat on the chair across from Luke and opened his bottle of iced tea. "Sally told me to invite you for supper. She's making her famous chicken and dumplings."

"*Danki*, but I have plans." Luke unfolded the paper and skimmed the articles.

"*Ya.* Sure." Mel snorted. "I can imagine what your plans are. You're going to work three hours past closing, go home, make yourself a turkey sandwich, and then putter around your shed until midnight. Then you'll go to bed and start all over again tomorrow."

Grimacing, Luke met his friend's pointed stare. "I don't do that every night."

"*Ya*, you do. You've done the same thing every night since your *dat* passed away." Mel set his bottle down and tapped the table for emphasis. "You nursed your *dat* for eight years. It's time you started living again. You're young, so start acting like it."

Luke blew out a sigh and turned his attention to the paper. He'd heard this lecture from Mel several times since Pop passed away eight months ago. Although Luke knew his friend was right, he just didn't know how to move on. He'd nursed Pop since he was twenty-one, so Luke didn't know how to "act young."

"You know I speak the truth," Mel said. "You should leave work on time tonight and come to my house. Enjoy an evening of friends, not solitude."

Luke shook his head and opened his mouth to respond, but the whooshing of the door opening derailed his train of thought. He gaped when he found a ghost from his past standing in the doorway.

"DeLana?" Luke stood, examining the tall, thin woman dressed in jeans and a black leather jacket. Her long, dark hair framed her attractive face, which was outlined with makeup.

"Long time, no see." She gave him a wry smile, her brown eyes sparkling. "How long has it been? Eight years?"

Luke nodded. "I reckon so." He motioned toward Mel. "DeLana Maloney, this is my good friend Mel Stoltzfus."

She smiled at Mel. "Nice to meet you."

Mel nodded, speechless.

She honed her gaze in on Luke. "Any chance we can talk? Alone?" She looked back at Mel again. "No offense."

"Uh, it's no trouble at all." Mel stood and started toward the door. He glanced back at Luke, looking puzzled, then closed the door.

Luke turned his attention to DeLana. "How have you been?" he asked.

"Good." She nodded. "How about you?"

"*Gut.*" He cleared his throat. "It's a surprise to see you here."

"I bet you thought you'd never see me again, huh?" She adjusted her leather purse on her shoulder.

Luke motioned toward the table. "Would you like to have a seat? I have a spare Coke if you're thirsty."

"No, thanks. I can't stay long." DeLana rooted around in her purse and pulled out an envelope. "I wanted to ask you about Peter."

"Peter?" Luke narrowed his eyes in question. "What do you mean?"

"I haven't heard from him in a few months. I've written him a few times, but the letters from him have stopped." She handed him the envelope. "I was going to mail this to him, but I was wondering if it's even worth it since he's cut me off. Do you know why?"

Luke stared down at letters addressed to Peter Troyer in Bird-in-Hand, Pennsylvania. "No, I don't. I haven't heard from him in years."

"It's strange." She shook her head, her diamond-studded earrings sparkling in the light of the gas lamps. "I heard from him every month like clockwork and then it all stopped about five months ago."

He glanced at the envelope again, his mind clicking with questions. "Bird-in-Hand? Is that where he's living?"

"Yeah. He said he worked at some Amish furniture place in town." She folded her arms, pondering. "Shoot, I can't remember the name of it."

His brow furrowed in disbelief. "He's working in an Amish furniture store? Are you certain?"

"Oh, yeah, I'm certain. He mentioned it often, talking about the different projects he was working on." She pursed her lips. "So you don't know anything?"

Luke shook his head, processing the information. Peter was living in Pennsylvania and working in an Amish furniture store. *Is he still Amish?*

"I'm sorry," he said. "Like I said, I haven't heard from him in years."

She pulled her car keys from her purse, and they jingled in response. "If you hear from him, would you ask him to contact me?"

"Of course." He held the envelope out to her.

"Would you please give that to him if you find him?" She glanced at her watch. "I'd better run."

"Let me walk you out." Luke followed her through the shop and out the front door to the parking lot, his mind flooded with questions about Peter. He shivered in the crisp autumn air.

"It was good to see you," she said.

"*Ya*, it was." He gripped the envelopes in his hand.

"If you hear from him, would you ask him to write or call me?" she asked. "He has my number."

"*Ya*, I will." He nodded.

"Thanks. Take care." She started across the parking lot.

"What was that about?" a voice behind Luke asked.

"Peter," Luke said, glancing toward Mel. "Letters from him have stopped, and her letters to him have gone unanswered."

"I'm confused," Mel said, coming up to glance at the envelopes in Luke's hand. "Why would Peter be exchanging letters with her?"

Luke waved as DeLana's SUV sped past, beeping on its way to the parking-lot exit.

"Apparently he's living in Pennsylvania and working in an Amish furniture store," Luke said.

"Amish furniture store?" Mel sounded as surprised as Luke felt. "He's still Amish?"

"That's what I said." Luke studied the envelopes again. "It looks like I'm heading to Pennsylvania."

"Why would you do that?"

"To find out what's happened to Peter. It's time for me to use the vacation time I've been saving for years." He headed toward the office to ask his boss for an extended leave of absence.

1

*S*moke filled Sarah Troyer's lungs and stung her watering eyes. Covering her mouth with her trembling hand, she fell to her knees while flames engulfed the large carpentry area of the furniture store.

"Peter!" Her attempt to scream her husband's name came out in a strangled cough, inaudible over the noise of the roaring fire surrounding her.

Peter was somewhere in the fire. She had to get to him. But how would she find her way through the flames? Had someone called for help? Where was the fire department?

A thunderous boom shook the floor beneath Sarah's feet, causing her body to shake with fear. The roof must've collapsed!

"Sarah!" Peter's voice echoed, hoarse and weak within the flames.

"I'm coming!" Sobs wracked her body as she crawled toward the back of the shop. She would find him. She had to!

Turning her face toward the ceiling, Sarah begged God to spare her husband's life. He had to live. She needed him. He was everything to her. They were going to be parents.

Their baby needed a father.

Standing, she threw her body into the flames, rushing toward the crumpled silhouette on the floor next to the smashed remains of the roof ...

Sarah's eyes flew open, and she gasped. She touched her sweat-drenched nightgown with her trembling hands. Closing her eyes, she breathed a sigh of relief.

It was a dream!

Stretching her arm through the dark, she reached across the double bed for her husband of three years; however, her hand brushed only cool sheets.

Empty.

Oh, no.

Sarah cupped a hand to her hot face while reality crashed down on her. Peter had died in the fire in her father's furniture store five months ago. He was gone, and she was staying in her parents' house.

Taking a deep, ragged breath, she swallowed a sob. She'd had the fire dream again—the fourth time this week.

When were the nightmares going to cease? When was life going to get easier?

She rested her hands on her swelling belly while tears cooled her burning cheeks. It seemed like only yesterday Sarah was sharing the news of their blessing with Peter and he was smiling, his hazel eyes twinkling, while he pulled her close and kissed her.

It had been their dream to have a big family with as many as seven children, like most of the Amish couples in their church district. Sarah and Peter had spent many late nights snuggling in each other's arms while talking about names.

However, Sarah had buried those dreams along with her husband, and she still felt as bewildered as the day his body was laid to rest. She wondered how she'd ever find the emotional strength to raise her baby without the love and support of her beloved Peter.

She'd believed since the day she married Peter that they would raise a family and grow old together. But that ghastly fire had stolen everything from Sarah and her baby—their future and their stability. Her life was now in flux.

Closing her eyes, she mentally repeated her mother's favorite Scripture, Romans 12:12: "Be joyful in hope, patient in affliction, faithful in prayer." But the verse offered no comfort. She tried to pray, but the words remained unformed in her heart.

Sarah was completely numb.

She stared up through the dark until a light tap on her door roused her from her thoughts.

"Sarah Rose." Her mother's soft voice sounded through the closed door. "It's time to get up."

"*Ya.*" Wiping the tears from her face, Sarah rose and slowly dressed, pulling on her black dress, black apron, and shoes. She then parted her golden hair and twirled long strands back from her face before winding the rest into a bun. Once her hair was tightly secured, she placed her white prayer *kapp* over it, anchoring it with pins.

Sarah hurried down the stairs and met her mother in the front hall of the old farmhouse in which she'd been raised. "I'm ready," she said.

Mamm's blue eyes studied her. "Aren't you going to eat?"

"No." Sarah headed for the back door. "Let's go. I'll eat later."

"Sarah Rose. You must eat for the *boppli.*" Her mother trotted after her.

"I'm not hungry." Sarah slipped out onto the porch.

"Did you have the dream again?" *Mamm's* voice was filled with concern.

Sarah sucked in a breath, hoping to curb the tears rising in her throat. "I'm just tired." She started down the dirt driveway toward the bakery.

Mamm caught up with her. Taking Sarah's hand in hers, she gave her a bereaved expression. "Sarah Rose, *mei liewe,* how it breaks my heart to see you hurting. I want to help you through this. Please let me."

Swallowing the tears that threatened, Sarah stared down at her mother's warm hand cradling hers. Grief crashed down on her, memories of Peter and their last quiet evening together flooding her. He'd held her close while they discussed their future as parents.

Rehashing those memories was too painful for Sarah to bear. She missed him with every fiber of her being. Sarah had to change the subject before she wound up sobbing in her mother's arms—again.

"We best get to work before the girls think we overslept," Sarah whispered, quickening her steps.

"Don't forget this afternoon is your ultrasound appointment," *Mamm* said. "Maybe we'll find out if you're having a boy or a girl. Nina Janitz is going to pick us up at one so we're at the hospital on time."

At her mother's words Sarah swallowed a groan. The idea of facing this doctor's appointment without Peter sharpened the pain that pulsated in her heart.

Pushing the thought aside, Sarah stared at the bakery her mother had opened more than twenty years ago. The large, white clapboard farmhouse sat near the road and included a sweeping wraparound porch. A sign with "Kauffman Amish Bakery" in old-fashioned letters hung above the door.

Out behind the building was a fenced-in play area where a few of the Kauffman grandchildren ran around playing tag and climbing on a huge wooden swing set. Beyond it was the fenced pasture. *Mamm's*, Peter's, and Timothy's large farmhouses, along with four barns, were set back beyond the pasture. The dirt road leading to the other homes was roped off with a sign declaring Private Property—No Trespassing.

A large paved parking lot sat adjacent to the building. The lot—always full during the summer months, the height of the tourist season—was now empty. Even though temperatures had cooled off for autumn, the tourist season had ended a month ago in Bird-in-Hand.

Mamm prattled on about the weather and how busy the bakery had been. Sarah grunted in agreement to give the appearance of listening.

After climbing the steps, Sarah and *Mamm* headed in through the back door of the building. The sweet aroma of freshly baked bread filled Sarah's senses while the Pennsylvania *Dietsch* chatter of her sisters swirled around her.

The large open kitchen had plain white walls, and in keeping with their tradition, there was no electricity. The lights were gas powered, as were the row of ovens. The long counter included their tools—plain pans and ordinary knives and cutlery.

Even though the air outside was cool, Sarah and her sisters still did the bulk of the baking in the early morning in order to keep the kitchen heat to a minimum. Five fans running through the power inverters gave a gentle breeze. However, the kitchen was warm.

Nodding a greeting to her sisters, Sarah washed her hands before pulling out ingredients to begin mixing a batch of her favorite sugar cookies. She engrossed herself in the task and shut out the conversations around her.

"How are you?" Lindsay, her sister-in-law's young niece, asked after a while.

"*Gut*," Sarah said, forcing a smile. "How are you today?"

"*Gut, danki.*" The fourteen-year-old smiled, her ivory complexion glowing. Although she'd been raised by non-Amish parents, Lindsay had adjusted well to the lifestyle since coming to live with Rebecca, Sarah's sister-in-law. Her parents had died in a car accident, leaving custody of her and her older sister to Rebecca. Lindsay quickly adopted the Amish dress and was learning the Pennsylvania *Dietsch* language as if she'd been born into the community.

Lindsay tilted her head in question and wrinkled her freckled nose. "You don't look *gut*, *Aenti* Sarah. Is everything okay?"

"I'm fine, but *danki.*" Sarah stirred the anise cookie batter and wracked her brain for something to change the subject. "You and Rebecca got here early this morning, no?"

"*Ya.*" Lindsay began cutting out cookies. "*Aenti* Rebecca was having some tummy problems this morning." She gestured toward her stomach, and Sarah knew the girl was referring to morning sickness. "She was up early, and I was too. So we just headed out. We had a couple of loaves of bread in the oven before *Aenti* Beth Anne and *Aenti* Kathryn got here."

Sarah glanced across the kitchen to where *Mamm* was whispering to Beth Anne and Kathryn, Sarah's older sisters. When her mother's gaze met Sarah's, her mother quickly looked away.

Sarah's stomach churned. She hoped her mother wasn't talking about her again. She was in no mood for another well-meaning lecture from her sisters. They were constantly insisting Sarah must accept Peter's death and concentrate on the blessing of her pregnancy. Over and over they told her it was God's will Peter had perished and the Lord would provide for her and her baby.

What did they know about loss? They both had their husbands and children, living and healthy.

"I best go check on the *kinner* on the playground," Lindsay said, wiping her hands on her apron.

Sarah picked up the cookie cutter. "I'll finish cutting out your cookies."

"*Danki.*" Smiling, Lindsay crossed the kitchen and disappeared out the back door toward the playground set up for Sarah's young nieces and nephews.

"Sarah," a voice behind her said. "How are you today? *Mamm* mentioned that you had a rough night."

Sarah glanced over at Beth Anne and swallowed a groan. "I'm fine, *danki.* And you?" *I wish you all would stop worrying about me.*

Beth Anne's blue eyes mirrored her disbelief, and Sarah braced herself for the coming lecture.

"You can talk to me. I'll always listen." Her older sister squeezed her hand.

"I appreciate that, but there's nothing to say. I didn't get much sleep last night, but I'm *gut*. Really." Sarah turned back to her cookies in the hopes Beth Anne would return to work and leave her alone with her thoughts.

"I know you're hurting," Beth Anne began, moving closer and lowering her voice. "However, you must let Peter's memory rest in peace. You need your strength for your *boppli*."

Sarah gritted her teeth and took a deep breath, trying in vain to curb her rising aggravation. Facing her sister, she narrowed her eyes. "I know you mean well, but you can't possibly know what I'm thinking or what I'm feeling. I lost my husband, and you have no idea how that feels. I know I need to let go, but how can I when Peter's *boppli* is growing inside me? Grieving is different for everyone, and it can't be rushed."

Beth Anne's expression softened. "I just want what's best for you."

"Then leave me alone and let me work." Sarah faced the counter. "I have a lot of cookies to make. We sold out yesterday."

"If you need to talk, I'm here." Beth Anne's voice was soft.

"*Ya. Danki.*" Sarah closed her eyes and prayed for strength to make it through the day.

Late that afternoon, Sarah lay on the cool, metal table at the hospital and stared at the monitor while a young woman moved her instrument through the gel spread on Sarah's midsection.

Sarah watched the screen and sucked in a breath while the ultrasound technician pointed out anatomy. Sarah wondered how many years of schooling it had taken for the young woman to figure out which was the spinal cord and which was the heart when it all resembled a bunch of squiggly lines.

Miranda Coleman, Sarah's midwife, interrupted the technician and moved over to the monitor. "Do you see that?" Miranda asked the young woman in a hushed whisper. "I believe that's . . ."

"Yeah, you're right," the technician said with a grin. "I think so."

"This is something." Miranda folded her arms and shook her head. "Well, that explains her sudden weight gain."

"What?" Sarah started to sit up, her heart racing with worry. "What's wrong with my *boppli*?"

Her eyes full of concern, *Mamm* squeezed Sarah's shoulder.

Miranda chuckled. "Nothing's wrong, Sarah."

Sarah held her breath and wished Peter was by her side to help her shoulder the news. "Please tell me what's going on."

"Sarah Troyer, you're doubly blessed," Miranda said with a smirk. "You're having twins. I guess one was blocking the other when we did the last ultrasound."

"*Zwillingbopplin?*" Sarah gasped. Lightheaded, she put her hand to her forehead.

How would she ever raise twins alone?

Later that evening, Sarah stood on the porch and studied the rain falling in sheets on the fields across from her parents' farmhouse. Rubbing her swollen abdomen, she swallowed the sorrow surging through her.

Zwillingbopplin.

The word had haunted her since it left Miranda's lips. Sarah had tuned out Miranda's voice while she discussed Sarah's prenatal care for the remainder of the pregnancy. She'd heard the midwife say Sarah was now "high risk" and would be referred to an obstetrician for further care. Beyond that, Sarah had just stared at her midwife and pondered the news.

Twin babies.

Two mouths to feed. Two babies for which to care.

Two children without a father.

How would Sarah bear the load? Of course, her family would help her, for it was the Amish way to care for one another. However, raising two children without Peter would be daunting, regardless of help from the extended family.

"Sarah Rose." Her mother's voice interrupted her thoughts. "How are you?"

"*Gut*," Sarah whispered, still rubbing her belly.

"*Zwillingbopplin.*" *Mamm* shook her head. "The Lord is *gut*. You are blessed."

"Am I?" Sarah snorted. The shock seemed to have deflated the blessing from the news.

"Why do you say that?" *Mamm's* eyes probed Sarah's. "*Bopplin* are a blessing. Daniel and Rebecca have waited fifteen years to have one of their own."

Sarah touched *Mamm's* warm hand. "*Ya*, I know *bopplin* are a blessing. You forget Daniel and Rebecca have each other." She gazed down at her stomach. "I'm alone. These *bopplin* will have no *dat*. They only have me."

"You're not alone. You have your *dat*, me, and the rest of our family. The community will take care of you. We'll all love and care for you and your *kinner*."

"But it's not the same." Sniffing, Sarah wiped a lone tear. "They'll know love but not their *dat's* love."

"You can tell them how much Peter loved them. We have many stories that will make them smile, and you'll smile again too." Leaning over, *Mamm* looped her arm around Sarah's shoulders. "You'll find joy again, Sarah Rose. God will make sure of that."

Nodding, Sarah wiped her eyes and cleared her throat in an effort to suppress her tears. She had to hold herself together. Dissolving into sobs wouldn't help the situation.

"When the time is right," *Mamm* began, "you may marry again."

"I doubt that." Sarah shook her head with emphasis. "I don't think I'll ever love any man as much as I loved Peter. That only happens once in a lifetime."

"Sarah Rose." *Mamm* took Sarah's hands again. "You're young. You may love again. Give your burdens up to God, and He'll see you through. Right now, just concentrate on your *kinner*. It will all come in time, God's time."

Sarah breathed deeply, hoping to stop the emotions that threatened. "Maybe someday, but not anytime soon. My heart still belongs to Peter." She stepped toward the door. "I'm going to go to bed. Good night."

"Good night." *Mamm* reached for Sarah's hand. "Don't rush yourself, Sarah Rose. God will see you through this. He's in control."

Sarah pulled her hand back and opened the screen door. "*Ya*," she whispered. "Good night."

Climbing the stairs to her room, Sarah closed the door and lowered herself down onto her bed, hoping to keep the world out. Lying there, she prayed for her family to stop nagging her. She needed room to breathe and figure out her way without their constant unsolicited opinions. She needed strength and guidance to make the right decisions for her twins.

As she moved her gaze to the ceiling, she let go of her breath and finally allowed her tears to flow, her sobs cutting through the painful silence of her bedroom. She opened her heart to God, begging Him to raise Peter as He raised Lazarus. If He'd done it once, why couldn't He do it again for Sarah, enabling her twins to have the father they needed and deserved?

She wiped her face with a trembling hand and closed her eyes. Why was she forced to live this lonely life? Didn't she deserve to be blessed with a loving husband and father to her children, like her sisters?

She tried to open her heart to God and beg again for guidance and patience, but her prayers jammed in her throat. Like so many nights in the past five months, she cried herself to sleep.

2

"How was your appointment?" Kathryn asked while standing at the counter with Sarah the following morning.

"*Gut.*" Sarah nodded and turned her attention to straightening the containers of baked goods before her.

"Just *gut?*" Kathryn moved closer to her. "Is that all?"

Hearing the rustling of skirts, Sarah turned to find Beth Anne and Rebecca standing behind her. Sarah wondered if her mother had already broken the news of her twins. Feeling as though she were backed into a corner, Sarah narrowed her eyes with the suspicion that they were pouncing on her like the stray cats she often found wrestling each other in the barns.

"How was your appointment, Sarah Rose?" Beth Anne asked, folding her arms in front of her apron.

"We hope it was *gut* news." Rebecca smiled.

"*Zwillingbopplin,*" Sarah whispered, self-consciously rubbing her belly.

Her sisters and Rebecca shrieked, pulling her close for a group hug and cooing about how blessed Sarah was. Sarah closed her eyes and wished she could find the joy her sisters felt. She prayed the cold, foreboding feeling currently enveloping her would loosen its grasp on her soul.

The bell signaling a customer's entrance into the bakery ended the group hug.

"This is wonderful *gut*, Sarah." Beth Anne's grin was wide as she stepped back toward the kitchen. "We must talk more when the shop is quiet."

"*Ya.*" Sarah forced a smile. "*Danki.*"

"I'm so happy for you." Rebecca gave Sarah one last squeeze. "Let me know if you need to talk," she whispered in her ear before heading into the kitchen.

"You don't look as happy as you should," Kathryn said under her breath in Pennsylvania *Dietsch* as a customer perused the containers of pastries lining the long counter in front of them.

"It's a shock," Sarah said.

"But it seems like something more. What's weighing on your mind?" her oldest sister asked.

"I don't think we should speak of it now," Sarah said, gritting her teeth with annoyance.

Kathryn jammed her hands onto her hips. "They can't understand us, Sarah Rose. They're English."

"I don't want to talk about it." Sarah faced her sister and lowered her eyes. "I'm still processing the news. I'm having *zwilling-bopplin*, and my husband is gone."

"May I please pay for these?" the English woman asked with an unsure smile.

"Of course, ma'am." Sarah scurried from behind the bakery counter and over to the register by the door. She felt her sister's judgmental stare while she rang up the pastries and took the woman's money.

When the sale was complete, Sarah busied herself with arranging the items at the cashier's station. Feeling watched again, she glanced up to find her older sister studying her.

"You can talk to me," Kathryn said, her expression warming. "I know you're scared, but you must remember your family will see you through this." Kathryn took Sarah's hand in hers. "We love you, Sarah Rose, and we'll help you and the *kinner.*"

Sarah's eyes filled with tears. "*Danki.*" She hoped she wouldn't cry, not here in public.

"Excuse me, miss?" an English voice asked. "Do you have more whoopie pies?"

Saved by the Englisher! Sarah blew out a sigh of relief. While Kathryn helped the English woman, Sarah lost herself in organizing the postcard rack in an attempt to calm her anxiety.

Sarah sipped a glass of cool water while gazing out over the field to where her nieces and nephews played at her parents' house.

Mamm squeezed Sarah's hand. "Before you know it, your *kinner* will be out there too."

"*Ya.*" Sarah touched her stomach and forced a smile. "Soon they will."

The clip-clop of a horse and crunch of buggy wheels on the drive stole Sarah's attention from her mother. "Who could that be?" she asked as the buggy headed for *Dat*'s barn.

"I think we have a visitor." Standing, *Mamm* patted Sarah's hand. "I'll get some iced tea." She stepped toward the door.

Glancing toward the barn, Sarah spotted Norman Zook chatting with her father and her brothers, and she smiled. Norman, who had lost his wife in childbirth a couple of years ago, had become a dear friend since she'd lost Peter. He seemed to be the only person in her church district who truly understood her grief.

Despite her protruding belly, she popped up to her feet and followed her mother through the door to the kitchen where they joined Beth Anne and Kathryn. It was only proper to have dessert when a guest visited.

"*Mamm,* do we still have some chocolate-chip cookies or cake left?"

"We have cookies." *Mamm* reached for a plate of cookies on the counter. "Let me put some on a tray for you."

"You have a visitor?" Beth Anne asked.

"*Ya,* Norman's here." Sarah lifted the tray of cookies.

"He's a *gut* man," Kathryn said with a smile.

"*Ya*," Beth Anne chimed in, coming to stand beside Kathryn. "He's a good *dat* too."

Sarah nodded. "He is, but we're just friends."

"Of course you are," *Mamm* agreed, pulled two glasses from the cabinet. "You two have a lot in common."

"It's *gut* to have a friend who understands," Rebecca said.

A slam yanked Sarah's attention to her brother, Daniel, standing with Norman by the back door. Norman's lips formed a tentative smile as his gaze met hers.

"Norman!" *Mamm* padded over to the widower. "It's *wunderbaar gut* to see you. Would you like to have a glass of iced tea on the porch?"

"*Danki*." Norman nodded. "That would be nice, Elizabeth." His eyes turned to Sarah. "How are you?"

"*Gut*." She held up the tray. "I hope you like chocolate-chip cookies."

"My favorite." He smiled.

Norman followed Daniel through the back door to the porch while *Mamm* grabbed the two glasses of iced tea from the counter. Sarah followed her out to the porch, where Norman sat on a chair next to the swing. His brown eyes met hers and then darted to the field where his children ran around, shrieking and playing with her nieces and nephews.

Sarah placed the tray of cookies on the small table in front of them and gingerly lowered herself into the swing.

"Here's some fresh-brewed iced tea," *Mamm* said, handing a glass to Norman. "Would you like a whoopie pie too? We have plenty left from the bakery. We always bring some leftovers home for the *kinner* to enjoy."

"No, *danki*." Smiling, Norman rested his hand on his abdomen. "We had a large dinner. I couldn't eat another crumb."

They sat in silence for a few moments, sipping their drinks, and Sarah relaxed. She appreciated their comfortable friendship. It was nice to not have someone telling her to let go of her grief. Norman understood her better than anyone, including her well-meaning family members.

"It's a beautiful evening," he said, breaking the silence.

"*Ya.* Beautiful. How was your day?" Sarah watched the youngest of Norman's four children, Gretchen and Marian, chase her nieces, and she wondered how the two girls were faring without their mother. Her chin trembled at the thought of children without a mother to cuddle and kiss them. His children were as needy without a mother as hers would be without their father.

"*Gut,*" he said. "How was yours?"

"Long but *gut.*" She absently rubbed her tummy, and her gaze moved to Norman, who was studying her.

"How are you feeling?" he asked, the warmth of his voice reflecting in his brown eyes.

The tenderness in his face caught her off guard, and for a moment she couldn't speak. "*Gut,*" she whispered. "I've been a bit tired, but that's to be expected."

"Your *mamm* mentioned you'd been to see the midwife recently."

"*Ya.*" She settled back in the swing.

"And it went well?" he asked.

"*Ya.*" She fingered the condensation on her glass. "I'm having *zwillingbopplin,* so I have to see a specialist now."

"*Zwillingbopplin.*" He smiled and pulled on his beard. "What a blessing. The Lord is *gut.*"

Sarah glanced down at her belly while her thoughts moved to Peter. How her heart cried for him now. She should be sitting on the porch discussing her pregnancy with him, not Norman.

"You will have your hands full when the *bopplin* arrive," he said, breaking through her musings.

"*Mamm* and I will manage," she said.

He was silent, and she glanced over to see him gazing at

the children again, his mouth forming a thin line instead of the wide smile she'd seen moments ago. She assumed he was remembering the difficult time he'd had adjusting to single parenthood after Leah had died.

She lifted the glass to her dry lips and took a long gulp of the cool water.

While Norman made mundane small talk about the weather and his busy dairy farm, Sarah's mind turned to Peter and their courtship. She'd met him at a youth gathering when she was nineteen, and she was smitten the moment she laid eyes on his handsome face and gorgeous hazel eyes.

Peter was mysterious, explaining only that he'd been raised by an older Amish couple in Ohio after his parents died in an accident, and he had no siblings. He'd sold his adopted parents' farm to pay off their debts after they died and then moved to Lancaster when he was eighteen to be closer to his adopted father's brother, who lived in a neighboring Lancaster County town. After moving to Lancaster County, he had mostly kept to himself.

Sarah knew nothing more about his background, and she'd never met his uncle before Peter died. But it didn't matter to her. She'd quickly fallen madly in love with Peter.

They'd courted for two years while he gathered enough money to build a small house on her parents' farm. During that time, Peter went to work in her father's store, where he impressed her family with his carpentry skills.

Once their small home was built, they'd married. For the first year, Sarah felt as if she were living in a dream. Peter was loving and attentive, and they rarely quarreled. However, their second year of marriage was different. Sarah had wondered if Peter had changed or if she'd finally seen him for who he was — mysterious. She wondered if she'd ever truly known him during their courtship.

"Sarah? Are you all right?"

"*Ya.*" Sarah shook her head. "Sorry. I was lost in memories."

He gave an understanding smile. "Would you like to share them with me?"

"No, *danki*. But I appreciate it. You were saying?" she asked, hoping to bring his focus back to his discussion of his cows. Her memories were too personal to share out loud.

Norman explained the idiosyncrasies of his new cow while Sarah lost herself again in thoughts of her husband and the questions he'd left her.

In the weeks before Peter died, he'd become quiet, standoffish, almost cold to her. She'd tried several times to get him to talk to her and open up, but he was always too busy, rushing off to work or disappearing into the barn. She hadn't had a chance to uncover what was wrong before he'd died.

Turning her gaze across the field, her eyes fell on the home she and Peter had once shared. Memories crashed down on her like a tidal wave—she could see Peter pulling her by her hand over the threshold the spring after they were married. She remembered the first night they'd sat down to supper in the small kitchen, and she could still smell his musky scent and feel his warm, taut skin as they lay awake in each other's arms . . .

"Sarah?"

She jumped, startled. Turning, she found Norman staring at her, his brown eyes full of concern. She flushed and covered her cheeks with her hands.

"Are you sure you're all right?" He touched her arm.

"*Ya.*" Sarah cleared her throat and pushed away the painful memories of Peter.

"You looked as if you'd entered another world."

Nodding, Sarah stared down at her lap. "I supposed I had. I apologize for not hearing everything you said." Gazing up, her eyes locked with his, and guilt surged through her soul at the genuine worry shining in his eyes. "It was very rude of me to not listen to you."

A tentative smile curled Norman's lips. "You forget I lost *mei fraa*. I understand the pain you feel."

He leaned in closer, reaching for her and then pulling back. "If you ever need to, Sarah, you can talk to me. I know the pain and the loss you're facing. It's not easy. With the Lord's help, time will heal your wounds."

Overwhelmed by his kindness, Sarah teared up. "*Danki*, Norman."

He stood, gazing toward where the children played. "*Ack*, I suppose I should get these *kinner* home. School comes early in the morning."

"*Danki* for visiting." Sarah began to hoist herself up, and Norman motioned for her to remain seated.

"Please sit. I can find my way to my buggy." He patted her hand. "You take care. I'll visit with you soon."

"I look forward to it." Sarah cradled her belly while watching Norman gather up his children and say good-bye to her brothers and father. Her mind swirled with thoughts of his friendship. Norman was a kind man, and he was a good father to his children. Maybe someday soon she would feel comfortable enough to tell him how she felt about losing her husband. For now, she would enjoy his company and the easy conversation.

L uke stared out the window as the taxicab motored down Route 340 in Bird-in-Hand. He had submitted the paperwork for a leave of absence and set out to solve the mystery of what had happened to Peter.

He glanced around at the small stores—most of them Amish themed—and the old, modest homes. His stomach tightened with anticipation when the car slowed in front of a building displaying a sign that read Kauffman & Yoder Amish Furniture. It was the store a young man at the farmer's market had suggested Luke investigate since it was the only Amish-owned furniture store in the town.

After paying the driver, Luke fetched his bag from the floor and climbed from the car. Standing at the curb, he studied the one-story white building.

He took in a deep breath, inhaling the scent of fresh paint. It was a brand-new building, which caused him to doubt if this was the wrong furniture store. DeLana had made it sound as if Peter had worked in the store for a long time. Perhaps Luke should've asked the driver to wait until after he spoke to someone inside instead of going through the hassle of finding another cab if it turned out to be the wrong place.

A handwritten sign taped to the front window read Reopened. Please come in. He wondered if business had been booming so much that they added onto the shop.

Luke climbed the steps and wrenched open the front door, causing a bell to ring in announcement of his presence. Large windows lined the front of the shop, and the walls were covered in crisp, fresh white paint. He glanced around the open area, impressed with the quality of the sample pieces, including mirrored dressers, hope chests, entertainment centers, dining room sets, bed frames, wishing wells, end tables, and coffee tables. The familiar aroma of wood and stain permeated his nostrils. It smelled like home.

A long counter covered with piles of papers and catalogs sat at the far end of the room, blocking a doorway beyond which hammers, saws, and nail guns blasted while voices boomed in Pennsylvania *Dietsch*. Luke crossed the room, his boots scraping the floor.

A tall man stepped through the doorway. With blond hair and a blond beard, he stood an inch taller than Luke, approximately six one. His dark shirt, suspenders, and trousers were covered in dust and stains.

When his gaze met Luke's, he squinted as if to study Luke's countenance. Luke could've sworn he saw recognition flash for a split second in the man's eyes.

"*Wie geht's?*" the man asked. He extended his hand and gave a cautious smile.

Luke shook his hand. "*Gut*, and you?"

"*Gut, danki.*" The man swiped his hands across his shirt, setting off a cloud of dust. "Is there something I can help you with? Were you looking to order something? We've just re-opened, so we're a bit backed up right now. However, if you're patient, we'd be happy to fill your order."

Pennsylvania *Dietsch* and nail guns continued to blast in the room behind him.

Luke cleared his throat and straightened his straw hat, mustering up the strength to ask about Peter. "Actually, I'm visiting from Ohio."

"Welcome to Bird-in-Hand." The man smiled. "What brings you here?"

"I'm taking some much-overdue vacation time." Luke yanked his straw hat from his head and fingered the brim.

"That's *wunderbaar.*"

"I noticed your store has just reopened," Luke said. "Did you do some remodeling?"

"*Ya.*" The man frowned, shaking his head. "We had to do some major reconstruction after the fire."

"You had a fire?"

"It was a tragic accident. One of our carpenters knocked over a lamp, igniting an oily rag. We lost everything." The man's gaze swept around the large room. "We had to completely rebuild."

"I'm sorry to hear that," Luke said. "When did it happen?"

"Nearly six months ago," the man said. "It's taken us a long time to get everything back on track with the shop. We're still sorting through missing orders."

"I was wondering if you know a man named Peter Troyer." Luke tightened his grip on the brim of the hat, anticipating the answer. "I heard he works in an Amish furniture store here in Bird-in-Hand."

"Peter Troyer?" The man's eyes widened. "Have you come here to see him?"

Luke nodded, his stomach tightening.

"I'm sorry, *mei freind*, but Peter perished in the fire."

Luke swallowed a gasp as bile rose in his throat. He fought to keep his emotions in check.

"It was a great tragedy." The man shook his head. "He was my brother-in-law."

"Your brother-in-law?" Despite his pain, Luke raised his eyebrows in surprise at the news Peter had been married.

"He was a *gut* man and husband. He also was one of our best carpenters."

Luke sucked in a breath, hoping to curb the surge of shock and grief coursing through him. "You own this shop?" he asked.

"It's a family business," the man said. "I'm Daniel Kauffman."

"It's nice to meet you. I'm Luke Troyer."

Daniel's eyes widened with shock. "Troyer? Was Peter your *freindschaft?*"

"*Ya*, he was my relative." Luke's voice was ragged with emotion.

Daniel's eyebrows knitted with confusion. "I didn't know Peter had relatives left in Ohio."

"He has relatives, mostly cousins," Luke said.

An older man, also covered in wood shaving dust, appeared in the doorway. He stepped through, followed by a man who resembled Daniel, only younger.

"Daniel, I thought Jake was running the front. Did he run to the supply yard again?" the older man asked.

"*Ya*, I think so. *Dat*, this is Luke Troyer." Daniel made a sweeping gesture toward Luke. "He's Peter's cousin visiting from Ohio. I just told him that we lost Peter in the fire." He turned to the older man. "This is my *dat*, Eli Kauffman."

Eli shook Luke's hand. "Welcome to Bird-in-Hand. Peter was a *gut* man. He was *gut* to my Sarah Rose."

"*Danki*." Luke blew out a trembling breath as the words sunk into his soul. Peter's wife was Sarah Rose—what a lovely name.

"This is my younger brother, Timothy," Daniel said, pointing to the younger man.

Luke held his hand out to Timothy, and the man hesitated before taking it. Luke thought he read shock and perhaps worry in Timothy's eyes.

Daniel patted Luke's shoulder. "Would you like to meet my sister? She can tell you more about Peter's life here in Bird-in-Hand."

Unable to speak, Luke nodded, grappling with the news Peter was dead and had left behind a widow.

"Let's take Luke over to the bakery. I'll go tell Elmer that we're leaving," Eli said, nodding toward the entrance to the shop.

Sarah handed an English woman her fistful of change. After thanking the woman, she leaned back on the counter behind her and groaned in response to her throbbing temples.

"You look tired." Kathryn rested her hand on Sarah's shoulder. "You should go sit. I can walk you home if you'd like. You need to take it easy for the babies."

Sarah shifted her weight on her aching feet. "I'll be fine. It's almost time for my lunch break."

"Excuse me." An English woman approached the counter. "Do you have any shoofly pie? I just love it. I'm heading back to Jersey this afternoon, and I promised my husband I'd bring him home a few pieces."

Smiling, Kathryn stepped over to the customer. "I believe we have some over here." She nodded toward the end of the counter. "How many pieces would you like?"

While her sister and the customer moved to the other end of the long counter, Sarah sighed and leaned forward. Her feet throbbed, and her head pounded. Kathryn's offer to walk her home was tempting.

But being alone in the house wasn't relaxing.

When Sarah was alone, memories of Peter overtook her, filling her heart with sorrow and regret. Remaining at the bakery and helping English tourists kept Sarah busy and silenced her numbing thoughts.

The whoosh of the door pulled Sarah from her mental tirade. Daniel stepped through the doorway, followed by Timothy, *Dat*, and another man. Timothy's face was creased with a frown, causing her to wonder why her brother was out of sorts. The men stopped to speak with *Mamm*, who was standing across the room with a frequent English customer.

The mysterious stranger pushed his straw hat back a fraction of an inch on his brown hair. His eyes scanned the bakery, and Sarah fixated on his clean-shaven face.

Her breath caught in her throat as she took in his familiar countenance. His cheekbones, the shape of his eyes and nose, and his complexion all mirrored Peter's. It was as though she were looking at her husband's face before they were married and he grew his beard.

Sarah gripped the counter and sucked in a breath while studying the stranger's tall, lanky build, wide chest, and broad shoulders. Even his physique and light-brown hair resembled her late husband's. He looked to be six feet tall, like Peter.

Dat said something to the man, and he turned and greeted *Mamm* with a smile.

Her heart hammered in her chest, and she cupped a hand to her burning face. Was she dreaming or had God raised Peter in response to her prayer?

"Sometimes I wish our English customers would open their eyes," Kathryn muttered in Pennsylvania *Dietsch*, coming up to Sarah. "The pie was right in front of her face, but I had to lead her to it. Then I had to hear the story of her life, and how she—"

"Kathryn," Sarah's voice came in a strangled whisper. She gripped her sister's apron and yanked her over, causing her to stumble. "Do you see that man over there talking to *Mamm*?"

"Sarah Rose?" Kathryn's blue eyes were wide with worry. "Are you okay? You're so pale. Sit." She took Sarah's clammy hands and pulled her toward a stool. "I'll call *Mamm* over here, and we'll take you home so you can rest."

"No!" Sarah wrenched her hands back and gestured toward the stranger, who was chatting with the others across the bakery. "Look at him, Kathryn. Please!"

Kathryn's eyebrows careened toward her blonde hairline as her gaze followed Sarah's pointed finger.

"Tell me I'm seeing Peter. Tell me God raised him like He raised Lazarus." Sarah wiped the tears that were suddenly escaping down her hot cheeks and wished her heart would stop pounding against her rib cage.

"He does favor Peter a little." Frowning, Kathryn took Sarah's hand in hers. "Sweet Sarah Rose, Peter has gone to be with the Lord and won't come back. I'm sorry."

Sarah swallowed a sob. In her mind, she knew her sister was right, but that man looked like Peter. Taking a deep breath, she willed her tears to stop flowing. "I think I need to get some air," she said. "Will you take care of the customers for me?"

"Of course." Kathryn's lips formed a sad smile. "Tell Beth Anne to come out front, and I'll walk you home."

"I'll be fine," Sarah whispered before racing through the kitchen, past her sister, and out the back door.

She wiped her eyes as she approached the small fenced-in play area where Lindsay sat with her nieces and nephews. Leaning on the fence, Sarah wished she could stop the pain strangling her heart. She prayed her soul would heal and stop playing cruel tricks on her, such as spotting Peter in the bakery. Hadn't she suffered enough without having hallucinations?

"*Aenti* Sarah?" Lindsay asked, stepping over to the fence. "Are you okay?"

Sarah nodded. "It's been a long morning. I needed to step out to get some air."

Lindsay reached for her. "Do you need help?"

Sarah shook her head. "No. *Danki*."

The children ran around playing tag and swinging on the elaborate wooden swing set that her brothers and father had built. Sarah contemplated the two babies growing inside her, wondering what they would look like and how much they would remind her of Peter. Would the sight of her newborns cause her more heartache or would they give her the comfort she craved?

"Sarah Rose?" a voice behind her called.

Turning, she faced her mother standing in the doorway.

"Would you please come here?" *Mamm* asked, her pretty face distraught.

Sarah headed for the door, wondering what had upset her mother. She hoped Kathryn hadn't told their mother that she was having a breakdown. The last thing she needed was another lecture about allowing Peter to rest in peace. It was much easier said than done.

Mamm stepped out onto the concrete. When the mysterious man followed her, Sarah stopped, frozen in place as she assessed him. He seemed to study her also, his brown eyes fixed on her as he sauntered toward her, the swing of his arms echoing Peter's movements.

Sarah remained cemented in place, feeling as though her shoes were sinking in quicksand. Her mouth dried, and her heart thumped madly in her chest. Was she hallucinating again, or was this man who resembled Peter advancing toward her?

Mamm and the man stopped near Sarah, and Sarah's gaze never left his. While Peter's eyes had been a deep hazel, the mystery man's were the color of mocha, reminding her of the milk-chocolate pies she loved to bake.

"This is Luke Troyer," *Mamm* said, breaking through Sarah's reverie. "Peter's cousin."

Sarah gasped and clasped her mother's arm to steady herself. She opened her mouth to speak, but no sound escaped. After clearing her throat, she tried again. "That's impossible," she whispered. "Peter had no family. There must be some mistake. *Troyer* is a common Amish name."

"He was my kin," Luke said. "His full name was Peter Jacob Troyer, and he was born on May 25 in Middlefield, Ohio. He had a strawberry birthmark on his upper left shoulder blade, and he was a talented carpenter."

Sarah's hands trembled as she stared into Luke's deep brown eyes. In her heart, she knew he was telling the truth, but doubt still filtered through her mind.

But why would Peter lie?

She wondered if this man who claimed to be Peter's relative was really just someone posing as a Troyer in order to gain something. But what could he be after?

"Anyone could've confirmed that information," Sarah said, hoping to sound more confident than she felt. "That doesn't prove you're his *Freindschaft.*"

He folded his arms across his broad chest. "Your brothers and father agree there's a family resemblance between Peter and me."

Unable to disagree, Sarah nodded.

"I'll leave you two alone to talk," *Mamm* said, her voice shaking with emotion. She disappeared into the bakery.

Sarah opened her mouth to protest her mother's desertion and then stopped. She cut her eyes to the tentative smile growing on Luke Troyer's lips, and her body tensed.

Suddenly her mother's favorite verse from Romans 12 echoed in her mind: *"Be joyful in hope, patient in affliction, faithful in prayer."*

She bit her lip while the words soaked through her being. Was Luke the source of hope she'd been begging God to send her?

No!

The internal response sent a jolt through her soul. He couldn't be the tranquility she craved. Having Luke here sent her already-crumbling confidence sinking into a black hole of doubt.

Who was this man? Why was he here when Peter had said he had no family left in Ohio?

She put her hand to her throbbing temples. "This is all too much," she muttered.

"Sarah Rose?" He stepped toward her. "Are you all right?" He held a hand out to her.

"Please don't touch me." She took a step back.

His eyes widened with shock, and he raised his hands. "I'm sorry. I didn't mean to make you feel uncomfortable."

"This is just a lot to take in." She gestured toward him. "I'm feeling a bit overwhelmed."

He glanced back toward the bakery and then at her. "Would you like to go for a walk?"

She hesitated and then nodded. "I guess it would be okay for a few minutes, but then I need to get back to work."

"That sounds fair."

Fastnachts (Raised Donuts)

2 cups milk
1/3 cup lard
3/4 cup sugar
1–1/2 tsp salt
2 eggs
1 yeast cake/package
1–1/2 Tbsp warm water
About 7 cups sifted flour
Oil for frying
Powdered sugar

Bring milk and lard to boiling point, but do not boil. Stir in sugar and salt and let cool to lukewarm. Beat eggs and add to the mixture. Soak yeast cake in warm water and keep warm. Sift and measure the flour. Combine yeast and mixture. Add enough flour until able to handle easily. Knead well by stretching and folding it over itself. Let rise overnight.

The following day roll dough out to 1/4–inch thickness. Cut into 2–inch squares and make a slit in the center. Cover and let rise for 45 minutes. Fry in deep fat until brown. While warm, roll in powdered sugar.

4

Timothy glanced out the kitchen window to where Sarah Rose and Luke stood talking. He gritted his teeth and swallowed a groan.

This can't be happening!

Ever since Peter's death, Timothy had worried he'd be caught in the lie of knowing about Peter's past. Now with this relative from Ohio showing up, the truth would be revealed, making Timothy look like a liar. His stomach roiled as he paced around the kitchen in front of his siblings.

"What's wrong with you?" Kathryn asked. "You got ants in your pants?"

While his siblings snickered, Timothy huffed. "We've got to be careful of this man. We can't know who he is for sure, and he's only going to upset Sarah Rose by bringing up the past—a past that Peter can't defend."

Daniel's brows furrowed with question. "What are you saying?"

Timothy gulped. *I said too much.* "I just meant that this man is coming at the worst possible time. Sarah Rose is in a very delicate condition. We don't need her upset right now. How can we even be sure he's truly Peter's *freindschaft?*"

"He's family," Beth Anne said. "You can see it in his eyes. He's a Troyer in search of other Troyers."

"Timothy has a point." Kathryn tapped her finger on the counter. "Why would he suddenly show up after his cousin is dead? Is he going to take advantage of Sarah in her fragile state?"

Timothy swallowed a sigh of relief. *Danki, Kathryn! Finally someone is listening to me.*

"No, he won't take advantage of her or upset her." Timothy crossed his arms. "I won't allow it. I'll watch him like a hawk. He needs to tend to his business and then leave."

"You're overreacting," Daniel said, raising his hands to calm Timothy. "We don't know if he's a liar, and we don't know what he's after. We need to give him a chance."

"We need to protect Sarah," Kathryn said. "She's still grieving for her husband."

Daniel lowered himself onto a stool. "He didn't even know Peter was married. I saw surprise in his eyes when I told him Peter had a widow."

"*Ya*, he seems genuine," Beth Anne said. "I'm a good judge of character."

Timothy shook his head. His siblings were always too quick to trust people. He knew all about how liars operated. Miriam Lapp, his ex-fiancée, had proved that when she shattered his trust along with his heart. He needed to make sure that Luke left and left soon, before he hurt Sarah Rose or, worse yet, convinced her to come to Ohio with him to be with the rest of the Troyer family. Sarah needed to be with the Kauffmans, not the Troyers.

"He could be a good actor," Timothy said. "People like that take you by surprise."

Meeting his gaze, Kathryn nodded with understanding. "*Ya*. It's the truth."

Beth Anne waved them off with a frown. "You two were always the skeptics of the family."

"And rightfully so," Timothy said, turning his stare toward

the door. "I'll make sure he doesn't hurt Sarah. She's been through enough, and it's our job to protect her."

Luke fell in step with Sarah as they moved across the parking lot toward a pasture beyond the bakery. He closed his eyes for a split second, checking to see if he'd been dreaming. However, when his eyes reopened, the blonde was still walking beside him, the sweet aromas of the bakery emanating from her like an invisible cloud. Luke shook his head with astonishment at the revelation.

Sarah was beautiful. No, she was stunning, almost angelic. Her skin was porcelain, and the hair peeking from beneath her prayer *kapp* was honey blonde, even lighter than her siblings'. Her eyes were powder blue and her lips a deep pink. When she spoke, her voice was soft and sweet, reminding him of the treats lining the counters and shelves inside the bakery.

He couldn't help but wonder how Peter had managed to court and marry such a delicate beauty.

Jealousy bubbled up inside of him. While Luke had put his own life on hold, Peter had managed to sweet-talk his way into this close family and win himself a lovely bride.

Somehow life didn't seem fair.

Sarah stood straight as an arrow, as if she were marching to her death. He could feel anxiety radiating from her.

"Peter never spoke of relatives in Ohio," she said, breaking the silence between them. "If I had known about you, I would've contacted you in time for the funeral. I'm sorry you missed it."

"It's not your fault. Daniel told me Peter claimed he didn't have any family." His eyes moved to her hands, folded across her abdomen, and he stopped short. He'd noticed her shape earlier, but the meaning of her size hadn't registered with him until that moment.

Peter was expecting a child.

No, life wasn't fair. Now Peter was gone, leaving a widow who would soon be a single mother.

"*Zwillingbopplin,*" she whispered, her blue eyes full of sadness. "Our first *kinner.*"

While it made his pulse kick with joy at the notion that he would still have family, a quick look at her face reminded him of her grief. "*Zwillingbopplin,*" he repeated. "Sarah Rose, I'm so sorry for your loss."

She nodded, glancing down at her stomach. "I am too." Her gaze collided with his again, her crystal eyes hardening. "Why would Peter not tell me about his family? It doesn't make sense. Family is the most important thing of all—aside from God, of course."

Luke scanned the pasture while collecting his thoughts. He couldn't tell her the truth. It would hurt her too much, and her condition was already delicate at best. He could tell by the sadness and anger in her eyes that his mere presence had rocked her to her very core.

It was best to just tell her what she needed to know, which was very little.

He spotted a wooden park bench near the fence that closed off a few horses from the open pasture. "Let's sit and talk, so you can get off your feet," he said.

They walked together. After she slowly lowered herself onto the bench, he sank down beside her. She smoothed the black apron over her black dress, a sign of mourning. When his eyes met hers, his heart sank at the hurt and turmoil he found there. He vowed not to tell her anything that would upset her. Her condition was paramount.

"What did Peter tell you about his past?" Luke asked.

"He said his parents, Hezekiah and Ruth Troyer, died when he was young and an older couple named Abner and Clara Yoder raised him." She stared down at her hands. "And he didn't have any siblings. He moved here after his adoptive parents had died. He sold the family farm to pay off their debts and then came to Lancaster County to be closer to his Uncle Ephraim, who lives in a neighboring town. I never met his uncle, but I understood he was the only family Peter had left."

Luke resisted the urge to shake his head with disappointment. Peter wasn't an orphan and had been raised by his biological parents.

"And Peter came to work for the family furniture store?" Luke prompted her to move on with her story.

"*Ya.* My *dat* was very happy with his work." Sarah's eyes glistened. She cleared her throat and placed her hands back on her belly. "Peter said his foster father taught him how to make cabinets."

"How did you meet Peter?" he asked.

Her expression softened, her eyes reflecting happy memories. "He had joined the church in Ohio, but he became a member of our church district since he quickly made friends here. We met at a singing one Sunday night. He offered to take me home, and I told him no since I didn't know him. But he pursued me." She laughed. "He was relentless. He actually got a job at my father's shop in order to get to know me. It took about six months, but I finally agreed to see him."

"Why were you so unsure of him?"

"He was new to our church district."

"When did you marry?"

"Two years later. Peter wanted to save money. We built a house on my *dat*'s land, and we moved in the spring after we married." She sighed, her smile fading. "He wanted a big family. At first, we didn't think God wanted us to have *kinner.* I only just found out we were having *zwillingbopplin* after he died. He never knew."

He stared across the pasture, wondering what kind of parent Peter would've been.

"Sarah Rose!" A strident voice behind them caused them both to jump.

Turning, Luke found Timothy charging toward them, his expression serious. He wondered if the guy ever smiled or if he was a constant killjoy.

"Timothy?" Sarah asked. "What's wrong?"

"I think you should come back inside and rest," her brother said.

"I'm sitting on a bench, Timothy. I think I'm resting just fine." Holding her back, she hoisted herself up. Her brother reached out to help her, and she swatted his hand away. "I'm fine. Don't suffocate me!"

Luke bit back a smile at her feistiness. Not only was she beautiful, but she was also strong.

"*Mamm* says we should offer our guest something to eat," Timothy said.

She faced Luke. "Are you hungry? Would you like some lunch?"

He stood. "That sounds nice."

"Let's go find you some of my famous pork chops and scalloped potatoes," she said. "*Mamm* and I brought it for lunch today. It was left over from last night."

As they strolled back toward the bakery, Timothy motioned for Luke to hang back with him. "Your being here is not the best timing," he said through gritted teeth. "My sister has been through enough after losing her husband."

Luke flinched at the sting of the words. "I'm not going to do anything to upset her. I'm just trying to find out what happened to Peter."

"I can tell you what happened. He passed away, and now we're all trying to pick up the pieces. My sister doesn't need you here upsetting her. She didn't know Peter had a life outside of Lancaster County, and you're opening up a can of worms that doesn't matter anymore." Timothy scowled. "I think it would be best if you just left. Peter is gone, and we'll take good care of her. We don't need you or the rest of your family."

Luke studied Timothy's expression. "So you know about Peter's past?"

"I know enough. If Sarah finds out, it will crush her." He lowered his voice. "I'm going to watch your every move. My concern is my sister and her welfare. Don't do anything that will upset her. If you do, then my brothers and I will escort you to the train station and send you on your way fast enough to make your head spin."

Raising his eyebrows, Luke nodded. "I understand."

Stepping into the kitchen, Luke wondered how close Timothy had been to Peter.

More important, just how much did Timothy know about Peter's past?

Sarah stepped back into the kitchen after serving lunch to Luke, Daniel, and her father on the porch outside the bakery. Worry and doubt played havoc with her emotions. She felt as if the very ground beneath her feet was shaking with the uncertainty in her heart. Who was Luke Troyer and why had he shown up now, nearly six months after Peter had died?

But the question haunting her the most was why, oh why, hadn't Peter told her he had family in Ohio? What else had he hidden from her?

Sarah had trusted Peter with her very heart and soul. Why would he lie to her?

Since she was a little girl, Sarah had dreamt of having a loving marriage modeled after her parents, who had met young and fallen head over heels in love with each other. She believed with all of her heart that there should be no secrets between a husband and a wife.

Hadn't Peter felt the same way?

Pushing the hurtful questions away, Sarah poured herself a cold glass of water from the pitcher in the refrigerator. After taking a long drink, she set the glass down on the counter. When a hand gripped her arm, she jumped, startled. She turned to face Timothy frowning at her.

"Why didn't you announce yourself?" she snapped with a glare. "I can't stand it when you sneak up on me."

"Sorry." He shifted his straw hat and wiped sweat from his brow.

"Why aren't you outside eating lunch with the rest of the men?"

"I wanted to speak with you alone." He scanned the bakery and then nodded toward the door. "Let's go outside for a minute."

Shaking her head with impatience, Sarah followed him out to the parking lot. "What's so important that we have to step outside? I have baking to do. You may get a day to goof off, but I actually work."

"This is important." Timothy leaned against the fence. "I want you to be cautious of Luke."

"Why?" Sarah's stomach roiled at the seriousness of her brother's words. She couldn't handle more distressing news of Peter's past. "What do you know about him?"

He shrugged. "It's just a feeling I have. I don't want you to upset yourself. You need to concentrate on the *bopplin* right now, not what some stranger from Ohio says."

He glanced across the pasture, and she wondered why he was avoiding eye contact with her.

"Timothy, is there something you're not telling me?" She studied his face, waiting for his gaze to meet hers, but he kept his eyes focused on the ground and kicked a pebble. "Please look at me."

Sighing, his eyes met hers. "Sarah, I'm just worried about you, is all."

She pursed her lips and studied him. Something was bothering her brother, and she was determined to get him to confess to her. "You haven't smiled once since you came into the bakery today. Has Luke upset you?"

He shook his head and repeated himself. "I'm just worried about you."

"You're not being forthright," she said. "You were Peter's best friend, Timothy, and, besides me, you knew him best."

He glanced across the pasture.

"Timothy? What is it?" She braced herself for his response. *Please, not more upsetting news about Peter's past.*

He touched her arm and trained his eyes on hers. "Sarah Rose, I miss Peter, and I also feel it's my duty to make sure you're well taken care of. I just don't want Luke to upset you or the *kinner*. That's all."

Sarah searched her brother's eyes for any hint of a lie and couldn't shake the feeling he wasn't being completely open with her.

"Sarah!" Beth Anne called. "Can you help me with this chocolate cake?"

Walking slowly back toward the bakery, Sarah sucked in a deep breath. A headache pulsed in her temple, and her body quaked with hurt and worry.

Closing her eyes, she sent up a prayer. *Please God, lead me to the truth about my husband's past. Give me faith in my future, and help me figure out who Luke Troyer is and why he's here now.*

5

Sarah's hands trembled as she puttered around her mother's kitchen later that evening. While she chopped lettuce for salad, her mind whirled with confusion caused by the afternoon spent with Luke Troyer. She kept asking herself why Peter would've claimed to be an orphan when he had family living in Ohio. Why would Peter want to hide his identity from Sarah, his wife? She and Peter had pledged to share all of their secrets and be loyal to each other.

Mamm opened the oven door, and the aroma of juicy meatloaf penetrated the warm kitchen, tickling Sarah's taste buds.

"I think it's just about done," *Mamm* said, closing the door.

Sarah nodded and scraped the lettuce into a large bowl.

"You've hardly said a word for the last hour, Sarah Rose," her mother said, wiping her hands on her apron. "Meeting Luke has to be difficult for you. You know you can talk to me, *mei Liewe*."

"I don't know what to think, *Mamm*. Everything is a big, jumbled mess. I don't understand why Peter would tell me he had no family in Ohio if it wasn't true. I don't know how to feel. But I do know that I'm hurt." Sarah's eyes flooded with tears. "Why did he lie to me, *Mamm*? Why couldn't he trust me, his wife, with the truth?"

"Oh, Sarah Rose." *Mamm* opened her arms, and Sarah folded herself into her mother's warm hug as the tears fell. "I'm so sorry you're going through this. But remember we all love you. Perhaps God sent Luke here to help you through the rest of the pregnancy."

Sniffing, Sarah looked up at *Mamm*. "What do you mean, 'help me through the rest of the pregnancy'? How could some stranger who claims to be Peter's relative help me through a pregnancy?"

Mamm pushed back a lock of hair that had escaped Sarah's prayer *kapp*. "The Lord may have plans for you and Luke to become friends and help each other through your loss."

Sarah wiped her eyes and nose with a napkin. "How do I know he's truly family? Peter said he had no family and then this mysterious man shows up months after his death. He knows Peter's middle name and his birth date. He even knows Peter had a birthmark on his shoulder blade. But that doesn't prove anything! A former schoolmate would know those things."

Leaning back on the counter, Sarah covered her mouth to stifle a sob. The confusion swelling in her mind was making her crazy. She wished life would return to normal, and that Peter would bound through the front door with a smile and kiss for her. *Ack*, she would even be happy to hear him fuss at her for forgetting to mend his favorite shirt or for burning supper.

"*Mei liewe*," *Mamm* began, rubbing Sarah's arm. "I think you know in your heart that he's family. Just look at his face, and you'll see the truth." She nodded toward the window above the sink. "See for yourself."

Sarah gazed out the window to where Luke stood with Timothy and *Dat*. She agreed Luke resembled her late husband, but the resemblance didn't answer the questions burning in her heart.

"But Peter said he didn't have any family." Sarah watched *Dat* pat Luke on the shoulder and laugh, and her heart thumped in her chest. This mysterious man was already worming his way into her family, and his presence nipped at her nerves. Was he a symbol of the untruths Peter had told her? Had she ever known her husband at all if he would lie about his family?

"Why would he show up now?" she asked, her voice trembling like a leaf in a gusty autumn wind. She grasped for someone to take the blame for her husband's dishonesty and settled on Luke. "What is Luke after? Does he want some of our land? Or does he want money?"

Mamm chuckled. "I doubt that. It isn't our way to go around looking for money after a *freindschaft* dies."

Biting her lip, she faced her mother, needing her reassurance and guidance. "Do you think my husband lied to me when he said he was an orphan?"

Mamm sighed while straightening the ties on Sarah's prayer *kapp*. "I don't know. Luke brings up some unanswered questions. Why would a husband deceive his wife about his family? What would be the purpose in that?"

"I can't imagine a reason to do that to me." Sarah swiped at a wayward tear, her voice still quaking. "If he could lie to me about that, then he could've lied to me about anything and everything. It's not fair that I can't ask him. Why did God have to take Peter when he was so young and in the prime of his life?"

Mamm shook her head. "I promise we'll get through this. The Lord will see you through. Remember Nahum 1:7: 'The Lord is good, a refuge in times of trouble. He cares for those who trust in him.'"

Sarah nodded, hoping her mother was right and that her emotions would calm before she had to sit at the supper table with this mysterious visitor.

Luke followed Timothy and Eli into the kitchen, which included a large gas oven, beautifully crafted cabinets, and a magnificent hutch in the corner. He assumed Eli had built the hutch and maybe even the cabinets; they were the products of a master carpenter.

The two men sat at the long table in the center of the large room, Eli at the far end and Timothy to his right. Timothy shot Luke another cool glance, causing Luke to wonder what Peter had said about him. Was Timothy simply overprotective of his younger sister due to her delicate condition, or had Peter told lies about Luke's character and integrity?

His attention turned to the savory smells penetrating the room. The fragrance of meatloaf awakened his appetite, causing his stomach to growl in response. He cleared his throat, hoping to shield his rude body in front of his new friends.

"I hope you like meatloaf," Elizabeth said, placing a pan on the table.

"It smells *appeditlich*," Luke said. "*Danki*."

"Don't thank me," Elizabeth said. "Thank Sarah Rose. She's the talented chef in the family." She smiled with pride toward her daughter.

Sarah shook her head as she handed a bowl of salad to her father. "Don't be *gegisch*, *Mamm*. You taught me everything I know." After calling her mother silly, her eyes met Luke's and then quickly darted away. "Have a seat," she muttered, nodding toward the chair next to her brother.

"*Danki*," he said, wondering if she was always shy or if his presence made her uncomfortable. He hoped he hadn't overstepped his bounds with Peter's family. Jealousy bubbled up inside him at the thought.

Did Peter even realize how lucky he was to have a family like this?

Ack, what Luke would've given to be surrounded by a large, loving family like the Kauffmans.

The women finished delivering the various dishes, then sat. Luke bowed his head in silent prayer along with the rest of the family and looked up when the sounds of cutlery banging against the dinnerware broke through the silence. He began to fill his plate, putting each entree on a different corner of the dish in order to prevent the food from touching—a habit he'd learned from his father when he was young. When he felt someone's eyes boring into him, he glanced across the table to find Sarah staring at his plate. Her gaze met his, and her eyes widened with astonishment.

Luke chuckled in response to her disbelief. "It's an old habit."

She nodded, the blood draining from her pretty face.

"You all right, Sarah Rose?" Eli asked, his face full of concern. "You look like you've seen a ghost."

She blinked and lifted her glass of water to her lips. Elizabeth whispered something, and Sarah averted her eyes to her plate. Luke wished he could read Sarah's mind. He hoped he wasn't the cause of her distress. Like Timothy, he was concerned for her welfare.

"How long do you plan to stay in Bird-in-Hand, Luke?" Eli asked, slapping mashed potatoes onto his plate.

"I'm not certain." Luke stabbed his meatloaf. "I thought I'd stay at least a couple of weeks to learn about Peter's life." In his peripheral vision he spotted Sarah watching him. When he looked up, she quickly glanced back at her plate. He wished she would look at him. He couldn't bear making her uncomfortable in her parents' home.

"Do you have a place to stay?" Elizabeth asked.

Luke shrugged. "I figured I'd find something out on that main highway. What is it—Route 30?"

"Route 30 out by the English tourists?" Eli asked. "Don't be ridiculous. We have plenty of room here."

Covering her mouth, Sarah began to sputter and choke.

"Sarah Rose?" Elizabeth leaned over and held her hands while her daughter continued to cough, tears streaming down her porcelain cheeks. "Lean forward," she ordered. Once she moved, Elizabeth rubbed her back. "It's all right. Just breathe easy."

After a few deep breaths, the coughing subsided.

"Take a drink," Elizabeth said.

"Are you all right?" Luke asked.

Sarah nodded. "Something went down the wrong way."

Her glance met his for a split second, and he saw something flash deep in her eyes—sadness or perhaps loneliness. Luke stood and picked up her glass from the table.

"What are you doing?" Sarah asked, her voice laced with annoyance.

"Refilling your glass," he said, wrenching open the refrigerator door.

"You're our guest," Sarah said. "You're supposed to sit while I refill your glass."

Luke topped off the drink and brought it back to her. "A simple thank you would suffice." He then returned to his seat.

Sarah studied Luke while Eli snickered.

"He told you, daughter," Eli said.

Sarah shot her father an evil look while Luke grinned. *Ack*, she was beautiful, especially when she was angry.

Turning toward Timothy, Luke found the man glaring at him. Luke cleared his throat and turned his attention back to his plate. He had crossed a line and gotten a cold stare for the effort. But he sure didn't regret it.

"I was thinking you could stay here," Eli repeated. "It would be wasteful to spend money on a motel when we have so much room."

Out of the corner of his eye, Luke spotted Sarah shooting her father a look of horror. His heart twisted with disappointment. He couldn't fault Sarah for being upset after hearing Peter had lied to her. However, he'd hoped they could somehow forge a friendship. He longed to be a part of her twins' lives, since they were his closest link to Peter.

Luke met Sarah's disapproving stare as he responded to her father. "Thank you for your hospitality, Eli, but I think it would be best if I stayed in a hotel."

Sarah's gaze was unmoving, challenging him. She sure was a feisty one!

"I won't allow you to waste your money," Elizabeth retorted. "You'll stay here. Why doesn't he stay at your house, Sarah Rose? It's been empty for six months now, and I'm sure the walls would enjoy some company."

Gasping, Sarah turned to her *Mamm.* "My house?" she asked. "The house that Peter built for us?"

"*Ya,*" Elizabeth said.

The women exchanged expressions, a silent and private conversation, before Sarah faced him again. "I'd be happy to host you," she deadpanned. "Please stay at my house."

"Are you certain?" Luke raised an eyebrow.

Sarah nodded and returned her attention to her supper.

"Where did you say you worked in Ohio?" Eli asked.

"A cabinet shop near my home," Luke said.

"Tell us about it," Eli said.

Luke swallowed a piece of juicy meatloaf and then told the Kauffmans about his life back home.

"How could you do that to me?" Sarah snapped while scrubbing a pot after supper. "How could you put me on the spot like that?"

"Whatever are you going on about?" *Mamm* asked, wiping off the table.

"What makes you think I want that man sleeping in my house?" Sarah shook her head and rinsed the detergent off the pot. "That was our house! The house I shared with my beloved Peter. I don't need that stranger—"

"He's not a stranger." Her mother's voice was calm.

"Yes, he is!" Sarah threw down the towel for emphasis. "I don't need him coming in here and stirring things up while I'm trying to create a life for my *zwillingbopplin.*"

"He was Peter's family, so that makes him the *zwillingbopplin's* family too."

"How do you really know that?" Sarah propped her hands on her hips. "What proof do you have?"

A smile curved *Mamm's* lips. "I know you saw it at supper. I witnessed the shock on your face."

Sarah shook her head. "I don't know what you're talking about."

"Sarah Rose, don't lie to me." *Mamm* wagged her slim finger. "You know exactly what I'm talking about. *Dat* even asked you what was wrong. He asked you if you'd seen a ghost."

Sarah gulped, knowing she'd been caught in a fib. "I did see it," she whispered. "He separated his food so it wouldn't touch."

"Peter did that at every meal I shared with him." Crossing the kitchen, *Mamm* pointed out the window. "Look at him, Sarah Rose. Tell me you don't see similarities in the way he walks and holds himself."

Licking her dry lips, Sarah turned her attention to the field where Luke stood by the barn, chatting with *Dat* and Timothy. Luke held onto his suspenders as he listened to *Dat*. Before speaking, he lifted his hat and smoothed back his hair.

"Peter always did that," she whispered, her voice croaking with emotion and memories. "He'd hold onto his suspenders and then smooth his hair when he was trying to remember something." Tears filled her eyes. "*Dat* was right when he asked me if I'd seen a ghost. I have seen one, and he's standing right there with my brother and *Dat*."

Mamm rubbed her back. "Embrace him as a friend. He's a connection to your Peter."

Sarah wiped her eyes. "But if I embrace him, then I embrace the knowledge that my marriage to Peter was a lie, *Mamm*," she whispered. "Don't you see how his presence here is breaking my heart? How do I know I married a man named Peter Troyer? His real name could've been something completely different.

Maybe he was really an English man posing as an Amish man to run from indiscretions he committed in his former life."

Mamm pulled her into a hug. "Peter was a *gut* man with a *gut* heart. Hold onto the happy memories, Sarah Rose. He's gone, but you know he loved you and loved your *kinner*."

"But he lied," Sarah said, resting her chin on *Mamm's* shoulder as she'd done as a little girl.

"There must've been a reason. I don't want to believe the worst."

Standing up tall, Sarah swiped her hand over her hot cheeks. "Neither do I, but the lies are here in the flesh of that man who looks like Peter and shares his mannerisms. How can I come to terms with that when it's staring me in the face? And how do I know my whole marriage wasn't a sham?"

Elizabeth took Sarah's hands in hers. "I don't have the answers, but I do know one thing for certain: Peter loved you. I could see it in his eyes every time he looked at you, Sarah Rose. I don't know why he would be dishonest with you, but I know his heart belonged to you and only you." She nodded toward the sink. "I'll finish the dishes. You go wash your face, then take Luke over to your house. Let him see where Peter lived and tell him about your life with him."

Sarah heaved a deep breath and headed toward the bathroom.

With her heart pounding, Sarah gripped the knob to the front door of the house she and Peter had shared for three short years. For a split second, she wished she'd taken Timothy up on his offer to accompany her and Luke to the house. However, she couldn't depend on her family to shield her from the pain for the rest of her life. She had to do this in order to start down the road to healing her shattered heart, for the sake of the twins.

Her soul swelled with grief when she pushed the door open and stared at the modest living room furniture on which she and her husband would sit and talk late into the evenings.

A husband who lied to me about his family!

Sarah closed her eyes. She couldn't deal with that now. She had to get through showing Luke the house. After a tour, she would retreat to her old room in her mother's house and try to sort through the stress of the day caused by the mysterious visitor.

Luke stepped past her into the room and dropped his duffel bag onto the floor with a loud thud. "Your house is real nice," he said, scanning the room. He sauntered to the doorway separating the living room from the kitchen and ran his long fingers over the molding. "Simple, but every piece fits perfectly. The moldings fit as if they were carved out of the wall. Peter's work. I'd know it anywhere."

Sarah rubbed her belly as Luke examined the baseboards. His mannerisms were so familiar. The way his hands swept lightly over the woodwork while he frowned, deep in thought, and how he rubbed his chin and squinted his eyes—it was so much like Peter that she almost felt her late husband's presence.

Sarah cleared her throat and crossed the room. "The kitchen is small, but I liked it." She gestured toward the oak cabinets. "He made them himself."

"*Wunderbaar.*" Luke rubbed the cabinets as if they were velvety-soft kittens. "Nice craftsmanship. I always told him he could open his own cabinet shop, but he wanted to concentrate on furniture. An uncle taught him how to make tables, chairs, and bed frames. Peter was a master at it."

"Uncle?" she asked, her voice small, weighed down with more hurt. "He had an uncle in Ohio too?"

He nodded. "*Ya,* he did."

Pain shot through Sarah's abdomen like fire, and she sucked in a deep breath.

"Sarah?" Luke rushed over to her. "Are you all right?"

Unable to speak, she held her breath, praying the cramping would subside.

"Sit," he ordered, pulling out a chair. He started to reach for her but instead pointed to the chair and she sat. He then knelt next to her, his eyes full of worry. "Should I run and get your *mamm*? Do we need to take you to a doctor?"

"No." She swallowed deep breaths. The pain eased, and she leaned back in the chair. "It passed," she whispered.

He nodded, concern still reflected in his face. "Want me to go get your *mamm*?"

She forced a smile and shook her head. "I'm *gut,* but *danki.*" She took short breaths in anticipation of any lingering pain. Finding none, she let her body relax. "Would you like to see the upstairs?" she asked.

He frowned. "Are you sure you can make it up the stairs?"

"I'm expecting *zwillingbopplin*. I'm not ill." She hoisted herself from the chair and started for the stairs. "Go get your bag, and I'll show you your room."

He grabbed his bag from the living room and followed.

Sarah took her time climbing the stairs and insisted she was doing fine when Luke again asked if she was okay. When they reached the hallway on the second floor, she leaned against the wall and breathed deeply, feeling as if she'd trotted across the back pasture in record time.

"Are you sure you're okay?"

"*Ya.*" She caught her breath. "I have two more months of this. I'd better make myself a bedroom on my parents' first floor."

"I think that would be wise," he said with a smile.

Sarah motioned toward the master bedroom. "This is our room." She paused. "I guess I should say this *was* our room." She scowled while studying her bed, which sat lonely and tidy, untouched since the morning Peter had perished. The beautiful green-and-blue log-cabin quilt her sister-in-law Sadie had crafted as a wedding gift seemed to mock her.

Closing her eyes, she concentrated on the last night Peter had held her close in the dark. She could almost feel his whiskers brushing her face, and she could almost smell his fresh, masculine scent.

But he lied! a small voice inside her chided. *Your precious husband died and took all of his secrets with him. You'll never know if anything he ever told you was true!*

"If this is too painful for you, we can move to another room," Luke's voice whispered close to her ear.

Sarah kept her eyes squeezed shut. If she concentrated, she could imagine the voice speaking to her belonged to Peter. She'd give anything to hear him say, "I love you, Sarah Rose" one last time.

And she'd give anything to find out why he'd been dishonest with her.

"Which room would you prefer I use?" he asked.

Sarah's eyes flew open, and she cleared her throat, forcing back the lump threatening to strangle her words. She had to find a way to let Peter rest in peace. She needed to pray for strength.

"Sarah?" he asked, stepping closer to her. "Do you need some time alone in here?"

"No," she whispered, surprised by his understanding, wondering if he could read her mind. "I need to face the memories in this house eventually, and there's no time like the present." She headed into the hall and pointed toward the room next door.

"This was my sewing room." Her eyes moved over the piles of material strewn about—the shirts and trousers she hadn't finished making for Peter, and the maternity dresses she had begun. Her sewing machine sat on a small desk in the center of the room.

"I need to clean up the mess. I'll have to tell Timothy to bring the material to *Mamm's*," she muttered, closing the door and moving to the next room, which contained a cradle and a few dressers. Bags of baby clothes from her sisters sat in the corner of the room awaiting sorting.

Her stomach twisted at the idea of being in this house, surrounded by bittersweet memories while organizing baby clothes for the twins who would never know their father.

And what would she tell her children about their father? Would she tell them they had more relatives in Ohio? Should she go to Ohio and meet the relatives herself before the babies were born?

She crossed the room and stared down at the cradle, wondering if she'd ever truly know who her husband had been.

Her thoughts turned to her own family.

"*Dat* made this cradle for my oldest brother, Robert," she said. "It's been passed down to each of the Kauffman *kinner* and *kinskinner*." Gingerly she pushed the cradle, which rocked back and forth, quietly scraping the floor.

"Eli does some nice work." Luke ran his fingers over the finish. "But you'll need a second cradle. Maybe I can make it for you."

Raising her eyebrows, Sarah met his gaze. "You want to make me a cradle?"

"Why not?" He tilted his head and shot her a crooked smile.

She noticed for the first time that Luke was handsome. Due to the strong family resemblance, she assumed he was Peter's first cousin. Perhaps their fathers had been brothers.

It didn't matter if they were first cousins or even distant cousins. How could Sarah even know for sure? What if the whole Troyer family was full of liars?

She headed for the door. "The guest room is here."

He stepped into the small bedroom and glanced around. "This is perfect."

Sarah moved to the bed and idly straightened the quilt. "It's nothing fancy, but it's functional."

"I'm Amish," he said with a chuckle. "I don't need fancy."

She lowered herself onto the edge of the bed. "*Ya*, that's true."

He lifted the dark-green shade and glanced out the window. "Who lives in that house across the field?"

"Timothy." Sarah held her stomach as the twins performed summersaults. "He built that house a few years ago."

"Is he engaged?" Luke straightened the shade and leaned back against the wall. His lanky physique filled the room, and she guessed he was taller than Peter by at least an inch.

"It was three years ago, but his girlfriend, Miriam, changed her mind a month before the wedding and left the community." She absently smoothed the quilt.

"She left the community?"

"*Ya.*" Sarah glanced up, meeting his surprised look.

"I guess she was shunned, *ya?*"

She shook her head. "She was going to join the church before they were married, but she left abruptly. Timothy was crushed. They'd been together a long time, and it took him a few years to work up the nerve to ask her to marry him. She'd always toyed with the idea of going to college, and she said she had to try to fulfill her dream. She longed to be a pediatric nurse."

He shook his head. "I'm sure he took that hard."

"He was angry for a long time. But he finally managed to move on by focusing on the furniture store." She hoisted herself up. "He works long hours and always takes on the larger projects at the shop. *Dat* tells him he's a workaholic, but that doesn't stop him. I think that's how he deals with his broken heart."

"He never met anyone else?" Luke asked, standing up to his full height, which meant he towered over her by at least six inches.

"No. I hope he does someday. He'd be a *gut* husband and *dat.*" She studied Luke's face and tried to guess his age. "How old are you?"

"Twenty-nine," he said.

"Two years older than Peter," she whispered.

"*Ya,* that's right." He rubbed his clean-shaven chin.

Studying his mocha eyes, she wondered who Luke Troyer was. Part of her wanted to stay distant from him and not get to know him, but another part of her wanted the truth—the real truth. Yet she worried Luke would reveal even more painful deception Peter had left behind without explanation.

"Why haven't you married?" she asked before she could stop the words.

A grin turned up the corners of his mouth. "You get right to the point, Sarah Rose."

"I'm sorry." Her face burned.

"It's fine." He waved off the thought. "I did have someone special back before my pop got sick."

"Your father was ill?"

"*Ya*, he had a stroke several years ago, and he died about eight months ago."

"And your *mamm*, is she living?"

He shook his head. "She died in an accident when I was young."

"I'm sorry to hear that. And you took care of your father alone?"

He leaned back against the wall again. "That's right. I split my time between work and Pop. My girlfriend got sick of waiting for me, and she moved on."

"Waiting for you?" She tilted her head in question. "I don't understand."

"She wanted me to choose between my pop and her. I couldn't leave Pop. He was my responsibility."

"Was she Amish?" Sarah asked.

"*Ya*. We grew up together." He tossed his straw hat onto the peg on the wall next to the bed.

She shook her head with disbelief. "How could she abandon you when you needed her most? It's our way to care for each other. Now that Peter's gone, it seems everyone wants to take care of me whether I want their help or not."

"Millie wasn't like that. I think she was too selfish to spend her time caring for my pop. She waited for a year and then married someone else—my best friend."

"And you never met anyone else?"

"I was too busy caring for Pop and working. I didn't have time for courting."

"You've had a lot of tragedy in your life. You've lost your *mamm*, your *dat*, and your true love. That's a lot for a person to bear." She stepped toward the door. "I'll let you get settled.

The bathroom is downstairs next to the kitchen. I'll go to the market tomorrow and get you some groceries. Feel free to come to my parents' house for meals."

Although Luke's presence had sent her emotions into a deep abyss of anger and hurt, she felt sorry for him and his loss. She didn't wish her sorrow on anyone, especially someone who was family.

"We'll be sitting on the porch later if you want to join us." She studied the exhaustion in his eyes and shook her head. "You look tired, though, so I'll understand if you'd rather sleep tonight. It's been a long day for you."

He raked his hand through his brown hair. "I think I may call it a day, but I appreciate the invitation."

"You're also welcome to use our horse and buggy," she added. "Timothy may have already introduced you to Molly in *Dat's* barn. Peter bought Molly before we were married. She's a very docile horse. You can use her to venture around town."

"*Danki*," he said.

"I'll see you tomorrow," she said. "Sleep well." Turning, she stepped through the doorway.

"Sarah!" Timothy's voice rang out downstairs. "Sarah Rose! *Mamm* is looking for you back at the house."

"Wait. I want to say something," Luke said.

He ran his hand through his hair again, reminding her of Peter when he was nervous. Her mouth went dry.

"*Danki* for everything," he said. "I appreciate how your family has welcomed me here."

"Sarah? Where are you?" Timothy called, boots scraping the stairs.

"I could only dream of having a family like this," Luke said.

His words brought tears to her eyes. This poor man had lost his family. He deserved her sympathy.

But how can I know he's telling the truth?

"Sarah?" Timothy said as he came up behind her. "We were

starting to get worried. You've been here quite awhile. *Mamm* is looking for you."

"I was just showing Luke the house," Sarah huffed, annoyed. "I was about to head back." Wasn't she old enough to take care of herself? She was sick of everyone hovering over her like she was a fragile little girl.

"Good night, Luke," she said. "I'll see you tomorrow."

"Let's go," Timothy said. Placing his hand on her shoulder, he steered her toward the stairs.

Later that evening, Luke stepped from the shower and snatched a towel off the rack on the wall. While drying himself, he reflected on the day, and exhaustion pummeled him. He was both emotionally and physically drained. His life had taken a turn he hadn't expected after arriving at the Kauffman & Yoder Amish Furniture store this morning. He'd discovered that not only was Peter dead, but that he had left behind a family—a real family with a wife, unborn twins, and a host of in-laws who'd cared for him.

Grief mixed with anger gripped Luke. He was filled with questions, and he wanted answers. No, he *needed* answers, and they were answers only Peter could provide.

But Peter was gone. He was dead.

Luke brushed at the moisture in his eyes and cleared his throat while unanswered questions swirled like a tornado in his mind. How had Peter—who had been anti-Amish and driven to become English, and who had left home in Ohio in a fit of anger—moved to another Amish community and quickly become a part of it? It didn't make sense.

Luke could tell the Kauffmans had loved and accepted Peter as one of their own. Peter had been a lucky man—probably luckier than he'd ever appreciated.

While pulling on his clothes, anger entangled with envy

surged through Luke. Peter had married sweet, angelic Sarah, and from the sound of her stories, he was a good Amish man.

He contemplated that for a moment. Perhaps Peter had rediscovered his belief in God. Peter had joined the church in Ohio before he left, and maybe he'd found renewed belief when he met the people here in Bird-in-Hand.

But still, it didn't seem fair. All Luke had ever dreamed of was a family—a real family, with a loving wife and many, many children. He'd given it all up to care for his pop. Yet Peter had walked away from his family in Ohio and into a brand-new one in Pennsylvania.

Balancing a kerosene lantern in his hand, Luke fetched his dirty clothes and moved through the kitchen toward the stairs. Scanning the room, he tried to imagine Peter and Sarah sharing a life in this house. He wondered if they'd been happy together.

The sorrow reflected in Sarah's eyes told him she missed her husband with all of her heart. Their home seemed haunted with a ghost of the love Peter had left behind. Luke's heart craved the love Sarah held for Peter. He hoped someday he could find a woman who was as sweet, loving, and kind as Sarah seemed to be.

Ascending the stairs, he focused on Sarah. Or, as her parents called her, Sarah Rose. How fitting her middle name was. She indeed was a delicate flower, but he'd also seen her thorns when she stood up to her family members. She was a complex woman. He hoped he could foster a friendship with her and be a part of her twins' lives. It was the least he could do to help her through her loss and the rough road ahead.

Luke yawned as he threw his dirty clothes into a pile on the chair near the bed. Tomorrow he would hitch up Molly and take a tour of Bird-in-Hand. Then he'd visit Eli and see if he could get some wood to start on that cradle.

He would have to tell DeLana the news of Peter's death, but first he wanted to find out more about the family Peter had left behind. He would contact DeLana when he traveled back to Ohio.

He snuffed out the lantern light and climbed into the double bed. Closing his eyes, he imagined Sarah's face. He prayed silently, thanking God for his safe passage to Bird-in-Hand and for the opportunity to find Peter's family.

7

"Sarah, is that chocolate cake ready yet?" Beth Anne asked as she crossed the bakery kitchen. "We have customers asking for one of your famous cakes."

"*Ya.*" Sarah swiped the knife over the icing one more time and then placed it on the counter. "Here you go."

"*Wunderbaar.*" Beth Anne lifted the cake plate. "Your best yet." She paused and turned her concerned eyes to Sarah. "How is Luke doing?"

Sarah shrugged. "*Gut*, I guess. I haven't seen him in a few days since I dropped off some groceries and supplies for him. But *Dat* says Luke's been visiting businesses and checking out Lancaster County. He's stopped in to see *Dat* every day and helps out with the projects at the shop."

"*Gut.*" Beth Anne touched Sarah's arm. "How are you feeling?"

Sarah yawned. "Tired."

"You need a break. Sit for a while, and I'll bring you some ice water." Beth Anne ambled toward the front of the bakery. "I'll be right back."

Sarah lowered herself onto a chair and took a deep breath. The past few days had been long. Although her mother had suggested she cut back on her hours at the bakery, Sarah couldn't bring herself to stay home. She'd rather be with her sisters, contributing to the family business.

Lindsay appeared with a glass and placed it in Sarah's hand. "Here's your water, *Aenti* Sarah."

"*Danki*," Sarah said, lifting it to her lips. The icy liquid was just the refreshment she craved.

While running her fingers through the cool condensation, she wondered what Luke had been doing since he'd arrived at Bird-in-Hand. Truth be known, she'd avoided him as much as possible, worried if she spent more time with him, she'd find out about more lies from Peter, crushing her already-broken heart.

Timothy insisted Luke would only hurt Sarah, and he encouraged her to avoid him. But while she wanted to stay away from Luke, Sarah still couldn't stop her mind from wondering about the questions Peter had left unanswered. The biggest was why Peter had left Ohio.

As curious as she was, she was afraid of the answers.

"Sarah Rose," Kathryn said, stepping into the kitchen through the back door. "You have a visitor."

Moving to the doorway, Sarah smiled when she found Norman standing outside.

His lips formed a tentative smile as his gaze met hers. "Sarah Rose. How are you?"

"*Gut. Danki.*" Sarah wiped her hands over her apron. "And you?"

"*Gut.*" He nodded.

"I'll let you talk," Kathryn said, moving into the bakery.

"Have you had lunch?" he asked.

Facing him, Sarah shook her head.

"Would you like to go to the Bird-in-Hand Restaurant?" he offered. "I'm sure you're very busy, but I promise I'll have you back soon."

Sarah blew out a sigh of relief. Getting out of the bakery and away from her overactive thought processes would be a blessing. She needed a nice distraction. "I'd love to join you for lunch."

Sarah studied the menu while sitting across from Norman at the Bird-in-Hand Restaurant and Smorgasbord. Stealing a glance over the table, she found Norman's attention fixed on her. She smiled and wondered what was going through his mind.

"Have you decided?" he asked.

She shook her head. "You?"

"I think I'll have my usual." He closed the menu and slapped it onto the table in front of him.

The server appeared with their glasses of ice water. Sarah lifted hers from the table and took a long drink while Norman gave his order—the Lancaster County Baked Ham.

"And you, ma'am?" the young Plain Mennonite woman asked.

"I'll have the same, thank you." Sarah handed her menu to the woman and sat back in the chair. "The weather has been nice, *ya*? I bet your herd is doing well."

He nodded, though his eyes seemed to be concentrating on something other than her words.

Enjoying the mundane conversation, she continued to babble. "My *dat* says it's hotter than usual this time of year. I really don't remember how hot it was last year this time. It seems normal to me." She drew imaginary circles on her glass. "An English customer the other day asked me if it was always this mild in October. I told her I thought so." She snickered. "Don't we always have a mixture of mild and cool weather in autumn? I guess she must've been from somewhere cold, like Alaska." She smiled. "You want to know something *gegisch*? I've always wanted to go to Alaska."

Norman took her hands into his. "Sarah Rose."

Glancing up, she met his gaze, and the warmth of his eyes caught her off guard. "Norman? Are you all right?"

"*Ya*, I am." He gave a sad smile. "I asked you here for a reason. I wanted to see how you're doing. I remember clearly the first half year after I lost Leah. I felt as if I were on a roller coaster. Waves of grief would drown me one moment and then the next moment I'd be remembering the happier times and laughing so hard my stomach hurt." He squeezed her hand. "How are you, Sarah Rose? How are you truly?"

Sarah licked her lips and sniffed back sudden tears while she wondered how Norman could understand her so well. The answer was obvious—he had lived through losing his own life partner, the person who was supposed to grow old with him as Peter was supposed to grow old with her.

"I'm *gut*," she whispered.

He raised an eyebrow. "Really?"

"No." Her voice croaked, and she cleared her throat. "I'm a walking time bomb, and I feel like I'll blow any moment."

He nodded. "I remember feeling that way. If you're comfortable sharing, I'd be honored to listen without judgment."

"*Danki*." She bit her lip and studied her glass, silently debating how much to share. Although she hadn't felt comfortable sharing her feelings in the past, she suddenly felt the strength of his friendship and trusted him. "My situation is a little more complicated than yours. I found out Peter omitted some information about his past."

"I'm sorry, but I don't understand."

Sarah explained how Luke had arrived from Ohio, proving that Peter in fact had family.

Their food arrived, and Sarah continued her story while they ate.

"Now I'm struggling with the realization that he lied to me," she said in between bites of ham. "It's made my grief so much deeper. I feel like my heart has been shredded. I don't know what to do with the pain."

Norman sipped his water and shook his head. "I'm sorry you're going through this. I don't know how to help you, except to say Peter did love you. It was obvious just by looking in his eyes."

Sarah studied Norman and blinked. "My *mamm* said the same thing to me."

He gave a sad smile. "Knowing and believing that won't take away the pain or the questions. But it may help you accept he's gone, and you may never know the answers. Just hold onto the belief and faith in the love you shared, a love that created your *zwillingbopplin*."

Sarah stared into his brown eyes and nodded. Norman was a good friend—a generous Christian man. God had blessed her with so many wonderful people in her life.

During the ride back to the bakery, Sarah lost herself in thought. Although *Mamm* and Norman had told her to hold onto the knowledge that her husband had loved her, their words didn't offer her any comfort. Anger and grief still surged through her. She wanted to speak to Peter face-to-face and tell him how much his lies had hurt her.

But she couldn't talk to him ever again.

Peter was dead. He was gone forever.

Sarah forced herself to concentrate on the scenery despite the renewed grief soaking through her soul.

"How was lunch?" *Mamm* asked as Sarah stepped through the door to the bakery.

"*Gut*," Sarah said, moving past her to the stove. "It was nice to get out of the bakery and talk for a while. Did Beth Anne finish another chocolate cake?"

"*Ya,* she did." *Mamm* sidled up beside her, her expression expectant. "Did you have a good talk at lunch?"

"*Ya.*" Sarah moved to the sink. "He just wanted to see how I was doing. He remembers what it feels like to lose a spouse." She washed her hands, careful to keep her expression nonchalant. She didn't want to rehash the whole conversation for fear of crying again. She'd cried enough tears to last a lifetime.

"I'm glad you have Norman to talk to. He's the best one to share your feelings with during this difficult time. I'm glad he's your friend. He's a *gut* man and a *gut* father." *Mamm* studied Sarah's face. "You seem preoccupied, Sarah Rose. What's on your mind?"

"Nothing." Sarah dried her hands and turned toward the counter. "I best get going on the next chocolate cake. I took a long lunch and need to get caught up."

"*Liewe.*" *Mamm* pulled her into a warm hug, then walked toward the front of the store.

Sucking in a deep breath, Sarah prayed for strength and answers to the riddle of Peter's life.

Funny Cake Pie

Top of cake:
1 cup sugar
1/4 cup butter or lard (shortening)
1/2 cup milk
1 beaten egg
1 cup flour
1 tsp baking powder
1/2 tsp vanilla
Pinch of cinnamon

Cream together sugar and butter. Add the milk and egg alternately with flour and baking powder. Add vanilla and cinnamon and set aside until lower part is mixed.

Lower part of cake:
4 Tbsp cocoa
1/2 cup sugar
1/2 tsp vanilla
6 Tbsp water

Mix together the cocoa, sugar, vanilla, and water. Pour into an unbaked pie shell. Over this pour the top part. The chocolate will come up around the outside edge, giving a nice crusty edge on the finished product. Bake at 350 degrees for 40 minutes or until firm (toothpick test).

8

"I thought Timothy would be back in time for supper," Sarah said while filling the kitchen sink with hot water.

"He said he had to stop by Norman's on his way home from the shop," *Mamm* said.

"Oh." Sarah faced her mother, who was balancing a load of dirty dishes in her arms. She wasn't surprised to hear Timothy had gone to see Norman; the two men had been friends since they were teenagers.

She thought about her lunchtime conversation with Norman. She wished she could take to heart Norman's assurance that Peter loved her. She knew if she could put aside her anger toward Peter and get to know Luke, she could ask him about Peter's past.

However, she was still afraid of finding out information that would hurt her even more.

Mamm shook her head and placed the stack of dishes in the soapy water. "You're a million miles away tonight. Come to think of it, you've been that way all afternoon. What is wrong, *mei liewe?*"

"Nothing." Sarah waved off the question with a dishcloth, avoiding the thoughts that haunted her. "Must be hormones from the babies. What were you saying?" She turned her attention to scrubbing the dishes.

"I said I guess Timothy stayed for supper." *Mamm* grabbed a cloth from the drawer and wet it.

"*Ya*. He must've." Sarah lined the clean dishes onto the drying rack. "I'm surprised Luke hasn't joined us for supper these past few days."

"*Dat* asked him that at the shop today, and Luke said he'd been eating a quick supper at the house at night. He mentioned something about working on a project at your house. You haven't visited with him lately, have you?" *Mamm* asked.

Sarah shook her head.

"Why is that?" *Mamm's* eyes were full of concern. "Are you worried he'll tell you more about Peter?"

"You mean more lies?" Sarah crossed her arms in front of her chest as if to guard her already-broken heart.

Mamm's face softened. "Sarah Rose, I can't pretend to understand how you feel, but I can offer you the intuition I feel in my heart. I know you're grieving, and I know you're hurt by what Peter told you and by what he didn't tell you. However, the only way you're going to heal is to face Peter's past, remembering his past came before he met you, and his future was with you and still is with you." She touched Sarah's stomach. "While he isn't here to defend the choices he made by not telling you the whole truth, he left part of his heart with you and you need to hold onto that."

Sarah swallowed and blinked back tears.

"I don't mean to patronize you." *Mamm* cupped Sarah's face in her hands. "But it's breaking my heart to watch you suffer so. Luke is only going to be with us for a short time. Perhaps you should give him a chance and hear what he has to say."

"Okay," Sarah whispered before clearing her throat.

Mamm gave her a quick hug and stepped toward the table.

Luke's boots crunched across the rocky driveway leading from

Sarah and Peter's house to Eli's. Covering his mouth with his hand, he blew out a deep yawn. Despite his better judgment, he planned to spend a few hours visiting with the Kauffmans on the porch instead of heading to bed for some much-needed rest.

He'd begun the day riding through Bird-in-Hand, and as if pulled by an invisible magnet, he found himself in front of Eli's furniture store.

He then spent the rest of the day helping Elmer Yoder's grandson, Jake Miller, build a dresser for an English customer. The store was still backed up with orders that had been placed before the fire. He enjoyed helping the carpenters get caught up since it made him feel an even stronger connection to the Kauffman family.

He'd enjoyed getting to know the family and their friends, and he felt closer to them every day. However, he still felt a chill from Timothy. The man never smiled, and he only offered one-word answers or terse instructions when he addressed Luke. Despite his best efforts, Luke hadn't been able to get Timothy to hold a cordial conversation with him.

When they closed up the shop at suppertime, Eli invited Luke to join him for the evening meal. Luke glanced down at his dust-covered clothes and decided it would be best if he cleaned up first. He promised Eli that he would make it to the Kauffmans' house in time for dessert.

Later that evening, Luke's gaze moved up the back steps to the small kitchen window, and he wondered if Sarah was washing the dishes. Guilt washed over him; he knew he'd been avoiding her. He'd wanted to sit her down alone and tell her the truth, the whole truth, about who he was and also about Peter's past. Luke knew in his heart he owed it to Sarah, but he was worried he would hurt her, just as Timothy predicted.

Luke cared about Sarah, and he worried about how she would cope without Peter. He knew her family would look after her, but he also wanted to be a part of her twins' lives. They were the closest chance he had left to enjoying a true family.

Those feelings haunted him every day, growing more intense each time he helped her father and brothers work in the new furniture shop. While surrounded by her brothers and father, Luke couldn't shake one thought—he longed to stay in Bird-in-Hand with the Kauffman family, even if only as a surrogate member. He'd picked up a paper during his travels through town and perused the real estate section. If he found an affordable home, he might consider staying.

He couldn't suppress the feeling that the Lord had held him in Bird-in-Hand for a reason, and he prayed about it every night. He wanted to be a part of the twins' lives, and he hoped to get to know Sarah. He prayed she would support his decision to stay.

Taking a deep breath, Luke sauntered up the path leading to the back porch of Sarah's parents' house.

The door creaked open, and his breath paused when he spotted Sarah, glowing in the low light of the kitchen behind her.

"Luke," she said, her eyes round with surprise.

"Good evening, Sarah." He stood on the bottom step. "Your *dat* invited me to come visit with him this evening."

"Oh. He had to tend to some chores in the barn." She smoothed her apron. "Would you like to sit on the porch and have some hot cocoa and some crumbly peach pie?"

"*Ya.*" He pushed his hat farther back on his head. "I'd like that very much. *Danki.*" He climbed the stairs. When she stepped back toward the door, he reached for her and then stopped. "How about you sit on the swing and I get the cocoa and pie?"

A sweet smile curved up her rosy lips. "And how will you find the cocoa and pie, *gegisch?*" she asked, her eyes twinkling with humor.

"Hmm. I guess you got me there." He rubbed his chin, trying in vain not to grin at the surprise of being called silly. Her cautious and cold demeanor seemed to have vanished, at least temporarily. Was Sarah finally opening up to him?

"*Ya.*" She laughed, the sound a sweet melody to his ears. "I do. Sit." She gestured toward the swing. "I'll be right back."

Luke lowered himself onto the swing, which creaked under his weight. Swaying back and forth, he breathed in the cool autumn air. His mind wandered with the idea of moving here and joining the community.

Since his father had passed away, he'd more than once considered selling his land to a developer who had been after his father to sell for years. Apparently the Troyer farm was prime property for an English housing development, but his father had never given in to the generous offering. However, Luke didn't feel tied to Ohio now that his immediate family was gone. He wanted to be near his only remaining Amish family: Peter's children.

The door opened and slammed with a bang, revealing Sarah balancing a tray with two mugs of cocoa topped with whipped cream, two plates with pieces of pie, forks, and napkins.

Popping up, he took the tray and motioned for her to sit. "Now I can serve you."

Pursing her lips, she let out a sigh. "You win." She lowered herself onto the swing. "*Danki.*"

He placed the tray on a small table in front of them and then sat beside her. Picking up a mug, he handed it to her. "The cocoa smells *wunderbaar.*"

"I hope you like it." Sipping the hot drink, she left a whipped cream mustache on her upper lip. She chuckled and licked it off. "*Ya*, it's *gut.*"

He sipped it and nodded. "Very chocolaty."

Her eyes twinkled in the low light of the kerosene lamp on the porch railing. "I heard you've been helping out at my *dat*'s shop. *Danki* for that. They've been struggling to fill back orders taken before the fire. You're a great help."

He became sheepish. "I don't mind. I enjoy getting to know your family." He placed the mug on the table and forked a piece of pie into his mouth, savoring the rich, sweet flavor. "Wow. This is the best peach pie I've ever eaten." He met her disbelieving stare. "I mean that."

She scrunched her nose in disagreement, and he couldn't help thinking she was absolutely adorable. "No." She shook her head. "I didn't get the filling right. Too much sugar."

"I disagree, Sarah. It's heavenly." Taking another bite, he groaned. "Wow. You're an amazing cook."

"Stop." She blushed. "You're embarrassing me." She sipped more cocoa and then shivered.

"You cold?"

"*Ya.*" She cupped her hands around the mug. "The temperature is dropping."

Luke put his plate back onto the tray and then slipped out of his coat. "Here. Take this."

"No." She waved him off. "I'm fine."

"I insist." Draping the jacket around her shoulders, he inhaled her sweet scent, which reminded him of cinnamon and lilac.

"*Danki.*" She took another sip and gazed out across the dark field. "It's finally autumn. I was just telling Norman today at lunch that it had been unusually warm. We were spoiled."

His stomach twisted at the thought of her having lunch with Norman. He frowned at the involuntary reaction. Was that jealousy? Why should he care if she had lunch with another man? He hardly knew her. "You had lunch with Norman?"

"*Ya,*" she whispered, studying her half-full mug. "He's a *gut* friend. He lost his *fraa* in childbirth a few years ago, so we have a lot in common. I enjoy talking with him."

"Oh?" He studied her. Why was she avoiding his stare? Was the warm friendship he'd felt earlier dissolving back into the cold front she'd had earlier?

She looked up at him, and something flashed in her eyes. Was it sadness? Or possibly worry? Her expression softened.

She placed her mug on the tray. "How do you like Bird-in-Hand?" She lifted her plate and took a bite of the pie.

"It's a beautiful place." Leaning back on the swing, he stretched his arm behind her. "I was thinking about staying awhile." He held his breath, awaiting her reaction, hoping for her approval.

"Really?" She turned to him, her eyes wide. "How long?"

"I'm not certain." He ran his fingers along the wood back of the swing. "I like it here, so I thought I'd see how it goes."

Her eyebrows knitted with confusion. "Are you going to move here permanently?"

He shrugged. "We'll see."

She turned back to the field, and a comfortable silence fell between them. He wished he could sit next to her forever, just enjoying her company.

After a moment, she took a few more bites of the pie, then returned the plate to the tray. With her eyes trained on the field, she took a deep breath. "I need to ask you something," she whispered.

Luke nodded. "You can ask me anything."

"You told me Peter hadn't been honest about his past, and I can see that truth just by looking at your face." Her voice was soft, her eyes still focused on the field across from where they sat. "I need to know more, but yet I'm afraid to ask. I'm worried that hearing my husband lied about … everything … will be too much to handle."

"I understand," he said. Sitting up straight, he prepared himself for the questions. He wanted to tell her the truth, and yet he didn't want to hurt her. He vowed to frame his answers in order to not cause her more pain.

She met his gaze, her expression cautious. "Were you and Peter close?"

He nodded. "We were."

"He wasn't an orphan, was he?" She bit her lip in anticipation of the answer.

"No," he shook his head.

Closing her eyes, she brought her hand to her temple and groaned. "Oh, Luke, I don't understand why he did this to me. It doesn't make sense. Why didn't he trust me?"

Luke started to reach for her and then stopped, knowing it was inappropriate for him to touch her, even just to console her. "I'm sorry I upset you, Sarah Rose. That's the last thing I wanted to do by coming to visit tonight."

She met his gaze. "It's not your fault." She looked toward to the field again. "Did he have siblings?"

Luke paused, knowing the truth would be painful, but not wanting to withhold information. Peter had already done too much damage to her heart with his deception. "*Ya*," he said.

"Are they living?" Her voice trembled.

"*Ya*," he whispered.

Her hands framed her stomach, and her expression was pensive. "My *zwillingbopplin* will want to know them."

"I agree." He prayed her questions would end before the answers became too distressing.

She faced him, her brows furrowed in question. "Why did he leave Ohio if he had a family? Did he have a falling out with a family member?"

Luke nodded. "*Ya*."

Her eyes widened with shock. "Who?"

Luke stared at her, wanting to tell her the truth, the whole truth. But his gut told him to filter the information and give only the bare minimum that she needed to know.

"His father?" she guessed.

Luke swallowed a sigh of relief, thankful she'd guessed correctly. "*Ya*."

Sarah shook her head, her expression softening. "How sad. I wish I had gotten to meet his family." She rubbed her belly. "But maybe the *kinner* will get to meet them. They may have lost their father, but maybe they can get to know his family."

Luke nodded, wishing he could tell her more without hurting her.

"How many siblings did he have?" she asked.

The clip-clop of hooves crunching up the rock driveway traveled toward them.

"It must be Timothy." She faced the oncoming horse. "He visited Norman tonight and must've stayed for supper."

Luke silently thanked Timothy for saving him from answering her question about Peter's siblings. Instead, he watched as Timothy stopped in front of Eli's barn and unhitched the horse.

Sarah cleared her throat.

"Sarah." Luke glanced at her. "Are you okay?"

Meeting his stare, she sighed. "I'll be fine. I'm trying to convince myself not to be angry, but I keep wondering if my marriage was a mockery. I feel as if I didn't know my husband at all."

He frowned, guilt nipping at him. "I'm sorry. I never meant to upset you. I just want you to know the truth."

She gave him a sad smile. "*Danki.* I appreciate it."

"*Wie geht's?*" Timothy's voice boomed as his boots scraped up the porch steps. He gave his sister a friendly nod and then frowned at Luke. "Isn't it a bit late to be visiting my sister?"

"I was just getting ready to leave." Luke folded his hands in his lap. "Beautiful evening."

"*Ya.*" Timothy turned back to his sister. "Could I possibly speak with you before you retire for the evening?" He shot another frown at Luke. "In private, Sarah Rose."

Not wanting to wear out his welcome, Luke stood. "I guess I should be heading back to the house."

Sarah placed her hands on the swing and started to heave herself up.

"No, no." Luke shook his head. "Don't get up. We can say good night here."

She pulled the coat from her shoulders and handed it to him. "Here. *Danki.*"

"You're welcome." He smiled. "Thank you for dessert and the pleasant conversation."

She nodded, and he wished he could steal the sadness from her eyes. Again, he wondered how Peter had snatched up such a lovely wife. Had Peter appreciated her? Perhaps not, since he hadn't told her the truth about his past. Or maybe he'd worried the truth would scare her away.

"I'll see you soon." He pulled on his coat. "Sleep well." Turning to Timothy, he nodded. "Have a good evening."

Timothy nodded in response.

"*Gut nacht,*" Sarah called as he headed down the stairs.

As he ambled down the rock driveway to Sarah's and Peter's home, he contemplated his evening with Sarah.

He wished he could take away the pain in her heart that the stories of Peter caused. However, he knew in the depths of his soul he was doing the right thing by telling her the truth. He hoped her questions and her openness were signs that she was beginning to trust him.

Sarah's gaze remained glued on Luke's silhouette as he strode through the shadows toward her house. She hugged her arms while concentrating on the information Luke had shared about Peter's past. While the news that Peter had lied about being an orphan caused her more heartache, another question came to the forefront: could she trust everything Luke had told her about Peter? She shivered.

Timothy took off his coat and sat next to her. "Would you like my coat?"

"No, *danki.* I'm fine." She shivered again.

"Don't be *gegisch.*" He covered her shoulders with his coat. "Your lips are turning blue." He chuckled at his joke.

"It's not that cold," she muttered, snuggling into the warmth of the jacket. "You were with Norman's family, yes?"

"*Ya.*" He glanced down at the tray. "I hope you saved me some crumbly peach pie. You know it's my favorite."

"Of course I saved you some," she said. "I always do."

"What were you thinking?" he said suddenly, his tone accusing.

"What?" She gave him a confused look.

"Why were you sitting out here in the dark, sharing dessert with ... *him?*" He spat out the last word.

"I was talking with our guest, Timothy. Why is that so bad?"

"Don't tell me you trust him, Sarah Rose."

"Please." She rolled her eyes and pushed an errant strand of hair back from her face. "You can let go of your *gegisch* accusations. Why wouldn't I trust him?" *At least, I hope I can trust him.*

Timothy's expression softened. "Please be careful, Sarah Rose. I don't want to see you get hurt. I'm worried about you and the *zwillingbopplin.*"

"Timothy!" *Mamm* appeared in the doorway. "Have some pie." She turned her gaze to Sarah and frowned. "Sarah Rose, get in here before you catch a cold."

Hoisting herself up, Sarah picked up the tray from the little table beside her and headed through the door. Stepping into the kitchen, she wondered if her life would somehow get easier. She yearned to squelch all of the confusing feelings that rained down on her. She hoped the Lord would lead her toward the truth about Peter's past—and also about Luke Troyer.

Sarah slathered cream-cheese frosting on another rhubarb cookie and yawned. The news of Peter's life in Ohio, along with her brother's words of caution about Luke, had haunted her throughout the night. Even more than before, she'd found herself doubting her marriage to Peter. Had she known him at all?

Had anything he'd told her been the truth?

Snippets of possible dishonesty flashed through her mind. She'd heard from family members that Peter had been spotted at the Bird-in-Hand post office at odd times during the day. He had also been very quiet and distant from her days before the fire.

What else had he been hiding from her?

The questions soaked her mind while she finished icing the cookies. She was wrapping the cookies in packages of three when her mother came up behind her.

"Those look absolutely scrumptious, Sarah Rose," she said. "Nice work."

"*Danki.*" Sarah wiped her hands on a towel. "I need to sit now."

"*Ya.* Let's find a quiet spot to sit and talk." Taking Sarah's arm, *Mamm* led her to the small back room that served as the bakery's office, with a desk, file cabinet, adding machine, and ledgers. A stack of receipts sat on the corner of the desk.

"Have a seat, Sarah Rose." *Mamm* gestured toward the chair in front of the desk. "Tell me what's on your mind."

Sinking into the chair, Sarah suppressed a groan at her mother's serious tone. She didn't want to be coddled. She had too much on her mind already. "I'm fine, *Mamm*."

Her mother's blue eyes were warm and supportive, breaking down the wall Sarah was building around her heart. "I can't help you unless you tell me what's going on. I know it's more than hormones, Sarah Rose. Won't you let me help you through this?"

Sarah's heart pounded in her chest, but she merely shrugged to shield her nerves.

Mamm touched her hands. "Sarah Rose, did Luke tell you something last night that upset you?"

Sarah's eyes immediately began to water. "He told me Peter wasn't an orphan. He was raised by his parents with siblings. He left Ohio and came here because he'd had a fight with his father."

"*Ack*, Sarah Rose." *Mamm* pulled her into her arms and held her close. "I'm sorry you're hurting."

"I'm trying to sort through it all, but I keep thinking my whole marriage was a lie." Her voice quavered as tears spilled down first one cheek, then the other.

"No, no. Don't say that," *Mamm* cooed in her ear.

"I'm remembering things Peter did that made me wonder if something was wrong. Perhaps the signs were there all along. He was so cold and distant the last few weeks before the fire. Maybe he was hiding more from me."

"Sarah Rose, you have to stop beating yourself up over this," *Mamm* said. He's not here to explain why he did what he did, and speculating will only cause your heart to hurt even more."

Wiping her eyes with the backs of her hands, Sarah looked

at her mother. "But what about the *kinner?* What do I tell them when they ask about their father? What kind of a man do I tell them he was when I don't know for certain myself?"

"The words will come to you when the time is right." *Mamm* rested her hands on Sarah's shoulders. "The Lord will lead your lips to the right words. Have faith in that."

"What is faith, *Mamm?*" Sarah wished her voice would stop trembling. "What is it really?"

"Hebrews 11:1 tells us, 'Now faith is being sure of what we hope for and certain of what we do not see.'" She squeezed Sarah's hand. "Does that help you at all?"

Sarah nodded to appease her mother, but the questions still haunted her. "And what about Luke? How do I know if I can believe him?"

"What does your heart tell you?"

"My heart is a jumbled mess. I'm not sure what it's telling me at all." Sarah gazed down at her lap. "I just keep thinking I'm too young to be a widow and a single mother. It somehow doesn't seem fair."

"But you have a family who loves you and will take care of you. That's more than some people have."

Sarah frowned, feeling like a heel for complaining. "*Danki.* I do appreciate and love you, but I'm not sure what to think about Luke."

"Listen to what he has to tell you and then see what your heart says."

Sarah nodded, but she still needed answers. She had to figure out how to get past her grief and understand what God's plan was for her and the children. *Please God*, she prayed silently, *please show me the right path for my zwillingbopplin.*

"You do good work," Luke said as he examined the triple dresser. "Your *grossdaddi* taught you well." Glancing around, he examined the shop, thinking how similar it was to his own back home.

The large, open area was divided into work areas separated by workbenches cluttered with an array of tools. The sweet scent of wood and stain filled his nostrils. The men working around Jake and him were building beautifully designed dining room sets, bedroom suites, entertainment centers, hutches, end tables, desks, and coffee tables.

Hammers banged, saw blades whirled, and air compressors hummed. Just like his shop back home, the air compressors powering the tools ran off diesel generators.

Returning Luke's nod, Jake Miller swiped the back of his hand across his brow. "Thanks for the compliment. You do good work too." He leaned back on the workbench and grabbed a bottle of water. After a long gulp, he placed it on the bench beside him. "So, you're from Ohio, huh?"

"*Ya.*" Luke sat on a bench and opened a can of Coke. "Middlefield."

"I didn't realize Peter had grown up in Ohio. I wonder why he didn't tell anyone about his family back home."

Rubbing his lower lip, Luke contemplated how much to reveal about Peter's history. "I guess you could say he was running from some things in his past."

"Why hide the past?" Jake wondered. "Peter had a great life here. He and Sarah seemed so happy. I can't see how telling where he came from would ruin that. I think it would be more detrimental and risky to create a web of lies you have to remember so you don't flub it."

A smile crept across Luke's lips. "You're a very wise young man."

Grinning, Jake stood. "I try."

"So, what's your story?" Luke asked.

"Well, I live about a mile up the road in half of a two-story house my uncle owns, and I love working on furniture. That's about it."

"Do you have a special *maedel* in your life?"

Jake shrugged. "I guess you could say I have a girl. At least, she's special to me. She moved back home to Virginia, but she's supposed to come visit in the spring."

"Oh?" Luke grabbed a can of stain.

"She's Lindsay's older sister, Jessica." Jake grabbed a paintbrush from his tool cart. "We met last summer when she came to live with Rebecca and Daniel. She wanted to go back home to live with her mom's best friend and finish high school. I'm hoping I can convince her to go to college in Pennsylvania, so we have a chance to get to know each other better. She's got another year of high school yet, though."

"She's English?" Luke asked.

"Yup." Jake grinned. "She's a great girl."

"You seem smitten." Luke shook the can of stain and then opened and stirred it.

The young man chuckled. "Yeah, I guess I am. I just wish she'd realize how smitten I am and give me a chance."

"Luke," a voice behind him called.

Turning, Luke spotted Timothy frowning near the door to the parking lot. He wondered idly if that man went through life with a dark cloud over his head.

"Can I speak with you for a moment?" Timothy asked, motioning toward the door.

"*Ya.*" Luke cut his eyes to Jake. "I'll be back to help you stain this."

Jake took the can of stain from him. "No problem. Take your time."

Luke crossed the shop and followed Timothy out to the parking lot, where they stood by a pile of scrap wood. "What's going on?" he asked.

"I'd like to know what your intentions are with my sister."

"My intentions?" Luke gripped his suspenders. "I reckon I intend to become her friend so I can be a part of her *zwillingbopplin*'s lives. That's as far as my intentions go. I don't see why you have a problem with that."

"My problem is, Sarah is in a fragile state, and she doesn't need you showing up here and confusing her." He gestured wildly for emphasis. "She's suffered a huge loss, and you don't need to be sticking your nose in her business."

Luke shook his head while trying to make sense of Timothy's anger. "I don't understand why you have this resentment toward me. I lost Peter too." He studied Timothy for a moment. "How much did Peter tell you?"

Timothy shrugged and looked away. "Enough."

"Why don't you try being more specific? I'd like to know why you know more than everyone else in your family. Were you and Peter close?"

"*Ya.*" Timothy met his gaze, sadness filling his eyes. "He was my best friend."

Luke's eyes widened. "Why didn't you tell me?"

"Because I can't let the rest of the family know how much Peter told me about his past. It makes me look bad."

"It makes you look like a liar," Luke finished his thought.

"Exactly." Timothy's expression softened. "You're his brother."

Luke knew he was caught. "I am."

Timothy snapped his fingers. "I knew it!"

Luke folded his arms in front of his chest. "What else do you know?"

"I know Peter left after having a horrible argument with your *dat*. And he regretted it very much."

"He did?" Luke raised his eyebrows in disbelief.

"He said he wished he'd had the courage to make things right between him and you and also him and your *dat*."

Luke scowled. "If he only knew what he put us through by leaving. Pop was so distraught that he had a stroke, and I nursed him until he died. I gave up everything to care for him. I lost my girlfriend and the chance to have a family of my own while Peter rebuilt his life here with a new family. It's hard for me to believe he had regrets when he had this." He gestured around the parking lot with his arms.

"I'm sorry. I truly am. But you have to believe Peter wanted to make amends before the *boppli* was born. He was talking about how to tell Sarah the truth." Timothy rubbed his chin and looked across the parking lot. "He was like a brother to me. We used to talk for hours."

"That's how it was before he abandoned Pop and me." Luke shook his head, disappointment mixed with resentment simmering through him. "Our address never changed. He could've written us. He had eight years to make things right."

"He wanted to make things right." Timothy shrugged. "I believed he would've done so if he'd had more time."

More questions bombarded Luke. "So why did he open up to you and no one else?"

"I told you—we were best friends."

"You knew the truth all along?"

Timothy shook his head. "No, I didn't know from the beginning. We quickly became friends when he got the job at the shop, but he didn't tell me he had family in Ohio until I met him at the post office one day about a year and a half ago. I found it strange that he had a post-office box. It seemed an unnecessary expense. Then he confided in me that he received letters there from his family in Ohio. He begged me not to tell Sarah. He said the news that he had family would crush her, and he wanted to tell her when the time was right."

"Did he say who the letters were from?" Luke braced himself, wondering if Timothy knew the truth about DeLana.

Timothy shrugged. "I had assumed they were from relatives, maybe your *dat* or even you. I never thought much about it."

Peter didn't tell him about DeLana.

"So where does that leave us now?" Luke asked. "You know who I am, but everyone else thinks I'm Peter's cousin."

Timothy's expression hardened. "It doesn't leave us anywhere different. You know I want you go to back home and let Sarah pick up the pieces of her life and move on. Your being here complicates things for her. She doesn't need to know any more about Peter's life back in Ohio. She belongs here with us."

Luke blanched. "You think I'm going to take her away?"

"I didn't say that. I don't want her to even consider leaving, which is why you need to leave."

"You also don't want me to tell the rest of the family you kept secrets from them."

Timothy frowned.

"It's up to you and your conscience to come clean with your family, but I can tell you this—those *kinner* are my family and my only connection to my brother. I have every right to be a part of their lives. They are as much my family as they are yours. You said Peter was like a brother to you and you lost him." Luke jammed a finger into his own chest. "Well, I lost him eight years ago when he chose to run out on my pop and me and start a new life without so much as telling us where he was living. I don't intend to hurt your sister. I only want to be her friend and be a part of her *kinner*'s lives. That's all."

"Sarah doesn't need you. She has the Kauffmans, and she belongs with us. You belong back in Ohio in your church district with your family. Peter must've left you for a reason."

Luke shook his head. "You're wrong. I think it's Sarah's decision if she wants me to stay or not."

Timothy's eyes narrowed to slits. "My sister is in no condition to make decisions like that. She's lost her husband and is about to become a mother for the first time. If you tell her who you really are and then ask her to decide if she wants you around, you'll hurt her even more. You'll probably crush whatever spirit she has left in her. Is that what you want?"

Knowing Timothy was right, Luke shook his head.

"Good. I'm glad we've reached an understanding. You need

to start packing and head back to Ohio. That's where you belong." Timothy turned and stalked back into the shop.

The crunch of tires on gravel pulled Luke's attention to a pickup truck steering into the back lot. Eli hopped out of the passenger seat while the English driver climbed out and circled to the back of the truck.

"Luke!" Eli called. "Would you help unload some supplies?"

"*Ya.*" Luke jogged over to the bed full of wood and lifted an armful.

"*Danki,* son," Eli said with a smile. "You're such a wonderful addition to our family."

Luke forced a smile. *Too bad your son doesn't agree.* "*Danki,* Eli."

"I hope you'll join us for supper tonight," the older man said.

"Of course." Luke suppressed a sarcastic snort. Timothy would not be glad to find him at supper once again.

10

Luke leaned back on the fence and laughed while Daniel shared another story about an English customer who'd ordered a triple dresser and wanted it within a week. It was obvious some of the customers had no concept of what went into making a beautiful piece of furniture. Creating a dresser wasn't about hammers and nails; it was creating a work of art that would be enjoyed for years and passed down through generations of families.

The aroma of livestock filled Luke's nostrils as he breathed in the crisp autumn afternoon air of the Esh family farm. Standing up straight, he righted his hat while trying to keep his focus on the men surrounding him. However, his eyes betrayed him for what felt like the hundredth time today, and he found his gaze trained on Sarah sitting on a bench across the yard and rubbing her abdomen while she watched the younger children play on the intricate wooden swing set.

He'd been fighting in vain all morning to avoid staring at Sarah, but it had been impossible. During the church service, his eyes kept moving from the bishop and ministers to Sarah sitting across the room on the backless bench with her sisters. She looked radiant—her cheeks pink and her eyes as bright a blue as the summer sky. A few times, she met his stare and graced him with a small smile, causing his heart to thump madly in his chest. He tried in vain to focus on God's Word.

Was he falling for her?

He pushed that idea away. She was his brother's widow. Any romantic feelings for her would be a sin.

However, he'd thought about her nonstop since their last meeting at her parents' house two nights ago. She invaded his head throughout the day and stole into his dreams at night.

"Did you hear me?" Daniel's voice penetrated Luke's daydream.

"*Ya?*" Luke met Daniel's questioning glance. "I'm sorry." Clearing his throat, he tried to ignore his heated face while the rest of the Kauffman men looked on with interest. "I wasn't listening."

"What has you so captivated?" Daniel asked with a smile.

"I think I know," Eli said with a sly grin. "It could be it's a certain *maedel.*"

Oh, no. Luke's stomach twisted. How could Eli know? *Is my ogling that obvious?*

Luke braced himself for a much-deserved tongue-lashing from the elder Kauffman.

"She's right over there." Eli looped his arm around Luke's shoulders and nodded across the yard toward a group of young women. "It's Naomi King, isn't it? She's a pretty thing. I tried getting Timothy to court her, but he thinks he's too good for her."

Timothy rolled his eyes. "Please, *Dat*. You know it's not that. She's too young for me. Besides, I'm through with courting. Miriam ended that for me."

"You have to move on, son. Miriam wasn't right for you."

"Let's leave the subject of my lack of a *fraa* for another day." Timothy stepped toward the house and held up his cup. "Anyone want more iced tea?"

Luke started to move toward Timothy to escape from the grilling, but Eli held him back.

"Look, Luke," he said. "She's smiling at you. You should go talk to her."

Luke glanced toward the brunette standing near the barn and found her grinning in his direction. His shoulders tensed. The last thing he needed to complicate his life was a girl with a crush on him in Lancaster County. He started toward Timothy. "I'll come with you. I could use some more iced tea."

Luke followed him into the large kitchen where more than twenty women chatted and cleaned up after the noon meal. Conversation flew through the air like confetti while they washed dishes and tidied up tables. Timothy refilled his and Luke's cups before they moved back out onto the concrete walk.

Luke stepped toward the gate leading to the playground and spotted Norman sitting with Sarah on the bench. She had been sitting alone when Luke had gone in the house.

A flicker of jealousy poked at him, and he stopped dead in his tracks. Where had that come from? Sarah and Norman were friends, which made perfect sense considering their circumstances. Why should Luke care who Sarah chose as her friends?

But his reaction made him think again: was he beginning to feel something more than friendship for Sarah?

He swallowed a groan. He didn't need the complication of feelings for his brother's widow.

"Luke," a sweet voice said. "I've been looking all over for you. I thought you'd run off."

Luke turned to find Naomi King beaming at him. She had deep brown eyes and matching brown hair that stuck out from under her white prayer *kapp*.

"Hi, there." He raised his cup as if to toast her. "I was just getting some more tea."

"*Ya.*" She smiled with a little too much mirth. "Elizabeth Kauffman makes the best iced tea." She stuck her hand out and shook his—hard, crushing his fingers in her grip. "I'm Naomi King. It's a pleasure to meet you."

"Luke Troyer." He pulled his hand back. "Nice to meet you too."

"Are you staying here in Lancaster County long?"

He shrugged. "Not sure yet." He glanced toward Sarah. She was still talking to Norman. "I guess I'll see how things go." He looked back at Naomi. The determined look in her eyes made him uneasy.

"I heard you're a carpenter."

He nodded. "That's true."

"There are plenty of carpentry businesses 'round here. You could make a nice living." When a gentle breeze blew her hair in front of her eyes, she pushed a wisp back from her face. "I bet Eli Kauffman would consider hiring you. He's short-handed since the—" She stopped short, turning pink with embarrassment at mention of the fire.

Luke sipped his tea and nodded. "Possibly. He could need help."

"I didn't mean to say—" Her face turned sad. "I'm sorry about your cousin. It was a tragedy. I heard you were close to Peter."

"*Danki*. I knew you didn't mean anything by mentioning the fire. It's quite all right." He cleared his throat and glanced toward the Kauffman men. Eli's wolfish grin annoyed him. Luke sure didn't need a matchmaker. "It was nice meeting you." He stepped toward the Kauffmans, but a hand on his arm, followed by a tug, stopped him.

His gaze collided with Naomi's bold smile.

She bit her bottom lip as if scheming. "Have you gotten a proper tour of our church district?"

"Well . . ." He searched for an excuse—anything—but came up blank. He was stuck.

"How about I give you one?" She pulled him toward the line of buggies in the field next to the second white barn. "I'll drive."

"I don't know if that's such a great idea," he began, scanning the yard for someone, anyone, to save him from an afternoon spent with an overly eager young woman he barely knew.

She stopped, blushing again. "Oh. Right." Turning, she called toward a group of young women gathered by the horse pasture. "Lizzie Anne! Lindsay! Let's go for a ride." She then faced Luke again. "We'll have two young chaperones so the rumors won't be too bad."

Before Luke could mount a protest against being kidnapped, a young woman resembling a younger Naomi trotted over, accompanied by Lindsay, Rebecca Kauffman's niece.

"Luke, this is my sister, Lizzie Anne, and you know Lindsay," Naomi said. "Okay, girls, let's give Luke a tour of our district." Turning, Naomi called to a young man, ordering him to retrieve her horse from the barn and hitch it to her buggy. Within several minutes, the horse and buggy were ready for the tour.

Plastering a smile on his face, Luke succumbed to the determined hand steering him toward the buggy. He hoped the district was small and the ride short.

Sarah smiled in response to the pleasant discussion of the weather Norman was providing from the bench seat beside her. As she listened, her eyes found Naomi King smiling, laughing, and batting her eyelashes at Luke across the yard. Sarah shook her head. Didn't Naomi realize she was making a spectacle of herself by flirting with Luke in front of the whole church district?

"Sarah?" Norman's voice broke through her mental tirade. "Are you with me?"

Her cheeks flushed. "I'm sorry. I was thinking about the *zwillingbopplin* again. Sometimes I just get caught up in my dreams of the future." She rubbed her belly, feeling a kick in response. A smile broke out across her lips. "Someone is awake."

Norman grinned. "Really?" He reached his hand out, then

swiftly pulled it back and frowned. "How forward of me. I apologize."

She smiled. He was such a gentleman.

A movement behind Norman distracted her, and she watched Naomi yanking Luke back toward her. What was that girl trying to prove by manhandling him? Was she going to force him to court her?

If he courted her, would he stay in Bird-in-Hand permanently?

Sarah analyzed her feelings about that. His staying would give the twins a connection to their father. However, how did she feel about his courting Naomi King?

Why was that her business anyway?

"Sarah?" Norman asked. "I've lost you again."

"Sorry," she whispered, glancing back at him. "You were saying?"

"Is something across the yard intriguing you?" Norman glanced over his shoulder toward the area where Luke stood with Naomi and then looked back at Sarah. His eyebrows arched in question. "Did you need to talk to Lindsay? Would you like me to call her?"

"No," she said, shaking her head. "I was just wondering what they were doing."

"Oh." He cleared his throat and his expression softened. "How have you been feeling lately?"

"I'm doing okay." She smiled. "*Danki* for asking."

"I've been concerned about you. Your due date is coming up fast. Is there anything you need? Anything for you or for the *kinner*? I have plenty of supplies up in my attic. Leah seemed to save everything from clothes to high chairs for the *kinner*. I'd be happy to turn them over to you."

She shook her head. "I'm fine with supplies, but *danki* for asking. My sisters are loading me up, but I appreciate it very much. You're a very thoughtful friend."

At the word "friend" something unreadable flashed in his eyes. However, his pleasant expression remained attentive and sweet.

Against her will, her attention moved across the yard again to find Naomi pulling Luke toward the field of parked buggies. Where was she taking him?

Sarah pushed the thought of Luke and Naomi away. How could she blame Luke for going out for a ride with a young, pretty woman like Naomi? Since he'd lost his true love when he was nursing his father, he deserved someone young and sweet like Naomi. He seemed so unhappy and alone. Perhaps Naomi would bring some joy into his life.

Sarah should be happy for him. And she should be happy her children would be born soon, putting a piece of Peter back into her life.

So why was something nagging at her? Some little, tiny feeling of unease creeping into her stomach.

Meeting Norman's gaze, Sarah smiled and patted Norman's hand. "What were you saying about the weather?"

Luke yawned and guided Molly up the driveway toward the Kauffman home, the horse's hooves crunching over the rocks. After Naomi had dropped him off at the Esh farm, Luke hitched up Molly and his buggy and headed back to the Kauffmans'. He breathed in the brisk evening air. As the scent of wood-burning stoves filled his lungs, he reflected upon his long afternoon of riding around the beautiful, rolling farmlands of Lancaster County. He'd listened to Naomi pointing out farms owned by families he didn't know while Lizzie Anne and Lindsay whispered and giggled from the back of the buggy.

Naomi was sweet and kind, but she was a little too eager, with her hand frequently brushing his and her girlish giggle bursting out at odd times. She'd invited him to come to supper tonight with her family, but he declined, hoping to not hurt her feelings. She seemed to want to court, but finding a mate was not the purpose of his trip. He'd come here to find Peter and what was left of his past.

The scent of cinnamon mixed with dew washed over Luke as the buggy approached the back porch of Elizabeth and Eli's home. He spotted the lamp still glowing in the kitchen and his thoughts turned to Sarah. He'd missed his chance to speak with her after the service, and he hoped she was doing well today.

He unhitched Molly, led her to the barn, and then stowed the buggy. He was locking up the barn when the back door swung open, revealing Sarah leaning in the doorway and squinting toward the barn.

Luke ambled toward the house, and when he stepped into the light from the kerosene lamp flooding the steps, she returned a cautious smile.

"*Wie geht's?*" He pushed his hat back on his head and rested his right foot on the bottom step.

"*Gut.*" She stepped onto the porch and gingerly closed the door. "You?"

"*Gut.*" He leaned forward, resting his elbows on his bent knee.

She gestured toward the swing. "Do you have a minute to visit before you head in for the night?"

"Of course." His boots clomped up the steps before he sank onto the swing next to her.

She cleared her throat and brushed a few stray golden strands under her prayer *kapp.* "Did you enjoy the service today?"

"*Ya.*" He nodded. "It was lovely."

"*Gut.*" She stared off across the dark field, and he wished he could read her mind.

"I was disappointed we didn't get to talk after the service," he said.

She looked at him, confusion clouding her pretty face. "You were?"

"*Ya.* I had every intention of visiting with you after the noon meal, but Naomi King had other plans for me."

"How was your ride with her?" Her expression gave no hint as to her thoughts.

He blinked, surprised that she'd seen him leave with Naomi. "It was nice. She gave me a tour of the area, pointing out Amish businesses and farms. She gave me a bit of a history lesson too." He shrugged. "I'm sure she was just trying to welcome me to the area."

"Were you gone all afternoon?" she asked.

"*Ya.*" He brushed a piece of lint from his trousers. "Did you stay at the Eshes' late?"

She nodded. "Norman invited me to join him and his family for supper, but I was too tired. The *zwillingbopplin* are wearing me out sooner these days."

No sooner had she said that than a small yelp escaped from her rosy lips, and she hugged her middle.

"Sarah?" He leaned over and touched her arm. "Are you all right?"

Meeting his gaze, her crystal-blue eyes beamed with pure elation. "That was the hardest kick yet. Want to feel?" Taking his hand, she laid it on her belly.

What he felt next sent his soul soaring with a rush of joy he'd never experienced in his life. Beneath his hand, a tiny bump-bump vibrated. Gasping, he looked up at her.

"The *zwillingbopplin*," she whispered. "They're awake. Sometimes I wonder if they're wearing boots." She gave a little laugh.

His eyes misted. How blessed he was to be sharing this moment with Sarah. Love for her twins, his brother's children, swelled in his soul, deeper than the ocean.

"I say a prayer of thanks every time they kick," she whispered. "*Kinner* are a gift from the Lord."

Luke wanted to agree, but his voice was stuck in his throat. They sat in silence for several moments while he felt the twins kick and tumble. He wished this moment could last forever.

When the screen door banged open, Luke and Sarah both jumped back, startled. He rested his hands in his lap feeling as if he'd been caught doing something inappropriate.

"*Wie geht's*, Luke," Elizabeth said, her expression curious as her eyes darted from him to Sarah.

"Hello, Elizabeth," Luke said.

"Sarah Rose," she said. "It's late."

Luke stood and straightened his hat. "I hadn't had a chance to speak with Sarah after service this afternoon, so I stopped by after putting Molly in the barn. I was just leaving."

Elizabeth nodded and turned her eyes to her daughter. "You remember what the doctor said. You need your rest now more than ever. You really should be in bed."

Sighing, Sarah rolled her eyes. "I know, *Mamm*."

"*Ya*, but I can't help but worry." Elizabeth glanced at Luke. "*Gut nacht*." She disappeared through the door.

"I'd best go." Luke took Sarah's hand and helped her to her feet.

"You'd think I was five, the way they treat me," she said, huffing as she stood. "I'm so sick of being treated like a child. I can make my own decisions. I'm going to be a *mutter*, for goodness' sake."

"It's just because they care about you," he said. "I can't blame them."

Her expression softened. "*Danki* for stopping by."

"I enjoyed it," he said. "*Gut nacht*."

"*Gut nacht*." She released his hand.

When he climbed into bed later that evening, he grinned as he remembered the vibration of the twins' kicks against his palm. Yes, children were a blessing from the Lord, and Sarah's friendship was a blessing as well.

Closing his eyes, he silently recited his evening prayers, adding a few extra for Sarah and her twins.

11

Sarah sat on a stool and sipped a glass of ice water, observing while Lindsay rolled out another batch of peanut butter cookies. Her thoughts wandered to last night and Luke's reaction to the feel of the babies' kicks. He appeared to be consumed by the twins, and she could've sworn she'd seen tears in his eyes. Did he truly care for the children?

Of course he did. Peter was his cousin, and the twins were his relatives.

"How's this?" Lindsay's question interrupted her musings.

"What's that?" Sarah asked, wiping the condensation on the glass.

"Is this size all right?" She gestured toward the circular cookie cutouts on the counter.

"Ya. Perfect." Sarah ran the cold glass over her flaming cheeks. "It's hot in here."

"It's not that hot in here." Lindsay's eyes filled with alarm. "Can I walk you outside?"

"No." Sarah shook her head. "I'll be all right."

Lindsay tilted her head, unconvinced. "You sure, *Aenti* Sarah?"

Sarah nodded and smiled at the girl's concern. "I'm fine."

Lindsay frowned in disbelief, but turned back to the cookies, loading them onto a sheet.

Biting her lower lip, Sarah contemplated asking Lindsay about the tour Naomi had given Luke yesterday. Would asking about it give Lindsay the wrong idea? But what was the wrong idea anyway? After all, Sarah was just curious. "Lindsay?"

"Hmm?" the girl asked, her stare focused on a stubborn cookie stuck to the cutting board.

"How was the ride yesterday with Naomi, Lizzie Anne, and Luke?"

"Oh, it was fun," Lindsay said. The knife freed the cookie, and she tossed it onto the sheet before facing Sarah and wiping her hands on her apron. "We rode all around the county, and Naomi pointed out different landmarks. She showed him the farmer's market where she sells her quilts, and where her family farm is. It was a lot of fun."

"Oh." Sarah took another long drink and then placed the glass on the counter beside her. She wanted to know more about the tour but struggled with what to ask. It wouldn't be appropriate to ask her niece if she thought Naomi and Luke were courting. "Did Luke enjoy the tour?"

"Oh, yeah." Lindsay smiled. "He seemed to have a great time. He and Naomi talked a lot." She turned back to the task at hand, flipping more cookies onto the metal sheet.

Sarah nodded. Naomi was so young and pretty; of course Luke had had a good time. Why should Sarah be surprised?

"I think Naomi likes Luke." Lindsay placed the last cookie on the sheet, then rolled out the remaining dough and began cutting more. "After we dropped him off, she told Lizzie Anne and me that she thought he was handsome. Then she said she was going to bring him lunch at work this week since her quilt store at the farmer's market is right across the street from the furniture store. I think she has a crush."

Sarah told herself it wasn't her concern. It was Luke's business whom he courted.

And why should she care anyway?

"Lizzie Anne said Naomi doesn't give up when she sets her mind to something." Lindsay cut out the last circle and proceeded to place the cookies onto the next sheet. "But I asked if she was sure he was even going to stay in town. Seems like she may be setting herself up to get hurt if she puts so much effort into trying to get him to court her and then he moves back home to Ohio."

"Good point," Sarah said, her voice brittle with something that felt an awful lot like jealousy.

"Done!" Lindsay smiled as she loaded the two full cookie sheets into the oven. She set the timer, hopped up on the stool next to Sarah, and grabbed her glass of ice water. After taking a long sip, she gave Sarah another concerned look. "You don't look so good. I think you should let me walk you outside or back to the house for a nap."

"I'll be fine," Sarah said, swiping the glass across her forehead.

"Lindsay's right, Sarah Rose," *Mamm* said behind her. "You should walk outside with me."

"Fine," Sarah muttered, lowering herself to the floor and schlepping outside behind *Mamm*. Her legs and feet ached, and her shoes were tight. She wished she could sleep for a week and awaken refreshed without any aches, pains, or swelling in her legs and feet.

She sank onto the bench outside of the play area. *Mamm* dropped down beside her and relieved Beth Anne from babysitting duty. They silently watched the children swinging and shrieking with delight.

After a few moments, *Mamm* turned her gaze to Sarah. "You look exhausted, Sarah Rose. You should go home and get some rest."

"No," Sarah said, shaking her head. "The house is too quiet, and it gives me too much time to miss Peter and think about the things Luke told me about his past. I'd rather stay here and keep busy. That way I can't think too much."

Sarah sank back on the bench and idly rubbed her belly. A rhythmic blip caused her to grin. "*Mamm*! Someone has the hiccups!" Grabbing her mother's hand, Sarah placed it over the bump.

"Oh, Sarah Rose." Tears filled *Mamm*'s eyes and spilled over her cheeks. "Oh, just *wunderbaar.*" A faraway look shone from her eyes. "I remember so clearly. Daniel had the hiccups the same time every morning like clockwork. You had them often too. I loved all of those little bumps and kicks."

"*Ya.*" Sarah smiled. "Sometimes when they're doing summersaults it feels like butterflies."

Mamm gave a soft laugh. "That's exactly how it felt."

They sat in silence for several moments, tuned in to the hiccups from the unborn twins and oblivious to the laughs and screams of the children on the playground.

When the hiccups ceased, *Mamm* sat back on the bench and sighed. "Before you know it, those little ones will be out here swinging and hollering with all of their cousins on the playground."

"*Ya.*" Sarah folded her arms over her stomach. "Time moves so quickly. It seems like only yesterday I found out I was pregnant." She waited for her mother to speak. When *Mamm* didn't continue, Sarah prodded her. "What's really on your mind?"

Mamm patted her hand. "I think it's time you stopped working. You've been so tired and hot all the time. I worry you'll get ill before the *kinner* come. You heard what the doctor said. You need to save your strength. You've only got two months to go."

Sarah knew her *mamm* was right. "I just can't face being at the house alone all day. When I think too much, I feel myself falling back into a bottomless pit of grief and anger. But the good news is that the nightmares about the fire have stopped."

"That's *wunderbaar,* but you still need your rest." *Mamm* squeezed her hand. "How about we have one of Robert's girls stay with you and help you get the room ready? Your nieces would love to help you. Nancy is a very sweet girl. I bet she would love to spend her days with you. She could sew and clean for you."

"You win." Sarah sighed. "It's a good plan."

"*Mamm*!" a voice behind them boomed. "*Dat*'s on the phone!"

Mamm stood and patted Sarah's leg. "I better go. Think about what I said. We can leave Sadie a message on her voicemail and ask her if Nancy would like to come stay with you. I know she would love it. "

Sarah nodded. "Sounds good."

"Did you want to come in?" *Mamm* asked.

"No," Sarah said, turning back to her nieces and nephews. "I'll stay out here and watch the *kinner*. It's nice and cool. I felt like I was going to pass out in the kitchen."

While *Mamm* ambled back into the bakery, Sarah watched her niece leap from the swing, landing in the mulch and collapsing in giggles. She imagined her children on the swings, laughing and singing with their nieces and nephews. Were her twins boys or girls or one of each? Soon she would know. A skitter of excitement coursed through her.

Her thoughts turned to Luke, and she absently wondered if Luke would sit with her someday, watching the children play. Would he stay in Bird-in-Hand long enough to see that? If so, would he perhaps be watching children play with Naomi instead?

Sarah settled back on the bench and focused on her niece dancing before her.

"That's great work." Daniel slapped Luke's shoulder as he studied the finished triple dresser. "You and Jake make a *gut* team."

Luke wiped the sweat from his brow. Glancing at the clock on the wall, he found it was nearing noon. He wondered if he could hitch a ride with an English customer and sneak over to the bakery to ask Sarah to lunch. He had awakened this morning remembering the feel of the twins kicking his hand last night. It was a sensation he'd never experienced; it was heavenly.

"Luke!" Jake bellowed from up front. "You have a visitor."

"A visitor?" Luke muttered, walking toward the front. Had Sarah beaten him to the punch and come to surprise him?

Stepping out into the showroom, he frowned as his eyes fell on Naomi standing by the counter. She was chatting with Eli while holding a picnic basket. He hoped she wasn't the visitor Jake had mentioned, but he knew in his gut he was wrong.

Naomi glanced up at Luke, and a coy grin spread across her lips. "Hi!" She held up the basket. "I hope you don't have plans for lunch."

"Well, I—" Luke searched for an excuse to work through lunch. He gave Jake a pleading look, but the young man simply shrugged. He made a mental note to clue Jake in on his feelings for Naomi.

Stepping behind the counter, Eli smacked Luke's shoulder. "Go on. Take a long lunch. You've been working hard, and you deserve it." He winked as if he and Luke shared an inside joke about picnic lunches.

Luke swallowed hard as he met Naomi's expectant stare. He was trapped yet again. How did he continue to find himself backed into a corner with this woman? She was pleasant and nice looking, but he didn't want to court her. And yet here she stood holding out a picnic basket and her heart for Luke's taking. How could he possibly hurt her feelings?

"I'll go wash up," Luke muttered, heading for the back room.

"*Wunderbaar*!" she called after him. "I'll get the picnic table by the pasture behind the shop set up for our meal."

"This is *appeditlich*," Luke said before biting into his chicken salad sandwich.

"*Danki*." Naomi lifted the bottle of iced tea and refilled his glass. "I thought today would be the perfect day for a picnic. It warmed up a bit." She set the bottle down and brushed a stray crumb from the tablecloth. Her brown eyes sparkled with something resembling expectation, or maybe hope. "It's *wunderbaar* that you're working here. Maybe Eli will offer you a permanent job. I visited Robert and Sadie's farm last night after supper, and Robert mentioned his *dat* was thinking of offering you a permanent job here at the shop."

Luke wiped his chin with a napkin. "Maybe. I haven't thought about that."

"Oh, if so, then you must stay! Do you want to stay here permanently?" she asked, her smile wide and bright.

"Eli hasn't offered me a job yet." Luke lifted the cup of tea. "And I haven't decided what I want to do."

Her eyes were wide, full of urgency. "Oh, you should stay, Luke. You said yourself you like it here."

He sipped his tea. "That's true. I do like it, but I like Ohio too. Ohio's always been my home, and I'm not sure if I want to pick up and move, leaving everything behind."

Naomi pushed the remaining crumbs of her sandwich around on her paper plate. "Is there someone special in Ohio?"

"You mean a *maedel*?" he asked.

Frowning, she nodded.

He almost chuckled. She couldn't be more obvious if she wore a sign declaring "Court me, Luke Troyer."

"No," he said, trying not to grin. "There's no girl."

Her smile returned. "So, there's nothing keeping you there."

"Nothing but memories, I guess. And some good friends, a couple of cousins, aunts, and uncles." He scooped another mound of homemade potato salad onto his plate. "How's business at the quilt shop today?"

"Busy. I took six custom orders this morning, so our quilting group will have to get busy." She retrieved a plate containing half of a vanilla crumb pie from the bottom of the basket. "I hope you have room for dessert."

"Wow." The scent of vanilla enveloped him. "That looks *wunderbaar gut*."

She grinned. "It is." After cutting two large slices, she slapped one onto his plate. "Enjoy."

He forked a piece into his mouth and savored the smooth, moist decadence.

"I'm a *gut* cook," Naomi announced, cutting up her piece. "I'm great at sewing and quilting, and I keep the house and farm in order. I take *gut* care of my eight siblings too."

Luke kept his eyes trained on the hunk of pie on his plate. He couldn't look her in the eye while she recited her résumé to him. He wasn't interested in her domestic skills.

"Do you ever feel like the Lord is guiding you?" she asked. "I mean, do you ever feel His hand on your back leading you to the way He wants you to go?"

Luke nodded. "*Ya*. Absolutely. He led me here."

Her smile widened, and he regretted the words immediately. He'd meant that the Lord had led him to Bird-in-Hand and Peter's new life, not to Naomi. Hoping to change the subject, he pointed the fork at the pie. "This is outstanding."

"*Danki*." Placing her elbows on the table, she rested her chin on her hand. "I'll be sure to remember this recipe for you."

An hour later, Luke walked through the back door of the shop with a full belly and a worried mind. Lunch had been delicious, but he felt guilty for giving poor Naomi the wrong idea. He would be happy to share a nice friendship with her, but he had no interest in courting her. Yet breaking the news to her would surely shred her heart. The last thing he wanted to do was hurt an innocent girl who enjoyed his company.

"Luke," Eli called, approaching. "How was lunch?" The older man waggled his bushy, salt-and-pepper eyebrows, and Luke sighed.

"*Appeditlich*." Luke hoped to leave it at that.

"She's a *gut* girl." Eli smacked his arm. "She'd be a *wunderbaar fraa*."

Luke pushed his hat back on his head and scratched his scalp. "I hope she's not getting the wrong idea. I'm not looking to court anyone."

"Take your time, son." Eli idly pulled on his beard. "I wasn't looking to court when I met my Elizabeth. The Lord has a way of leading us to roads we never imagined we'd take. Just keep your heart and mind open to endless possibilities."

Luke nodded and then headed over to Jake's work area, where the young man studied plans for another project. "So, what are we starting now?" he asked.

"My grandpa asked me to take a look at this new design for a hope chest. It's similar to the one you helped me finish last week before you completed that triple dresser." Jake pushed the papers over to Luke.

"Hey, Troyer." A strong hand on Luke's shoulder nudged him backward.

Luke turned to find Timothy smirking.

Timothy gestured toward the back door. "I see you were getting cozy with Naomi King at lunch."

"We're friends," Luke said. "That's all. Now, if you'll excuse us, Jake and I have work to do."

"I thought you weren't going to stay here permanently," Timothy said, his expression hardening. "Don't you have a job, family, and friends to return to in Ohio?"

"I'm not sure what I'm going to do, but I know for sure I'm

not ready to court anyone." Luke turned his attention back to the plans, hinting it was time for him to leave.

"Don't forget our conversation," Timothy said. "I think you know what would be best for everyone involved."

Luke met Timothy's stare. "I know what you're saying, and I'm not promising you I'm going to stay, and I'm not promising I'm going to leave. I'm going to wait and see what feels right to me. But I can promise you one thing: I won't hurt Sarah."

Timothy shook his head. "You're making a mistake if you stay here. You will hurt her, and no one in my family will be happy." He turned on his heel and stomped back over to his workstation.

Luke stared after him and gritted his teeth with frustration.

"What was that about?" Jake asked.

"Timothy is convinced my being here is detrimental to Sarah because I remind her of how Peter lied about his past. He wants me to leave, and he won't let me forget it." Luke looked back at the plans, hoping his stomach would stop churning.

"I think Timothy needs to leave the future to God and let it go," Jake said. "You're not the type of person to hurt anyone, and you know how precious life is since you've lost your parents and your cousin."

Luke met the young man eyes and smiled. "You are wise beyond your years, Jake. I wish more people thought like you." He then studied the plans. "All right, we better get to work before your grandpa gets impatient."

Apple Ring Fritters

1 cup sifted flour
1/4 tsp salt
1–1/2 tsp baking powder
1 egg
3/4 cup milk
4 large apples
Shortening
2 Tbsp cinnamon (For use after draining on paper towel)
2 Tbsp sugar

Sift together flour, salt, and baking powder. Add egg and milk. Beat well. Peel and core apples and slice into rings about 3/4–inch thick. Dip rings in batter and drop into skillet containing 3/4 inch of hot melted shortening. Fry until golden brown on both sides. Drain on paper towel. Mix sugar and cinnamon together and sprinkle over fritters. Makes 18 to 20.

12

Sitting across from Naomi Friday afternoon, Luke popped another large piece of vanilla crumb cake into his mouth. The cake was superbly moist and sweet, just like it had been the previous four days this week.

He smiled while Naomi prattled on about amusing English customers and new quilt designs. She had appeared in the showroom of the furniture store precisely at a quarter of twelve each day with her basket and a delicious lunch. Each day he accepted her invitation, even though he knew by spending time with her he was leading her to believe he wanted to court her. Yet he couldn't seem to form the words "I want to just be friends" or "I don't want to court you." Extinguishing her hopes and dreams felt wrong, but so did letting her believe he wanted to be more than friends.

Today Naomi had brought a mysterious large black garbage bag, which she'd refused to allow him to carry to the table for her—and which she also refused to open. It sat next on the ground at her feet like a loyal pet.

"Would you like to join my family for supper tonight?" she asked, a tentative smile spreading on her lip. "I'm making my *appeditlich* ham loaf."

"Oh," Luke said, setting his fork down on the empty plate. "I wish I could, but I can't."

She frowned. "That's a shame. I guess you already have plans?"

"*Ya,*" he said quickly, hoping a half truth wasn't too much of a sin. "I'm going to join the Kauffmans tonight. I haven't made it over to their place all week, and Eli's been asking me to come by."

It wasn't a complete lie. He hadn't had a chance to make it to Eli's because he'd been working late helping Jake with a project for a loyal customer, and he'd been working on Sarah's cradle late into the night at the house. He'd longed to see Sarah all week, and while her father hadn't invited him over, he hoped to pop in and see her around suppertime tonight.

Naomi suddenly brightened. "I plan to get on your schedule soon. Perhaps you can join us Saturday night."

"Perhaps." Luke cleared his throat and began piling up their dirty plates. "I'd best get back to work before I lose my job." He put the dirty dishes into a small bag and then added the used cups.

Smiling, she hefted the bag onto the bench beside her. "I brought you a gift." She untied the knot and pulled down the sides of the bag. "Since you're all alone in Sarah's old house, I thought you might get cold at night." She slowly lifted a white quilt with purple-and-blue panels. "It's my favorite design, Log Cabin. I thought you might like deep purples and blues."

"Oh, Naomi." Reaching across the table, he ran his fingers over the soft material and intricate stitching. Guilt nipped at his soul as he imagined her slaving over this beautiful blanket for him. "You shouldn't have done this for me."

"Don't be *gegisch,* Luke." Her eyes were trained on his—intent and purposeful. "I wanted to."

"*Danki,*" he whispered. "I'm not worthy."

"But you are, Luke. You truly are." She gave him a hopeful smile. "I hope you'll stay here in Bird-in-Hand."

He nodded, overwhelmed by her frank admission of feelings

and her generous nature. "I guess we'll see what God has in store for me."

"I can hardly wait," she whispered with a smile.

"Naomi," he began. "I appreciate your friendship. You're a lovely *maedel*, and you'll be a *wunderbaar fraa* someday."

He paused to gather his thoughts, and her smile fell in anticipation of his unspoken "but." Leaning over, he took her hands in his. "I'm not sure what my future holds or where I'll wind up living, so you shouldn't waste your time waiting to court me. You should find someone who is available for you now."

She shook her head and pulled her hands back. "No, no. I want to wait for you, Luke. I'm willing to wait as long as it takes you to move here. You're the one for me. I can feel it." She placed a hand over her heart. "I know in my heart God wants us together. I truly believe that."

Luke sighed, lamenting that he had to be more direct. "Naomi, I'm not ready to court anyone. Please don't wait for me." He nodded toward the quilt. "I can't accept that quilt from you."

She frowned, and her eyes glistened. "I'll wait as long as I need to. You are the one for me, and you must take the quilt. I insist."

"Naomi, please look into my eyes." He held her hands tight. "I want to be your friend."

Her lip trembled. "Are you breaking up with me?"

He paused, debating how to respond. "I want to be your friend. I enjoy spending time with you, and I enjoy our lunches. Right now, I'm trying to figure out where I belong. Please don't wait for me. You're a beautiful *maedel*, and I'd hate to see you wasting your time on me."

She sniffed and wiped her eyes. "You're not a waste."

He gave her a sad smile. "*Ya*, I am." He touched the quilt. "That's a beautiful quilt. I'm honored you made it for me, but I can't accept it."

Clearing her throat, Naomi forced a smile. "We're friends, *ya*?"

"*Ya*, we're friends."

She raised her eyebrows. "Friends give each other gifts, *ya*?"

A smile crept over his lips. "You're not going to let this go, are you?"

"Nope." She lifted her glass of iced tea.

"*Danki*." He smiled. "I appreciate the gift."

They chatted about the weather and their weekend plans until it was time to head back to work. She packed up her basket and then stood.

"*Danki* for having lunch with me."

He folded the quilt into the bag and rose alongside her. "*Danki* for the *appeditlich* meals and fabulous cake. I will cherish the quilt."

"Can friends have lunch together sometimes?" she asked as they walked toward the front of the store.

"I don't see why not."

"*Gut.* Enjoy your afternoon." She gave him a quick hug.

Before he could respond, she trotted across the street toward the farmer's market.

Sarah wrapped a quilt around her shoulders and stared off across the dark pasture toward her former home. She breathed in the fresh scent of wood burning in the fireplace, mixed with the newly harvested hay.

The past month had dragged by at a turtle's pace. At the doctor's orders, she'd spent most of her time on the sofa with her swollen feet and achy legs keeping her from baking the dishes she loved and sewing clothes for the children. Her sweet niece, Nancy, had waited on Sarah and worked around the house. While she loved spending time with Nancy, she missed the bakery.

Gazing across the fields, she thought about Luke. She had expected him to stop by to visit or for supper. However, she hadn't seen him once since Thanksgiving dinner last week. She wondered what had kept him away all week. They'd chatted briefly after Thanksgiving supper, and he'd asked how she was feeling. After that he was dragged outside to the barn for the usual men talk.

She'd found herself missing him all week. She longed for their previous conversations on the porch and hoped she hadn't scared him off by being too bold that Sunday when she had shared the twins' kicks with him. She had felt at the time their friendship allowed for that level of intimacy, but she must've been wrong. Letting him touch her may have been too much for him. She hoped he didn't think she was ... forward. Or, worse yet, loose.

She pushed that idea away and reflected on her week. Norman had dropped in for supper on Wednesday, and they'd spent the evening chatting about the children. She enjoyed their time together and appreciated his friendship. However, she sensed something more in his eyes lately. More than once, she'd found him staring at her with an intensity that made her uncomfortable.

Sighing, she cradled her belly and smiled when a baby kicked in response. Hearing her twins' heartbeats at the doctor's had deepened the excitement she already harbored for them. In a couple of weeks or so, she'd be holding them in her arms and gazing into their eyes

Cupping a hand over her mouth, she tried in vain to stifle a yawn. The screen door squeaked open and banged shut, and Timothy's boots scraped across the porch before he sank into a chair nearby.

"It's cold out here," he said, hugging his coat to his chest. "You should go inside."

"I will soon enough," she said through a second yawn. "I was just enjoying the cool air for a moment." She nodded toward her house. "I'm surprised Luke hasn't stopped by this week. Have you talked to him at all?"

"He's been real busy at work. Tonight he's working late helping Jake with a project that's due to a customer tomorrow."

"That's nice he's helping Jake," Sarah said, ignoring the disappointment flickering through her. She wondered if Luke and Naomi were still friends. She hesitated, since the question would sound like she was gossiping, which was a sin, but her curiosity won out. "Does Naomi come by the shop at all?"

"She brings Luke lunch sometimes," Timothy said. "She was by a couple of times this week."

"Oh?" Sarah pushed the rocker back and studied her dark house across the pitch-black pasture.

"I think she would like to court him," Timothy said. "But I have the feeling Luke isn't going to stay around here."

She looked at him. "You don't think so?"

Timothy shook his head. "He belongs in Ohio."

"He said that?"

Timothy shrugged. "In not so many words, but *ya.*"

Sarah battled the disappointment bubbling up inside her. "I thought he might stay to be with the *kinner.*"

"He'll probably be gone right after Christmas. He'll stay long enough to see them born and then head back home to live his own life." Yawning, Timothy stood and started down the stairs. "I reckon I should hit the hay. The alarm goes off early in the morning. *Gut nacht.*"

"*Gut nacht.*" Sarah heaved herself from the swing and started toward the door.

Climbing the stairs to her room, she wondered what would become of Luke Troyer. Somehow she couldn't imagine losing him. And yet, she couldn't figure out why she felt so attached to him.

What do you think, *Aenti* Sarah?" Nancy nodded at the poinsettia she'd placed on the mantle in preparation of Christmas dinner tomorrow night. "Do you like the flower there?"

"Oh, it's love—" Sarah gasped and groaned, her words stolen by a unexpected sharp stab of pain, slicing through her lower back like a knife.

She sucked in a breath and rubbed her stomach as a cramp radiated through her abdomen. All week she'd endured pressure and occasional cramps. Today they felt more intense as she sat in her father's favorite easy chair.

"*Aenti* Sarah!" Nancy yelped, rushing over and dropping at Sarah's feet. She grasped Sarah's hand in hers. "Are you all right?"

Sarah could only manage a slight nod as the pain radiated again, more intense than ever.

"Katie!" Nancy yelled. "Katie, come quick! We need help!"

Her older sister trotted in from the kitchen. "What's wrong?"

"Something's wrong with *Aenti* Sarah." Fear shimmered in Nancy's big, blue eyes.

"I think it's time," Sarah whispered, her voice raspy and breathless. "I think I'm in labor. Please get help."

Katie pulled Nancy to her feet and pushed her toward the kitchen. "Go! Run! Get help!"

Katie then looked at Sarah. "I'll get you a glass of water and a compress for your head." Her expression was calm, her words steady and even—evidence she'd been present when her *mamm* delivered her younger siblings at home.

"*Danki,*" Sarah whispered. She sucked in a breath when another cramp gripped her.

Katie returned with a cold washcloth and swiped it over Sarah's clammy forehead and cheeks. She then held a glass of water to Sarah's lips. Sarah held her breath through more cramps while Katie brushed Sarah's hair back from her face and chatted about their plans for Christmas dinner.

After what seemed like an eternity, the back door slammed open and *Mamm* entered, followed by Rebecca and Lindsay. Sarah only heard the echo of voices as another cramp hit, stronger and more intense this time. The pressure on her abdomen felt like fire and stole her breath.

"Sarah Rose!" Her mother's voice cut through her fog of pain. "I'm with you now. Everything's going to be just fine. We've called Nina, and she's on her way. We'll have you to the hospital soon, *mei liewe*. I promise."

Pulling up a chair, Rebecca sat next to Sarah and took her hand. "Squeeze when it hurts."

"I'll get your bag." *Mamm* hurried up the stairs.

Sarah stared into Rebecca's eyes and gripped her hand. "It's time."

"*Ya.*" Rebecca smiled, pushing a wet wisp of hair that had escaped Sarah's prayer *Kapp* back from her face. "It's time. I'll stay with you the whole time. I promise."

"*Danki.*" Sarah sucked in a breath as another cramp set in.

Rebecca quietly counted.

When it released, Sarah felt a dribble between her legs and gasped. "I think my water just broke."

Rebecca squealed and squeezed her hand.

Closing her eyes, Sarah said a silent prayer the labor would be smooth and the twins would be healthy. She couldn't help but wish Peter were with her.

The following afternoon, Christmas Day, Sarah stared down at the beautiful baby girl in her arms. After twenty-four hours of labor, she had delivered two perfect babies, each weighing a little over six pounds.

"A boy and a girl," *Mamm* cooed while holding Sarah's son. "They are just precious, Sarah Rose, just precious."

"I'm so blessed," Sarah whispered. Her heart had been bursting with love and joy ever since she'd laid her eyes on her twins. "I had no idea being a *mamm* would be like this. There's no joy like it." She glanced over at *Mamm* and wiped a tear. "*Danki.*"

Mamm chuckled. "Why are you thanking me? You're the one who delivered them."

"No." She held her free hand out, and *Mamm* leaned over the hospital bed and took it. "*Danki* for being here. I couldn't have done it without you."

"You're welcome, Sarah Rose." *Mamm* squeezed her hand and then pulled back, staring down at her new grandson.

Sarah studied her daughter. The baby's chubby, pink face was accented with bright eyes. Her bald head was shielded by a pink stocking hat, and her little body was covered in a white blanket trimmed in pink and blue. "I've decided on names."

"Oh?"

"Rachel Elizabeth and Seth Peter." When *Mamm* didn't answer, she glanced over to find her wiping her eyes. "*Mamm?*"

"*Danki,*" her mother whispered. "I'm very touched."

Sarah looked down at her daughter just in time to see her yawn. Her little mouth opened wide, revealing bright pink gums and a matching little tongue. Sarah grinned.

If only Peter were here to see his beautiful twins.

No, she would not be sad now. He was in her heart and in the eyes of her babies.

Rachel fell asleep, and Sarah ran her finger over the baby's head. While she watched her daughter sleep, she opened her heart to God, silently thanking him for her two wonderful miracles, her children.

For the first time since Peter's death, she felt true happiness.

Turning to *Mamm*, Sarah found her humming softly to Seth, who slept in her arms. *Mamm* met her gaze and smiled.

They sat in silence for a few moments. Sarah stared down at her baby girl, thinking of Peter. He would've been elated.

"Merry Christmas, Peter," she whispered. "I wish you were here to hold your babies. They are a gift from God, the perfect Christmas gift to fill my heart."

"*Ya*," *Mamm* whispered, her voice trembling as she wiped again at her eyes.

A knock sounded from the door.

"Come in," Sarah called.

The door squeaked open, and a knot of Sarah's sisters and nieces paraded through into her room, oooing and ahhing with love. The littlest nieces pushed forward and stood on tiptoes to view the new babies.

Sarah smiled, scanning the crowd and finding her brothers standing near the door. She searched the sea of faces and a twinge of disappointment hit her when she didn't find Luke there.

Kathryn appeared from the crowd, her arms extended, and her face expectant. "May I?"

"Of course." Sarah handed over Rachel and sighed.

"Merry Christmas and Happy Birthday, little one," Kathryn cooed, rocking her niece to her chest.

Luke paced outside Sarah's hospital room, gripping the brim of his hat. Laughter and voices rang through the door. Although he knew most of her family members were there celebrating the birth of the twins, he felt like an intruder. Or perhaps he felt more like a fraud, since he was posing as a cousin to the children when he was really an uncle. However, he was so knee-deep into the falsehood that there was no turning back for fear of being ostracized.

Nevertheless, it wasn't a lie. He'd never said he was a cousin; the family had assumed it. Just the same, he hadn't corrected them either ... which made him a liar.

Taking a deep breath, he marched to the door and knocked. Receiving no response, he pushed the door open to find a crowd of Kauffmans surrounding Sarah, who was propped up in the bed, smiling and laughing with her family.

She looked breathtakingly beautiful dressed in a blue hospital gown with her golden blonde hair hidden under her prayer *kapp*. He couldn't help but wonder if his brother had ever spent time staring at her and contemplating how something so perfect existed in nature. God had blessed Eli and Elizabeth when He created their youngest daughter.

Her eyes met his and lit up as if her heart swelled with joy. His smile broadened at the thought that he could bring her such happiness.

"Luke." She extended her hand in his direction. "I'm so glad you came. I was hoping you'd heard the news." She beckoned him over.

He weaved through the knot of visitors and stood next to her. "You didn't think I'd come?" He wished he'd brought her something—a bouquet of flowers or a small gift. However, the gift he had waiting for her at home would be special enough.

"I was afraid no one told you." She started to adjust herself in the bed and then winced in pain.

"Are you okay?" He reached for her hand but stopped himself from touching her.

"*Ya.*" She forced a smile. "I'm a bit sore."

Elizabeth leaned over her daughter. "You want me to call the nurse for more medicine?"

Sarah shook her head and waved her mother off. "I'm fine. It passed." She then faced Luke. "Have you seen them? Aren't they exquisite?"

Luke nodded, staring at the baby in Beth Anne's arms.

"That's Seth Peter." Sarah beamed. "Doesn't he look like Peter? It's uncanny. His eyes are the same shade of hazel." She pointed to the baby in Kathryn's arms. "Rachel Elizabeth has blue eyes, like me."

Luke studied his nephew, and warmth washed over him. His eyes filled with tears as he was overwhelmed with a mixture of love and grief for his brother. He fought the urge to flee the room in order to deal with the confusing emotions in private.

A gentle hand encircled his arm.

"Luke? Are you okay?" Sarah asked.

The concern and affection in her eyes caused the emotions within him to churn. He cleared his throat and wiped his eyes, hoping to stop the tears.

"I'm fine. It's just warm in here." He hoped he sounded convincing.

Beth Anne angled the baby boy toward Luke. "Would you like to hold him?"

"No," Luke said, shaking his head in protest. "I don't want to—"

"You won't hurt him," Sarah said with a chuckle. "*Bopplin* are resilient."

"I couldn't," he said. "I don't know the first thing about them."

"Don't be silly." Sarah hoisted herself up from the bed, wincing slightly as she moved toward him.

His eyes raked over her, taking in how tiny she was.

She lifted the baby from her sister's arms and held him close to Luke. "Seth, meet your *onkel* Luke."

His eyes snapped to hers at the word *uncle*. Did she sense the truth? Did she know who he was?

"Oh, I'm sorry." Her pretty face flushed a bright crimson. "It's just automatic for me to say *onkel* since I have three brothers."

"It's okay," he whispered, his voice quavering. He cleared his throat, but emotion ruled his words. "They can call me *onkel*."

"I think the *zwillingbopplin* would be happy if you were their *onkel* Luke." Her smile was bright, and he feared he might shed a tear or two after all. She held Seth out to him, her arm resting against his, mixing their body heat. "Would you like to hold him?"

"I don't think I could," he whispered.

"It's not so hard, Luke," Daniel chimed in. "I've held my nieces and nephews plenty."

"It's good practice," Rebecca said with a grin.

"Just don't drop 'im," Timothy added, and the crowd laughed in response.

Luke succumbed to the request and took the tiny child in his arms. His heart felt as if it would overflow with love as his brother's tiny offspring opened his hazel eyes, yawned, and fell asleep again.

Lowering himself into the chair next to the bed, Luke held the baby. The rest of the world disappeared, and he was alone with the boy who would never know his father.

At that moment, Luke silently vowed to help raise his niece and nephew, in honor of his brother, whom he missed more than words could express. He was going to stay with the twins in Bird-in-Hand. There was no doubt in his mind or his heart; this was where he belonged.

14

Glad to be home from the hospital, Sarah climbed the stairs, taking each with care due to her lingering aches and pains. She followed *Mamm* toward her room.

The twins' cries echoed from downstairs where her sisters tended to them. She stopped and started toward the stairs.

"Sarah Rose!" *Mamm* chided. "Your sisters can handle the *kinner*. You need to get some rest."

"But they're crying ..." Sarah bit her lip.

Mamm gave a knowing smile. "Babies cry, *mei Liewe*. They will be fine. You need your rest. You just gave birth three days ago."

Sighing, Sarah hobbled to her room. Stepping in, she glanced around at the familiarity of the room that had become hers since Peter died and she moved out of her house. She stopped in her tracks when something out of place caught her eye.

On the floor next to the cradle her father had made was the most exquisite cradle she'd ever seen. It was simple yet elegant, with a pattern engraved in the sides. It was stained a deep cherry color and sparkled in the low light of the lamp. A large red bow hung over the side.

Sarah gasped and crossed the room. She bent and touched it, and it rocked back and forth, scraping the wooden floor with a quiet whooshing sound.

"You kept your promise, Luke," she whispered, running her finger over the slick wood and sniffing back tears. "*Danki.*"

"It's your Christmas gift from Luke," *Mamm* said. "Actually, he said it was for you and the *zwillingbopplin*. He had intended to give it to you himself on Christmas, but the *kinner* had other plans. Since he's at work today, he asked *Dat* to give it to you for him."

"It's perfect," Sarah said, meeting *Mamm's* gaze. "How *wunderbaar.*"

"I think he loves those *kinner*, you know." *Mamm* dropped Sarah's bag onto a chair by the bed. "He said he'd come by to visit when you were ready to have company."

"He can come any time." Sarah crossed to the bed and lowered herself onto the side.

"You get some rest. The babies will be fine with your sisters and me."

Sarah nodded. "Okay."

"Call me if you need anything." *Mamm* disappeared through the door, gently closing it behind her.

Rolling onto her side on the bed, Sarah closed her eyes and drifted off to sleep, dreaming of Peter, the babies, cradles ... and Luke.

Sarah yawned as she lounged on the sofa with Rachel in her arms. She hadn't achieved much rest last night since the babies had their days and nights mixed up. Although *Mamm* had helped with the middle-of-the-night feedings, Sarah still found herself awake most of the night.

Sarah was thankful to have *Mamm's* help during the night. And since the bakery was only open part-time during the winter, she was also grateful to have *Mamm* home to help along with her nieces most days.

It was hard to believe she'd been home a week with the

twins. She'd expected to have a house full of visitors; however, only her sisters and a few of her friends from the church district had stopped by and brought food and gifts for the children.

If Sarah were honest with herself, she'd admit she was disappointed one guest in particular hadn't stopped by at all, and that guest was Luke. She'd asked Timothy if he'd seen Luke, and her brother had explained Luke hadn't missed a day of work.

While she was rocking Rachel back to sleep early this morning, she'd pondered the question of why Luke had been staying away. She couldn't get the image of Luke at the hospital out of her mind—the way his brown eyes had filled with tears when he saw the children touched her deep in her soul. She wondered if his absence had anything to do with the emotion he'd displayed then. Was seeing the twins too difficult for him because they reminded him of his beloved cousin?

She hoped Luke wouldn't stay away. For some reason she craved Luke's presence even more now that the children were here. Was it because he was her only connection to Peter beyond the twins? Or did she miss his friendship? Her gut told her it was a combination of both. Sarah felt a connection to Luke that was unlike any other friendship she cherished.

A flurry of activity and a chorus of children's voices sounded from the kitchen, announcing the arrival of visitors.

Mamm entered the living room with a smile on her face. "You have a visitor. Or rather, you have visitors."

"Send them in." Sarah adjusted a sleeping Rachel on her shoulder and then ran her hand over her prayer *Kapp* to make sure she was presentable. She felt silly for fussing over her appearance. After all, she was a sleep-deprived woman who'd given birth less than two weeks ago.

She hoped Luke was among the visitors, but a quick glance at the clock on the mantle showed it was shortly after four and too early for Luke to arrive on a weekday.

Mamm disappeared into the kitchen and a few moments later, Norman appeared in the doorway followed by his daughters.

"Norman." Sarah smiled. "It's so good to see you."

He glanced down at Seth sleeping in the cradle and then back at Sarah, who turned slightly, angling Rachel toward them.

Norman smiled at the babies. "Beautiful," he whispered. "Congratulations. God is good."

"*Ya*," Sarah said, rubbing Rachel's back. "He is."

The girls stood over the cradle and cooed at the babies.

"Why don't you two go back in the kitchen and have cookies with Nancy and Katie?" Norman asked. "Sarah and I are going to visit, and the babies are sleeping."

The girls retreated to the kitchen.

"Please have a seat." She gestured toward the chair with her free hand.

"*Danki*." Norman folded his stocky body into the sofa across from her. "How are you feeling?"

"Exhausted but happy." She covered her mouth to shield a yawn. She then adjusted Rachel on her shoulder, which had started to ache.

"Are they sleeping well in the night?" he asked.

Sarah snorted with sarcasm. "No, not yet. *Mamm* says I slept through the night at three months. I'm hoping these two figure out their nights and days faster than that. If not, then I may pass out soon from exhaustion."

Norman's eyes trained on Seth, and a smile broke through his pleasant countenance. "How does it feel to be a *mamm*?"

"It's more *wunderbaar* than I ever imagined." She ran a finger over Rachel's soft cheek. "I stare down at my *kinner* and can't believe they're mine."

"Blessings from God," he whispered.

"Absolutely." She shifted to the edge of the chair and gently placed Rachel into the cradle next to Seth. Sitting back in the chair, she sighed and rubbed her shoulder. "Little ones weigh more than you think."

Norman smiled.

They fell into an easy conversation, discussing everything from the weather to the children.

After an hour, he stood. "I reckon I should get back home and feed my own *kinner* before they start grumbling."

Sarah walked with him to the kitchen. "I can whip up something to feed all of us."

"No, no." He touched her arm. "I wouldn't want to do that to you. You have your hands full."

"Don't be silly." She glanced at *Mamm*, who was sitting at the table talking with *Dat* and the children. "Do we have something we can throw together for supper for everyone?"

Mamm stood and went to the refrigerator. "Of course we do. Let me see. I can make this stew quickly. It's plenty for everyone."

"No, I couldn't impose." Norman snatched his coat from the rack by the door and glanced at his daughters. "Get your wraps on. We're heading back home."

"Norman, don't be silly." Sarah touched his arm. "I haven't seen you in a couple of weeks. I'd be happy if you and the girls stayed."

"Another night. I promise." He glanced at his girls, who were ready at the door. "Say good-bye to everyone. We'll see them very soon." He said his farewells to her parents and then steered his girls out the door.

Sarah followed close behind, hugging her arms to her chest as the January wind sliced through her caped dress. She inhaled the chilly air, breathing in the aroma of wood fireplaces.

Norman directed his girls to the waiting buggy and then turned to Sarah. "You best get inside before you catch a cold."

"*Danki* for visiting," she said through her chattering teeth.

"We'll have dinner together very soon," Norman said, his

expression flickering with an intensity she'd never seen before. "I'd like to see you more often."

Unsure of the meaning behind his words, Sarah was rendered speechless for a moment.

"*Gut nacht.*" He paused for a moment and then touched her arm. "Take care of those *wunderbaar zwillingbopplin.*"

Norman clattered down the porch steps and loaded the girls into the buggy. Sarah waved as they drove off toward the road.

The crunch of stones drew her gaze toward the path. Spotting Luke heading for the porch, she rushed down the stairs toward him.

"Why don't you have a coat on, Sarah Rose?" he scolded, shaking his head in disapproval.

She stopped in her tracks and scowled. "And it's nice to see you too."

He gave a bark of laughter, and she grinned.

"How are you?" he asked.

"Angry with you."

He raised an eyebrow.

"Why haven't you been by to see me and the *zwillingbopplin*?" She folded her arms across her chest. "I feared you'd moved back to Ohio without any notice."

His smile disappeared. "You think I'd leave without telling you?"

She shivered.

He nodded toward the house. "How about we take this disagreement inside?"

They climbed the porch steps side by side.

"Did you hear the news?" she asked. "Daniel is a father. Rebecca gave birth to their son, Daniel Jr., last night."

"I did hear." Luke's smile was genuine. "Eli told me this morning."

"I can't wait to see my new nephew." Sarah's heart swelled with love. She knew Daniel and Rebecca were elated to welcome their first child into the world after fifteen years of marriage. It was a miracle.

Her thoughts turned to cradles, and she stopped short of the door.

Luke reached for the doorknob, and she blocked it. "Sarah Rose, you're going to catch a cold or, worse yet, pneumonia."

"That's not the first time I've heard that tonight," she quipped.

He reached for the knob again, and she stopped him by taking his hand in hers. The warmth of his skin took her by surprise, and she pulled back.

"I need to tell you something in private," she said, shivering again.

"Tell me quickly. I don't want to see you back in the hospital." His eyes were full of concern.

"The cradle you made is beautiful. It's the most *wunderbaar* gift I've ever received, and I love it. *Danki.*" She looked into his eyes and for the first time since she'd met Luke, her stomach fluttered. She tamped down the feeling and turned toward the door.

"Wait." He touched her shoulder, and she faced him. "I'm glad. I wanted to do something special for the *kinner* in memory of Peter. I'm very happy you like it."

"It's perfect. No, it's better than perfect. It's magnificent."

He nodded, his eyes intense.

They stared at each other for a long moment and then he broke away and turned the doorknob.

Sarah stepped into the kitchen and took in the delicious scent of *Mamm's* stew.

"Sarah Rose!" *Mamm* snapped. "What on earth were you doing out there without a coat? Did you forget it's January?"

Sarah sighed, and Luke snickered.

"Luke!" *Mamm* stepped toward him. "You're just in time for supper. Take off your coat and make yourself at home."

"*Danki*." Luke hung his coat on a peg by the door and greeted *Dat* and Sarah's nieces.

Sarah touched his arm. "Would you like to see the babies?" she whispered, noticing his warm scent.

"Are you kidding? I really only came to see them, not you." His crooked grin was teasing.

She laughed and led him into the living room, where the babies were fast asleep in their cradles. She stood back while he squatted between the cradles and gazed between them. His smiled faded, and his expression turned to reverence.

For a moment, Sarah wondered if she should leave the room and give him privacy. When he reached for Seth and then pulled his hand back, she stepped over by him.

"You can touch them," she whispered. "I promise they won't break."

He glanced at her in disbelief.

"Go ahead. Don't be afraid. Touch them."

Leaning down next to Luke, she lifted his hand to place it on Seth's back. Liquid heat coursed through her veins at the touch, and for a split second, she couldn't breathe. She pulled her hand back as if to stop the fire burning within her.

Again his eyes bored into hers, and they studied each other for a brief moment.

Standing, she folded her arms as if to guard her confused heart.

Luke glanced back at the babies and, placing his free hand on Rachel's back, he caressed their backs simultaneously. His expression was filled with emotion, similar to the day in the hospital. His eyes glistened.

Feeling like a voyeur, she backed toward the door to the kitchen. "I'm going to go help *Mamm* with supper," she whispered, gesturing toward the kitchen.

"Don't go." His eyes locked with hers.

She stopped and wracked her brain for something to break

the protracted silence between them. "Why haven't you visited until now?"

"I didn't know if it was proper to come see you when you first got home." His smile was back. "I'm new at this whole *boppli* thing."

"I was afraid it was too much for you at the hospital."

He stood, his eyebrows raised in question. "What do you mean?"

"You seemed so emotional at the hospital when you held Seth. I was afraid the *bopplin* scared you off."

"Are you joking?" He stepped toward her. "You couldn't beat me away with a two-by-four. I want to be a part of their lives."

"Supper's ready," *Mamm* said from the doorway. "Robert's here for the girls, and he's going to join us."

Sarah followed her *mamm* into the kitchen, where they served the meal to the guests. While they ate, Sarah was aware of Luke studying her, and she wondered if he'd always been so observant of her or if she'd only just noticed it.

After supper, Robert and the girls headed home. Sarah excused herself to her bedroom, and her parents helped her carry the babies and cradles upstairs, where she fed and rocked the babies until they fell asleep.

Returning to the living room, she found Luke chatting with her parents. She sat on the couch with *Mamm* and joined in the easy conversation. She again found Luke's eyes honed in on her. What surprised her the most was that she enjoyed the conversation and the attention from Luke.

What was wrong with her? She didn't feel this awareness or excitement when she was with Norman. What was different about Luke Troyer?

And why did she like it so much?

Sarah didn't know the answers to those questions, but she knew one thing for certain—she hoped Luke would visit again soon and often.

Luke said good night to Eli and Elizabeth and thanked them for supper before they disappeared upstairs.

Turning to Sarah, he found her standing by the kitchen doorway with a comfortable smile on her face, and his heart turned over in his chest. She was different tonight—more at ease and more intent on him. He wondered where the change came from. Had giving birth to the children released stress for her?

He wasn't sure what had made her different, but he knew that he couldn't take his eyes off her tonight. Although she'd been beautiful when she was pregnant, she was even more stunning now. Her body was petite, and her eyes seemed brighter. And when their hands touched, something had ignited between them. Had she felt it too?

"I had a nice time tonight," she said.

"Me too." He rose and crossed the room. "I reckon I should get on home, and you should get to bed."

She sighed. "*Ya.* Those *bopplin* will have me up most of the night, so I might as well get some sleep while I can."

He studied her, wishing he could read her thoughts. "Your nieces are helping you during the day, *ya?*"

She nodded as they walked to the kitchen. "Robert brings Nancy and Katie by every morning, and they stay all day. *Mamm* is only opening the bakery every other day, so she's here too. It's nice to have help. I can nap a little during the day since I don't sleep much at night."

"That's *gut*." He glanced out the dark window and remembered a question he'd wanted to ask. "I saw a buggy leaving when I was walking over. Who visited here earlier?"

"Norman came by to see the babies." She yawned, cupping a hand to her pretty face. "Oh, excuse me. It's not the company making me yawn. It's lack of sleep that's tiring me out."

Jealousy twisted his gut at the mention of Norman's name. Why was he jealous of her friend? "I better let you get some sleep. I've taken enough of your time."

"You're welcome anytime," she said. "You're family."

"*Danki.*"

He felt an insatiable need to touch her. No, more than that, he found himself resisting the urge to kiss her forehead.

"*Gut nacht,* Sarah Rose." Snatching his coat from the peg by the door, he slipped his arms into it.

"*Gut nacht.* I hope you'll come back again soon." She opened the back door and handed him a lantern. "You best not stay away too long next time."

He smiled, stepping onto the porch and shivering in the whipping wind. "I promise I'll see you again before the week's out."

"I'm going to hold you to that." Glancing across the field, her eyes widened. "Is that snow?"

Luke held his hand out and smiled when large, fat flurries danced over his fingers. "*Ya,* it is. You better get inside before you catch a cold."

"You hurry home too."

"Stay warm." He hopped down the porch steps and rushed through the wind toward the house.

Glancing up, he smiled as the flurries kissed his face. The evening had been like a dream, spending time with Sarah, her parents, and her precious children—his niece and nephew, his only living link to his only brother.

For the first time since his *mamm* died, Luke felt like a part of a family, a real family. He understood why Peter had stayed in Bird-in-Hand—he had been surrounded by people who loved him. Luke wanted that too. Being with the Kauffmans was a dream come true.

Life was pretty close to perfect.

In his heart, he knew he longed to be more than a friend

to Sarah, but those thoughts were inappropriate. His brother hadn't been gone a year, and it was disrespectful to even consider courting Sarah.

Aside from that, coveting his brother's widow was a sin in itself. However, even if he could never be more than a friend to Sarah, he would be satisfied. Just knowing her and the twins was a gift from God after losing his parents and brother.

What happens when she finds out you're her brother-in-law and not her husband's cousin? How will that knowledge change her feelings for you? Will she ever trust you again?

The questions came from deep within his heart and slammed him back to reality. He didn't know the answers, and he dreaded the day when she found out the truth.

Loping up the front steps of the house, he glanced over his shoulder and saw a light burning in Elizabeth's kitchen. He wondered if Sarah was watching him walk home. He hoped she would remember this evening with as much happiness as he did.

The wind shifted, and his teeth chattered as the air sent a frosty shudder through him. The snowflakes picked up, and he glanced up at the sky, feeling the very air around him changing, as if a big storm was coming to Bird-in-Hand.

15

Sarah awoke with a start after a night of jumbled dreams and nightmares. She'd dreamed she was sitting on a stool in the kitchen of the bakery and telling Peter about the twins. Then she was in a strange house in Ohio, and Luke was telling her about Peter's past. Next she was in the nursery of her former home rocking one of the twins to sleep while Luke stood at the window overlooking the pasture, holding the other baby.

When she sat up in bed, she felt a burning desire to go to her other home and sort through Peter's clothes. She couldn't explain why, but she needed to hold one of his shirts and inhale his scent—if any remained on his clothes. Perhaps his scent would make her feel close to him again.

Nancy and Katie had planned to come by today to help Sarah while her parents kept to their Saturday routine of running errands and visiting the market. Sarah fed the babies and then dressed. She was gathering up the babies' supplies when the girls appeared in the doorway, eager to help. Together, they brought the twins and their things downstairs and then ate breakfast while the children rested in their cradles.

Once the girls were settled with the children, Sarah asked them if they were comfortable staying alone with them while she ran to her house to get a few things. They both told Sarah to take her time and not worry about the children.

Slipping on her cloak, Sarah hurried down the gravel lane to her former home. The dream was still vivid in her mind, and her heart thumped in her rib cage as she climbed the front steps to the porch. The brisk February wind soaked through her shawl, and she shuddered.

Taking a deep breath, she wrenched open the front door, wondering if she'd find Luke at home. She'd seen him nearly every day for the past three weeks when he'd stopped by after work to hold the twins and visit.

"Hello?" she called, her voice echoing throughout the downstairs. "Luke? Are you home?" The floorboards creaked beneath her shoes as she wandered through the living room, laundry room, pantry, kitchen, and bathroom. Finding them all empty, she gripped the banister and headed to the second floor.

"Luke?" she called. "Are you here? Hello?" Sarah stuck her head into her former bedroom, sewing room, and nursery. Again, each was empty.

Standing before the closed spare bedroom door, her pulse skipped at the idea of finding Luke asleep in bed. What would she say to explain an awkward situation such as that? Lifting a trembling hand, she gingerly knocked on the door.

"Luke?" Her voice quavered with embarrassment. "Luke? Are you here?" After waiting a brief moment, she turned the knob and the door creaked open. The room was quiet, and the bed was made. No sign of Luke.

"I guess you got an early start this morning too," she muttered.

She crossed the room and peered down at a pile of his clothes. The dark-colored trousers and shirts lay neatly folded and piled on the hope chest by the window. A spare pair of boots sat in the corner, lined up symmetrically like corn in *Dat's* field.

Looking at Luke's clothing brought back thoughts of how Peter kept his personal belongings. Sarah's lips curled in a melancholy smile. A love for the neat and orderly ran in the Troyer family. Peter used to get frustrated if the cans weren't lined up perfectly in the pantry—labels all facing the same way.

She smiled at the memory before padding back down the hallway to her former bedroom. Her stomach flip-flopped with anticipation when she opened the doors to Peter's armoire. Although a part of her had hoped to see Luke, she was also relieved to have privacy while delving into Peter's things for the first time since his death. Shaking her head, she tried to fathom the nine-month period since he'd died. Where had the time gone?

Her hands shaking like dandelions in a spring breeze, she pulled out Peter's favorite dark-blue shirt. She closed her eyes and buried her face in the fabric as if it were the oxygen her lungs needed to sustain her life. A faint whiff of his scent filled her soul. He'd always smelled like wood, stain, and a hint of earth.

Tears of mourning began to sting her eyes, and she was dragged back in time to their last conversation on the morning of his death. He'd kissed her lips on the porch and told her to have a good day. She'd held onto him and asked him to wait a few more minutes since she'd wanted to clear the air between them. He'd been cool and withdrawn toward her for a week, and she couldn't take it any longer. She'd needed to know what was on his mind.

Her hopes of a meaningful talk were derailed when his ride pulled into the driveway. Before trotting off to the car, he promised they'd talk later.

However, later never came.

Looking back on that time, she wondered again if Peter's cold behavior had something to do with the lies he'd told her. She dug deep into her memories, searching for other signs of his deception. When they'd first met, she'd ask him about his family, and he'd give quick, evasive answers and then change the subject. Perhaps the signs had been there all along, and she'd chosen to ignore them because she was so consumed with love.

She pushed her thoughts away, leaving them in the past where they belonged. Wiping her eyes, she set the shirt down on the end of her bed and ran her fingers over the sleeve while studying the garment. It served no purpose keeping the clothing in the armoire. She wondered if Luke would want to pick out a few pieces to keep and then she could give the rest to her nephew Samuel. He was growing up so quickly and would wear them soon enough. She would also hold a few shirts back for Seth, who would want to know about his father when he was older.

With memories raining down on her, Sarah sorted through the remaining shirts in the top of the armoire. Finally she stood before the armoire, ready to conquer the drawers of socks, underwear, and suspenders. When she leaned down to open the drawer, she spotted what looked like a long, flat wooden box stuck in the back of the emptied shelf. She fetched it and sank down onto the chair next to the bed.

The box was stained a deep cherry, and the hinges were simple but elegant—no doubt Peter's work. She flipped the tiny latch on the front and lifted the top, revealing stacks of letters, all addressed to Peter in beautiful handwriting accented with flourishes—obviously written by a woman. The return address on each letter was "D. Maloney" in Middlefield, Ohio.

Sarah bit her lip, and her stomach tightened as questions swirled through her mind. She'd never heard of a person named D. Maloney, and she had never known of Peter keeping in touch with someone in Middlefield, Ohio. Who from Ohio had been writing to Peter, and why would he keep this secret from Sarah?

Her stomach roiled, and she groaned. *Oh no! More lies!*

Sucking in a deep breath, Sarah examined the top envelope. The postmark was from ten months ago, a month before he died. Pulling out the letter, guilt nipped at her. She felt as if she were invading his privacy, but the question rang through her mind: why had he kept this from her?

Holding her breath, she read the letter.

Dear Peter,

    I hope you and Sarah are doing well. Congratulations on your news! You must be so excited to be expecting a baby. Cody is doing well and is excited to be finishing up first grade. In fact, he's counting the days until summer break. I'm enclosing a snapshot of him in his soccer uniform. Thank you for the check. It will help pay his summer camp tuition.

Take care,
DeLana

Sarah's brow furrowed while she reread the letter, wondering who Cody was. From the letter, she deduced he was English. She'd never heard of an Amish boy named Cody, and Amish children didn't go to summer camp. Why would Peter secretly send money to a strange English child?

Sarah fished the photo from the envelope and studied it. A boy with light-brown hair and bright hazel eyes, clad in a blue shirt and matching shorts, grinned while holding a soccer ball. The shape of his face, his smile, his eyes, and the color of his hair were all very familiar.

Then it hit her.

She gasped.

No, it couldn't be.

But it was.

He looked like Peter.

"No, no, no." Her voice croaked with worry and hurt. This child couldn't be Peter's son. There was no way! Peter would've told her.

Would he have?

Could her husband have been so deceitful?

Yes, he could have. He lied about his childhood.

One by one Sarah pulled out the letters and read them; each was similar to the previous. This mysterious DeLana wrote short, one-page notes, telling Peter how Cody was doing in school, including that he excelled in math but abhorred reading and that he loved to play sports, especially soccer. She would always wish Peter and Sarah well and end with thanking him for the check.

The checks.

Money Peter and Sarah had earned for their own family.

Sarah blinked back tears, and a lump swelled in her throat. How could Peter send their money to another family every month and not tell her?

How could he have a child and not tell Sarah!

The realization of the growing web of his deceit drowned her in a deluge, and she couldn't fight the hurt anymore. Hugging the letters to her chest, Sarah dissolved into tears as sobs wracked her body and soul.

As she succumbed to the emotion rioting within her, one question echoed through her mind:

Had she known her husband at all?

Luke's boots scraped the porch steps to Peter's home, a counterpoint to the conversation from the morning that replayed in his mind. He tried in vain to suppress the excitement coursing through his veins. It seemed too good to be true, but he had asked the farmer to repeat the offer to him twice, and the price for the house and twenty acres was only half of what the developer had offered Luke for his farm in Ohio seven months ago.

If the offer still stood, he could sell his farm in Ohio and move to Bird-in-Hand with money in his pocket to start a cabinet-making business in town. The farm was about a mile up the road; therefore, Luke would be close to Sarah and the twins.

Entering the living room, Luke tossed his hat onto the peg

by the door and then shucked his coat and hung it next to the hat. He ambled toward the kitchen, but stopped dead in his tracks, thinking he'd heard a voice coming from upstairs. He listened, and again he heard the sound of a moan, or perhaps a sob.

"Hello?" he called. He waited for an answer and then ascended the stairs, his boots clomping up the hardwood. The sound of the voice grew louder when he reached the hall. It was a woman crying.

"Hello? Are you all right?" Luke called. "Who's there?"

He stepped into the master bedroom and sucked in a breath at the sight of Sarah slouched in a chair and crying while holding a stack of crumpled envelopes. A pile of men's shirts littered the bed.

He shook his head. Memories of Peter must have shattered her.

"Sarah!" Crossing quickly, he crouched before her and took her hands in his. "Are you all right?"

Meeting his gaze, she threw herself into his arms, sobbing on his shoulder. He leaned forward to balance his weight on the chair while he rubbed her back. The warm, sweet scent of her hair reminded him of vanilla mixed with hyacinth, and his pulse quickened. Holding her was almost too much for him; it felt like a sin. But she needed him. How could he push her away?

"Sarah Rose," he whispered. "It's okay. The hurt will get better. I promise. I know he's gone, but your heart will heal. You have to be strong for your *zwillingbopplin*. You can show them all of the love that Peter gave you."

Her body trembled against his, and his throat tightened. Despite the exhilaration of holding her close, he concentrated on consoling her.

Suddenly, she pulled back, and fire flashed in her blue eyes. "He has a son. How could he not tell me?" Fresh tears pooled in her eyes. "Why didn't you tell me, Luke? Why did *you* lie to me?" She smacked his arm, and he jumped back with a start. "You're just as bad as he is!"

Shaking his head with shock, he stood. "Cody," he whispered.

"Yes, Cody! I was going through Peter's clothes, and I was going to offer you some of his shirts as a memory of him. I found a box hidden behind the clothes, and it contained these letters." She shook the envelopes in front of his face for emphasis.

Standing, she marched across the room, pacing. "I guess the Troyer family is full of liars! He was sending her money without telling me."

She threw the letters onto the bed. "I trusted you, Luke. I trusted you to tell me everything. I knew all along you were holding something back. But I thought you were my friend." Her voice trembled. "I really trusted you." The tears overtook her again, and she wilted against the wall, sobbing, her hand at her mouth.

"Sarah Rose." He gathered her into his arms, and she wrapped herself around him. "I'm so sorry. I thought it would hurt you if I told you, but finding out this way was much worse than I ever imagined."

"Oh, Luke," she whispered, her voice quavering along with her body. "I don't know who my husband was. I'm so confused. How could he keep this from me?"

"I think he was afraid of losing you." Stepping back, he placed his finger under her chin, lifting her eyes to meet his. He wiped a stray tear from her soft cheek and suppressed the urge to kiss the sadness away. "Why don't I make you some tea and we'll talk? I'll tell you anything you want to know."

She nodded, her expression softening. "I'd like that."

Sarah sat across from Luke at the kitchen table and cradled the warm teacup in her hand. Biting her bottom lip, she tried to mentally sort through the letters she'd read, but she couldn't grasp the idea that Peter had withheld from her the fact he had a son he was supporting in Ohio.

Her eyes fell on the small wooden box full of letters and her mouth trembled. "I just don't understand," she whispered, her voice thick with emotion. "Peter has a child?"

Luke studied the wood grain on the table. Why was he avoiding her gaze? Was he filtering what to share?

"Please, Luke. Tell me everything. I can handle it." Reaching over, she touched his hand.

"Peter met DeLana when he was seventeen," Luke began. "We both were working in our uncle's cabinet store, and her father owned the local wood supply shop. Peter made a supply run one day with the English driver, and DeLana was working in the office. From what he told me, it was love at first sight."

Sarah's stomach tightened. As ridiculous as it seemed, the idea of Peter falling in love with another woman caused her stomach to sour. How silly was it to be jealous of a person from Peter's past?

She knew the answer—the woman meant so much to Peter that he'd never told Sarah about her. The thought made Sarah's stomach churn with a mixture of jealousy, anger, and betrayal.

"They courted in secret for a long time, probably close to a year." Luke ran his fingers over the grain in the table, his mocha eyes lost in the past. "He would sneak out his window late at night and meet her in the barn behind her father's house. Sometimes he would say he was at a singing but drive out to a field near her house instead."

Sarah sipped her tea, wondering if she was going to wake up from this nightmare of deceit. Peter meeting an English girl in a field or in a barn late at night ... She gripped the mug.

"Then one day—" Luke stopped and cleared his throat. "Then one day," he began again, "his father found out and was furious." He sighed, shaking his head. "They argued, and his father forbade Peter from seeing her. Peter stormed off, saying his father had no right to run his life."

He raked his fingers through his hair, a gesture she'd seen Peter do a thousand times when he was anxious. "From what my uncle told me, DeLana's father found out and came to the shop one day, ranting about how the Amish had no right to mingle with the English girls. His father agreed, and they made a pact to keep the two of them apart. So he told Peter he would withhold all of the money Peter had made working in the shop for the past two years unless Peter joined the church and stopped seeing DeLana."

Sarah tilted her head in question. "How could he do that?"

"He had control of the money." He slouched in the chair and folded his arms. "The accounts were in his name at the local bank. So Peter's dad laid the law down, and Peter went crazy. And that's when he revealed DeLana was pregnant."

Groaning, Sarah shook her head.

"His dad muttered something about how disappointed his *mamm* would be, and Peter went to pieces. He left on foot and walked for miles."

Tears spilled from Sarah's eyes. "He must've felt so alone."

Luke laid his hands on hers. "Before he ran off, I tried to talk to him, but he locked himself in his room. He told me he tried to see DeLana, but her parents kept her prisoner in her house. They took her car and drove her to and from school. She was in her senior year of high school. They had dreams of her going to college and marrying a rich *Englisher*, so they were determined to keep her away from any Amish man. They wanted her to give the *boppli* up for adoption."

Sarah swallowed, hoping to wet her dry throat. "What happened?"

"Peter joined the church the following spring and he kept working at the shop. He and his father barely spoke. Then one day, months later, he ran into DeLana at the market. She was married to an *Englisher* and had kept the *boppli*, Peter's son. The child's name was Cody Alexander Maloney. Her husband adopted him without Peter's consent." Luke frowned. "When he looked into his child's face, he crumbled. He came home that night and had it out with his father. It nearly came to blows. That was when he left and never came back."

Sarah shook her head with disbelief. "Why didn't he tell me the truth?"

Luke squeezed her hand. "He probably didn't want to tell you because he was afraid you would think lowly of him."

Sarah stood, grabbed the two mugs, and walked to the sink. With tears streaming down her hot face, she washed the mugs and placed them on the counter. Questions surged through her. The story seemed so surreal.

How could Peter keep this secret for so long? How could he walk away from his son in Ohio and act like it never happened? It just didn't make sense.

She obviously had never known her husband at all.

Grief, anger, and betrayal drenched her soul. She felt as if he'd died all over again, the grief was so raw, so penetrating, so new.

"Sarah Rose." Luke's voice was millimeters from her ear. "Talk to me. Don't hold your feelings inside."

Sucking in a deep breath, she turned, finding his chest inches from her.

"I feel so betrayed," she whispered, her voice quavering again. Why couldn't she stop crying? She wished she could rein in her emotions. "I don't understand why he would keep something like this from me. I was his wife."

She pointed to her chest. "I shared everything with him— my heart, my soul, and my love. I lived our wedding vows, but he lied to me. He sent out our money every month to his son without telling me. How could he not tell me he had a son? I don't understand. Why, Luke?" Her voice broke on the last words, and then she was sobbing again. She closed her eyes and covered her face with her hands.

Strong arms pulled her to his hard chest, and his voice was comforting in her ear. "It's okay to cry, Sarah," he said gently. "But I'm sure he loved you. He was the luckiest man on earth to have you as his *fraa*."

"You're so different from him," she whispered with her head on his shoulder. She contemplated the story Luke told and wondered about a detail he'd missed. She stood and faced him. "What happened to Peter's parents?"

"They're gone. Both have passed away."

"When?"

"*Mamm* died when Peter was little." He blew out a sigh and raked his hand through his hair. "Pop blamed himself after Peter left. He tried to find Peter, but couldn't. The guilt was too much for him. He suffered a massive stroke and died about a year ago."

The story clicked together in Sarah's mind. "Oh, my goodness." She gasped, cupping her hand to her mouth.

"What?" Luke's eyes fill with concern. "What's wrong?"

"You nursed him." She pointed at him. "You nursed him because he was *your* father too."

Something resembling fear flashed in Luke's eyes. "Wait. I can explain—" He reached for her, and she backed up.

"Don't touch me!" She held her hands out, blocking his. "You're a liar, Luke Troyer! You're not Peter's cousin. You're his brother!"

"Sarah, give me a moment to explain. I never lied." Luke stepped toward her. "I never said I was his cousin either. Everyone assumed it."

"But you never told me the truth." She leaned back on the counter and shook her head. "It all makes sense now. How could I have been so stupid?"

He frowned. "You're not stupid."

"How could I have missed the obvious? It was right before my face just like Peter's deception." She gestured toward Luke. "You look like him. You sound like him. When I first saw you in the bakery that day, for a split second, I thought you were him."

He raised his eyebrows in surprise. "You did?"

She ticked off a list of similarities in her mind. "You hold onto your suspenders and then smooth your hair when you're trying to remember something, just like Peter. You run your hands through your hair when you're nervous, just like Peter. And you separate your food on your plate so that it doesn't touch, like Peter did."

She ignored his shocked expression and continued her rant. "And you know the intimate details of his life. A cousin wouldn't know the details of every conversation that goes on in inside a home. You said you tried to talk to Peter, and he locked himself in his bedroom. A cousin wouldn't know those things. My nieces and nephews don't live with me."

"Sarah Rose," he began, reaching for her. "I wanted to tell you, but every time I shared a story about his past, it seemed to hurt you. The last thing I wanted to do was hurt you even more than Peter did."

"So you thought lying was the answer?" She gestured widely. "Don't you realize you did exactly what Peter did to me? You omitted the truth, Luke. That's the same as lying!"

"But I wanted to tell you, Sarah Rose. I really did." His eyes pleaded with her, tugging at her heartstrings.

"You could've told me at any time," she snapped. "We spent plenty of time talking and sharing." She groaned, contemplating how much she'd shared with him. "I feel like such a fool for trusting you, Luke."

"No, no." He placed his hands on her arms. "Don't feel like a fool. You know me. You know the real me." Taking her hand, he held it to his chest. "You know my heart."

She pulled her hand back to her side. "Don't touch me! I don't know you at all. You're a liar just like your brother!"

Stomping over to the table, she grabbed the box of letters and held it up. "See these letters? That's what Peter did to me for years. He never told me he had another child, a son, in Ohio. That's the same as not telling me who you really are. You're my brother-in-law, the uncle of my *zwillingbopplin*. No wonder you gave me a surprised look in the hospital when I called you *onkel*. You were afraid you were caught."

Luke gave her a pained expression. "That's not true, Sarah Rose. I was afraid of hurting you. Timothy warned me not to tell you who I was or share more about Peter's past for fear it would break your spirit even more."

Her eyes widened. "Timothy knew too? My own brother kept the truth from me?"

"He didn't know about DeLana, but he knew about me."

Sarah sniffed, fighting tears at the realization she'd been betrayed by Peter, Luke, and Timothy. "You and Timothy have managed to break my heart once again."

She started for the door. Then she stopped short of it and faced him. "Tell me one thing, Luke, and I want to know the truth."

He nodded. "Anything. I'll tell you anything you want to know, and I promise to tell the whole truth this time, not leaving one detail out."

"How many siblings did Peter have?" She ignored the quaver in her voice and held her head high, giving the pretense that nothing more would hurt her.

"Only one—me." He pointed to his chest.

"*Danki*." She turned her back to him and started for the door.

"Sarah Rose, please wait."

Ignoring his pleas, she slipped on her cloak and stalked out the front door, nearly walking into *Mamm*, who was coming toward the door.

Coconut Chews

½ cup butter

2 cups brown sugar

Melt butter in saucepan, then stir in sugar until dissolved. Cool.

Slightly beat in:

2 eggs

1 tsp. vanilla

1 cup flour

1-1/2 tsp. baking powder

½ tsp. salt

1-1/2 cups coconut

Pour batter into a greased 9x13 pan lined with wax paper. Cut in squares. Bake for 35 minutes at 350 degrees.

16

Sarah Rose?" *Mamm's* eyes filled with worry. "I was concerned when I got home from the market and the girls told me you'd been here for a couple of hours. Are you all right?"

"No, I'm not. Follow me home." Sarah marched down the stairs.

"Sarah Rose!" Luke rushed out onto the porch. "Wait!"

Ignoring him and the pain surging through her soul, Sarah continued on, her head held high. The betrayal would not steal her confidence. She had to think of the twins and be strong for them.

"What's going on?" *Mamm* asked.

"He's a liar, just like his brother," Sarah snapped through gritted teeth.

"What?" *Mamm* yanked Sarah to a stop. "Like his brother?"

"*Ya*, like his brother—Peter." She sucked in a breath, willing her body to stop quaking.

"His brother?" *Mamm* gasped, her hand at her mouth. "Oh, my word. I had no idea. Why didn't he tell us?"

"Because he didn't want to hurt me. Instead he lied and hurt me even more."

Sarah hugged the wooden box to her chest. Her husband had been supporting a child she never knew existed, and now the man she'd considered a dear friend wasn't who she thought he was. He'd turned out to be deceitful, just like her husband.

Her heart ached with renewed grief.

Whom could she trust?

Her eyes filled with fresh tears.

"What's that?" *Mamm* pointed to the box.

"I found it in Peter's armoire," Sarah said, her voice hoarse. "It has letters from his English girlfriend."

"An English girlfriend?" *Mamm's* eyes widened with shock.

Sarah wiped her eyes, trying in vain to stop the tears. "He was with her before he abandoned his father and Luke and came here to start a new life."

Mamm's voice clouded. "What do the letters say?"

"He was sending her money."

"Why would he do that?"

Opening the box, Sarah fished out a photo of the boy and handed it to her. "This is why," she whispered.

Mamm studied the photo, then glanced at Sarah. Brows furrowed in confusion, she shook her head. "Sarah Rose, I don't understand."

"That's his son," she said, her voice trembling as much as her body.

Mamm's eyes rounded as she inhaled.

Sarah sobbed, and *Mamm* pulled her into her arms. "There, there, Sarah Rose." She patted her back. "We'll get through this. *Kumm*. Let's go home."

Sarah fingered the crumbs left from her homemade bread while sitting across from *Mamm* at the kitchen table. She'd just finished telling her *mamm* the details of the letters and the story Luke had relayed regarding Peter's past.

Mamm had listened with wide eyes. Taking a bite of bread,

she shook her head with disbelief. "I don't know what to say. I never imagined Peter had such a troubled past."

"I don't understand why he didn't tell me," Sarah said, pushing back a strand of hair that had escaped from her *Kapp*. "It was bad enough he lied about his family, but now I found out he lied about a child he was supporting. I don't know who my husband really was, *Mamm*. I never imagined he was a liar."

Mamm took Sarah's hand in hers. "I know this is difficult, but you must forgive him. I'm sure he had his reasons. Maybe he worried that you wouldn't love him if you knew he'd made mistakes in the past."

"That's what Luke said." Wiping more tears with her free hand, Sarah shook her head. "But I would've loved him anyway, *Mamm*. It doesn't make sense. There should be no secrets between a husband and wife. I was never dishonest with him."

"Never?" *Mamm* raised her eyebrows in disbelief. "Not even when you bought extra material for a new dress without checking with Peter first? Or when you bought a little gift for one of your nieces without telling Peter? Or how about when you bought a few extra books to read without checking your weekly budget?"

"That's different." Sarah yanked her hands back and folded them on the table. "Buying a few extra things at the market is not the same as hiding information about your past—especially information about a child you're supporting."

She pictured Luke, and her anger simmered. "I'm so upset with Luke for not revealing his identity. He said every time he shared more of Peter's past, I seemed more and more hurt and upset. But not telling the whole truth is lying too." Her eyes narrowed. "And to make it even more hurtful, he said Timothy has known all along that Peter had family in Ohio. My own brother kept the truth from me. Why did they all lie? I could've handled the truth, *Mamm*. I'm a strong woman."

"You just gave the answer, Sarah Rose." *Mamm* patted her

hand. "They didn't want to hurt you. Luke and Timothy could see how much you were hurting after Peter died and then you found out that he wasn't an orphan as he'd said."

"It's wrong to be deceitful. It's a sin." She swabbed a napkin across her cheeks and then her nose.

"Sarah Rose, you must remember the words of the Bible. In Luke 6:37 we read, 'Do not judge, and you will not be judged. Do not condemn, and you will not be condemned. Forgive, and you will be forgiven.'" *Mamm* covered Sarah's hands again with her own. "Peter was wrong; he never should've kept those secrets from you. But he was human just like you and me. You must forgive him. He's not here to defend himself. We can only assume he did it to protect you."

"Protect me from what?" Sarah snapped.

"He loved you and didn't want to hurt you."

"How can you be so sure he loved me?" Sarah tried to clear the knot in her throat. "Love means you're open and honest. Love means you trust your spouse completely."

Mamm sighed. "You're hurt, but you can't deny he loved you. I saw it in his eyes every time he looked at you and every time he held your hand or hugged you. He wore a smile on his face for weeks after the day you were married. He walked around with a glow on his face when he found out you were expecting a *boppli*."

Sarah blew out a quivering breath as she thought back to those days. Then it clicked, like the latch on the back gate. Everything suddenly made sense. "That could be why he stopped talking to me. Maybe he felt guilty for not telling me he had a son in Ohio when he found out we were having a child of our own."

Mamm gave a sad smile and a slow nod. "That could very well be it, Sarah Rose. And you must forgive him. And you also must forgive your brother and Luke. They care about you too."

Sarah nodded, even though it was easier said than done. But

forgiveness was the Amish way, and she knew she had to let go. Somehow.

"I'll forgive them, but I won't trust them again, especially Luke. He took advantage of me. I thought we were friends." She shook her head. "He'll be a part of the *bopplin's* lives because they're family, but that's it."

"Don't be so hard on him, Sarah Rose. Now that you know he's Peter's brother, you must remember he's grieving too."

"That's all the more reason why he should've told me the truth. I thought we were close. I shared so much with him, and now I feel betrayed and used."

Mamm squeezed her hand. "He cares for you. I can see it in his eyes. I'm sure he felt he was justified in not telling you the whole truth."

Sarah glanced down at the remaining crumbs on her plate. "And I'm going to have a word with Timothy."

"Go easy on your brother. He's been hurt too."

The sound of infant cries rang from the living room, and Sarah jumped up. After warming two bottles, she and *Mamm* headed for the cradles.

She lifted Seth and snuggled him close while feeding him. *Mamm* sat next to her and hummed a lullaby as she fed Rachel.

Sarah traced a finger along Seth's soft chin and contemplated the news of Peter's older son. The photograph of Cody was burned into her memory, and she could see a resemblance between Seth and Cody—they both looked like Peter and Luke.

She wondered how DeLana had felt raising Cody without his biological father and how Cody would feel if he knew Peter had been his father. The three children—Cody, Seth, and Rachel—would never know what their father looked like or hear the sound of his voice or see the color of his eyes.

Sarah sighed. The children would want to know each other. She would have to contact DeLana and see if she would feel comfortable getting the children together.

Her thoughts moved to Luke, and she frowned. She would allow him to be a part of the twins' lives, but that was as far as her relationship with him would go. She could no longer trust him with her heart. She'd believed their friendship was special, and she'd even felt a teensy hint of affection for him, but those feelings had dissipated today. The children had a right to know their uncle, but Sarah would no longer allow him into her heart.

And her last issue was with her brother Timothy. She would address his lies the next time she saw him.

Pushing her hostility away, Sarah concentrated on the beautiful baby boy in her arms. Closing her eyes, she thanked God for her healthy twins. Even though her heart was broken by the deception she'd received from those she cared about, her heart swelled with love for her children, a true miracle and gift from the Lord.

Luke trudged up the gravel driveway to Eli's house, hoping to see Sarah sitting on the porch. The memory of the anger in her eyes had haunted him all day. Her sadness and her devastation at finding out about Cody and then finding out about his own identity had broken his heart. He wished he could take away the pain he and his brother had caused. He worried he had lost her friendship forever. He couldn't stand the thought of not being her friend, and he longed to make things right between them.

His hope deflated when he found Eli and Elizabeth sitting on the porch without their youngest child.

"*Wie geht's,*" Eli called with a bright smile.

"*Gut,*" Luke said, climbing the stairs. "How are you both tonight?"

"*Gut,*" Eli responded, looping his arm across the back of the swing and behind his wife. "Right, *mei fraa?*"

Elizabeth gave a sad smile. "*Ya,*" she said.

"I wanted to check on Sarah," Luke said, leaning against the porch railing. "She was a mite bit upset earlier."

"*Ya*, she was," Elizabeth said. "She's fine now. She's resting since the *zwillingbopplin* are sleeping. She has to get her sleep whenever she can."

Luke nodded, wondering if Elizabeth was telling the truth. Was Sarah truly resting well or was she still distraught, crying alone in her room or sitting alone, contemplating how much he, Peter, and Timothy had hurt her. "I'm sorry that my brother hurt her so much. And I'm sorry I wasn't upfront with all of you about being Peter's brother. I should've told you the first time I met you. I only did it because I was afraid of hurting her more. I wish I could make it better. I was wrong, and I regret it with my whole heart."

"She'll be just fine." Elizabeth's expression softened. "She's stubborn like the rest of the Kauffmans." She elbowed her husband, who shrugged. "She'll be angry for a few days, but I'm sure she'll get through it. We just need to give her time."

Eli glanced at his wife, his eyebrows careening with feigned anger toward his hairline. They exchanged a private conversation without words, and she smiled.

Luke longed to have a loving relationship like theirs. He'd thought he and Sarah had that kind of friendship, where they could poke fun of each other and almost read each other's minds; however, he'd ruined it by not telling her the truth from the beginning. Now it was all lost, and he was alone—again.

Elizabeth eyed Luke. "Have you eaten? We have leftover meatloaf and chocolate cake."

Luke considered the offer for a moment and then shook his head. It was obvious he'd worn out his welcome with Sarah Rose. In order to regain her trust, Luke knew he should keep his distance and give her time to heal, as much as it would hurt his heart to stay away from her and the twins.

"*Danki*, but I ate a little bit earlier." He stood up straight.

"I just wanted to make sure she was okay. Please give her my regards."

"Will do, son." Eli smiled. "You have a *gut* night."

"You too." After a quick nod, Luke descended the stairs and walked slowly back toward the house.

Climbing into bed that night, he prayed for Sarah, asking God to comfort and bless her and her twins and to find room for Luke in their lives. He prayed giving Sarah space would help him win a place in her family.

Sarah hugged Rachel closer to her body and swung gently back and forth on the porch the following afternoon, enjoying an unusual break in the normally bitter-cold February weather. *Mamm* sat beside her with Seth while Rebecca held Junior on the chair beside the swing.

Gazing out over the yard, Sarah spotted her nieces and nephews racing to and fro, screeching and laughing during a competitive game of tag. Her sisters sat nearby chatting while her brothers leaned on the fence by the pasture. The sights and sounds were all fitting for an off Sunday without church service, and normally it would be a comfort.

However, today it was anything but comfortable. Instead, Sarah glanced around the scenery and gave a shuddering sigh.

After crying most of the night, her tears had dried up. Numbness had settled in her soul around four this morning. Betrayal and disappointment filled the hole in her heart that had been left after Peter died. She felt like an empty shell of the woman she once was.

Her gaze trained on Timothy, and her stomach soured. She planned to give him a piece of her mind the first chance she had to speak to him in private.

Junior fussed, and Rebecca stood. "I'm going to go in and feed him."

Sarah and *Mamm* nodded as Rebecca disappeared through the door with her infant.

"How are you?" *Mamm* asked.

"*Gut,*" Sarah said, but her voice was flat and devoid of the emotion she'd hoped to convey.

Mamm patted her arm. "It will get better. Have faith, Sarah Rose."

Sarah let the words soak into her as she stared across the pasture toward the house where Luke was staying. Bitterness and disappointment rolled through her.

The clip-clop of a horse and the crunch of wheels on gravel yanked Sarah back to the present. She glanced toward the barn as Norman and his family emerged from their buggy. Timothy greeted Norman. The children joined her nieces and nephews in their game of tag, the eldest girls caring for the younger children.

Sarah plastered a smile on her face as Norman and Timothy sauntered toward the house, talking. Norman met her stare and gave her a sincere smile. She was thankful for his friendship.

Something she'd thought she shared with Luke.

The men climbed the stairs, and Norman greeted her mother and sisters before turning to Sarah. "*Wie geht's,*" he said, his eyes warm.

"*Gut,*" she said.

"How are the *zwillingbopplin?*"

"They're sleeping better at night. I'm getting almost four solid hours of sleep." Sarah angled a sleeping Rachel toward him.

"*Ack,* she looks just like you." Norman's face beamed. "She's beautiful."

Sarah felt her face heat at the compliment.

Mamm stood with Seth asleep in her arms. "Would you like me to take the *zwillingbopplin* in so you can talk?"

"You can't handle them both." Sarah stood. "I can take Rachel in."

"Don't be silly." Her *mamm* turned toward the older girls sitting on the other side of the porch. "Katie, would you please help me put the *zwillingbopplin* to bed?"

Katie hurried over and took Rachel from Sarah's arms.

"*Danki,*" Sarah said as *Mamm* and Katie disappeared through the door with the sleeping children.

"Would you like to go for a walk?" Norman offered.

"That sounds nice."

Sarah followed him down the steps, and they walked side by side on the path toward her former home. Her heart fluttered at the idea of seeing Luke, considering how hurt she was by his actions.

"What's on your mind?" Norman asked. "You seem preoccupied."

She silently marveled how well Norman could read her emotions. He seemed to have a gift. "I found out some more disturbing things about Peter's past yesterday."

"Would you like to talk about it?"

Sarah frowned. "I feel bad for dragging you into my problems."

Norman stopped and stared into her eyes. His expression was serious. "Sarah Rose, I want to help you. You forget I also suffered a loss, and I know how difficult it can be to wade through the grief, bitterness, and anger after someone you love leaves you. I want to help you through this."

"*Danki,*" she whispered. "I appreciate your friendship more than you know."

Something flickered in his eyes, but she wasn't sure what it meant.

"While I was going through some of Peter's things yesterday, I found some letters written to Peter from a woman in Ohio." Sarah paused, choosing her words. "I discovered he was sending the woman money to support his son—a son they'd had together."

Norman's mouth gaped.

"The woman is English, and they had an affair when Peter was seventeen. His father broke them up, and the girl married someone else. Peter left his family after he found out she'd married someone else. While he and I were together, he was writing her and sending her money every month to help care for the boy." Sarah shook her head. "There was a photograph of the boy. He's handsome and looks just like Peter and Luke."

"He looks like Luke?" Norman's eyebrows knitted in confusion. "Why do you say that?"

"Because it's true. That's the other detail I uncovered. Luke is Peter's brother, not his cousin." She glared toward Timothy across the pasture. "I found out Peter, Luke, and Timothy have all lied to me."

"What do you mean?" Norman asked.

She met his confused expression. "You already know about Peter's deception about his past. Luke also omitted the truth that he's Peter's brother, and Timothy has known about Peter's past for some time. I'm going to have a few words with my brother when I can get him alone."

"Timothy never said anything to me about it, but I know he and Peter were close when Peter was alive."

Sarah wrung her hands together. "I've been trying to sort through it all and figure out how to get past the hurt."

Norman took her hands in his. "Give your burdens up to the Lord, and He will see you through. Have faith that He is leading you down the path toward happiness."

She gazed into his brown eyes, astounded by his strong faith. "You are so calm and faithful."

He smiled. "It took me a long time to get here after losing Leah, but I'd like to help you find your strength." His expression became serious. "I would like to spend more time with you, Sarah, and help you through this."

"I appreciate you so much, Norman. *Danki*." She led him

back toward the path to her parents' house. "Let's go see if there's any chocolate cake left."

Later that evening, Sarah tiptoed down the stairs after rocking the twins to sleep. Heading toward the kitchen, she heard soft masculine voices. She stepped into the doorway and found her *dat* and Timothy sitting at the table. Her expression hardened as Timothy saw her.

"Sarah Rose," *Dat* said. "I thought you were asleep."

"I was just coming down to get a drink before heading to bed." She crossed the kitchen and poured a glass of water. Standing at the counter, she sipped it while her *dat* and brother discussed the weather. Anger swirled in her while she studied her brother. Sensing her observation, he raised a brow in question, and she scowled in response.

"I reckon I better head to bed," Timothy said, standing and stretching. "Work comes early in the morning."

"*Ya*, it does." *Dat* also rose. "It was *gut* talking to you, son."

"You, too, *Dat*." Timothy headed for the door. "*Gut nacht*."

Dat said good night and disappeared through the doorway toward the stairs.

"What was that look for, Sarah Rose?" Timothy said, crossing his arms and leaning on the door.

"I found out some interesting information yesterday." Placing her glass on the counter, she stood before him, hoping her eyes resembled the daggers she felt in her heart.

"Oh?" His expression was one of teasing, despite her harsh words. "Please, enlighten me."

She ignored his attempt at a joke and got to the point. "First of all, I found out Peter was sending money to an English girl in Ohio."

Timothy's eyebrows careened toward his hairline. "What are you talking about?" he questioned, shocked.

"*Ya.*" She gave him a smug smile. "Your best friend was sending money to support his son in Ohio. His *Englisher* son."

Timothy gasped. "Peter had an English son? Are you certain?"

"Absolutely. I found the evidence: a box full of letters from DeLana Maloney." She studied his dumfounded appearance. "I can show it to you if you'd like."

"I believe you, but I had no idea."

"I also found out Luke is his brother, and you knew *that* all along, Timothy." Her voice was thick. "That brings the total number of men whom I trusted and who have lied to me to three." She counted them off on her fingers. "Peter, Luke, and you, my brother."

"Whoa, now, Sarah Rose." He held his hands up in protest. "I didn't know about DeLana and this boy you're talking about."

"But you knew Peter had family in Ohio, and you knew Luke was his brother." Her voice shook. "How could you do that to me, Timothy? You're my brother. I trusted you! You've been hurt before, and you know what it's like to lose someone you love."

His expression softened. "I only meant to protect you."

"Your big plan to protect me wound up hurting me even more!" Disgusted, Sarah started toward the stairs.

"Wait!" Timothy caught her arm and pulled her back. "Hear me out."

She yanked her arm out of his grasp and glared at him.

"Peter was my best friend, and I miss him every day." Timothy pursed his lips. "You have to know he loved you, and he hated lying to you. He told me the truth about a year before he died. I saw him coming out of the post office one day, and I think he felt he had to explain why he was there. I didn't know about the letters to the girl in Ohio, but I knew he had family back there. He told me he had an older brother he looked up to because he was so loyal to their family and faithful to God.

He said Luke was everything he wanted to be but knew he couldn't."

Sarah sniffed. "Why didn't he tell me, Timothy?"

"He wanted to, Sarah. He wanted to tell you the truth. He said he knew he had to be honest with you since you were expecting a child. He was planning to find the right words, but he ran out of time. He wanted to make things up to his family too — his *dat* and his brother."

She wiped her tearing eyes and shook her head. "I would've forgiven him. I loved him."

Timothy touched her arm. "He loved you too."

She wished she could speak to Peter herself and hear those words from him one more time.

"Can you forgive me?" Timothy's eyes were hopeful.

She frowned. "I don't have a choice. You're my brother."

He shrugged. "I'll take that as a yes."

She nodded toward the door. "Go home. The *zwillingbopplin* will have me up soon enough for a feeding."

"How are things with Norman?"

She faced him. "What?"

"You and Norman, you're close, *ya*?"

"*Ya*," she said with a nod. "We're *gut* friends. What's wrong with that?"

He waved off the question and started toward the door. "See you tomorrow."

"No." She rushed after him. "What are you implying, Timothy?"

"I'm not implying anything at all. Talk to you later." He patted her head. "Stop worrying so much."

She rolled her eyes. "I'm so tired of being treated like a child." She headed for the stairs. "Good night, Timothy."

Climbing the stairs, Sarah let Timothy's words sink in. Peter had truly loved her, and he'd wanted to tell her the truth. He'd planned to tell her the truth before he'd died. The words warmed her and settled her heart. And, yet, she still felt betrayed by Timothy and Luke. They'd known the truth and kept it from her.

She yawned as she entered her room. It was too late to figure out her feelings. However, she knew one thing for certain: her brother's question about Norman had her stumped. Why would he ask about their friendship? Why did he care?

17

Luke dried his hands and stepped from the restroom into the shop hallway. Deep in thought regarding Sarah and her well-being, he jumped when a strong hand on his shoulder stopped him mid stride. Turning, he found Eli frowning at him.

"Eli," he said. "You startled me."

"Sorry. Can we talk?" The older man nodded toward the door leading to the parking lot.

"Of course." Luke followed him outside, his stomach in knots of anticipation.

They walked to the far end of the lot, where Eli leaned against the fence and sighed.

"Is everything all right?" Luke asked. "Are you feeling okay?"

"I wanted to ask you why you haven't been by the house since Saturday," Eli said. "You left abruptly, and we haven't seen you since. Did something offend you?"

Luke stuffed his hands in his pockets and kicked a stone while contemplating how to respond. He couldn't tell Eli that he had strong feelings of affection for Sarah and was giving her space in hopes of her forgiving him.

"Luke?" Eli asked. "What is it?"

Glancing up, Luke gave a tentative smile. "I was afraid I'd worn out my welcome after Sarah found out about my brother's past and found out I'm her brother-in-law. I thought I should give her a few days to come to terms with the news and figure out how she felt about the rest of the Troyer family."

Technically, he wasn't lying. He was worried about how she felt about the rest of the Troyers—especially him, since he hadn't been upfront with her about Cody from the beginning.

Eli nodded and looked at something past Luke's shoulder. "Don't stay away too long. Elizabeth was right when she said Sarah was stubborn, but she'll get over her hurt. I know you've been a good friend to her, and I'm sure she misses you."

Luke nodded. He missed her too ... a lot.

"I was surprised you didn't have lunch with Naomi today," Eli said.

"What?" Luke asked, surprised by Eli's quick change of the subject. "Naomi?"

"*Ya*, Naomi." Eli grinned. "You know, the *maedel* who brings you lunch a few times a week." His smile clouded. "Did you two have a disagreement?"

Luke shook his head. "No. I think everyone got the wrong idea about us. We're just friends."

Eli gave him a look of disbelief. "Does Naomi know that?"

"I told her that back in December before Christmas."

"Oh. How'd she take it?"

Luke kicked another stone, trying to suppress the guilt. "She wasn't happy. She had her heart set on courting me. But we decided to stay friends, and she insists on bringing me lunch. I guess she has other plans today."

"It's *gut* that you're friends. Maybe your friendship will develop into something more as you get to know each other. She's a sweet *maedel*." The older man smacked Luke's shoulder. "I just wanted to tell you not to be a stranger. Come by the house and see us." He started for the door. "I reckon I better get back to work. I have quite a few impatient customers."

"I'll be there in a minute." Luke leaned on the fence, staring out over the field behind the shop while he pondered Eli's words. Maybe Sarah only needed a few days to mull things over, and he'd have a chance to win back her friendship . . . hoping it would turn into more.

Luke made up his mind that he would visit the Kauffman house tonight. He missed the twins. He'd made a promise to be a good uncle to the twins in honor of his brother's memory, and he intended to keep that promise. And of course he also missed Sarah. He needed to show Sarah he cared for her and had only lied about his identity to save her more heartache.

Luke climbed the steps of Eli's porch later that evening. The warm glow of a kerosene lamp illuminated the kitchen. After taking a deep breath, he rapped on the back door. Elizabeth peered through the glass and frowned at him before opening the door.

"*Ya?*" she asked. "Oh, hello, Luke. How are you? We haven't seen you in a few days."

"Hello, Elizabeth," he said. "I hope you're doing well this evening. May I speak with Sarah?"

"I think she's putting the *zwillingbopplin* to bed."

"Oh." He frowned. "I'm sorry I missed seeing them."

"I'll check for you. Just a moment."

"*Danki.*" While she disappeared into the house, he paced, his heart pounding and his mind searching for the right words to express how he felt about Sarah's friendship and how special the children were to him. He prayed for the right words. He didn't want to cause her more pain; as Eli said, she'd been through so much already. His soul would shatter if he continued to be another source of sorrow for her.

The door squeaked open, revealing Sarah clad in a black cloak with a white gown peeking out at the bottom.

"What do you need, Luke?" she asked, her voice flat and her expression tired, as if the life had been sucked from her.

His heart broke as he remembered the life dancing in her blue eyes the night they had spent visiting with the children and her parents.

"Have a seat." He gestured toward the swing.

"I'll stand, *danki*." She hugged her arms to her chest. "Why are you here?"

While her tone cut him to the bone, he kept his expression even, hoping to shield the hurt she caused him. "I'm here to apologize again." He leaned back against the railing. "I'm sorry for not being forthright about my identity. You and the *zwillingbopplin* mean more to me than you know. I want to be a part of their lives since they're my only link to my brother. I'm very sorry, and I hope you can let me back into your life, Sarah Rose. I care for you."

Sarah paused, her eyes flashing with emotion before returning to their flat blue. She angled her chin in defiance of his comment. "You'll always be a part of my *kinner's* family. You're welcome to visit them any time. However, our friendship will never be the same. I've lost all trust in you."

He flinched. Where was the sweet, suffering Sarah who had sobbed in his arms on Saturday? How had she transformed into this cement statue, devoid of warmth?

"Is that why you came here?" She gestured as if to dismiss him. "To try to prove to me that you're a trustworthy man after you deliberately posed as my husband's cousin instead of his brother?"

Frustrated, he shook his head. *Why are we beating this subject to death?*

"Sarah Rose, I never posed as a cousin. I just didn't tell you I was his brother. There's a difference between pretending to be something you're not and omitting information."

She blinked and then frowned. "Your standards of truthfulness astound me. I guess lying runs in the Troyer family. I can only hope my *kinner* take after the Kauffmans."

"And lie like Timothy?" He couldn't stop his smug expression.

Her mouth gaped with shock.

Elizabeth appeared in the doorway. "Sarah Rose," she said. "Seth is screaming again."

"*Ack*." Groaning, she shook her head. "I'll be right in." She glanced back at him and nodded curtly. "I have to go. I think Seth is getting his first ear infection. We've had a long day."

"Oh, no." Panic gripped him. "Is he going to be okay?"

"*Ya*." She waved off his worry. "*Bopplin* go through this. He'll be just fine. It's more exhausting than anything else." She started for the door.

"Can I come see them?"

Hesitating, she nodded. "You can visit them anytime. I'll give you some time alone with them when you're here. That way you can really bond." She squeaked open the door.

He couldn't let her go. Not like this. "Sarah."

She faced him, her eyes exhausted, no doubt due to the sick baby. However, her beauty glowed in the low light of the lanterns.

He knew at that moment he loved her, truly loved her, but he couldn't form the words to tell her so.

"I care about you," he whispered, stepping toward her and hoping she understood. "I mean that."

She blanched. "I don't understand."

Their eyes locked, and his heart skipped.

"I'm not sure how you can't understand. I care about you, Sarah Rose."

"And how would Naomi King feel if she heard you tell me that?" she whispered, her voice quavering. "I've heard that you and Naomi have lunch together frequently."

"What does Naomi King have to do with my feelings for you?" he asked.

"I have to go," she whispered. "*Gut nacht*."

Before he could respond, she slipped through the door, which slammed behind her.

Strolling back to the house, Luke felt his heart splintering into a million pieces, like a thin piece of wood shattered with a hammer. He wanted to tell Sarah he loved her and wished he could care for her and the twins; however, her cold stare had prevented the words from forming on his lips. His feelings for Sarah had taken him by surprise. He'd never felt love like this before. It was overwhelming and all-consuming. He was truly in love for the first time in his life.

Stepping into the house, he wondered if he should remain in Bird-in-Hand. While he had found a farm to purchase and had a possible buyer for his home in Ohio, he couldn't bear the thought of Sarah avoiding him when he visited the twins.

Luke shook his head as he climbed the stairs to the bedroom. While dressing for bed, he contemplated why Sarah had mentioned Naomi King. Were rumors floating around the community about his relationship with her?

Climbing into bed, he turned his cares over to the Lord. He prayed God would lead Sarah toward a life of love and laughter, not one of misery and regrets. He also prayed he would find his own way in the world and figure out where he truly belonged— in Ohio or in Pennsylvania.

Sarah snuggled down under the quilt and closed her eyes. She felt as if the world were crashing in around her. In just a matter of days, she'd discovered her late husband was supporting a child she never knew existed in another state. Then she'd found out her own brother had lied to her about her husband's past to "protect" her. To make matters worse, Luke had stopped by this evening to try to apologize for his deceit and then told her he cared for her.

She frowned. *How dare he!*

Sarah pulled herself up to a sitting position, then swung her legs over the edge of the bed. She crossed the room and snatched Peter's wooden box from her bureau. Sinking into a chair, she opened the box and stared at the letters in the low light of the kerosene lamp.

She fished a stack of photos of Cody from the box and stared at the child's face. He was the spitting image of Peter with his bright hazel eyes and light-brown hair. Even his dimpled smile reflected his late father. She also saw Luke's features in the boy's delicate face. He was a Troyer, through and through. Seth would probably resemble him as well.

Sarah closed her eyes and tried to conjure Peter's face in her mind's eye. She searched her memory, concentrating on the week before she lost him. She tried to remember the details of his face, his eyes, his nose, his lips.

But only one face kept coming to mind ... *Luke.*

Huffing out her frustration, she stood, dropped the box onto the chair, and padded to the window. She lifted the dark-green shade and stared across the jet-black pasture toward her former home. A soft light glowed from the living room, leading her to wonder what Luke was doing up so late.

Tears filled her eyes as she remembered their conversation earlier. He'd had a lot of gall coming over and trying to apologize after what he'd done.

She sat on the edge of the bed as his voice echoed in her mind. She could still see the genuine warmth in his eyes when he'd said he cared about her. Why had he said that? He didn't mean it. He was seeing Naomi King. It was the talk of the community. She'd heard from more than one person at church service that Naomi brought him lunch a few times each week. He'd probably marry Naomi, and they would live together happily, having babies of their own.

Sarah believed Luke cared for the twins because they were his only living link to Peter. He didn't truly care for Sarah as more than a friend or a family member. And she didn't care for him either.

At that, she gave a sarcastic laugh. Her inner voice challenged her: *If you don't care for him, then why are you crying? And why does Luke's voice and face fill your dreams at night?*

Why did all of her thoughts of Peter end with visions of Luke? Why had her hands trembled and her heart skipped a beat when Luke pulled her into his arms and consoled her?

She grimaced with disgust. She needed to put Luke Troyer out of her mind and concentrate on her future with her twins. They were all that mattered.

Standing, she crossed the room and lifted the box from the chair, then slipped the photographs back inside. As she placed it on the bureau, she heard something metal clink against the side of the box. She opened it again and removed the letters and photographs, stacking them on the bureau until the box was empty. A small brass key lay on the bottom.

Picking up the key, she examined it. It was inscribed with "U.S.P.S. Do Not Duplicate" followed by a series of numbers.

"Post office box," she whispered, closing her fingers around the cool key. Her stomach tightened. "Another secret."

After dropping the letters and photographs back into the box, Sarah lay the key down on the bureau, snuffed out the lamp, and climbed back into bed. She closed her eyes and silently recited her evening prayers.

God, please lead me down the right path for my and my zwillingbopplin's future.

18

Thank you for coming with me," Sarah said, stepping into the post office with Kathryn the following afternoon. "I convinced Nancy and Katie I needed to run to the market, but *Mamm* knew the truth when she left for the bakery this morning."

"Did you really think I would let you come here alone?" Kathryn looped her arm around Sarah.

"I'm just glad *Mamm* let me come without her. She's been so worried about me. I know she thinks I should just let Peter's memory go and concentrate on the future. But how can I when I have so many unresolved questions?" Her chin wobbled.

Kathryn gave her a sad smile and touched her shoulder. "Sarah, it's okay to cry. And it's okay to ask questions. You need to understand the past before you can concentrate on Rachel and Seth's future."

"*Danki.*" Sarah hugged her sister. "You're the only one who understands."

They took their place in line, and Sarah studied the key, wondering what secrets that little brass clue held about her late husband's past. When they reached the counter, Sarah pulled the key and a stack of letters from the concealed pocket in the back of her apron.

"May I help you?" a young man in a postal uniform asked.

"Yes," Sarah said. She placed the key and letters on the counter, trembling with anxiety about the secrets the key would reveal to her. "My husband passed away in the fire at the Kauffman & Yoder furniture store almost ten months ago."

He frowned. "I'm sorry to hear that, ma'am. I'm very sorry for your loss."

"Thank you." She cleared her throat, and Kathryn placed a hand on her shoulder, silently encouraging her to continue. "I found a box with this key and these letters. I would like to clear out his box and close it."

"Is your name on the box, ma'am?" he asked.

Sarah shook her head. "I had no knowledge of the box until I found the letters and key."

The man grimaced, tapping the counter. "What's your name, ma'am?" he asked.

"Sarah Troyer." She twirled her finger around the tie to her cloak. "My husband was Peter Troyer."

The man took the key, studied it, and then examined the letter. "Excuse me for a moment while I get my supervisor. I'll need permission since your name isn't on the box." Taking the keys and letters, he disappeared into an area behind the counter.

"Don't worry," Kathryn whispered. "They'll understand. This can't be the first time a spouse has found a post office box."

Glancing to her left, Sarah spotted a young English woman mailing a package while a toddler boy sat in a stroller and whined. Sarah smiled.

She was still thinking of her twins when the young man returned to the counter, accompanied by a middle-aged man holding the key and letters.

"Mrs. Troyer," the older man said. "I'm so sorry for your loss. I was so saddened to hear about the fire. I bought a hope chest for my daughter at Kauffman & Yoder, and I've known Eli Kauffman for years." He handed her the letters.

"Thank you." Sarah nodded and slipped the letters into the pocket of her apron. "Eli is my father. This is my sister, Kathryn Beiler."

The man smiled at Kathryn. "It's a pleasure to meet you." He glanced back at Sarah. "I understand Mr. Troyer didn't have your name on the box. It's not our policy to allow other folks access to the box. However, under these circumstances, I can make an exception. Mr. Troyer had paid for the box a year in advance. I'll get a form for you, and you can close the box and receive any remaining mail."

"Thank you," Sarah said.

With the key in his hand, he disappeared behind the counter.

Kathryn rested a hand on Sarah's shoulder while they waited for the man to return. Sarah's mind swirled with questions. Would the box reveal only letters from DeLana Maloney or would there be more secrets? Could Sarah stomach the lies the letters would share with her? Her heart ached with worry. She prayed the letters would only confirm what she already knew — that Peter had a son named Cody Alexander Maloney whom he was supporting. Sarah didn't want to know any more than that.

A few minutes later, the postal worker returned with a stack of three letters and a form. Sarah filled out the form, closing the box and forwarding any remaining mail to her parents' home. Thanking the man, she and Kathryn headed out to the parking lot where Nina Janitz waited to drive them back to the bakery.

After they climbed into the car, Sarah examined the three unopened letters. Each one included DeLana's return address. Her hands trembling, she slipped them into her apron, deciding to open them later when she was alone.

Leaning over, she touched Kathryn's arm. "*Danki.*"

"*Gern gschehne,* sweet Sarah Rose." Kathryn patted her hand. "Give yourself time to heal and figure things out. Don't feel rushed to accept Peter's past. Remember the verse from the service last week? It was 2 Corinthians 1:3: 'Praise be to the God

and Father of our Lord Jesus Christ, the Father of compassion
and the God of all comfort.'"

"*Ya.*" Leaning back in the seat, Sarah closed her eyes and
thanked God for the support from her wonderful family members, especially Kathryn.

Luke wiped his brow and retrieved his can of Coke from the
workbench. He glanced down at the entertainment center he
was sanding and heaved a sigh that seemed to carry the weight
of the world.

The entertainment center wasn't his best work, and he owed
it all to one distraction—Sarah. Their disagreement and the
sadness in her eyes had haunted him since they spoke last night.
He couldn't sleep. He couldn't eat. He couldn't concentrate. It
was shattering his soul.

Glancing across the shop, he spotted Eli weaving through
the projects and carpenters toward Luke's workbench. Taking
a long gulp of Coke, he imagined what Eli would say about the
entertainment center. "Try again" was the most likely comment.
Luke set the can on the workbench and hopped up on a stool.

"Great work, Luke," Eli said, studying the furniture piece. "I
think Mitch Harrison will love it."

With a brow arched in disbelief, Luke glanced at Eli. "You've
got to be kidding me. Those corners aren't perfectly square. I
figured you'd tell me to start over."

Eli chuckled, patting Luke on the shoulder. "You're way too
hard on yourself. You remind me of myself at your age." His
expression softened, becoming serious. "You know, losing your
brother was a huge blow to our family. He was like a son to me,
and he meant the world to my Sarah Rose. He also did great
work, just like you."

Luke lifted the can and took another long drink, willing the
emotions within him to settle. Hearing about his brother this

way caused his stomach to tighten and a lump to swell in his throat.

"What I want to say, Luke, is I'd be honored to have you as a part of our family here at Kauffman & Yoder. I've spoken to Elmer about it, and we want you to stay here and work for us." Eli gave him a hopeful smile. "Please, son, say you will. We need you."

Luke took another swig and then set the can down again. "*Danki* for asking me. It means a lot." He took a deep breath, searching for the correct words. "But I can't accept."

Eli frowned. "Why not? Don't you like working here?"

"*Ya*, I do." Luke slowly rose from the stool. "But I'm thinking it's time I head back home."

"Home?"

"Back to Ohio. I'm just not sure I belong here." Luke studied the piece of furniture, staring at the corners he should've squared better. *Pop would turn over in his grave if he saw this poor excuse for an entertainment center.*

"You're talking nonsense." Eli smiled and patted Luke's shoulder. "You think about it and get back to me on Monday." He looked back at the entertainment center and shook his head. "You did a great job on that. I don't know what you're bellyaching about."

Luke rubbed his bottom lip, considering Eli's offer of a permanent job. It was tempting to stay, but it would torture him to see Sarah with anger in her eyes, silently accusing him of being a liar, time after time, when he visited the Kauffmans or went to church services.

But how could he walk away from his brother's children? He supposed he could always visit periodically, and he could call and write letters to keep in touch. Perhaps he could keep in touch through Eli.

He lifted the can to his lips again and glanced at the piece of furniture. Maybe leaving was the best choice. He could sand

and stain the entertainment center this evening and ask Jake to finish it for him next week. He had forged a great friendship with the young man, and Luke imagined Jake would be happy to help him complete the project.

Gazing across the shop, his eyes settled on Jake walking to his workbench, a wide grin splitting his young face. Luke tossed the empty can of Coke into the trashcan and then weaved through the shop to Jake's workbench, giving him a friendly smack on the back. "Hey, there, Jake. Do you have a minute to talk?"

"Sure thing." Jake nodded toward the door. "Outside?"

"*Ya.*" Luke followed him out to the parking lot, where they sat on the concrete step. "What are you grinning about?"

"I just talked to Jessica." Jake folded a piece of gum into his mouth and held the pack out to Luke, who took a piece. "She's coming to visit soon. She said she's doing real well in school, and she misses me." His grin was back. "She's planning to come to visit her sister, and she can't wait to see Sarah's twins."

"That's *wunderbaar,*" Luke said, slipping the cinnamon gum into his mouth and the wrapper into his pocket. "You're pretty crazy about her, *ya?*"

"Oh, yeah." Jake's face became serious. "You know when it just feels right? It's like everything clicks between you and your girl, and you just know in your gut that it's right?"

Luke nodded. He knew exactly what Jake meant. He only wished Sarah felt it in her gut too.

"I hope I can convince her to go to college here. I can't imagine having her so far away for four more years. Just waiting for her to finish school is going to be next to impossible." Jake chewed his gum and sighed. "I guess only time will tell, though. She's a stubborn one."

Luke snorted, thinking he again knew just what the young man meant. *Stubborn* was the perfect word to describe Sarah Rose Troyer.

Jake bent his legs and rested his elbows on his knees. "You didn't invite me out here to discuss how nuts I am about Jessica. What's up?"

"I was wondering if you would finish that entertainment center for me next week," Luke said. "I'll stay late tonight and get it stained and all. I was just wondering if you would put the clear coat on and then the hardware."

Jake nodded, chewing the gum. "Sure thing. Are you starting something else?"

Luke shook his head. "I'm leaving, heading back to Ohio."

"Oh?" Jake looked surprised. "For good?"

Luke nodded. "*Ya*, but I'll visit."

"It's none of my business, but why?"

Luke chewed his gum, debating what to tell him. He hated to lie, but the truth was too personal. "I need to get back to my old job and my house. It's just time."

"I hate to see you go, but I guess you gotta do what you gotta do." Jake slapped Luke's arm. "You better keep in touch or I'll come find ya."

Luke gave him a sad smile. "You know I will."

Jake stood and headed into the shop while Luke remained and stared across the parking lot. The sound of boots crunching on the gravel drew his attention to Timothy walking from the supply truck toward the back door.

"Sitting down on the job again, huh, Troyer?" Timothy quipped as he approached.

"Yup, that's what I do—goof off all day long." Luke stood and shook his head. "You don't need to worry about me anymore. I'm heading back to Ohio."

Timothy's face mirrored his surprise. "And what made you change your mind about staying here?"

"I don't belong." Luke said, deciding to tell Timothy the truth since Timothy already knew the whole story about Luke's identity. "Sarah has decided I'm a liar like my brother, and I can't bear to stay under those circumstances. I'll keep in touch with my niece and nephew and maybe visit a couple of times a year."

"I can't say I'll regret seeing you go since you already ratted me out." Timothy rubbed his chin.

"What do you mean?"

"Sarah thinks I'm a liar, too, thanks to you. I thought you were going to keep our little secret to yourself, but you've blown it for both of us."

Luke shook his head with regret. "I'm sorry. I never meant to get you into trouble with her too. It just slipped."

"Right." Timothy shrugged. "I guess I'll see you when you visit the *kinner*."

Luke studied Timothy. "Why do you hate me so much?"

"I don't hate you." Timothy's expression softened. "You just remind me of all I lost when we lost Peter."

"Why can't we be friends, since you and Peter were? I didn't come here with a chip on my shoulder, but you've certainly had one from day one."

"You did just what I worried you'd do—made me look like a liar in front of my family. That's what I've always feared."

"You're her brother, Timothy. She'll forgive you. I'm nothing to her now. What I thought we had was ruined when she realized I wasn't a cousin. I lost everything, but you have her love as a brother."

"She'll eventually forgive you." Timothy smiled. "Things are about to get better in her life. Pretty soon it will be a year since Peter died and she can court again. I'm fairly sure she'll be getting married here shortly. Maybe she'll get married this spring, since it'll be the second marriage for both, and they won't have to wait until fall."

Luke's stomach roiled. "She's getting married?"

Timothy folded his arms. "She and Norman are becoming really close, and I have a feeling he's going to ask her soon. He's had feelings for her for a long time, but he's kept it to himself so as not to pressure her."

"Norman?" Luke asked, his stomach churning with jealousy.

"It makes sense for them to get together, don't you think? They've both lost their spouse, and they have *kinner* to raise. It's the perfect partnership."

Luke swallowed his disgust.

"It's not public knowledge, so don't get me in trouble with this one, okay? Norman's told me he's going to propose, but he hasn't even asked Sarah yet." Timothy pointed to Luke's chest. "Promise me, all right?"

"Your secret is safe with me." Luke couldn't fathom saying those words aloud.

"And for the record, I don't hate you. I'm sorry I came off that way." Timothy held his hand out and Luke shook it. "Friends?"

"*Ya.*" Luke stared after Timothy in disbelief as he disappeared into the shop.

Bile rose in his throat at the thought of Sarah marrying Norman. He was sure that was a sign for him to leave Bird-in-Hand. He couldn't stand to watch her marry another man. Luke's decision was made for him—he was going home to Ohio.

Later that evening, Sarah stared at the letters in her hands, rereading the words for what felt like the hundredth time. Each of the three letters had the same overall message from DeLana to Peter. She asked if he was okay and if he had forgotten to send the child support. DeLana requested that Peter call her to let her know everything was okay, and her cellular phone number was scrawled at the end of each note. Sarah had committed the number to memory.

She couldn't stop the overwhelming urge to call DeLana.

She wanted to hear DeLana's voice and ask her several questions, such as how she and Peter had met, how long they courted, why they broke up, if they truly loved each other, and why Peter had walked away from his son.

Sarah closed her eyes and hugged the letters to her chest. She had to know exactly what had happened between Peter and DeLana and verify that Luke's version of the story was accurate. The questions would haunt her until they were answered.

A knock on the door startled her. Sarah slipped the letters into the pocket of her apron.

"Sarah Rose?" *Mamm's* anxious voice sounded outside the door. "Are you all right?"

"*Ya.*" Sarah rose from the chair. She wiped her eyes, and adjusted her prayer *Kapp* on her hair. She then forced a smile and opened the door. "I was just resting. Is *Dat* ready for devotions?"

"No." *Mamm's* eyes studied Sarah's. "Norman's here for a visit. Are you well enough to come see him?"

"*Ya.*" Sarah straightened her dress. "The *zwillingbopplin* are fast asleep in the nursery." She stepped past *Mamm*, but a strong hand on her shoulder stopped her.

Mamm didn't look convinced. "You've been quiet all day. What did you find out at the post office?"

Sarah paused, debating what to say. "I closed out his box and I got a few more letters. All from DeLana."

"Did the letters upset you?" *Mamm* touched her hand. "You must let go of all of this hurt. Please do it for your heart and for the *kinner.* They can sense when you're sad, *mei liewe.*"

"I'm fine." Sarah took *Mamm's* hands in hers. "I promise you I am. Let's go see our guests, *ya?*"

Sarah and *Mamm* met Norman and his family in the kitchen, where they ate dessert and talked late into the evening. While the children played games in the living room, Sarah and Norman retreated to the porch and sank onto the swing.

Wrapped in a blanket, Sarah breathed in the chilly air and stared toward her dark house, wondering where Luke was. Was he working late? Had he not made it home safely? Was he still angry with her? Did he feel the same ache in his heart for her as she did for him?

Against her will, Sarah heaved a heavy sigh that carried the weight of her regret for snapping at him.

"Sarah?" Norman asked with a chuckle. "I'm boring you to tears, no?"

"*Ack*, I'm so sorry." Sarah sat up and smoothed the blanket. "You're not boring me at all. I'm just tired. It was a long day."

"*Mei freind*," Norman said, squeezing her hand. "You don't have to explain yourself to me. I know this is all overwhelming for you. You lost Peter not even a year ago. Please don't make excuses for yourself. You're permitted to be a bundle of emotions."

Sarah forced a smile. Norman continued his conversation about his extended family that had visited today from Gordonville, and Sarah tried to concentrate on it.

The clip-clop of a horse and crunch of tires rolling up the lane stole Sarah's attention from Norman's voice. Her heart flip-flopped in her chest when the buggy stopped in front of *Dat's* barn and Luke emerged from the driver's seat.

While Luke unhitched Molly, Sarah clasped her hands together and sucked in a deep breath. He stowed the buggy and Molly and then emerged from the barn.

Part of Sarah hoped Luke would just disappear down the lane to the house without so much as a greeting for her, while another part prayed he would stop by and say hello.

His tall, slender silhouette sauntered toward the porch, and Sarah's pulse quickened. When the light of the lamp kissed his chiseled countenance, her breath caught in her throat.

"*Wie geht's*," Norman said. "It's good to see you, Luke."

"You too." Luke nodded at Norman. He then turned to Sarah, and his brown eyes sizzled with hot emotion. Was it anger? Or was it passion?

Sarah cleared her throat.

"Sarah Rose," Luke said, his voice cool.

She nodded in response, her voice still lost in her throat.

He tapped the railing. "I'll leave you to visit. Have a nice evening." He then turned and started down the gravel toward her former house.

"You too," Norman called after him. "*Gut nacht.*" After a few beats, he rubbed Sarah's arm. "He's a *gut* guy."

Sarah nodded and cleared her throat, hoping to stop the tears that threatened. She couldn't stop the foreboding feeling that Luke was walking out of her life.

Luke threw his bag on the bed and tossed his shirts into it. His heart pounded in his chest while anger, resentment, and regret rioted in his gut. Seeing Sarah sitting on the porch with Norman's arm around her had sent his blood pressure soaring. To make matters worse, she never spoke to him, never even acknowledged him beyond a slight nod. It was as though he meant nothing to her now that she had her future husband, Norman.

Timothy's words stung his ears—it made sense for her to marry Norman since he was a widower and had children to raise. Perhaps Timothy was right. However, he couldn't shake one question: did Sarah even love Norman? If so, she'd never expressed it to Luke.

Sarah had made her choice, proving Luke didn't belong here. The Lord was telling him he was wrong to covet his brother's widow, and it was time he faced up to that fact. By going home, he could find a way to heal his heart and move on without any reminder of what Peter had left behind.

He packed up his clothes and then moved to the master bedroom where the pile of Peter's shirts still sat patiently waiting for a new home. Tears stung Luke's eyes as he sifted through the clothing.

Memories of his brother crashed down on him—holidays

with their parents before their *mamm* died, playing volleyball in the back pasture with friends, walking to school together, and sitting in the loft of the barn late at night and talking about everything from girls to their deep faith in God.

He allowed the memories to carry him back to a less complicated time, and the mourning he'd held at bay since he learned of his brother's death assaulted his emotions. The release was cleansing, but it left Luke feeling like a cold, empty shell of who he'd once been.

After choosing four shirts, Luke tossed them into his bag. His thoughts then turned to the twins. His heart ached at the realization of leaving them, but he couldn't bear to watch their mother, the woman he loved, marry someone else.

The pain was too much for him. He felt as if he was breaking a promise to Peter by leaving, but it was the best choice for Luke. He would visit the children and keep in touch with them. They would know their uncle Luke; he'd make certain of it.

Needing to exit the house in an attempt to clear his head and quell his emotions, Luke grabbed his coat and stalked out the front door. The cold air kissed his face and filled his lungs with the heavy aroma of wood fireplaces.

He lowered himself onto the porch steps and reflected on the events of his four-month stay in Bird-in-Hand. The reality of leaving filled him with regret. He'd enjoyed being a surrogate member of the Kauffman clan, and he would miss their closeness. Yet he had good friends in Mel and Sally. It wasn't as if he would be alone back in Ohio. He also had a few cousins, aunts, and uncles.

He had to get out of Lancaster County while he still had some of his heart and soul intact. Tomorrow would be the day. He needed to be on that first train.

Something flashed in his peripheral vision, and Luke turned toward Eli's home. A Coleman lamp held by a tall figure floated near the large barn. Judging from the height of the silhouette,

Luke deduced it to be Eli—just the man he needed to arrange for a ride to the station.

Luke hopped up and jogged toward the barn, reaching it just as Eli finished locking the large doors. "Eli," he called. "Do you have a moment?"

"Luke." The older man gave a surprised expression. "What are you doing out this late?"

"I couldn't sleep." Luke jammed his hands into the pockets of his coat. "Do you have a minute to talk?"

"Of course." He nodded toward the porch. "Would you like to have a seat?"

Luke hesitated. Scanning the property, he found Norman's buggy was gone; however, he feared Sarah might be awake. Luke didn't want her to overhear his conversation with Eli and find out he was leaving.

"Something wrong?" Eli asked.

"How about we walk along the fence?" Luke asked. "It's a beautiful night."

Eli eyed him with suspicion. "It's a bit cold for a leisurely walk. Let's go back into my woodshop. We'll have privacy there."

"Danki," Luke said, wondering if his apprehension was more transparent than he feared.

He followed Eli around the back of the barn and into a shed converted into a carpentry shop, complete with several workbenches, stools, and a sea of tools. An unfinished bookshelf and an end table sat in the corner awaiting stain. The scent of wood and paint filled Luke's nostrils as he hopped up onto a stool.

Eli set the lantern down, leaned against the bench, and studied Luke. "What's bothering you, son? You seem preoccupied, like you're wrestling with the meaning of life."

Luke hugged his arms to his chest; however, the cold seeping into his bones seemed to be more than the temperature in the shed. "I was wondering if you'd arrange for me to get a ride to the train station early tomorrow morning."

A frown clouded Eli's face, and he fingered his beard, deep in thought. "I guess my suggestion for you to wait before making a decision didn't help, no?"

"I appreciate all you and your family have done for me, but I feel like the Lord is telling me that it's time to go home." Luke leaned back against the workbench and ran his fingers over the grain of the wooden top. "I'll be back to visit the *zwillingbopplin*."

Eli was silent for a moment, still rubbing his beard and studying Luke. His expression softened. "This is about Sarah Rose, isn't it?"

"No," Luke said, shaking his head. "I just feel it's time to go home. That's all."

"Don't deny it." Eli gave a knowing smile, folding his arms across his muscular frame. "You love my Sarah Rose."

"No, I don't," Luke said with a shrug, hoping he appeared nonchalant.

Eli rested a foot on the rung of a stool. "Why are you retreating to Ohio when your heart will remain here?"

Luke blew out a sigh and glanced around the shop in an attempt to avoid Eli's knowing expression. The question left Luke's lips before he could squelch it: "How do you know where you truly belong?" He glanced down at his lap and then met Eli's warm gaze.

"You know in here." Eli pointed to his heart. "God fills our heart with clues for what He wants us to have in life. If something seems to fit, then we know it's what God wants for us."

"But I feel like I should go home." Luke crossed his arms and shivered. "I don't feel like I belong here."

"Are you sure?" Eli raised his eyebrows in anticipation. "Is that really what your heart is telling you? Is that what you came to tell Sarah Rose the other night when you found out she was still angry with you?"

Luke blanched. "How did you know—"

"Elizabeth told me. She overheard some of the conversation." Eli's eyes probed Luke's. "Are you sure you want to leave?"

"*Ya.* I think it's best." Luke nodded with emphasis.

"Then you best give me your contact information. I'd like to keep in touch." Eli fetched a notepad and pencil from the bench behind him and passed it to Luke.

"I'll be in touch and visit. I want the *zwillingbopplin* to know me. I'm their only connection to Peter." Luke recorded his address and the phone number to the shop where he worked. He then handed the notepad back to Eli, who slipped it into his coat pocket.

"You don't have to run." Eli touched Luke's shoulder.

"I'm not running. I'm doing what's best for me and also for Sarah. She's my brother's widow." He shook his head. "It's just not right for me to even think of her that way, and I would guess she knows it. I'm sure my being here brings back memories she needs to forget."

Luke sighed. "I messed things up for her by telling her the truth about Peter's past and who I was. I did nothing but hurt her. The best thing I can do for her now is to leave and let her live a new life. She deserves happiness, not bad memories and lies Peter selfishly left for her to sort through."

"There's a verse I read during our devotion time the other night that reminds me of this situation. It was 1 John 4:18." Eli squeezed his shoulder. " 'There is no fear in love. But perfect love drives out fear, because fear has to do with punishment. The one who fears is not made perfect in love.' Don't fear your love for Sarah Rose. See where it takes you."

Luke shook his head despite the warmth the verse gave his soul. "No. I need to go before I cause her more pain. Will you help me get a ride to the train station tomorrow?"

Dropping his hand to his side, Eli frowned and blew out a defeated sigh. "If that's what you want, then yes. But think about what I said."

"*Danki.*" Luke walked back to the porch with Eli.

The door opened revealing Sarah standing in a white robe

tied tightly over a white nightgown. Her golden hair hung in waves touching her waist. He'd never seen her with her hair down before, and thought she resembled an angel. Her flawless beauty was so striking that his heart pounded in his chest. He'd give anything to hold her in his arms, kiss her, and tell her that he loved her.

But she was marrying another man who would hold her in his arms and love her.

He frowned, and his stomach twisted at the thought of Norman touching her.

All the more reason to go home to Ohio.

Sarah shivered as she ambled onto the porch. She looked at her father standing at the bottom of the porch stairs with Luke, and her throat dried.

"*Dat?*" she asked, ignoring Luke's stare. "What are you doing out here so late?"

Dat turned to her, his eyes wide. "Sarah Rose! Get inside before you catch pneumonia!"

"Are you coming in?" Sarah asked. "You don't need to be out here either."

Dat trotted up the stairs and opened the door. Turning back to Luke, his expression softened. "Think about what I said. Don't make any hasty decisions."

Luke nodded and started down the gravel drive to her former home.

"Sarah Rose?" *Dat* asked, holding the door open. "Are you coming inside?"

Her eyes darted toward Luke. She couldn't squelch the urge to talk to him, even though she didn't know what she wanted to say.

Dat pulled off his coat and handed it to her. "Here. You'll need this if you stay out here and chat." He then placed the lantern on the small table next to the swing.

"*Danki.*" She put on the coat and then stepped to the edge of the porch as the door shut behind her. She spotted Luke's tall, slim silhouette stalking through the dark to her former home. "Luke!" she called. "Luke! Wait!"

Luke stopped and faced her, and she wished she could read his expression through the dark. For a moment he hesitated, and she was certain he was going to go back to the house without talking to her.

Holding her breath, she prayed he'd come back and talk to her. However, considering the way she'd treated him the last two times she'd seen him, she couldn't blame him if he decided to continue back to the house.

When he started back toward the porch, her heart turned over in her chest. He came to the bottom step of the porch. His dark eyes shimmered in the low light of the kerosene lamp as they studied hers.

"*Ya?*" he asked, his voice soft but intense.

She cleared her throat and wracked her brain, trying to think of something to say. She'd called him back to her, but now she was dumbstruck, unsure of how to open a conversation with him. The sight of his chiseled features rendered her speechless.

He folded his arms. "What is it, Sarah Rose?"

"What were you discussing with my *dat?*" she asked, twirling a strand of hair around her finger. She realized she was clad in her father's coat over her robe and nightgown, and she suddenly felt exposed. Only a woman's husband should see her hair, and she wished for her prayer *kapp* or a shawl to cover her head. Yet there she stood exposed in the late February night with her brother-in-law's intense eyes probing her.

He frowned. "It was nothing you need to worry about. *Gut nacht*, Sarah Rose." He started for the house again.

"Wait!" She hurried down the porch stairs, holding onto the banister for balance. She couldn't let him go, but she had no idea why she was so panicked at the thought of his leaving.

He stopped. Facing her, he sighed with frustration. "It's late, and it's cold. Your pop's right, and you should go inside before you catch pneumonia. There's nothing left for us to discuss. *Gut nacht.*" He gestured toward the door. "Go in where it's warm."

"Don't dismiss me like some child!" She frowned with her hands on her hips. "I wasn't finished talking to you."

"What on earth could you possibly have to say to me? You already told me our friendship is over and I'm a liar like my brother." His eyes flashed with anger. "I know where I stand in your life."

"Do you?" She held her breath in anticipation of his answer.

"*Ya.* I'm somewhere around that annoying gum that gets stuck on the bottom of your shoe."

She gasped at his biting tone. "How could you say that?"

"How could I say that?" He gave a sarcastic laugh. "You didn't even have the decency to speak to me earlier tonight when I saw you on the porch with Norman. That told me how important I was to you. I'm not worth your breath. Our friendship means nothing to you anymore."

"Luke, that's not true." Her voice quavered, betraying her attempt to appear cool and collected.

He shook his head and grimaced. "Don't worry, Sarah Rose. I won't butt into your business anymore."

"What do you mean?" She wiped at the tears that had appeared without her knowledge.

"I'm leaving tomorrow." He jammed his hands into the pockets of his coat. "I'm going home to Ohio. That's where I belong."

"What?" She stepped toward him, feeling as if she'd been punched in the stomach. "You're leaving?"

"I am. I'll be in touch." His expression softened. "I'll want to see the *zwillingbopplin.*"

"If you cared so much about them you'd stay." She glared at him.

He shook his head. "You just don't get it, do you?"

"What don't I get?" She sniffed. "I don't understand what you mean."

"Forget it, Sarah Rose." He nodded toward the house. "Go inside before you get sick."

"Fine." She slapped her hands to her sides. "Just walk out of my life. Walk out of the *zwillingbopplin*'s life. That's what you Troyers do best, right? Peter walked away from his son, and you're walking away from Peter's *kinner*."

His eyes flashed with fury. "Don't compare me to my brother," he said, seething. "I never would've lied to you, and I never would've walked away from you. But you wouldn't give me the chance."

She gasped as more tears streamed down her cheeks.

"Good-bye, Sarah Rose. May God bless you and your *zwillingbopplin*." He turned and stomped toward the house.

Hugging her arms to her chest, she sobbed while he left her standing in the bitter cold.

19

Luke sank back in the seat and closed his eyes in an attempt to shut off his brain and sleep to the monotonous click-clack of the train. He'd spent a restless night tossing and turning in bed and then pacing around the room.

His heart ached when he thought of Sarah. He wished he could take back the words he'd said to her, but the hurt had boiled over from his soul after carrying it for so long. She was wrong, so wrong, to run after him and act like she cared for him after the way she'd treated him. Perhaps she was the liar instead of Luke.

To make matters worse, no matter how hard he tried, he couldn't shut off the echo of Eli's words in his head. He kept pondering what Eli meant when he said Luke was running. Was Luke running back to Ohio out of fear of his love for Sarah?

Was going back to Ohio a mistake?

But Luke kept coming to the same conclusion: if Sarah loved Luke, then she wouldn't marry Norman. It was a simple assessment. Being with her felt so right, yet it was so wrong. It was a sin, and she was marrying another man. It made more sense for Luke to forget her.

Luke imagined Sarah's beautiful face—her ivory skin, sky-blue eyes, and pink lips. She would be a beautiful bride. Norman was the luckiest man on the planet.

Yet he couldn't deny the affection for her that surged through his heart and his soul.

And then there were the twins. When they were born, Luke had made a vow to be the uncle they needed and deserved. Yet here he was retreating to Ohio with his tail between his legs because he couldn't face Sarah marrying another man. He was breaking his promise to Peter's children, but he couldn't stand the idea of seeing Sarah with Norman.

How on earth would Luke be able to let the twins and Sarah go and move on with his life?

Staring out the window at a wide-open field rushing by, Luke opened his heart to prayer, asking God to lead him down the right path. He hoped he could arrive back in Ohio thankful for his days in Bird-in-Hand and, somehow, through a miracle only God could provide, with his heart and soul glued back together.

After getting the twins settled in their cradles, Sarah joined *Mamm* at the breakfast table and lowered her head in silent prayer. Lifting her gaze, she scooped scrambled eggs from a bowl onto her plate and then handed the bowl to *Mamm*. "Where's *Dat?*" she asked.

"He had to run an errand. He should be back shortly." *Mamm* passed the plate of rolls to Sarah. "How did you sleep last night?"

Sarah shrugged, studying the contents of her plate. "*Gut.* The *zwillingbopplin* only had me up twice."

It was a bold-faced lie, but she couldn't bring herself to tell the truth. *Mamm* would worry if she knew Sarah had been up praying and crying between feedings. She'd spent the night drowning in guilt for yelling at Luke. She'd deserved the cruel words he'd spat at her.

She remembered how he'd stalked off. The anger in his eyes

had split her heart in two, and she had to face the fact that he hated her.

She'd prayed most of the night, begging God to convince Luke to stay. Yet she feared the inevitable—that he would go back home to Ohio to forget her and the twins forever.

Sarah tried to smile but worried her lips formed a grimace instead. She buttered her roll while *Mamm* yammered on about her plans for the day. Sarah nodded at the appropriate times.

The door opened and slammed, and *Dat* slipped into the chair next to *Mamm*. "Smells *appeditlich*!" He reached across the table aiming for a roll.

"Eli Kauffman," *Mamm* scolded, slapping his hand. "Wash your hands!"

"*Ack*, my hands are clean." He rolled his eyes and schlepped to the sink. After scrubbing, rinsing, and drying his hands, he returned to the table and then bowed his head in silent prayer.

Finishing, he looked up and smiled. "How are you this morning?" he asked Sarah while loading his plate.

"*Gut*." She forked some egg from her plate. "Where did you have to run to so early?"

"I had to meet Mike Gray to get someone to the train station." He buttered a roll. "What do you ladies have planned for today?"

"Train station?" Sarah's stomach plummeted. "Mike Gray gave someone a ride there? Who had to take a train?" She knew the answer before he reported it.

"Luke went home." He said the words as if they were mundane, but something in his eyes revealed more. It was as if he knew how she felt. How could he know? Had Luke told him about their argument last night?

Speechless, Sarah stopped chewing and studied her father. Out of the corner of her eye, she spotted *Mamm* watching her, a curious expression clouding her face.

"He asked me to arrange for a ride, so I took him to Mike's

early this morning." *Dat* shrugged, but his eyes were more honest—they were filled with hurt. "He said he felt like it was time to go." He brightened. "But he'll keep in touch and wants to come visit the *zwillingbopplin*."

Sarah's stomach twisted.

Luke was gone. Gone for good.

And she had pushed him away.

And he hated her.

Her throat dried and her eyes stung. Setting her fork next to her plate, she pushed back her chair.

"Sarah Rose," *Mamm* said. "You must finish eating and keep your strength up so you can care for the *zwillingbopplin*."

"I'm not as hungry as I thought." Standing, she took her dishes to the sink. "I need to go lie down for a bit. I'll finish the dishes later."

Mamm rose and took Sarah's arm. "Please sit. You must eat."

"Maybe later." Sarah gently pulled her arm back. "I need to go rest." She headed for the stairs, avoiding her parents' stares.

"I thought you wanted to go to the market with me," *Mamm* called after her. "Your *dat* can watch the *kinner*."

"Later," Sarah called back, her voice thick. She hurried up the stairs, reaching her room just as the tears began to splatter.

Flopping onto her back on the bed, she sobbed, silently scolding herself for pushing Luke away. Would she ever see him again? Did she even deserve to see him again?

No, she didn't, after the way she'd treated him.

Covering her face with her hands, Sarah wished she could turn back time to the day of the fire. If only she'd convinced Peter to stay home with her that day and talk, then maybe, just maybe, he'd still be alive. If she hadn't lost him, she'd never have wound up in the mess she was in now—alone and confused, raising two babies without a husband.

She never would've met Luke.

And she never would've loved Luke either.

Applesauce Cake

1 cup granulated sugar
1/2 cup shortening
2 tsp baking soda
3 cups flour
1 cup raisins
1–1/4 cups nuts
1–1/2 cups sweetened applesauce
Pinch of cream of tartar
1 Tbsp cooking sherry
1/4 tsp salt
1–1/2 tsp cinnamon
1/2 tsp cloves
1/2 tsp allspice
1/2 tsp ginger

Cream sugar and shortening. Sift in baking soda and flour. Add raisins and nuts, then add remaining ingredients. Bake in a greased 9-inch square pan at 350 degrees for 35 to 40 minutes.

20

Sarah stared down at the ledger and frowned. At *Mamm's* request, she was balancing the bakery books in preparation for the start of the tourist season at the end of the month.

Although she tried to concentrate on the numbers, her mind repeatedly wandered to Luke—how he'd chatted in the den with the family after meals, how he'd looked every time he gazed down at the twins with love in his eyes ... how he'd smiled at her during their conversations on the swing ...

Leaning back in the chair, she covered her face with her hands. Why was Luke still haunting her nearly two months after he'd left? She'd attempted to engross herself in the *zwillingbopplin*. However, time and time again, her thoughts meandered back to Luke. She could see the pain in his eyes the night before he left. She could still feel his anger, hear it in the tone of his voice.

She'd hurt him. How could she have hurt the one man who made her feel safe? Why did she push away the one man she could possibly love?

But how could she court her late husband's brother? It was wrong to covet him. Nevertheless, she couldn't stop her mind from constantly concentrating on him and dreaming of him every night.

Sarah closed the ledger and stared out the window at the

light rain cascading down from heaven and soaking the field behind the bakery. Spring was on its way to Lancaster County. She wondered if the temperature was warming in Ohio yet.

Was Luke working late tonight at the cabinet shop? Was he thinking of her and the twins? Why hadn't he contacted her since he'd gotten home?

Her mind turned to Peter, and she stood and moved from the office into the kitchen. She wondered when Peter had planned to tell her the truth about his past. Would he have taken her to Ohio to meet Luke or Cody?

Pulling a letter from the pocket inside her apron, Sarah stared down at DeLana's cellular phone number for what felt like the hundredth time.

Sarah had considered calling DeLana several times over the past two months since the woman had a right to know why the checks from Peter had stopped coming. Sarah wondered if Luke planned to tell DeLana what had happened to Peter, although she knew it wasn't his responsibility. This was something Sarah should do.

She walked out to the front counter and stared at the phone hanging on the wall. She was alone in the bakery and had the perfect opportunity to make the call. She just needed the strength.

A knock on the glass door sounded through the silence of the empty bakery. Sarah looked up and found Kathryn grinning at her and hugging her cloak to her chest. Sarah unlocked and held open the door.

"Hi," Kathryn said, stepping in and shaking the raindrops from her arms. "Spring is coming to Bird-in-Hand."

"What are you doing here?" Sarah asked. "Don't you have to cook for your family?"

"*Ya.*" Kathryn rolled her eyes. "I forgot to grab my change purse." She padded back to the kitchen. "I took it out to give Lindsay some money earlier and forgot it," she called from around the corner. "Here it is." She reappeared and pulled her cloak closer to her body. "The *kinner* are waiting for me at *Mamm's* house. I told them I'd be right back."

Sarah forced a smile, only half listening to her sister's chatting.

Kathryn shook her head. "I'm so scatterbrained lately. David says I need to slow down, but there are only so many hours in the day and so much to do. Running a farm and taking care of *kinner* is a full-time job. And then I have to work in the bakery. I mean, just yesterday I had a difficult time—"

Her sister stopped mid-sentence, her expression clouding. "Sarah Rose, what's wrong?" She touched the ties to Sarah's prayer *kapp*. "You look as if you're carrying the burden of us all on your little shoulders."

Sarah leaned against the counter and shook her head. "You need to get home to your family. Don't worry about me."

"Don't be *gegisch*." Kathryn led her to two chairs in the back of the kitchen and motioned for her to sit. "I always have time for you. What's wrong?"

Sarah pulled out the letter and handed it to Kathryn. "I feel like I should call DeLana and tell her why Peter's checks stopped."

Kathryn shrugged. "So call her. Want me to dial?"

"That's not it." Sarah shook her head. "I want to go to Ohio. I want to see DeLana and talk to her, face-to-face, about Peter. I need to know more. I need to know the details. I have to understand it all before I can move on."

Kathryn nodded, taking in her words. "That makes sense. I understand."

"I know you do." Sarah sighed. "But *Mamm* never will. She'd never let me go. But I can't leave the *zwillingbopplin* without telling her."

Her sister took Sarah's hands in hers. "Do you want me to go to Ohio with you?"

"You're sweet and so thoughtful." Sarah dabbed away the sudden moisture in her eyes. "But I need to do this alone."

"So, do it," her sister said. "Call DeLana and then go ahead and plan a trip to Ohio. Find out what you need to know and let your heart mend, Sarah Rose."

Kathryn stood and steered Sarah to the phone. "Call Nina and ask her to take you to the train station early in the morning. I'll come over and care for the *zwillingbopplin*. I'll tell *Mamm* you had to take care of some business. If she's angry, she'll just have to forgive us. You need to listen to your heart, Sarah, not everyone else." She lifted the receiver and dialed the number. She then handed Sarah the phone. "I'll wait in the office so you can have privacy."

Sarah put the receiver up to her ear and held Kathryn's arm. "Stay." She leaned against the counter and stared at the numbers on the cash register.

The phone rang several times and then a voice spoke. "Hello?"

"Hello," Sarah said, her voice shaky. "Is this DeLana Maloney?"

"Yes. Who is this?"

"My name is Sarah Troyer."

DeLana paused as if contemplating the name. The voice of a child rang out in the background, and Sarah imagined it was Cody. The noise softened, and Sarah assumed DeLana had moved to a quieter area.

"Sarah," DeLana said. "Sarah Troyer?" Her voice rang with recognition. "Peter's wife?"

"*Ya*," Sarah said. "I mean, yes." She nervously drew circles on the counter with her fingertip. "I hope it's okay I'm calling you. I wanted to tell you some news, and it didn't seem appropriate to write you a letter due to the lag time of the mail system."

"Of course it's okay that you called," DeLana's voice was gentle. "What's going on?"

226

"You're probably wondering why your child support money has stopped." Sarah took a deep breath. A hand on her shoulder gave her the support she needed to trudge on. "I'm sorry to tell you that Peter ... Well ..." Her voice quavered. "Peter died in a fire almost a year ago."

"Oh, Sarah, I already knew." DeLana's voice was full of concern and sympathy. "Luke, Peter's brother, called me about two months ago and told me. I'm so, so sorry."

"Luke told you?" Her heart fluttered as she said his name. Sarah glanced at Kathryn, who gave her a sad smile.

"Yes, he did," DeLana said. "I'm so very sorry for your loss."

"Thank you."

"How are you coping?" DeLana asked.

"God is seeing me through it. My family has been my strength." Sarah wiped her cheeks. "I'm sorry I didn't contact you sooner, but I found your letters when I was going through Peter's things. I didn't know about you or Cody until fairly recently and then I had to find the strength to call you. It was a shock to find out about Cody. I had no idea."

DeLana sighed. "I'm sorry about that. Peter said he wanted to keep it a secret because he didn't want to hurt you."

Sarah bit her bottom lip. It seemed now was the time to ask. "I was wondering if I could come meet you. I have some questions I would like answered."

There was a pause, and a few awkward moments of dead air on the line. "You want to come visit me?" DeLana's voice was full of surprise.

"If it's okay with you ..." Sarah cut her eyes to Kathryn, who squeezed her hand.

"Well, sure. Why not? When would you like to come?"

"Would Thursday be too soon? I can catch a train tomorrow and meet you Thursday afternoon." Sarah held her breath, expecting a lame excuse for her not to come.

"That sounds perfect."

Sarah grabbed a notepad and pen and wrote down the particulars of where to meet DeLana. Then she thanked her and hung up.

Turning, she pulled Kathryn into a warm hug. "Thank you for giving me the strength to do it," she whispered. "I'm meeting her at a restaurant in Middlefield on Thursday."

"You're welcome." Kathryn rubbed her back. "Now you need to call Nina to arrange for a ride early tomorrow morning. I'll plan to be there and care for the *zwillingbopplin* for you."

Later that evening, Sarah climbed the stairs of her former home and entered the master bedroom. Tomorrow morning she would head to Ohio, and she wanted to bring a gift for Cody. Someday he might want to have something from his biological father, if DeLana ever told him who his biological father was.

She found the pile of shirts arranged neatly by color. Not at all resembling the way she'd left it. Luke must've gone through the pile and picked a couple for himself.

Considering, she lifted a shirt, inhaling a faint scent of Peter still clinging for dear life to the fibers. She chose two for Cody and draped them over her arm. She then headed down the hallway and stepped into the spare bedroom where Luke had slept.

Standing in the middle of the room, her mind flooded with memories of the night she'd given him a tour. She sank onto the bed and lifted the pillow to her nose. The faint aroma of Luke, stain and wood mixed with earth, washed over, and her pulse skipped. Again she wondered if he'd thought of her since he'd gone back home. Did he miss her?

Glancing at the ticking clock on the wall, Sarah realized it was time for devotionals. Her parents would suspect she was up to something if she missed the nightly Kauffman ritual.

She rushed back to the house, making it just in time. But

while her father read from the Bible, her mind kept wandering to her trip to Ohio and how it would feel to meet DeLana.

When her father finished his reading, they bowed their heads in silent prayer. Sarah then excused herself for the evening and rushed to her room. She packed a small bag of clothes and then wrote her parents a note she would leave in the kitchen on her way out the next morning.

During the night, Sarah tossed and turned in between feedings, unable to sleep due to the anxiety of her trip.

Elizabeth rushed down the stairs the following morning, her heart beating like a racing horse. She bounded into the kitchen where Eli sat drinking his coffee. "Eli, I can't find Sarah Rose. Her bed is made, but she's not in it. And the *zwillingbopplin* are gone too."

"She's gone," he said.

"What?" Elizabeth stared at her husband in disbelief. "What are you saying?"

"She's gone and Kathryn is in the living room with the *zwillingbopplin*. They're sleeping in their cradles, and she's fast asleep in my chair alongside them. You must've rushed right past them in your haste." He passed her a note. "I found this by the coffee machine. It will explain everything."

Elizabeth held up the note, and her eyes rounded with shock as she read it.

Dear Mamm and Dat,

I left early this morning to go to Ohio to meet with DeLana Maloney. Forgive me for not telling you ahead of time, but I knew you would try to talk me out of it. I have some questions I need answered about Peter's past before I can move on with my life. Nina is going to take me to the train station this morning, and I'll arrive in Ohio tomorrow. Kathryn will be here to

*help with the zwillingbopplin until I return. I'll get the first train
back and be home late Friday night. Please don't worry about
me. I'll be just fine.*

*I love you,
Sarah Rose*

Elizabeth's eyes filled with tears. "My *boppli* is traveling all
alone." She glared at Eli. "How can you sit there like everything
is okay?"

"Because it is, Elizabeth." He sipped the coffee and set down
the mug. "She's a grown woman, and she'll be just fine. Just
have faith."

She threw her hands up in frustration. "Why would I expect
you to understand? You're a man!" Muttering under her breath,
she headed for the peg by the door and slipped on her cloak.

"Elizabeth!" Eli bellowed after her.

She glowered at him.

"Sarah Rose is a capable young woman, just like the rest of
our girls. She's confident, like you." Moving toward her, he took
her hands in his as a smile softened his countenance. "Elizabeth, I married you because you're beautiful, intelligent, confident, and a smart business woman. I see you reflected in our
girls' eyes. That's why I trust that our Sarah Rose will come
back to us in one piece, and she'll have settled some things that
are preventing her from moving forward. Trust her."

Elizabeth sniffed. "I worry about her every night. I pray for
her for hours, begging the Lord to guide her and take care of her
and her *zwillingbopplin*."

"The Lord will provide. The Lord will bless her and her
zwillingbopplin. Trust Him." Leaning down, he brushed his lips
against hers. "*Ich liebe dich, mei fraa.*"

A sad smile curled her lips. "I love you, too, Eli." Closing her
eyes, she wrapped her arms around his neck and sent up a silent
prayer to the Lord to protect their youngest daughter.

21

Luke straddled a chair in the break room, popped open a can of Coke, and opened the latest copy of *The Budget*. While scanning the articles, he tried in vain to concentrate on the words, yet his mind wandered to Sarah—again.

Ever since he'd arrived back in Ohio, it seemed he couldn't make it through five minutes on any given day without falling into memories of her—her face, her smell, her gorgeous blue eyes, the sweet lilt of her laughter, the way the sun highlighted the wisps of hair cascading from under her prayer *kapp*, and the way she—

"So, how long are you going to mope, Troyer?" Mel's voice wrenched him back to the present.

Luke frowned as Mel sat down across from him and fished a snack-sized bag of pretzels from his pocket.

"Who's moping?" Luke asked.

Mel snorted with sarcasm. "Please. You've done nothing but work and mutter since you got back from Bird-in-Hand. Sally keeps accusing me of not inviting you for supper, but the truth is I can't get you to come."

"I don't mutter." Luke trained his eyes on the paper, still not comprehending the words in the articles, or even the headlines.

"*Ya*, you mutter. A lot." Mel munched the pretzels. "What happened in Bird-in-Hand? It's been two months, and you still haven't told me anything except that you found out about Peter."

Luke sighed and folded the paper. "I met his family. They were *wunderbaar*. They were warm. They made me feel as if I were a part of their family too."

Mel raised an eyebrow. "That doesn't sound so bad."

"It wasn't." Luke ran his thumb over the cool can. "I met Peter's *fraa*."

"Oh?"

"She's . . . incredible." Luke lifted the can and took a swig.

"Oh?" Mel's eyebrows rose.

"I can't believe Peter snatched her up." Luke studied the can to avoid Mel's probing stare. "She had *zwillingbopplin* on Christmas Day. A boy and a girl, and they're beautiful. Perfect."

His gaze collided with Mel's, and he found his friend grinning like the cat that ate the canary.

"You're in love with her." Mel pointed at him, wagging an accusing finger. "I haven't seen you light up about a *maedel* since you were with what's-her-name."

"My former girlfriend's name was Millie." Luke glowered. "Peter's *fraa* is Sarah Rose, but don't plan my wedding. Her year of mourning is up next month, and she's marrying someone else, a man I don't think she even loves."

"Why aren't you stopping her?"

"Because I'm here in Ohio, and she's in Bird-in-Hand, Pennsylvania."

Mel drew an imaginary map on the table with his fingers and pointed out the spots. "We're here. She's there." He connected the two areas by running his finger in a straight line between them. "You get on a train and go back to Bird-in-Hand." He shrugged. "Simple answer. Now tell me—What are ya doing here?"

Shaking his head, Luke sighed. "Are you listening to me? She's marrying someone else. That's why I'm here. I'll visit my niece and nephew, but it would be too painful to live there and watch her with another man. I can't do it."

"So, you're just going to give up, *ya?*" Mel clicked his tongue. "That's a shame."

Luke glared at him. "I didn't give up. She didn't give me a chance."

"I guess she wasn't worth fighting for." Mel crunched another pretzel.

Luke opened the paper again. "The night before I left, we argued. I said some pretty awful things to her. I wouldn't be surprised if she hated me now."

"So go tell her you didn't mean it."

Luke looked up. "It's not that simple."

Mel grimaced. "Why isn't it? Life is short. You lost your parents and your brother, so you know how short life is. Go to her before you wind up an aging single guy without a *fraa* or a family. Before you know it, you'll be a bitter old man."

"Like my pop, right?" Luke scowled at him.

His best friend shrugged. "I didn't say it. You did."

"I didn't expect you to understand." Luke pushed back his chair and stood. "You have Sally. You don't remember what it's like to court. You never knew what it was like to live alone. I'm almost thirty, so it's not like I can go to a singing and find a group of girls to pick from. It's not easy when you're older."

"You have to decide how important she is to you. If you can just walk away from her like you never met her, then it's not meant to be." Mel lifted another pretzel to his lips. "End of story."

"Right. End of story." Luke tossed the empty can into the trash. "I better get back to work." He headed for the door.

Sauntering to his workbench, he wondered what Sarah was doing and if she'd thought of him since he left. Did she miss him as much as he missed her?

Sarah fingered the ties of her prayer *kapp* and glanced around the diner. The large dining area was full, evidence of the lunchtime rush. Outside the wide front windows, large, sloppy raindrops danced through the air on their way down from heaven.

The aroma of hamburgers and fries filled Sarah's nose, and the grumblings of conversations swirled around her. Dishes and utensils clanged, and waitresses weaved through the sea of tables taking and delivering orders.

Glancing through the menu again, Sarah's stomach tightened. She wondered if she'd made a mistake traveling this far just to ask DeLana a few questions. Perhaps it would've been more intelligent and economical to have interviewed her over the phone.

Sarah didn't know DeLana, and she may have been naïve to trust a stranger. She also wished she'd remembered to ask DeLana what she looked like. Or maybe she should've asked Luke for a description of the woman she was going to meet.

Luke.

She bit her lip. Ever since the taxi had pulled into town, she'd wondered where he was. Where was his shop located? Had he thought of Sarah since he'd left Bird-in-Hand?

Scanning the dining area, Sarah's eyes found an Amish family seated in a corner. The young couple looked to be in their late twenties. A toddler sat at the table eating a dinner roll while the parents chatted and enjoyed their lunch. The woman's belly was round.

Sarah sighed. If Peter were still alive, they might've resembled that family now. Perhaps they would've been blessed with a large family in the making too.

Sarah tried to imagine sitting at a restaurant table with another Amish man, maybe a friend from her community such as Norman, but the image didn't come into focus. Instead, she saw herself sitting with Luke while her *zwillingbopplin* smiled from their highchairs ...

Why did her musings always lead her back to Luke? Was God trying to tell her something?

She frowned at her silly thought.

How ridiculous ... Luke hates me.

"Sarah?" A voice beside her asked. "Sarah Troyer?"

Turning, Sarah found a tall, thin woman with a long dark ponytail and brown eyes smiling down at her. "DeLana?" She stood from the seat.

DeLana gave her hand a firm shake. "It's so nice to meet you." She shrugged out of her heavy gray parka, dotted with fresh raindrops, and hung it on the back of the chair across from Sarah.

"I'm sorry I'm a few minutes late. This rain has everyone driving like crazy. There were a few fender benders near my house. You'd think we never get rain here." She set a small tote bag on the floor next to her chair and then sat down. "So, how was your trip?"

"*Gut.*" Sarah nodded, trying to imagine Peter with DeLana. The woman sitting across from her was very attractive. She wore a tinge of makeup to accentuate her bright eyes and rosy lips.

Sarah couldn't help but wonder if Peter had yearned to be English. How much was there that she'd never learned about her husband? Regret nipped at her soul.

A waitress appeared and took their drink order.

When the girl disappeared, DeLana gave Sarah a sad smile. "I'm so sorry for your loss. I know Peter loved you very much. He spoke very highly of you in his letters."

Sarah swallowed the lump forming in her throat. "Thank you."

"May I ask what happened? Where was the fire?"

Praying for strength, Sarah explained the events that had taken place the day of the fire.

When she finished, DeLana shook her head. "I'm so sorry.

I had no idea. I was surprised when the letters and checks stopped. He'd been so faithful sending them over the past several years. I could count on receiving a short letter with a check on or about the fifteenth, no matter what."

"How long had he been sending them?" Sarah fiddled with a napkin on the table.

DeLana's eyes took on a faraway look as she tried to remember. "I got the first letter and check when he got his first steady job in Lancaster County. Cody was about two, so I guess that was seven years ago. I was really surprised. He sent this short note saying he wanted to help provide for his son. I was pleasantly surprised."

Sarah nodded, letting the words soak in.

"I'm sorry he never told you." DeLana hesitated, then reached over and took Sarah's hand. "He never wanted to hurt you. That's why he kept it a secret. I think he was afraid you'd leave him if you knew he'd fathered a child outside of wedlock."

"That never would've happened," Sarah whispered, her voice ragged. "We don't believe in divorce."

Pulling her hand back, DeLana nodded. "True, but I think he was afraid for your happiness. He didn't want to lose you emotionally. It really bothered him that you didn't know — especially since you were expecting a child. In his last letter, he told me he was contemplating telling you the truth. He just didn't know how." She touched Sarah's hand again. "I want you to know he felt terrible not telling you the truth. Peter loved you more than life itself."

Sarah blinked back tears, hoping she wouldn't dissolve into sobs in front of DeLana and the whole restaurant.

She was relieved when the waitress arrived with their drinks and took their lunch order. Since she hadn't taken the time to read the menu, Sarah chose what DeLana ordered, hoping the soup-and-sandwich special would warm her freezing heart.

Sarah took a long drink of iced tea and then cleared her throat. "Would you tell me about how you met Peter?"

DeLana explained the story, similar to how Luke had told it. DeLana had worked for her father at a large wood wholesaler, and she'd met Peter when he accompanied his English driver on a supply run one hot summer day.

According to DeLana, it was love at first sight. Peter had invented excuses to handle the supply runs once a week during the next month, and he eventually worked up the courage to ask DeLana to meet him after work one day. That first meeting led to frequent secret dates and then a secret courtship that ended when their parents discovered the relationship.

"According to Luke, your parents didn't want you to see someone who was Amish, and Peter's *dat* didn't want him to see an English girl." Sarah ran her fingers down the cool glass of tea.

"That's right." DeLana smiled. "I'm glad you got to meet Luke. I knew Peter had cut off his family when he moved to Pennsylvania. It's good you connected."

Sarah nodded. "I had no idea Peter had any family until Luke showed up in October."

"Interesting." DeLana tapped her glass, deep in thought.

The waitress dropped off their food, and Sarah took a bite of the ham sandwich despite her dissolving appetite.

"I heard their father died last year, and I felt bad," DeLana said. "Despite all that happened, I think he was an okay guy. He was just really controlling and overbearing." She grinned, lifting her sandwich. "He was just like my dad."

"When did you find out you were expecting your son?" Sarah asked.

"After we broke up. I managed to meet him in secret one night," she began, "and I told him the news. He begged me to run off and marry him, but I knew it would lead to disaster. We had no money and nowhere to go. My parents had convinced me to go to college and give the baby up for adoption."

Between bites of her sandwich, DeLana explained how furious her parents were when they found out she was going to have

Peter's baby. They forbade her from leaving the house except to go to school. Peter's father did the same and also took away money Peter had saved up to pay for his first home.

"And that was the night he had the fight with his father and ran off?" Sarah asked.

"No." DeLana shook her head while wiping her mouth with a napkin. "That was later on. I decided to keep the baby, against my parents' wishes, and I met Alex soon after."

"Alex?" Sarah asked.

"My husband. We met while I was pregnant. I had gone out shopping with a friend one day, and he was at the mall. I was able to hide my stomach with a large shirt. When I told him I was pregnant, I figured he wouldn't have anything to do with me, but he saw past that." DeLana smirked. "I upset my parents when I told them I was going to scratch their college idea, keep Cody, and get married. But they got over it. Alex is a good guy and a great father. He wanted to marry me and raise Cody as his own. Since I had lost Peter, I felt lucky to meet someone who loved me despite my past."

Sarah nodded, wondering how all of this had affected Peter. "So you ran into Peter after Cody was born."

"That's right. I was at the market one day with Cody, and Peter was there with Luke. He saw me and Cody, saw my wedding ring, and went nuts. That night he had it out with his dad and then left town." DeLana frowned. "I hate that I hurt him, but we just weren't meant to be. He tracked me down through the phone book in the library and sent a letter with a check about a year later. We've appreciated the money. Alex owns his own garage, and some months are rough. It seems like folks want their cars fixed in spurts. The child-support checks helped pay for extras, like Cody's soccer fees and summer camp—things like that."

"Had you kept in touch with Luke?" Sarah asked, her breath held in anticipation of the answer.

DeLana shook her head while chewing. "Not since the night Peter ran off. My dad had run into him a few times, but I never saw him."

Sarah stared down at her soup, taking in all that DeLana had said. The stories overwhelmed and confused her. Peter had truly loved DeLana and wanted to provide for his child. Why hadn't he ever told Sarah the truth? She would've found a way to understand it all. He had a right to love his child.

Was the problem that his heart had still belonged to Cody and DeLana even when he was with Sarah? The thought caused her heart to sink.

"How are the twins?" DeLana asked, snapping Sarah back to the present.

Glancing up, Sarah found DeLana smiling. "*Wunderbaar.*"

"Luke told me that they were just exquisite. He was very excited about them. Congratulations."

"Thank you." Sarah was overwhelmed Luke had been excited enough about her children to mention them to DeLana. Perhaps he truly cared—although it meant he cared for the children, not for Sarah.

"That's so cool you have a boy and a girl," DeLana said. "I want to have another one, but the time never seems right. My mom says we should just go for it, but I don't know. Kids take so much time and money."

"They're a gift from God," Sarah said, lifting a spoonful of soup.

"Yeah. They are." DeLana pulled an envelope from the bag below her chair. She set it down in front of Sarah. "I know the Amish don't believe in photographs because of the whole 'do not make a graven image of yourself' verse from the Bible, but I thought you might like these. They're photos of Peter and also some of Cody."

Sarah's mouth gaped. "Photos of Peter?"

"Yeah." DeLana opened the envelope and out slid a stack

of photographs. "They were taken while we were dating." She handed Sarah the pile. "I found them when I was looking through some old albums last night. I took a little trip down memory lane."

Sarah gasped as she stared at a photograph of Peter with his arm around DeLana while they stood in front of a large oak tree. His smile was wide, almost electric, and he was clad in jeans and a dark T-shirt. His hat was also missing. DeLana's smile was equally bright. Their love was obvious in their eyes.

Sarah glanced up, meeting DeLana's gaze. "Peter dressed English?"

DeLana smiled sheepishly. "We did a lot of things our parents would never have approved of."

Sarah flipped through a half dozen photos of Peter, some with him hugging DeLana, others with them sitting on a pier near a lake, and a few of him alone, just smiling while posing on stairs or in a hay loft.

She then sifted through photos of Cody, stopping when she came to one at the bottom of the pile. She studied his eyes, his nose, his mouth. The child resembled Peter, but he also looked like Luke.

She couldn't get Luke out of her mind's eye. She again wondered if she should visit him. Would he be happy to see her or would he tell her to go home?

"Is Luke's shop far from here?" Sarah asked, placing the photos on the table.

DeLana shook her head and finished chewing. "No. It's just on the other side of town." She sipped her iced tea. "I was surprised he never married that girl he was dating. I can't remember her name now. Was it Maddie? Maggie?" She snapped her fingers. "Millie! That's it. I wonder why they didn't get hitched."

Sarah stared at her half-eaten sandwich. "He took care of his ill father, and his girlfriend broke up with him. She didn't want to have to nurse him too." She explained how Luke and Peter's father had had a stroke after Peter left and died eight years later. "It's a shame he never married," Sarah whispered, her voice thick. "He's a *gut* man. He'd be a *gut* husband and father."

"I bet it was hard for him to find out about his brother by showing up at the shop where he died." Frowning with sympathy, DeLana shook her head. "I can't imagine how that felt."

"He was stunned. He didn't know about me, and I didn't know about him. It must've been hard on him to face losing his brother when he moved away, losing his *dat* to the illness, and losing Peter all over again when he found out he had died." Sarah stared down at the napkin she had folded by her plate. "Luke deserved better than that. He's such a kind, sweet, gentle man. He deserves a loving family. He has so much to give. He shouldn't be alone."

Glancing up, she found DeLana studying her with a wide grin and round, laughing eyes.

Sarah's face warmed. Could DeLana sense her feelings for Luke?

"How long did Luke visit?" DeLana asked, still smiling.

"Four months."

DeLana leaned forward on the table as if Sarah were going to share a juicy secret. "You guys got pretty close, huh?"

"Well, no. We visited and then he had to go home to get back to work."

"Have you two kept in touch?" DeLana asked.

"I haven't heard from him, and I haven't contacted him either."

DeLana's eyebrows rose in question. "How come? It sounds like you became close friends."

Sarah thought her cheeks might catch on fire as she searched for the answer to explain why Luke probably wouldn't contact her. DeLana was more outspoken than the English customers she'd encountered in the bakery.

"I don't think he would—" Sarah began.

The waitress appeared and cleared their dishes. "Did either of you save room for dessert?"

Sarah resisted the urge to kiss the waitress for interrupting her stammering. She glanced at DeLana, who shrugged. "Feel like some awesome chocolate cake?" she offered.

"Why not?" Sarah rubbed her flat middle. "It's not like I have to watch my figure. I lost quite a bit of weight after having those twins."

They both laughed, and Sarah realized she felt strangely at ease with this English woman from her husband's secret past. They drank coffee and enjoyed large slabs of rich, moist chocolate cake while discussing their lives. DeLana bragged about how well Cody was doing in school while Sarah told her about the twins, the bakery, and her father's carpentry shop.

An hour later, the coffee and cake were gone, and DeLana paid the check, refusing to take any of Sarah's money. They walked outside together. The rain had slowed a bit, and small drops tickled Sarah's nose and soaked her cloak as they maneuvered through the parking lot.

"I have an hour before Cody gets out of school," DeLana said, hitting the Unlock button on the keyless remote for her SUV. "Would you like a quick tour before I take you to the train station?"

Sarah shook her head. "Thank you, but I better get back and buy my ticket." She opened the door and climbed in. "My family is expecting me home tomorrow night."

"You sure?" DeLana folded herself in the driver's seat. "I can take you by Luke's shop."

"No, thank you." Sarah buckled her belt.

DeLana turned over the ignition. "We have time. I could even take you by his house so you can see where he and Peter grew up. Then we can drop by his work. Don't you want to see him? You came all this way, Sarah."

"No, thank you. I'd better get to the station and buy my

ticket." Sarah kept her eyes focused on the passenger window. "The rain is beautiful, yes? I always loved running through puddles when I was a girl. My brothers, and sisters, and I would run through the mud in the back pasture, and—"

"Sarah." DeLana touched her arm. "You don't have to hide it from me. I know you want to see Luke."

Sarah met her gaze, hoping her voice wouldn't defy her. "I really don't want to. I need to get home to my babies."

DeLana nodded. "Fine. Suit yourself." She chatted about the scenery as she steered through the town.

When a sign for "Amish Custom Cabinets" came into view, Sarah's heart pounded. She glanced at DeLana, who kept droning on about the weather and her hopes for a warm spring as she steered into the parking lot of the cabinet shop.

"This is where Luke works," DeLana said, pulling the SUV into a spot in front of the building. "This is your last chance to go see him."

Sarah gaped at her, wide eyed. Who did this woman think she was? Sarah had said no more than once.

DeLana folded her arms and grinned. "You don't have to lie to me, Sarah. I can see it in your eyes."

"You can see what?"

"Love."

"Love?" Sarah shook her head. "I don't understand what you mean."

"Sarah, I hear regret in your voice when you talk about Luke."

Sarah gasped. "You do?"

"Yes, you do," DeLana said. "Luke makes you happy, and you deserve happiness. I know it's none of my business, but you've been through so much. I'd hate to see you lose someone who can make you happy."

Sarah stared at the front door of the shop and took a deep breath. She absently wondered if DeLana could read her mind.

"Alex makes me happy," DeLana whispered, "but a tiny part of me regretted not running off with Peter that night he begged me to. We had a terrible fight, and we both said some horrible things and threw around nasty accusations. We didn't speak again until that time I saw him at the market. I saw remorse and hurt in his eyes, but it was too late to try to rebuild what he and I once had. I don't want you to live with that kind of sorrow, Sarah. You've lost Peter too. You know how short and precious life is."

"I can't face Luke," Sarah said, her voice trembling. "I said some terrible things to him."

"Sure you can face him. Just apologize and tell him you love him."

"You don't understand. I can't take back the hurt I caused him. I saw it in his eyes." Sarah stared straight ahead at the shop.

"He'll forgive you. They were only words." DeLana touched her hand. "Think about your life."

Sarah faced DeLana, tears filling her eyes. "We had an argument the night before he left Bird-in-Hand. He said some horrible things to me too, and I deserved them all." She sniffed and swiped a hand across her wet cheeks. "I was awful to him. I lost any chance with him."

DeLana gave her a sad smile. "If he loves you, he'll forgive you, and you can work it out. Don't make a mistake you'll regret the rest of your life, Sarah. You deserve some happiness."

Sarah turned back to the shop and stared at the sign above the door. "I can't see him. Please just take me to the train station."

"Suit yourself." DeLana put the truck in gear, and they drove to the train station in silence. The rain increased, and drops pelted the windshield, sounding like a chorus of hammers banging in unison.

When the windshield fogged, DeLana punched a series of

buttons on the dashboard, sending air hissing through the vents to fill the thick silence between them.

The train station came into view, and DeLana maneuvered the SUV through the lot, parking one row from the entrance.

Sarah hefted her small tote onto her lap and fished Peter's shirts from the bottom of the bag. "I wanted to give these to you for Cody. They're not much, but they were Peter's. If you ever tell Cody about his biological father, then please give these to him as a memento."

DeLana's face lit up as if Sarah had just handed her a treasure. "Thank you. They're beautiful." Her lips turned up. "Actually, I do want to tell Cody about Peter soon. I wanted to ask you if we could keep in touch. You have Cody's only siblings, and I'd love for them to meet and foster a friendship."

Sarah smiled. "That would be *wunderbaar gut*. After all, they're family."

DeLana pulled a card from her purse, snatched a pen from the console, and jotted some numbers on the back. "Here's my number at work. I do the books for Alex's shop. You can reach me during the day if you'd like. Let me know how you and the twins are. We can meet up sometime in the summer if you'd like. I'd be happy to come see you next time."

"I'd like that. Thank you for everything." Leaning over, she gave DeLana a quick hug.

"Thank you too." Pulling back, DeLana gave her a stern look. "Don't give up on Luke. He's a good guy." She tapped her own chest. "Listen to your heart."

Sarah nodded even though she disagreed. Her heart told her that she'd lost him forever.

"Promise me, Sarah." DeLana wagged a finger at her.

"I promise. Good-bye." Sarah wrenched the door open.

"Call me!" DeLana said.

Rushing through the rain, Sarah entered the train station and purchased a ticket to go home, leaving behind Peter's past and Luke too.

Her heart swelled with a mixture of regret and hope as she headed toward her departure gate. She contemplated Cody, her twins, and their future relationship. She knew one thing for certain—Peter would live on through his three children.

22

The following evening Sarah thanked Nina, hoisted her bag on her shoulder, and trekked up the gravel driveway toward the porch stairs.

During the long trip home, she'd analyzed all that DeLana had told her and stared at the photographs. Although the man in the photos resembled her late husband, he felt like a stranger. She'd never imagined Peter had had a love affair with an English woman and considered running away with her. The Peter Troyer she'd married wasn't who he'd seemed to be, and she still wasn't sure how to open her heart to accept the past.

And yet, she'd felt a new sense of hope when she'd heard DeLana explain Peter had planned to tell Sarah the truth. According to her, Peter had lived with worry and regret for not being truthful with Sarah from the beginning, and he planned to make things right before the twins were born. DeLana's words had mirrored Timothy's, which only proved they were true.

Sarah smiled at that realization. Peter truly had loved her, and he'd planned to make things right.

Just knowing that settled her heart; she felt as though a weight had been lifted from her shoulders. Perhaps her anger and betrayal toward Peter could be put to rest.

Was this the faith her mother had suggested Sarah find?

With prayer, Sarah had found the answers to the riddle of Peter's past—it was a past he regretted and had wanted to share with Sarah, his true love.

Sarah hurried up the porch steps. She longed to see the twins and had missed them every moment she'd been away.

As she approached the back door, she stopped when she heard a chorus of voices sounding from within the kitchen. She had only expected to come home to her parents, Kathryn, and the children, yet it sounded like the entire Kauffman clan awaited her arrival.

Taking a deep breath, she pushed the door open, and a sea of eyes focused on her. Scanning the group, she spotted her parents, Timothy, her sisters, her brothers-in-law, nieces, nephews, Norman, and his children. Then everyone began speaking at once—yelling questions, wanting details of her visit, asking if she'd seen Luke.

Sarah held her hand up. "Please. Everyone."

A hush hovered over the crowd.

"I'm home. I'm safe. I had a nice trip." She gestured toward the stairs. "Now, if you don't mind, I'd like to see my *zwillingbopplin*. I've missed them. *Gut nacht*." Sarah ambled toward the stairs.

"Sarah Rose!" *Mamm* scurried after her. "You can't go to bed without telling me about your trip."

"I promise I'll tell you tomorrow," Sarah said, squeezing her hand. "I'm just wiped out. It was a long and bumpy ride home, and I couldn't sleep." She started up the stairs, ignoring voices calling her name.

Reaching her room, Sarah pulled off her cloak, tossed it onto the end of the bed, and let her bag fall to the floor with a *thwap*. She then hurried next door to the nursery and leaned down over her sleeping babies. She rubbed their backs and whispered her love for them before returning to her room.

Boots scraping in the hallway announced an approaching

man. Sarah hoped it wasn't one of her brothers coming to lecture her about leaving without warning and worrying *Mamm*. Exhaustion filled her.

Glancing toward the hallway, her eyes widened when Norman appeared to stand frowning in her doorway. "Norman," she whispered.

"Hello, Sarah. I know it isn't appropriate for me to be up here alone, but I told your *mamm* I needed to talk to you. I'll keep our conversation short." He leaned against the door frame, folding his arms across his wide chest. "You gave your family and me a real scare running off like that."

"I didn't run off." She sat up straight and gestured toward a chair. "Have a seat."

"*Danki.*" His expression softened. Stepping into the room, he lowered himself into the chair next to her. "Your *mamm* was a bundle of nerves. Timothy came and told me you'd gone to Ohio, and I was really surprised."

"I know it was wrong not to tell her I was going, but I didn't want her to talk me out of it." Sarah fingered the hem of her apron. "It was something I had to do. I wanted to do it alone without any suggestions or advice."

"I care about you. Had I known you were going, I would've offered to accompany you to Ohio. I could've helped you through this ordeal."

"*Danki,*" she said. "I appreciate the offer, but this was something I had to do on my own. Kathryn offered, and I told her I preferred she help with the *kinner* instead of going with me."

Leaning forward, his warm hands covered hers. "I'm not sure you know how much you mean to me."

Sarah studied the fire in his dark eyes, and her heart fluttered with panic, wondering what he was going to say.

"I think of you all the time, Sarah Rose," he said. "You're very important to me. I hope you can learn to trust me with your worries and your burdens in your heart. We're going to be lifelong partners."

"What did you say?" she asked, sitting up straight. "Lifelong partners?"

"*Ya.*" His eyebrows rose in question. "I want to marry you, Sarah Rose. Your year of mourning will be over next month, and I hope I can court you. We can be married in the spring, or we can wait until fall and do a traditional wedding."

"Wait a minute." Sarah popped up from the edge of the bed and stared at him. "What are you saying?"

He shook his head with confusion and stood before her. "I love you. I've always loved you. I thought you knew that."

"No." She shook her head as guilt rained down on her. How could she have missed his feelings? "I thought we were friends. Good friends."

"We are." He smiled. "And I love you. I want you to be my *fraa*. We both have *kinner*, and we can provide a good, strong, Christian home for them together." Again he took her hands in his.

She shook her head, and the warmth of his eyes burned her soul. He was such a good man. Marrying him was tempting. But Sarah didn't love him.

She knew in her heart she loved Luke.

Norman deserved someone who loved him with her whole heart; not someone like Sarah who couldn't fathom sharing his marriage bed.

"I never meant to hurt you or lead you on," she whispered, her voice quavering with guilt. "I want to be your friend, Norman, but I can't marry you."

His smile faded. "Oh. I had assumed our friendship was leading to a wedding date. I thought, from the long talks we've had, you loved me. Those conversations have meant so much to me."

"They've meant the world to me, too, but I'm not ready to get married."

He shrugged. "I can wait."

She smiled. "No, Norman, don't wait for me. I want to

be your friend, but that's all I want. Just your *wunderbaar* friendship."

He paused. Then he opened his mouth to speak and then paused again, his expression falling to a deep frown.

"I see." He stepped toward the door. "If you ever need someone to talk to, please let me know. I'm here whenever you need me."

"*Danki.*" She smiled.

"*Gut nacht.*" He opened the door. "I'm glad you're home safe."

She swallowed her guilt. "*Gut nacht. Danki* for checking on me."

He exited the room, gingerly closing the door behind him. Sarah collapsed on the bed. She cried herself to sleep, praying that she could find a way to forget her love for Luke and let go of her guilt for not loving Norman Zook, the one who loved her in return.

Sarah lounged on her bed the following afternoon and skimmed her Bible while the twins slept.

During breakfast this morning, Sarah had filled her parents in on her trip to Ohio, telling them the highlights of her conversation with DeLana. They listened with wide eyes when she explained how Peter had met and courted DeLana and detailed the events that led to their breakup.

Sarah shared the photographs, and her parents gasped at the shots showing DeLana frolicking with Peter clad in English clothing. She did not share the conversations about Luke, but she did explain she and DeLana wanted to keep in touch for the sake of the children since they were family.

Mamm and *Dat* were supportive, and elated to hear she had forgiven Peter. Sarah also noticed that her father seemed more attentive than usual. There was something in his eyes telling her he understood more than she knew.

As she lay in bed reading from her Bible, she wondered exactly what *Dat* was trying to tell her with his wordless expressions.

Sarah had considered telling *Mamm* and *Dat* about Norman's proposal, but she couldn't form the words. The guilt over turning him down still haunted her, and she couldn't admit to them she'd told him no. Logically, she and Norman would make the perfect couple with their blended family.

However, Sarah knew her heart belonged to Luke, a man who hated her after the way she'd treated him.

Sarah was reading from the book of John and trying to ban Norman and Luke from her thoughts when a knock sounded on her door.

"Come in," she called.

The door squeaked open, and Kathryn stuck her head in. "Hi. Can I come in?"

"*Ya*." Sarah sat up and patted the edge of the bed next to her. "Please."

"How are you?" Kathryn closed the door, crossed the room, and lowered herself onto the edge of the bed.

"*Gut*. Tired. How are you?" Sarah closed the Bible and placed it on the end table.

"*Gut*." Kathryn touched Sarah's hand. "I'm worried about you. Tell me how things went."

Sarah opened her heart and shared everything with Kathryn. With her eyes brimming with tears, she pulled out the photographs and explained all the stories about Peter's past. She even shared the conversation she and DeLana had had while sitting outside the cabinet shop. She ended with telling Kathryn that she and DeLana would keep in touch so that the children could meet someday.

Kathryn wiped her eyes and shook her head. "DeLana sounds like a *gut* person."

"She is." Sarah cleared her throat. "I can see why Peter loved her."

"You love Luke, don't you?" Kathryn took Sarah's hands in hers.

"*Ya*," Sarah whispered, admitting it aloud for the first time. "I do. I can't stop thinking about him. I miss him so much that my heart aches."

Kathryn gave a sad smile. "You need to call him and tell him."

"No." Sarah shook her head. "I never could. It's not right. We don't belong together."

"Why not?"

"Because he only wants to be with me for the sake of the *zwillingbopplin*. He doesn't want to be with me because of his feelings for me."

Kathryn raised an eyebrow in disbelief. "How do you know that?"

"He feels a responsibility to take care of his brother's *kinner*. That's the only reason he wanted to be here."

"That's ridiculous." Kathryn waved off the thought. "When I saw him with you, he was attentive to you. I don't believe for a second he would only want to be with the *zwillingbopplin*."

Sarah shook her head. "We also argued the night before he left, and he said some nasty things. I'm convinced he hates me."

Kathryn scoffed. "Please. I don't believe that man could ever hate you, Sarah Rose."

Sarah told Kathryn the details of the argument.

"I think he said those things out of frustration." Kathryn squeezed Sarah's hands. "He was hurt and angry, but I don't think he hates you."

"You didn't see his eyes, Kathryn." More tears spilled down her cheeks. "I've never seen him that angry."

"I've made David that angry before, and he still loves me."

Her sister frowned. "You should call Luke and give him another chance."

"There's more," Sarah said. "Last night Norman came up to see me after I got back. He asked me to marry him."

"What!" Kathryn gasped. "You're kidding!"

"Shh," Sarah warned her. "If you wake the *kinner* our visiting will be over."

"Sorry." Her sister giggled. "I'm stunned. I had no idea he was interested in you."

"I didn't know either," Sarah said, crossing her legs under herself. "I thought we were just friends."

"What did you say when he asked?"

"I told him no. I said I cherish his friendship, but I could never be his wife. I think I broke his heart." Sarah sighed. "I wonder if I made a mistake. Luke doesn't love me, and I may spend my life alone. Maybe it makes sense for me to marry Norman since we both lost our spouses and have *kinner* who need two parents. It's logical, really. We're *gut* friends already. Maybe I could learn to love him."

"*Ack*, don't say that." Kathryn squeezed her hands. "You did the right thing. You shouldn't marry the wrong person. Marriage is for life, and you should be happy, Sarah Rose. You've lost Peter. Don't marry for the sake of having a husband. Marry for love."

"But Norman is so *gut* and kind. He's a *wunderbaar dat*. He'll love me and my *zwillingbopplin* for life."

"But do you love him?"

Sarah shook her head.

"There's your answer." Kathryn nodded. "You made the right choice by telling him no. You need to listen to your heart and not make a mistake you'll regret the rest of your life. He'll still be your friend. He's a loyal man."

"But I don't think God's plan is for me to marry Luke."

"How do you know that?" Kathryn's smile was smug. "What is your heart saying?"

"I'm not sure." Sarah brushed away a tear. "I'm so mixed up. All I know is that I can't stop thinking about Luke, and it feels like a lost cause, a silly fantasy."

"Listen to your heart," Kathryn said again. "Close your eyes, open your heart, and pray for hope. Then listen to what God tells you. You'll get your answer, Sarah Rose. I promise the Lord will guide you to the right path."

Sarah pulled Kathryn into a hug. "I thank God for my wonderful family, especially you."

23

Elizabeth rolled the finished whoopie pies in individual pieces of plastic wrap. She hummed her favorite hymn to herself while the swirl of Pennsylvania *Dietsch* from her daughters filled the bakery kitchen around her. She smiled to herself. This bakery had been her dream when she was a young wife. Sharing it with her daughters, granddaughters, and daughter-in-law was more than a dream come true—it was a gift from the Lord.

"How's Sarah?" Kathryn asked. She hoisted herself up onto a stool beside Elizabeth.

"She seemed fine when I left this morning. Nancy and Katie were helping her with the *zwillingbopplin*." Elizabeth stacked the wrapped whoopie pies in a basket in preparation for taking them out front to the counter. She then faced her daughter and wiped her hands on a rag. "I'm worried about her. I think something is bothering her. She's been different ever since she got back from Ohio last month." She frowned. "I think that English girl said or did something to her. I'm not happy."

Kathryn bit her bottom lip and averted her eyes.

"What is it, Kathryn?" Elizabeth touched her shoulder. "You know something you're not telling me."

Her oldest daughter frowned. "I'm sorry, but I can't betray her confidence. I couldn't bear it if she didn't trust me."

"Please, Kathryn." Elizabeth pleaded with her eyes. "Of course I have to know what's wrong with my *dochder*."

Kathryn glanced around the kitchen.

"No one can hear you," Elizabeth said. "They're all baking and chatting. They have no idea what we're discussing over here."

"Sarah's miserable." Kathryn held Elizabeth's hand as if to convince her. "Norman proposed to her, but she doesn't love him. She feels horrible about telling him no, but it doesn't feel right."

Elizabeth gasped. "Norman proposed?"

"You can't tell anyone, *Mamm*." Kathryn's eyes were serious.

"When did he ask?"

"The night she got home from Ohio. She was caught off guard."

Elizabeth shook her head. "I had no idea. I wish she'd told me."

"She feels horrible about it because he said he loved her, but she doesn't love him." Kathryn shook her head, frowning. "She feels like she broke his heart because it may seem logical for them to marry. She said he's a *gut* friend."

"Why does she feel bad if she doesn't love him? No one is forcing her to get married. She can stay with your *dat* and me for as long as she wants."

Kathryn gave a knowing smile. "That's not it. She loves someone else."

"What did you say?" Elizabeth raised an eyebrow. "Who does she love?"

Kathryn nodded. "She loves Luke."

Elizabeth tilted her head in surprise. "Are you sure?"

Kathryn nodded again. "She's miserable over it. She said she can't stop thinking about him, and she feels horrible about the argument they had the night before he left."

Cupping a hand to her mouth, Elizabeth lowered herself

onto a stool. "I feel wretched for not knowing this about my own *dochder*. How could I not know she's been suffering?"

"It's not your fault, *Mamm*." Kathryn placed a hand on her shoulder. "I'm just telling you so you can help her. She listens to you and looks up to you. I'm worried she's going to sink into a deep black hole in her heart. She's finally accepted Peter's past, which is *wunderbaar* and healthy for her. She can move on with her life now, but she's stuck because she thinks Luke hates her."

Elizabeth shook her head. "I hope I can help her."

"Just listen to her." Kathryn put her hand on Elizabeth's arm. "Please listen and really hear what she has to say."

Elizabeth nodded. She would do anything to help her youngest daughter find happiness again.

Later that evening, Elizabeth found Sarah propped up in bed reading her Bible. Glancing up, Sarah smiled, and Elizabeth's heart warmed with hope. Maybe Kathryn was wrong, and Sarah was okay.

"Hi, *Mamm*." Sarah set her Bible down. "How are things at the bakery?"

"*Gut*." Elizabeth lowered herself onto the edge of the bed, which creaked under her weight. "The question is how are you?" She patted Sarah's hand.

Sarah shrugged. "All right. Just tired." She covered her mouth and yawned. Nodding in the direction of the nursery, she grinned. "They've been active today. They're wearing me, Nancy, and Katie out. I'm thankful they're sleeping now so I can spend some time with the Scriptures."

"I'm glad you had a *gut* day. The girls seem to like coming here to help you."

"We have a *gut* time together." Sarah glanced toward the window with a faraway expression. She looked as if she were a million miles away.

"What's on your mind, Sarah Rose?" Elizabeth asked. "You seem to be preoccupied."

Blinking, her youngest daughter met her gaze. "How do you know what God wants for you? How do you know if you're on the right path?"

Elizabeth squeezed her hand. "You follow your heart and listen to what it tells you. Sarah Rose, what's really bothering you? You've been different since you came home from Ohio."

Sarah hesitated.

"Is something wrong?" Elizabeth searched her eyes, wondering if Kathryn's assessment was correct. "Is there something you're not telling me?"

Sarah took a deep breath and then shook her head.

Elizabeth studied her daughter's eyes. Was she lying? Did she really love Luke?

"Sarah Rose," Elizabeth said, holding her hands. "You can talk to me. I'm here to listen. Kathryn told me today she's worried about you too."

Sarah's eyes flashed with something resembling fear and worry at the mention of Kathryn's name.

"If something is worrying you, you can tell me," Elizabeth said. "If you don't want to talk about it with me, then you can always open your heart to God. You know what I always say."

"Yes, *Mamm*." Sarah's voice croaked with emotion. "You always tell us your favorite verse, 'Be joyful in hope, patient in affliction, faithful in prayer.'"

"That's right." Elizabeth smiled. "You can always pray about it."

Sarah wiped her eyes. "*Danki*. I'll do that."

Elizabeth nodded, hoping Sarah would open up to her. However, Sarah settled against the pillows and didn't speak. Elizabeth patted her daughter's hands and stood. "You call me if you need anything."

"*Danki, Mamm*." Sarah picked up her Bible from the end table and opened it.

Elizabeth climbed into bed later that evening and watched Eli change into his nightclothes. She'd spent all evening worrying about Sarah and contemplating Kathryn's words. She wondered if Kathryn had been telling the truth. If so, then why hadn't Sarah confessed her feelings for Luke?

"Sarah Rose was quiet during devotions," Eli said, crawling into bed next to her.

She wondered if he'd read her mind. "I'm worried about her," Elizabeth blurted before she could stop the words.

"She seems unhappy," he said. "I've noticed it." Angling himself onto his side, he fluffed the pillow before lying down facing the wall.

"Kathryn has a theory." Elizabeth snuggled under the quilt and rubbed his back.

"Oh?"

"She insists Sarah Rose is in love with Luke. Do you think that's possible?"

Moving onto his back, he faced her and nodded. "I watched a beautiful friendship bloom between her and Luke, and I tried to encourage him to stay."

"What?" She gasped. "He was courting Naomi King, but you encouraged him to pursue Sarah Rose?"

"No, no, no." He blew out a sigh. "Elizabeth, I never said that." He reached over and patted her hands.

"First of all," he began, "Naomi King was trying desperately to court *him*, and he was just being nice. At first I thought there might be a romance. But I could see the frustration in his eyes every time Naomi showed up—uninvited, mind you—for lunch. And yes, when he came to me and said he wanted to go home, I encouraged him to stay. I told him I could see the love in his eyes for Sarah Rose. He didn't confirm my theory, but he also didn't deny it. He said Sarah Rose had made her choice by harboring her anger for not telling her he was Peter's brother when he first came, and he felt he had to leave because she didn't love him in return."

"Do you think they belong together?" she asked.

"If that's what God has planned for them, *ya*."

"Norman asked Sarah to marry him."

"He did?" In the dark Eli sounded surprised.

"She turned him down. Kathryn thinks it's because Sarah loves Luke."

"That could be," Eli said.

"I just want Sarah to be happy," Elizabeth whispered. "I want to see her smile again. It seems like she hasn't smiled since Luke left."

Eli's breathing became deep and rhythmic, and she knew he'd fallen asleep. It was typical that he would nod off when she felt the urge to talk to him.

Staring up at the ceiling through the darkness, she closed her eyes and considered what Eli had said. She agreed Sarah and Luke had formed a special friendship. She had thought it was merely the bond they'd shared through their love for Peter and the twins. Were they meant to be more than relatives?

She blew out a sigh and then began to silently pray, asking God to guide Sarah's heart to the right path.

Pound Cake

1 cup shortening
1–1/4 cups sugar
5 eggs
2 cups flour
1/4 tsp salt
1/8 tsp nutmeg
1 tsp vanilla

Cream shortening and sugar together. Add eggs, beating well after each egg. Add flour, salt, and nutmeg. Add vanilla and beat thoroughly. Bake in greased loaf pan at 350 degrees for 50 minutes or until done.

24

Eli's conversation with Elizabeth the night before rang through his head all morning as he tried to concentrate on running the front desk, answering the phone, and taking customer orders. When Jake offered to take over, he was happy for the break. He weaved through the shop and stepped out the door to the back lot hoping to clear his mind.

Staring over the pasture, Eli contemplated his youngest child, wishing he could take away her pain. Losing Peter had been a blow to their family, but it was devastating to his sweet Sarah Rose. During Luke's time with them, however, Eli had seen Sarah Rose's genuine smile and heard her true laugh for the first time since Peter's death.

Eli leaned on the fence and considered how he could help Sarah Rose through this rough time. The girl had suffered enough after losing Peter. She deserved happiness.

"Busy up front?" a voice behind him asked.

Eli turned just as Timothy came up to him. "*Ya*. Very. I needed to step out and clear my head." He gestured back toward the shop. "How do you think production is? Jake mentioned he's swamped. I'm thinking about trying to hire another carpenter."

His son shrugged. "I think we're *gut*."

"Don't you think projects really piled up after Luke left? He was a *gut*, fast worker and a talented carpenter."

Timothy averted his eyes. "Luke is back where he should be. The shop is fine. We can handle it."

Eli studied his son. "Why do you look away when I mention Luke?"

"He hurt Sarah by telling her all of the stories about Peter's past. He should've quit while he was ahead. I encouraged him to go back to Ohio, away from us."

Anger boiled in Eli and his eyes narrowed. "Are you telling me you drove Luke away?"

"I didn't drive him away, but I encouraged him to go." Timothy folded his arms. "He lied about who he was when he first got here, and it just did more damage to Sarah, who was already in a fragile state. Besides, Sarah is going to marry Norman anyway."

"What did you say?"

"I said Sarah and Norman are going to get married. She doesn't need the distraction of her past around all the time when she's going to start a new life."

"No, they aren't getting married," Eli snapped. "She turned him down a month ago."

"She did? He never told me." Timothy grimaced. "I told Luke Sarah was going to marry Norman. They're *gut* friends, and it just seemed like they would."

"No wonder Luke left in such a hurry. He thought Sarah was going to marry Norman." Eli shook his head and stalked back toward the shop, fury roaring through his veins.

"*Dat*!" Timothy trotted up beside him. "Hang on." He tried to stop Eli, but Eli yanked away and kept walking. "Let me explain. Please."

Eli halted and glared at Timothy. "Do you have any idea what you've done? Sarah is miserable. She's almost as distraught now as she was after Peter died."

His son's eyes rounded like an animal caught intruding in a pasture of crops. "If you'll just let me explain." His folded hands pleaded for forgiveness. "I thought Norman was going to marry her. He told me he was going to propose, and I figured they belonged together. They were good friends, and it seemed natural for them to—"

"You thought wrong." Eli jammed a finger in Timothy's chest. "Do us all a favor and only think for yourself. You made the choice to be alone and not court after Miriam left you, but you have no business making Sarah Rose's decisions for her." He left his stunned son in the parking lot while he marched through the shop to his office.

Closing and locking the door, he sank into his desk chair and wracked his brain for a solution that would make Sarah smile again.

After several minutes, an idea lit his mind like lightning illuminating the midsummer sky. He fished the piece of paper with Luke's contact information from his jacket pocket, pulled out a notepad, grabbed a pen, and began to write a letter.

When he finished the letter, he folded it, deposited it into an envelope, and then sealed and addressed it. As he was angling a stamp in the upper corner, a soft knock sounded on the door.

"*Ya?*" Eli called.

"*Dat*, please let me in." Timothy's voice sounded humble on the other side of the door. "I need to talk to you."

Frowning, Eli rose and unlocked the door. Wrenching it open, he glared at his son. "You better be here to apologize."

Timothy nodded. "I am."

Eli studied him, waiting for an explanation.

"I thought I was doing what was best for Sarah," he said. "I wanted to protect her from enduring more pain. We all loved Peter, but seeing her suffer was the most horrific thing I've ever experienced." He sighed. "She's my baby sister, and I want her to be happy. I don't care about what happens to me, but I want to see my siblings happy."

Eli crossed his arms and rubbed his beard. "You had no right meddling between her and Luke. They love each other. Because of your actions, she may give up on love altogether and wind up alone."

"That's just it, *Dat*." Timothy stepped into the office and leaned against the wall. "Norman loves her, and he'd be *gut* to her. I wanted to see them get together because I care about both of them. Norman is a *gut* friend, and Sarah is my sister. I thought they would make a good team since they've both experienced losing their spouses."

Eli shook his head in disbelief. "But that's not for you to decide. Sarah Rose has the right to choose her own husband."

"I see that now. My heart was in the right place, but I was making the wrong choices. I should've backed off." Timothy placed a hand on his father's shoulder. "I messed up. What can I do now to make it right?"

Eli held up the letter and shook it. "I'm hoping this will do the trick."

Timothy studied the address. "You wrote Luke a letter?"

"*Ya*." Eli shook a finger at him as a warning. "Do me a favor and keep this between us. You've already done enough damage."

"*Ya*." Timothy nodded. "You can trust me. I've learned my lesson."

"Say a prayer this works." Eli smacked his son's arm.

"I will, *Dat*. I will."

25

Luke leaned against his workbench and glanced across the empty shop, pondering what had possessed him to agree to come in to work on the weekend. Of course, it wasn't as if he had anything to do at the house.

He'd spent last night visiting with Mel and Sally, which meant he spent the entire evening eating too much and longing for the close, loving relationship his best friend shared with his beautiful wife. And those desires conjured up thoughts of Sarah that had haunted him all night long.

Taking a deep breath, he sauntered to the other side of the shop to Mel's work area where a half-finished cabinet sat. Grabbing a sander, he set to work, hoping to finish the project for his friend as another way to thank him for the delicious meal.

Luke was deep at work, struggling to tune out memories of Sarah and concentrate on the hum of the tool, when a tap on his shoulder startled him.

"You scared me half to death!" he hissed at the teenager who ran the front of the store. "What is it?"

"You have a visitor out front." The kid jerked his thumb toward the show room.

"A visitor?" Luke set the tool down on the workbench.

"Yeah." The kid shrugged. "Some girl."

"Girl?" Luke's stomach flip-flopped. Had Sarah come to see

him? Had she finally realized she belonged with him and not Norman?

Rushing out front, Luke stopped dead in his tracks when he spotted an English woman leaning on the counter. "DeLana?" he said. "How are you?"

"I'm good." She smiled. "How are you doing?"

"Fine. What brings you out here today?"

"I was hoping we could talk." She nodded toward the front door.

Luke glanced out the showroom window toward the large drops raining down on the pavement. "It looks a bit wet out there. How about we talk in the break room?"

She shrugged. "All right."

He led her through the shop and into the small room in the back, where she sat at the table. He fetched two cans of Coke from the refrigerator and sat across from her, handing her one.

"Thanks." She popped open the can, which fizzed and hissed in response. She then took a long drink before setting it on the table and meeting his gaze. "I had an interesting conversation with someone about a month ago. I've been meaning to stop by, but things kept coming up at work. Today I made it my business to come by and tell you about my special visitor."

"Anyone I know?" He took a long drink, enjoying the cool carbonation on his dry throat.

Her smile was smug. "Oh yeah. She's a pretty blonde who is all into you."

He looked at her with curiosity. "Who was it?"

"Sarah Troyer." She lifted her can and took another drink while he stared at her, unable to breathe for a moment.

"Sarah?" His voice was ragged. "How ... Where ..." He shook his head, trying to figure out what she meant. "I don't understand."

She grinned. "I gotcha."

"DeLana," he began with frustration. "I don't have the time or patience for games. How on earth did you meet Sarah?"

"She came to see me. She had some burning questions about Peter's past, so I filled her in." DeLana explained how they'd visited in a restaurant and she'd told Sarah the history of how she and Peter met and about the night he left.

Hurt radiated through Luke's soul at the realization Sarah had been a few miles from his shop only a month ago.

"She came all the way out here but didn't stop to see me," he muttered. He ran his hand through his hair as the truth sank in—Sarah never loved him, and he was kidding himself by thinking he'd ever had a chance with her. Maybe she really did love Norman.

And maybe she did hate him.

He swallowed a groan.

"That's where you're wrong." DeLana's smirk was back. "I drove her out here, but she was too afraid to get out of the car."

"Afraid?" He snorted. "Please. Have you ever known me to be intimidating?"

"No, but her feelings for you are."

He studied her eyes, finding no sign of a lie or a cruel joke. He needed to know more. "What do you mean?"

"It was obvious when she talked about you that she had feelings for you. I tried to encourage her to come and see you, but she insisted the feelings weren't mutual." She pushed back a lock of dark hair. "She was afraid you hated her since you had an argument the night before you left. She was in tears over you. It was difficult to watch her break down. She's such a sweet, innocent thing. I wanted to pull her into a hug."

The image of her crying in his arms twisted his heart. He pushed the memory away. Frowning, he shook his head. "It doesn't matter anyway. She's marrying someone else."

DeLana gave a look of surprise. "She is? She didn't mention that to me."

Luke nearly dropped his can. "She didn't mention a guy named Norman?"

She shook her head. "No, she didn't mention anyone named Norman. But she was very emotional when she talked about you. It's obvious, Luke, that girl has the hots for you."

He frowned in disbelief, but his heart thumped in his chest at the possibility that DeLana was right. "She has 'the hots' for me? That's funny, because she accepted it when I told her I was leaving, and she hasn't contacted me. Her father has my information. She could get my number from him or look it up in the phone book at the library. There are ways to contact people. And you said it yourself that she went home without seeing me."

"You're just as stubborn as your brother was, Luke. You're not listening to me. She hasn't contacted you because she thinks you hate her." DeLana leaned forward, her eyes serious. "I got the feeling she would love for you to come after her. She needs the fairy tale, Luke. You have to ride in on your white horse and sweep her off her feet like a Disney movie."

He looked at her in confusion, and she snapped her fingers.

"I forgot." She chuckled. "You aren't allowed to watch movies or television. Just trust me on this. She wants you to come and save her, but she doesn't know how to reach out to you. I think she's afraid of being hurt again."

Luke leaned back in the chair and raked his fingers through his hair, letting her words soak into his mind. He crossed his arms and studied her expression. "Why are you telling me this?"

She placed the can on the table. "To be honest, I'm not sure what possessed me, but I've had a nagging desire to come and tell you all this. I guess it's because I let your brother slip through my fingers eight years ago, and I didn't want it to happen to you. I love my husband, and I don't regret marrying him. However, as I told Sarah, sometimes I wonder what would've happened if I'd run away with Peter the night he begged me to leave town with him. I don't want you to let the love of your life slip through your fingers too."

He narrowed his eyes, challenging her. "What makes you think she's the love of my life?"

DeLana snorted, lifting the can again. "It doesn't take a rocket scientist to see your expression or hers and figure it out." She leaned forward and lowered her voice for effect. "Luke, don't be a dunce. You're wasting your life away living like a hermit here in Ohio. Go back to Pennsylvania and marry that girl."

His mouth gaped. How on earth had she figured out so much about him? While he studied her, she pulled an envelope from her purse.

"I brought photos of your nephew. He's almost nine now." She slapped a few photographs onto the table in front of him.

Luke flipped through the photographs, silently marveling at how much Cody looked like Peter. Warmth filled his heart. How could he have lived in the same town as his nephew for nearly nine years and never contacted him? He needed to be the uncle the child deserved and the uncle the twins deserved too.

"He's grown up so much," Luke said. "It's amazing how time flies."

"I'd love for you to meet him sometime."

He glanced up at her. "Really?"

She nodded. "Alex and I are going to tell him about Peter soon. We want him to know his other siblings, and Sarah promised to keep in touch."

"I'd love to meet him." He stared at the snapshots.

They chatted about old times, swapping funny stories about Peter. After nearly an hour, DeLana stood and said she had to get home. Luke walked her to the show room.

"It was great seeing you again." DeLana pulled him into a quick hug.

"You too." He rubbed her arm. "Thank you."

She gave him a wicked grin. "If you want to thank me, then go to Pennsylvania and tell Sarah how you feel about her before it's too late." She winked and then rushed out the door into the blowing rain.

Luke stood at the window while DeLana climbed into her SUV and sped through the parking lot, her tires leaving their wake in the puddles.

His stomach tightened while he contemplated all she'd revealed about her visit with Sarah. While it cut him to the bone that Sarah had visited DeLana without seeing him, he felt a ray of hope that she could possibly love him.

For a split second, he considered calling a taxicab, leaving the shop, and heading to the train station.

But how could he truly know Sarah wanted to be with him and not Norman?

It just didn't make sense. Why would Sarah share her true feelings with DeLana, a stranger who had shared an intimate love affair with her late husband, but not tell Luke how she felt?

He considered the thought. Then another idea struck him— why would DeLana come to see him after all of these years to share a lie?

A headache throbbed in his temple while he considered all of the possible motives for DeLana's visit. All he knew for sure was he was more confused than ever.

On Sunday evening, Luke sank into a kitchen chair and flipped through the letters he'd piled up on the table over the past couple of days. He'd been so consumed with his conversation with DeLana he hadn't bothered to open his mail or read the newspaper.

He glanced through the usual bills without much interest and then stopped when he found a handwritten envelope with a Pennsylvania postmark. His heartbeat leapt when he read "Kauffman" in the return address.

Ripping it open, Luke held his breath as his eyes scanned the block handwriting.

Dear Luke,

I hope this letter finds you well. The shop has been busy since you left. We sure could use your hands around here these days. Please remember the job here is always available for you if you decide to come back.

The real reason why I'm writing isn't to tell you about the business at the furniture store. I wanted to tell you that the person who misses you most of all is Sarah Rose. She hasn't been the same since you left. I haven't seen her smile or heard her laugh in weeks. She spends most days in her room, reading her Bible and not talking to anyone.

If you can find it in your heart to come back to Sarah Rose, please do it as soon as possible. I'm sure she loves you. In fact, she admitted to Kathryn that she does. If you come back, I think you both would realize you're meant to be together.

May the Lord bless you and keep you in His tender care.

Sincerely,

Eli Kauffman

Luke stared at the letter, reading and rereading it until he'd committed it to memory. Eli's words were so similar to DeLana's.

Then it struck him like a ton of bricks—was God trying to tell him something? Was he, Luke, wrong to think Sarah belonged with Norman and not him? Was he wrong to think it was a sin for him to covet Sarah?

The questions rang through his mind all night and lingered into the early morning as he rode to work with his English driver.

Luke cornered Mel in the parking lot and filled him in on DeLana's visit and then handed him Eli's letter. He held his breath while he waited for Mel's reaction. When Mel met his gaze with a grimace, Luke's heart sank.

"Are you dense, Troyer?" Mel asked, handing the letter back to Luke.

"What do you mean?"

"What are you doing here?" Mel gestured around the parking lot. "What are you waiting for?"

Luke shook his head. "But isn't it a sin to covet my brother's *fraa*?"

His best friend raised an eyebrow. "A sin? Why would it be a sin? There's a verse about it. Let me think …" Mel snapped his finger. "That's it! It's from Romans, and it goes something like, 'By law a married woman is bound to her husband as long as he is alive, but if her husband dies, she is released from the law of marriage.'" He shrugged. "So, where's the sin in coveting her? Peter was her past." He gestured toward Luke. "You could be her future."

Luke's stomach lurched with excitement. "You think so?"

"What are you doing waiting here?" Mel gestured toward the pickup truck sitting by the entrance to the shop. "Go! Get packed and rush to the train station. Go to Sarah before she marries Norman."

Luke gave Mel a quick hug. "*Danki*." He trotted toward the English driver. "I'll call you!"

26

Luke drummed his fingers on the door of the taxicab as it rolled down Route 340 toward Kauffman & Yoder. The train ride had seemed longer than the last time, due to his excitement. Even though Eli didn't mention a wedding in his letter, Luke prayed he wasn't too late to tell Sarah he loved her and not to marry Norman.

When the cab pulled into the furniture store lot, he tossed money to the driver, snatched his bag from the floor, and jogged into the showroom, finding Jake on the phone.

Jake looked up and grinned. Ending his call, he rushed around the counter and smacked Luke on the shoulder. "Hey, man! I knew you'd be back. You just couldn't stay away, huh?"

"*Ya.*" Luke forced a smile, anticipation bubbling in his gut. "Is Eli around?"

Jake shrugged. "Should be. Head on back. You know the way."

"*Danki.*" Luke hefted his bag on his shoulder and stepped into the shop. The familiar scents of wood and stain washed over him, and the booming sounds of tools rang through his head as he scanned the sea of men working on various projects. He missed the variety of building furniture.

Nodding greetings to his former coworkers, he steered to the back of the shop and knocked on Eli's office door.

"Enter," Eli called over the chorus of tools.

Luke wrenched open the door, which squeaked its protest.

When their gaze met, Eli's eyes rounded, and he jumped from his chair. "Luke!" Grabbing his hand, he shook it. "It's so *gut* to see you."

"I got your letter." Luke's voice trembled. "*Danki.*"

The older man smiled. "I'm glad you came."

"How is she doing?" Luke's stomach clenched.

A knowing smile parted Eli's lips. "I think she'll be fine." He shrugged into his coat. "Let's call a driver and head to the house now. She'll be glad to see you."

Sarah smiled and hugged her arms to her chest while she observed Jessica holding Rachel and Lindsay snuggling Seth. She was so glad Jessica had come to visit after finishing high school for the summer.

"He's so tiny," Lindsay said, running her finger over his hand. "Check out those teensy fingers, Aunt Trisha."

Trisha leaned over the chair and smiled. "So beautiful. Hey, little buddy."

Jessica grinned down at the baby girl. Rachel scrunched her face and yawned in response.

"You are just too cute." Jessica glanced up at Sarah and then back at Rachel. "She definitely looks like you. She has your chin."

Sarah chuckled. "*Danki.*"

"I see Peter in him," Trisha said with a nod.

"You know what's weird?" Lindsay gave Sarah a serious look. "I see Luke in him. I guess it's the family resemblance."

Sarah's heart thumped at the sound of Luke's name.

"That's not weird," Trisha said, rubbing Seth's cheek. "My husband is a dead ringer for his uncle Poochie."

"Uncle Poochie?" Lindsay guffawed, and the baby squirmed.

"It's a long story," Trisha said. "I'll have to tell you some other time."

"Have you seen Jake yet?" Sarah asked Jessica.

Jessica shook her head and her face flushed. "Not yet. He thinks I have another week of classes. I'm going to surprise him at the shop."

"He'll be excited to see you," Lindsay said. "He always asks about you. He's still crazy about you."

"Don't rush it," Trisha warned with a serious expression. "You're young and have your whole life ahead of you."

"*Ya.* That's right," Sarah agreed with a nod.

An engine rumbled outside, and Sarah peered out the window as *Dat* and another man climbed from the cab of Mike Gray's pickup truck. "*Dat's* home early."

Settling back in the chair, she took in the sight of the women cooing to her twins, who were almost six months old. It was hard to believe Peter had been gone nearly thirteen months.

Life had changed so much since the Christmas morning they'd been born. She'd lost her friendship with Luke and turned down a marriage proposal from Norman. It seemed things were changing daily.

She couldn't help but wonder what tomorrow would bring. She hoped she'd soon find happiness for her and the twins.

Luke glanced around the Kauffman's kitchen, and his pulse pounded. He wondered if he'd made a mistake coming here.

"She's up in the nursery visiting with some out-of-town relatives." Eli gestured toward the stairs. "Go on."

Luke gnawed his lip, facing her father. "What if she's not happy to see me?"

Eli gave a knowing smile. "She will be. Trust me." Taking Luke's arm, he steered him toward the stairs. "Go."

"But we argued the last time we spoke. I said some awful

things to her." Luke adjusted his hat on his head. "She probably hates me."

"She doesn't hate you, Luke." Eli made a sweeping gesture toward the stairs. "Go tell her how you feel and listen to her."

With a deep sigh, Luke climbed the steps to Sarah's room. His heart was pounding so hard in his chest he was sure Sarah would hear it. Doubt mixed with worry swirled in his gut. What if she told him to leave?

What if she said she loved Norman?

Approaching her room, his palms trembled, and sweat beaded on his brow. The next few moments would change the rest of his life.

Sarah had the nagging sensation of being watched. Glancing toward the doorway, her eyes focused on Luke. She gasped. "Luke?" she whispered, her voice quavering with a mix of shock, awe, and affection.

His handsome face displayed a tentative smile. "May I come in?"

"Please." She gestured toward the twins. "Your niece and nephew have missed you."

Misty-eyed, he stepped over toward Jessica, who held out Rachel. "I've missed them too. Hello, *mei liewe*."

Sarah's heart swelled when he called Rachel "my love." He did love the children.

But did he love Sarah too?

"Would you like to hold her?" Jessica asked with a smile.

He glanced at Sarah for permission, and she gave a quiet laugh. "Of course. You're her *onkel*."

Jessica passed the tiny bundle to him. He held her as if she were the most precious little person in the world, and Sarah's heart turned over at the sight. He looked so natural with Rachel in his arms. He looked like a father.

She suppressed the thought. He didn't love her.

Lindsay rose and handed Seth to Sarah. "We'll go downstairs and let you visit alone. We can run by the shop and see Jake." She motioned to Jessica and Trisha. "Luke, this is my sister and my aunt Trisha."

"Nice to meet you." He nodded as they exited the room. His eyes then met Sarah's, and the intensity in them caused her pulse to double. "It's so good to be back with you and the *zwillingbopplin* again."

"We've missed you." Sarah's mouth dried.

"They've gotten bigger. Rachel still looks just like you."

"Lindsay says Seth looks like you." She sidled up to him. He leaned over, and she inhaled his scent, so familiar, so warm.

"No," he said. "He's still my brother, through and through." He smiled at her, and her heart somersaulted.

She resisted the urge to touch his sweet face.

Questions swirled through her mind as she watched him with her baby. First and foremost, she wanted to know if he was back for good, but the answer scared her. She took a deep breath before she spoke.

"Why are you here?" Her voice was thick as fear slithered through her—fear that he'd say he wouldn't stay long.

"Your *dat* wrote me." He kept his eyes trained on the sleeping child snuggled in his large arms like a precious doll.

"What?" She studied him. "Why?"

"He asked me to come back and see you because you've been unhappy." He ran a large finger over Rachel's chin, and she sighed in her sleep. A loving smile graced his lips. "And DeLana came to visit me at the shop."

"DeLana?" Sarah's eyes popped wide open.

"She also said you missed me, and I should come back." He grinned. "She said I should ride back on my horse and sweep you off your feet like a fairy tale in some movie."

"Oh." She studied his eyes, trying to discern if he was laughing at DeLana's analogy or if he was saying he wanted to be with her. She had the sinking feeling that he was laughing, and he wasn't going to stay after all. She feared he was only here to visit and see the twins.

She needed to find out what his intentions were, but they couldn't talk with the children sleeping. Since Seth was already asleep, she placed him in his cradle. She then removed Rachel from Luke's arms, and placed her in the other cradle. Taking Luke's warm hand in hers, she led him into the hallway, gently closing the door behind her.

Still holding his hand, she guided him into her mother's sewing room, closing the door behind them. Once there, she stood before him. She knew she had to apologize to him, and she wracked her brain for the right words.

His eyes scanned her face, and she looked down, suddenly self-conscious.

"Why are you staring at me?" she asked, running her hand over her prayer *kapp* to be sure it was straight.

"I can't believe I'd forgotten just how beautiful you are." His face and eyes were serious.

"*Danki*," she whispered, her body trembling at his intense expression. Squeezing his hand, she cleared her throat. She had to apologize before she lost her nerve. "I'm sorry, Luke." Her voice quaked. "I'm sorry for everything I said. You're not a liar, and I never meant to compare you to Peter."

His expression softened, and he touched her face. "No, I'm sorry. I was wrong to say you regarded me as gum on your shoe. I know you don't."

Tears began to drip down her cheeks. "You're so much more than that to me, Luke. So much more. I've missed you."

"I'm glad you feel that way." He swiped away a tear with his thumb. His touch was so gentle and so loving. "I didn't arrive here on a horse like the fairy tale DeLana mentioned, but I would like to sweep you off your feet."

Her pulse quickened in her veins, and her breath caught in her throat. "I think you've definitely swept me off my feet."

He cupped her face in his hands. "I'm here to ask you not to marry Norman." His eyes pleaded with her. "Please don't marry him, Sarah Rose. Please."

Her voice failed her for a moment. "What are you talking about? I was never going to marry Norman."

Luke raised his eyebrows in shock. "You weren't?"

She searched his eyes. "Who told you I was going to marry him?"

"Timothy said Norman was going to ask you when May arrived, and it was only natural for you to marry him since you're such close friends."

She groaned. "It wasn't true. There were no plans. Norman asked me to marry him the night I arrived back home after visiting DeLana, and I told him no. I said I only wanted to be friends."

She studied his brown eyes, drinking in the warmth she found there. "I told him I couldn't marry him because I didn't love him. When I looked into the eyes of my *kinner* I knew I couldn't raise them in a loveless marriage. They need so much more, and I do too."

Taking her hands in his, he pulled her to him. Her pulse pounded like a horse trotting through town.

"Sarah," he began, his voice ragged. "I'm miserable without you. I think of you day and night." Leaning down, he brushed his lips over her cheek, and her knees buckled. "*Ich liebe dich*, Sarah Rose. I want to come back here and stay. I already have a buyer for my land. He's been asking me for years to sell so he can build an English housing development." He released one of her hands and ran his thumb over where his kiss had fallen. "Will you marry me?"

She blinked back tears. "Luke, I love you too," she whispered, her voice quaking. "Yes, I'll marry you."

A smile broke out on his lips. "I am the happiest man on earth." He leaned down again. His lips brushed hers, sending her stomach into a wild swirl.

He pulled her to him, and she buried her head in his chest, listening to the sound of his beating heart. She let the feel of his lips soak into her heart.

"At first I thought being with you would be a sin," he said.

"You did?" she asked. "What made you change your mind?"

A smile formed on his lips. "My best friend Mel. He reminded me of a verse in Romans." He rubbed her back. "He made me realize my brother was your past, but I could be your future."

"*Ya.*" She buried her face in his chest again. "I'd like that, and so will the *kinner.*" Closing her eyes, she said a silent prayer, thanking God for her beautiful twins and for Luke.

He held her close. "Your parents named you right. You're my beautiful rose. My perfect, lovely, sweet rose."

Sand Tarts

1 cup butter
2 cups sugar
4 eggs, separated
1 cup flour
1/2 cup cinnamon
1/2 cup almonds

Work in butter and sugar. Mix in 2 eggs. Use flour to make stiff dough. Roll thin, cut out small squares. Wet top with two beaten eggs, sprinkle with extra sugar, cinnamon, and chopped almonds. Bake on cookie sheet at 350 degrees for 10 minutes.

27

This is the best chocolate cake I've ever had," Luke said, sitting across from Sarah at her parents' supper table later that evening. "It's so moist."

Sarah gave him a teasing glare. "I didn't make it. You better say it's not the best you've ever had or I'll never make you another chocolate cake."

"*Ack.*" He feigned a serious frown. "It's the second-best I've ever had."

"Well, that does it." Beth Anne gave him a mock glare. "You'll not have any more of my chocolate cake."

The rest of the Kauffman family laughed while a group of grandchildren raced through the kitchen on their way outside. Lindsay, Jessica, and Jake followed them out to the porch.

"Slow down," Robert called. "You don't want to fall down the porch stairs!"

"Luke," *Dat* said, forking more cake. "How long do you plan to stay this time?"

Luke gave Sarah a sideways glance. He was so handsome that her heart skipped in her chest.

"I was wondering if your offer of a job was still open." Luke wiped his napkin across his mouth and gave *Dat* a serious look. "Are you still looking for a carpenter?"

Dat's eyes rounded in surprise. "Are you here to stay?"

"I'll have to go home and take care of some things, but then I'll be back to stay." He met Sarah's gaze. "For good."

Beth Anne and Kathryn gasped and gave Sarah a surprised expression. Sarah's cheeks flamed.

Dat stood and crossed the room to Luke. "That's *wunderbaar*, son." He patted his shoulder. "You have a job. You know that."

Mamm stood and began gathering the dirty dishes, and Sarah and the rest of the women followed suit. The men headed for the porch.

Before stepping outside behind her brothers, Luke looked at her and gave her a loving smile. She mirrored his expression, and her heart warmed again.

He mouthed the words "I love you" and then disappeared outside. Joy flamed in her soul.

"It's so *gut* to see you smile again, Sarah Rose," *Mamm* said, wiping the counter.

Sarah smiled.

"She's glowing," Beth Anne chimed in.

"When's the wedding?" Kathryn asked with a grin as she filled the sink with soapy water.

"*Ya.*" Beth Anne looped an arm around her shoulders. "We'll have to get started on a dress."

"You're marrying Luke?" Sadie asked, coming up to her. "I had no idea you were courting."

"Slow down." Sarah placed the dishes on the counter and then held out her arms. "We have no formal wedding plans."

"Not yet?" Sadie asked with a grin.

Sarah met *Mamm's* surprised expression. "We haven't set a date yet, but I don't see where there's any hurry. We can wait until fall if we need to. It will be a real transition with the *kinner.*"

"I'm so happy for you, Sarah Rose," *Mamm* said, squeezing her hand. "I'm glad you listened to your heart."

Beth Anne, Sadie, and *Mamm* began to talk at once, commenting on Luke and their future. While they prattled on, Kathryn crossed the room to her.

With a smile, Kathryn pulled Sarah into her arms. "I'm so glad for you," she whispered. "You deserve happiness."

Cries erupted from upstairs, and Sarah pulled back. "I think the *zwillingbopplin* are hungry."

Kathryn chuckled. "*Ya.* I'd say so."

Sarah gestured toward the stairs. "Would you like to join me?"

"I'd love it." Kathryn looped her arm around Sarah.

She smiled. "Before you know it, my *kinner* will be running through the kitchen and out the back porch with the rest of them." Joy bubbled over in her heart at the realization of raising her children with her family, including Luke.

Luke leaned on the porch railing and glanced over at Sarah's father, brothers, and brothers-in-law. While the men chatted about the furniture store, Luke smiled to himself, imagining his future with his Sarah Rose. His heart swelled at the thought of spending time with her and the twins.

Crossing his arms, his glance collided with Timothy's, who was studying him intently.

Timothy stepped over to Luke and nodded toward the stairs. "Can I talk with you for a moment? Alone."

"*Ya.* Why not?" Following Timothy down the steps toward the pasture fence, Luke dreaded Timothy giving him another lecture about how wrong it was to be back and spending time with Sarah.

They reached the fence, and Timothy leaned forward on it, resting his foot on the bottom rung while staring across the lush, green pasture.

Luke glanced back toward the house, his eyes focusing on

the men visiting on the porch. He suppressed a smile while thinking of how he would be visiting with them more often— as a member of the family.

"So, you're back for good, *ya?*" Timothy asked, breaking through Luke's thoughts.

Luke crossed his arms and leaned back on the fence. "That's the plan."

"And you're courting my sister." Timothy kept his eyes trained across the pasture.

"*Ya.*" Luke rubbed his chin, wondering where Timothy was going with this.

"*Gut.*" Timothy met his gaze, his expression softening.

"*Gut?*" Luke raised his eyebrows, waiting for Timothy to say something negative.

Yet the man just nodded. "It's good to see my sister smile again. *Danki* for coming back."

"You're welcome." Luke tried in vain to suppress his surprise.

"I'm sorry about everything I did to make you leave." Timothy faced him.

"What do you mean?"

"I was wrong when I told you she was going to marry Norman. I assumed she'd marry him because they're good friends and have both suffered the same loss, but I was dead wrong." He paused and looked at his boots and then up at Luke. "I had no idea you and Sarah were so close. I was totally out of line. I'm sorry." He held his hand out. "I hope we can start over as future brothers."

A smile of relief curled Luke's lips as he shook Timothy's hand. "*Danki.* I appreciate your honesty."

"My sister has a right to decide who she'll court and who she'll marry, and judging by the smile you've brought to her face, I assume it will be you." Timothy smacked his arm. "*Danki* for making her smile again. She's been through a lot, but I think she's finally found happiness."

"*Gern gschehne.*" Luke crossed his arms. "It's my pleasure."

"Luke!" Kathryn called from the porch. "Sarah would like to see you upstairs."

"Duty calls." Luke turned to Timothy. "Thanks again." He trotted across the driveway, up the porch, through the kitchen full of women chatting, and up to the second floor.

Stepping into Sarah's room, he found her rocking Rachel and humming. Glancing up at him, she smiled, and his pulse skittered in his veins. She was the picture of beauty. He couldn't believe she'd agreed to marry him. He was more thankful than he could express in a prayer.

He lowered himself onto the hope chest next to her, rested his elbows on his knees, and smiled over at her. "Fast asleep?"

She nodded. "I just fed them, and they fell asleep."

Reaching over, he ran his finger down Sarah's arm. She looked at him, and her sapphire eyes simmered with an intensity that made his insides stiffen.

"My family is very happy you came back," she whispered.

"And are you?" he asked.

"What do you think?" She gave a coy smile. "*Ich liebe dich,* Luke."

"I love you, too, Sarah Rose. *Ich liebe dich.*"

Her eyes grew serious. "I think I finally understand something my *mamm* told me a few months ago."

"What's that?" he asked.

"She said Scripture tells us 'Faith is being sure of what we hope for and certain of what we do not see.' When Peter died, I lost my faith. I was drowning in a deep abyss of sorrow and thought I would never find my way out." She paused, and her expression brightened. "Now I see God was with me all along. God had a plan for me, and His plan for me was you."

Reaching over, she cupped her hand over his. "Despite everything I thought was wrong, the Lord made sure everything was going to be all right for the *zwillingbopplin* and me. I should've had faith all along."

His heart filled with love for his future bride. "I know exactly what you're saying, Sarah Rose. The Scripture is true. I, too, was drowning in sorrow when I found out I'd lost my brother, and I was also envious of the family he had here. Now my faith in God is renewed, and I'm so thankful for what I've found in you."

Leaning over, he gently took her face in his hands, and she closed her eyes, smiling. Brushing his lips against hers, his heart swelled with joy. He silently thanked God for blessing his life with Sarah Rose, Seth, Rachel, and Sarah's loving family.

Epilogue

While Luke trotted up the porch steps, Timothy leaned back against the fence and reflected on the conversation they'd shared.

A huge weight had dissolved from his conscience when Luke accepted his apology. He hoped Luke and Sarah had a long, happy life together. His younger sister deserved a life of joy after the pain she'd endured.

A buggy clip-clopped up the drive and stopped in front of the barn. Titus King climbed from the buggy and began to unhitch his horse. While *Dat* and Timothy's brothers gathered around to chat with Titus, his wife, Irma emerged. She greeted the men and then headed for the house while their children hopped out of the buggy behind them.

The youngest of them ran off to play with Timothy's nieces and nephews. Naomi leaned down and said something to her younger sister, Lizzie Anne, and handed her a large cake plate covered with foil. Lizzie Anne jogged toward the house with the plate, and Naomi turned, meeting Timothy's gaze. She waved, and Timothy nodded in response.

She walked over to him, and he noticed for the first time that she had the prettiest brown eyes he'd ever seen. Her expression brightened as she approached, and he spotted a dimple in her right cheek. Why hadn't he seen that before?

"Hi." Naomi hugged her apron to her body.

"Hi." Timothy smiled.

"Pretty night." She glanced across the pasture.

"*Ya*. Real pretty."

She gave him a shy smile. Why hadn't he ever observed how attractive she was? Too bad she was eight years his junior.

"I made an apple walnut cobbler." She jerked her thumb toward the house. "My sister carried it in."

He folded his arms and rubbed his chin. "Are you trying to get a job at my *mamm's* bakery?"

She laughed. "Somehow I don't think my *mamm* would let me leave the quilt business."

He nodded in agreement. "Don't blame her. You make a mighty fine quilt."

Her eyes lit up. "Really? You think so?"

"I saw the one you gave Luke. It was *wunderbaar.*"

Her smile faded. "*Ya*, that was a bit immature of me. I thought Luke had wanted to court me." Her cheeks flushed, and he couldn't help but think she was adorable. "I was a bit silly with him. My *mamm* chastised me for being so forward. I'm embarrassed by it now."

"We all make mistakes." *I've sure made enough to last a lifetime.* He nodded toward the house. "Would you like something to drink? I'd love to try some of your cobbler."

Her smile was back. "That would be nice."

As they walked toward the house side by side, *Dat's* voice echoed in his mind. Perhaps Naomi King wasn't too young for him after all.

Discussion Questions

1. As the story progresses, Sarah discovers more and more about her late husband's past. Her anger toward him grows throughout the book. She isn't able to forgive him until after her twins are born. Why do you think her children helped her forgive Peter?

2. Think of a time when you were betrayed by a close friend or loved one. How did you come to grips with that betrayal? Were you able to forgive that person and move on? If so, then where did you find the strength to forgive? Share this with the group.

3. Timothy assumes Sarah will marry a man she does not love. While his intentions are good, he is not taking into consideration what Sarah truly wants. Think of a time when you may have had misguided intentions for a child or loved one. Share this with the group.

4. Luke is overwhelmed when he discovers the life Peter has left behind. Although he wants to be a part of Sarah's family, he struggles to find his place. Think of a time when you felt lost and alone. Where did you find your strength? What Bible verses would help with this?

5. Peter feels he's saving Sarah from hurt by not sharing his past with her. However, after he dies, Sarah is left with lies and deception. Do you think Peter's intentions were justified?

6. Have you ever known anyone who lied in order to save someone's feelings? How did that situation turn out?

7. Read Nahum 1:7 (print out the verse). Has this verse ever helped you when you're struggling to accept a loss in your life?

8. Which character can you identify with the most? Which character seemed to carry the most emotional stake in the story? Was it Sarah, Luke, Elizabeth, Eli, Timothy, Naomi, or even DeLana?

9. Read 1 John 4:18 (print this out). What does this verse mean to you? How does it apply to the book?

10. What did you know about the Amish before reading this book? What did you learn?

Acknowledgments

This book wouldn't have been created without the help of my fabulous plotting partner and best friend: my mother, Lola Goebelbecker. Thank you, Mom, for your patience with my incessant plot and character discussions. Also, thank you for all you do for our family. We would be lost without you, and we love you.

To my mother-in-law, Sharon Clipston: thank you for buying all the copies of my books in Hampton Roads, Virginia, and for sharing them with friends and family. I truly appreciate your support of my writing career. Thank you also for all you do for us.

Eric Goebelbecker is the coolest big brother in the world! Love you!

To my wonderful aunts, Trudy Janitz and Debbie Floyd: thank you for your love and encouragement.

Thank you also to my wonderful friends who were willing to edit, proofread, and critique for me—Margaret Halpin, Sue McKlveen, and Lauran Rodriguez. You all offered wonderful suggestions, and you cleaned up my endless typos. Love you!

There aren't enough words to express how much I appreciate all that Sue McKlveen has done for me. You're like a sister to me. Thank you also to Ruth Meily and Betsy Cook for their help with Lancaster County knowledge. I appreciate your friendship so much!

Thank you also Pastor Tim, PJ (Pastor John), and the rest of my wonderful church family at Morning Star Lutheran in Matthews, North Carolina. Your encouragement, prayers, and love mean so much to my family and me. Thank you also for making my book signings such a great success!

Thank you to John and Carol Ionescu, who offered guidance on twin pregnancies. Congratulations on your two beautiful baby boys, John Cristian and Nicolae Daniel!

Thank you also to my Old Order Amish friend who continues to share her friendship and the details of her life in Pennsylvania. You and your family are in my prayers daily.

I'm more grateful than words can express to the Zondervan team. Thank you to my amazing editors—Sue Brower and Becky Philpott. I appreciate your friendship and your fabulous talent polishing my books. I've learned so much from you both. I am also thankful to the amazing marketing team, especially Karwyn Bursma and Jessica Secord. Thank you also to Joyce Ondersma and Jackie Aldridge for your support and friendship. I'm so blessed to be a part of the Zondervan family.

To Mary Sue Seymour—you are the best agent in the world! Thank you for believing in my writing.

Zac and Matt, you are the most amazing boys on the planet. I love you with all my heart. Thank you for bringing sunshine into my life. There's nothing better than dancing in the garage to Michael Jackson and watching Disney Channel with you. And remember, the zombies in "Thriller" aren't real. If they were, then they wouldn't have any sense of rhythm!

To my husband, Joe: there aren't words to tell you how much I cherish you. Thank you for putting up with my mood swings and crankiness when I'm burning the midnight oil and writing until 3:00 a.m. You're my rock. Thank you for reminding me to always have faith. You handle your illness with more grace than I could ever fathom. I pray we have a matching kidney for you soon so you can get on with your life. You're my inspiration; you're my "Luke." I love you. Always.

I'm also eternally thankful to my readers. I appreciate the wonderful emails you send me telling me how much you enjoy my stories. Thank you also for praying for my husband during his illness.

Thank you most of all to our Lord Jesus Christ for granting me the words and the opportunity to share my faith through my books.

Special thanks to Cathy and Dennis Zimmermann for their hospitality and research assistance in Lancaster County, Pennsylvania.

Cathy & Dennis Zimmermann, Innkeepers
The Creekside Inn
44 Leacock Road—PO Box 435
Paradise, PA 17562
Toll Free: (866) 604–2574
Local Phone: (717) 687–0333
Fax: (717) 687–8200
cathy@thecreeksideinn.com

A Gift of Grace

A Novel

Amy Clipston

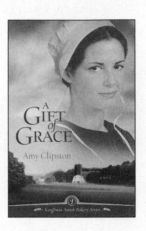

Rebecca Kauffman's tranquil Old Order Amish life is transformed when she suddenly has custody of her two teenage nieces after her English sister and brother-in-law are killed in an automobile accident. Instant motherhood, after years of unsuccessful attempts to conceive a child of her own, is both a joy and a heartache. Rebecca struggles to give the teenage girls the guidance they need as well as fulfill her duties to Daniel as an Amish wife.

Rebellious Jessica is resistant to Amish ways and constantly in trouble with the community. Younger sister Lindsay is caught in the middle, and the strain between Rebecca and Daniel mounts as Jessica's rebellion escalates. Instead of the beautiful family life she dreamed of creating for her nieces, Rebecca feels as if her world is being torn apart by two different cultures, leaving her to question her place in the Amish community, her marriage, and her faith in God.

Available in stores and online!

A New Curtain Rises in the Heart of Lancaster County's Amish Country.

For more than 40 years the Smucker Family has been treating the world to Grandma Smucker's favorite Pennsylvania Dutch recipes and fruits, vegetables and meats harvested from local farms. Along with clean, comfortable lodging for all styles and budgets, they have also opened doors to their Anabaptist faith through experiential dining and special Smucker Socials.

In September 2011 the Smuckers raised the curtain on the Bird-in-Hand Stage: a whole new way to experience Bird-in-Hand and learn more about its Amish and Mennonite neighbors. Its first performance — Beverly Lewis' "The Confession: A Musical" — shares an adaptation of a trilogy of the Lancaster County native's bestselling Amish novels. Don't miss this uplifting Amish love story and its soaring melodies and inspiring lyrics September through November 2011 and 2012. Tickets and meal and lodging packages are available, along with discounts for groups of 12 or more.

Bird-in-Hand Family Restaurant & STAGE

2760 Old Philadelphia Pike, Bird-in-Hand, PA 17505-0402

(717) 790-4069 • www.Bird-in-Hand.com

Experience
- people
- food
- culture

Amish Visit-in-Person Tours

Traditional Amish Farm Feast

Heritage Amish homestead tours

www.AmishExperience.com
www.PlainAndFancyFarm.com

the Amish

Experience

the amish experience at plain&fancyfarm

- ten pristine acres on an AAA scenic byway -

discover luxury with a view at www.AmishViewInn.com